THE CHILD WITHIN US *LIVES!*

by

William Samuel

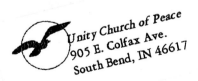

FIRST EDITION

Main entry under title:

The Child within us lives

1. Philosophy—Science.   2. Physics—Metaphysics
3. Metaphysics—Religion.   4. Cosmology.
I. Samuel, William.

ISBN 0-938747-00-2
ISBN 0-938747-01-0

Type set in Baskerville
Manufactured in the United States of America

*This book is dedicated
to the carefree, joyful, triumphant Child
within each of us.*

THE CHILD WITHIN US *LIVES!*

by
William Samuel

ACKNOWLEDGMENTS

This book could not have been written without the help and patience of many lovely people. For the past twenty years I have lived the ideas written here, with little tangible means of support, else I could not know for a fact that one who thinks subjectively can survive in the objective world, asking payment for nothing and giving whatever he receives to others.

In particular, I thank those who recognized the physical necessities that Rachel and I required to bring a book such as this into tangible expression—giving us a typewriter, copier, envelopes, stamps, food, love and supporting words of encouragement, knowing we are not a part of the world's organizations and receive nothing from them but the hard lessons they teach.

I should also thank the "principalities and powers" that worked so vigorously to prevent the publication of this volume. Without their opposition, I'd not have tried so diligently to prove their powerlessness to prevent the Truth's rediscovery.

My gentle wife, Rachel, has worked hard on this volume with me. As helpful as her intellectual assistance, has been the marvelous atmosphere of calm and non-judgmentalism that surrounds her—and her continuing confidence that I would one day string these words. Rachel kept me going during those days when I didn't think I could write another word—nor dared to try.

Besides Rachel, there are David Manners and John Barone, Laurel Carriel and Dorothy Finch, Bruce Dubin and Jo Ann Stewart, William Jillson, Susanne Shreeve, Terry Albee, Michele Finck, Michael Weintraub, Jan Schultz and so many others.

Especially, there is Janice Winokur, my primary editor, without whose patience, talent, inspiration and repeated trips to Woodsong from her teaching post, these words would not have been written so clearly.

Finally, I thank God for the Glimpses and love that allow all of us to participate in this continuing adventure together.

TABLE OF CONTENTS

INTRODUCTION 1

OVERVIEW 5

BOOK ONE 13

I   MANKIND'S SEARCH FOR TRUTH 15
    Da Shan, Mythical Mountain of Seeking and Finding

II DEVELOPMENT OF COSMOLOGY 35
    Da Shan and the Mist

III UNDERSTANDING THE HUMAN EXPERIENCE 49
    Transcending Dualism

IV OUR REAL IDENTITY 61
    The Child Guide

V   OUR REAL IDENTITY, BEYOND THEORY 77
    Recognizing And Feeling The Child Within

VI THE LIGHT OF TRUTH BREAKING THROUGH .. 91
    Glimpses and Glimmers

VII THE CHILD LIVED IN THE WORLD 103
    Interface and Journal Tending

VIII INCREASING THE FLOW OF LIGHT 119
    Sharing Glimpses and Glimmers

IX THE BALANCE BETWEEN ACTION AND NON-
    ACTION 133
    Living Subjectively in an Objective World

X   THE SECRET OF SUPPLY 151
    Giving and Receiving, Two that are One

XI PROFOUND SIMPLICITY 167
    The Child and the Child's Equation

XII ILLUMINATION 179
    "Line upon line, precept upon precept"

BOOK TWO 193

RELATED PAPERS 199
BOOK CONCLUSION 397
EPILOGUE 409
POSTSCRIPT 410
PUBLISHER'S WORD 412

INTRODUCTION

QUANTUM MAN, THE GUIDED MISSILE

Something enormous is soon to happen in the world; there is no sensitive person who doesn't feel this deeply. In every field—science, religion, philosophy, government, business, or whatever—a strange sense of disquiet is growing, a feeling of Something Imminent. As we look about us, we can see that the world is off course. Many who think they understand, point to drugs, overcrowding, pollution, the overload of information, corrupt government and any number of other possible causes. But what is happening now has a more significant and, as yet, undreamed of cause. *The recognition of this deeper dimension comes with a solution for the world's problems!* This book is about that.

If we think of mankind in quantum terms—as a single organism—we might picture civilization as a missile moving through time and space. This missile has been on its way for many thousands of years, headed for a special destination for mankind. Its internal guidance mechanism was turned on when the great religions and philosophies arrived to give humane guidance to men. For Western society, the missile's central system was activated at the time of Judaism's declaration of one God, and that declaration, along with similar statements from other cultures, has been the primary directive for society thus far.

When Christianity arose and broke from the popular Judaism of the day, the missile received input that altered the course, much as our satellites today are given in-flight corrections as they move to do their work in the universe. With each discovery or development in history, Eastern or Western, exter-

1

nal and internal, have come new adjustments in civilization's direction. None of the developments in this long line of progression have been accidental or "bad," despite the human tendency to judge them so. Everything that has happened has been driving us relentlessly to this present moment and to the events shortly to begin.

Now, imagine the missile of collective civilization nearing its target, ready to receive its final redirection for the next and perhaps last phase of the trip—not unlike the "smart missile" that sees the target ahead and directs the internal mechanism to drive itself straight to the destination. For mankind, the destination is a *rediscovery of simple subjectivism,* a new mark in non-space and non-time, a fulfillment of the Original Purpose for tangible life on earth.

As far as the relationship between time and space and their interconnections to tangible life goes, the end-game's corrective information is presently being received within the quantum body of civilization. This information is intended to adjust and correct society's major systems for their final movement as mankind comes to discern the true nature of things—particularly *time, space, matter and awareness (life).* In many ways science, the vanguard of human wisdom, has nearly reached that comprehension already.

What does this final corrective feel like to you and me here in the old-world scene of things? It comes as a new clock turned on within us; as new sensitivity; an increasing intuitiveness; a new perception within us; as certain unfamiliar anxieties, disquiets, stresses and discomforts; as inexplicable fear and depression. Anyone can look at the human scene and see the lids popping off here and there with acts of insanity and people trying to satisfy impossible urges. Who is to say what the northern geese feel before they assemble to make the trek south? Or the butterflies before they start their long upwind search for their ancestral birthplace? I know that dramatic course-altering input is presently arriving within mankind; the sensitive feel it especially. This arrival is not unlike the way the ability to perceive color has developed in mankind in recent millennia. We are told this sense is one of the latest developments of the human brain—but what is presently happening is at a deeper level of mentation. What is it? The arrival of the *truly subjective nature of mentation*—quantum man's capacity for ever greater introspective self-examination.

At this moment, civilization is a little like a field of cotton beginning to bloom: first a boll here, another there, then more and more until one morning we look out and the entire field is abloom. Or, it is like popcorn popping. One kernel pops, then another and another until there is a veritable explosion of the rest. Hard pressed, shaken together and running over, mankind is coming into a conscious knowledge of a subjective sense of things which is certain to alter the course of civilization. The first "blooms" have been the prophets, the seers, the avatars, the insightful, those with eyes to see and ears to hear. Now the field is turning white with the ability to perceive subjectively. Confusion abounds at the unrecognized newness of it all. Now that subjectivism is here, no one knows what to do with it. The major divisions of human activity have not made the necessary adjustments to allow the missile the freedom to change course. Neither education, government, religion nor metaphysics has made the full turn demanded of them—and the time is short. In certain areas, science, with the help of subjective quantum mechanics, has adjusted reasonably well as it goes along searching the vistas of tangibility, but it remains to be seen what scientists will do with their information once it becomes clear that they are now, and always have been, *examining consciousness.*

People are individually willing to adjust, as their intuitions and feelings come into focus, but the controlling groups to which they belong, are vigorously holding to the old ways, refusing to listen to the New Sounds within. Either the institutions of mankind adjust to allow men to change mental course, or there will be a sociological anguish unparalleled in human history.

Pertaining to this subjective capability within myself, I have come to perceive special things about time, space, and matter that seem to be generally unknown; yet it is essential that Everyman begin to understand them. Like so many of the things that have been shown to me in the past, I know that mankind and his science will find them soon.

THE MOUNTAIN

I left the woodland's edge and looked at the mountain. No one had prepared me for the sight. No one had said that such a mountain existed. I stood there transfixed, my heart saying, "Hey! This is a mountain *to climb!*" Except for that moment, there was no wait. With no more than a broken pencil, half a tablet of paper and the clothes on my back, I struck out for the top. I take no credit for this climb because anyone who saw what I saw would have begun his climb as well—and immediately, exactly as I did. But, these years later, the same mountain stands at the edge of the same woodland and there are few who have made the trek to the top. If they knew the view from the peak of that mountain, they would not wait to find it or to make the climb.

THE RIVER

I found the river as I found the mountain, unexpectedly. No one had told me about the river; it wasn't on the map. This was a strange and beautiful river, one to explore. Except for the time required to build a raft, there was no waiting to set out and follow the river wherever it went. Pushing away from the bank, I began a long journey to Somewhere. It was a coincidence, perhaps, that I began the journey that day with no supplies but the clothes on my back, a single pencil and half a tablet of paper. I am sure many persons have made the same journey, but to this day, I find few who even know of the river.

THE COTTON FIELD

Rachel and I found the special field one day when we took a wrong turn on the river. We walked out into the newly plowed ground of a cotton field and saw a white stone glistening in the light. I remember the yelp of joy when we realized that the stone shining in the sunshine was an ancient projectile point. Ten thousand years before, as linear time goes, someone had stood where we were standing, holding a long spear tipped with a white quartz stone. Ten thousand years later, we held the stone in our hand—and there were no other hands intervening—nor years.

THE FIVE TREES

I have been back to the cotton field many times during the past twelve years and have taken others there. There are five huge twin oaks that surround the field. I have become friends with those trees and have learned their secrets.

The mountain climb, the time on the river and the experiences in the cotton field are the subject of this book. It is a difficult story to tell because all of these events, while separate in linear time, are happening simultaneously in non-time for all of us. Each event has its own story and I have written a book about each one—but now, in a wonderful and simple way, the stories have become one Story, intricately interwoven with the tangible world and its people, its poets and dreamers, its scientists and sophisticates, its wise and simple seekers and all their gentle things—birds and kittens, children and ancients.

More, each of these stories is already woven into the experience of the reader who reads this book, whoever he or she might be. Not everyone who reads these words will understand all they have to say, but those who understand the least part of them will never be the same again. They will see from atop my great mountain; they will flow with my river; and they will find a white stone in a white field that is ready for harvest. That field will be harvested soon.

OVERVIEW

THE LIMITS OF PHYSICAL LIGHT AND SCIENCE

Science has nearly reached the limits of tangibility at both ends of the scale, first and last, large and small. Presently our physical instruments are looking out to the very edges of the tangible universe of light and inward to the limits of the particle's apparent beginning in time and space—to a billionth of a billionth of a second, it is said. These two views are one View. Human views will give way soon to the Reality of things. The government of Godhead—not the government of man and his religion—will arrive palpably right here in man's finite measure because It is here already in simple, timeless Truth, albeit not quite seen, recognized or confirmed yet. As the Lights of the world have said, the New Covenant *is* written in the hearts of men already. There IS to be a breakthrough and a breakout into childlikeness and simplicity. Beyond that, there is something for the Child of us to do in this world. This book is about that as well.

THE MYSTICAL EXPERIENCE

The experience of "illumination" is a genuine event awaiting most of us. Exactly what this much touted and nebulous event is, among other things, is *the subjective nature of consciousness breaking through our ordinarily objective thought patterns.* These "solipsistic" experiences are moments when we catch a *conscious* glimpse of our own (or God's) subjective nature as it relates to the world. Most of us desire these happenings mightily—and have them long before they are recognized or understood.

So much has been written about illumination that no thinking person still questions its existence, albeit, many have searched for it without success, and many more have wandered into anguish, confusion and metaphysical gridlock trying to make a preconceived concept happen for themselves. Many more have been led astray by the fanciful accounts of those in high places who would like us to believe they know what they are talking about. The experience of gnosis is not uncommon—but it is often misunderstood or ignored by organized, dogmatic Christianity and Judaism. In Western metaphysics it is ignored, spoken of in hushed circles and frequently distorted. Illumination is better understood in the East, but misconceptions abound there as well. This quiet event actually happens often for everyone in unrecognized ways, much more frequently than it is *understood.* Light is our birthright. That experience has taught me that my Experience is everyone's experience; that what is true for me is true for the rest of myself—including those who read these words.

THE MOVE TO SIMPLICITY AND CHILDLIKENESS

After half a lifetime, I began to understand that every breakthrough and breakout was accompanied by a personal move toward simplicity and childlikeness. Again and again, when my affairs had grown complex, a glimpse of Light arrived, reducing earlier frustrations to new simplicities, and revealing an underlying unity. Somewhere along the line of our inner development, simplicity and childlikeness become primary. Science has perceived this move toward simplicity, but neither science, religion nor metaphysics has seen the equation between simplicity and childlikeness—the untouched Child within us. The recognition of this will be part of the explosion soon to come.

In a marvelous and mysterious way, an Overtruth takes care of our affairs. But, until I was *convinced* of this, the inner workings of science, religion, mind and metaphysics were disconnected and confusing. As each glimpse of Light arrived, the complexity was understood and seen beyond, and a new simplicity came into view; then the process began again and still another simplicity arrived to explain itself within another view more basic than the last.

I call these simplifying insights "Glimpses," and we will have much to say of them later in the book. They are extremely important. Surely, for all of us, the study of truth becomes a knot of intellectualism until Something bursts through to help.

SCIENCE CONFIRMS THIS PROCESS

The new sciences, embracing metaphysics to a degree, are making breakthroughs into a comprehensive simplicity. Each breakthrough produces questions that proliferate into areas of confusion, and then comes another Glimpse and a sudden turn toward an underlying, more fundamental unity.

When the final answers are known in this world, the Divine Simplicity of the Primal One (Godhead) will be "all there is," and human intellectualism will not only have reached its limit, but will have run its course as well. The intuitive knowledge of a primal Simplicity behind everything sparks the scientist's search as surely as the metaphysician's.

Now, as the twentieth century winds down, one can see that human searching has nearly reached the limits of human measure, but woe, the heart of us, the soul of us, remains where it was, just beyond the reach of the intellect. Neither religion nor metaphysics has performed as it promised. The "heart and soul"? Yes. The *real* of us, the Christlike truth of us, the Child of us, the ultimate Identity seems as far from our grasp as ever. Clearly, the fullness of Godhead remains beyond the limits of intellectualism and its organizations, but the wisdom about God that *can* be understood lies rooted in a knowledge of Identity, the Self made in the image of God. Certainly, Identity includes the heart and soul.

OLD LANDMARKS AND IDENTITY

Many years ago, believing I had left the hallowed halls of theology forever to explore the loftier towers of metaphysics, I wrote a long paper on Identity. It was a hundred pages of theological and metaphysical discussion that few, if any, including myself, fully understood. Then, years later, nineteen years ago, after many Glimpses of new light, many Gordian Knots untied, retied, and untied again, I wrote of my most "absolute" discoveries and of the subjective views they permitted. That book had but a single chapter on Identity.

Today, having found that one does not leave old landmarks but takes their wisdom with him to continually resurvey a single Scene from ever higher perspectives, I write once more of Identity—what it is, where it is, what it does, how I found it *and what I learned to do with it when it was truly found.*

Now I speak of Identity in a single word—Child. What I did to find Myself can be written in a simple, old/new equation. While it isn't certain how many will find the word or understand the equation, it is important that these things be written, clearly and simply, so they will be meaningful to those who are SEARCHING.

QUANTUM MAN TODAY AND THE RIVER OF LIFE

Present civilization and its organizations (religious, philosophical, educational, scientific, financial) are like the great bend in the river of life just before the shallows ahead—just before the unsuspected turbulence of subjectivism when life roars through the narrow passages. Historic education—religious education in particular—has paid little attention to its prophets. It has deemed subjectivism too unsettling and difficult to teach. Our temptation is to hang on to the old ways where few demands are made and the familiar pacifies us. But the River of Life is moving relentlessly in growing, ongoing *information*, and the River of Life *includes the rapids of metaphysical subjectivism* whether churchdom and science want to examine it and tell of it or not. As content as we might be in our religious views—or in avoiding spiritual matters altogether as so many do—the end of the quiet time looms for everyone. We are approaching a New View of things. The world is already caught in the swift flow of quantum information leading to new knowledge and strange, startling vistas.

For the new perspectives being thrust upon us, *neither* the objective studies of religion nor the subjective studies of metaphysics, *as they are presented today*, will be adequate. The tumult we are already facing insists that mankind, if he is to survive, *begin to think in a new way.* Humanity, with its physical sciences leading, is soon to confirm the insubstantial nature of matter and time.

PROUD SCIENTISTS AND METAPHYSICIANS

Even *beyond* the turbulence of subjectivism, there are sticking places where physical scientists and metaphysicians are loitering along the banks, wading in the shallows of arrogance and self-superiority. In this world of appearances, metaphysicians wax, wane and suffer no less than anyone else and, in the end, they find their brands of subjectivism inadequately meeting their own needs, much less the needs of the world. Caught in the sterile void of "absoluteness," the suffering subjectivist faces an awful anguish and wonders why his metaphysics does not work as it did in the beginning, why his organizations languish and why there are no more answers now than a hundred years ago. This book is for the metaphysician, the physicist and astronomer who want more Light— and the *answers* to those questions.

Once I wrote of the chemical insanity that would smash the world—and it did. Now I speak of a new madness in the name of pseudo-metaphysics to shake the world, wherein much of mankind will find its faith in *everything* shattered, unable to find God's good in anything, anywhere, outside *himself*. Completely unaware of it, the bastions of *legitimate* subjectivism face an attack from every quarter by an insecure and threatened "religion," in the NAME of religion which isn't working either. The only ones who won't be conquered in the melee already begun, objectivist and subjectivist alike, will be those who *have moved onward in their studies to FIND the Light of the Child within themselves and follow Its leadings rather than the world's.*

THE TREE OF LIFE IS SOON TO BLOOM

In the days ahead, when the flowering begins, *those who run with the Child will be part of the flower and the seed.*

As time goes, physical science will soon understand what time and space are actually about. In a very literal sense, we are approaching the end of human ignorance. If the prophets are right—and they have been remarkably right to date—our reach to the limits of light, human understanding, corresponds to a period of tumult in personal and world affairs. Therefore, we have only a short time remaining to turn from our self-limiting views, slough off the old sense of ignorance with its cherished notions, and awaken to the Child of Identity and Its birthright.

But that isn't the end of things either. Humanity is soon to make a spiritual and metaphysical breakout into a new day, a new time and space. Those who find the Child within, and listen to Its Covenant, are *to DO what they have been intended to do from the beginning of linear history.* Another "dimension" is to be added! This book is about that.

The reader has a role to play in these events. This volume

would not have come into your hands unless you were to be a part of the story soon to unfold.

HOW TO READ THIS BOOK

Dear Reader,

Truth, however it is expressed—whether it is the physics of the world or the jargon of the mystic—contains layer upon layer of meaning, addressing every human condition and state of comprehension. Consider David's Twenty-Third Psalm. His words "I shall not want" mean something to the trusting child, to the fearful heart of the soldier, to the anguished lover, the worried business man, the invalid, the mother and father. It is a meaningful statement to the aging heart of one grown weary of the world or to any human condition one might imagine. Isn't that true? If those four words can mean so much to so many, is it any wonder that some meanings may elude us for the moment?

Reader, do not struggle with this book. Read gently. If something seems vague, do not puzzle overmuch, but read on. Things that aren't clear immediately will become clear later, and when you have an opportunity to reread small sections, you will be delighted to find that the book has become new again. Repetition is not necessarily repetition. With each Glimpse the entire book is new—and so is our world—because it is yet to be surveyed in the light just discovered. There is more to read on each topic in the RELATED PAPERS section of the book.

There is a saying that nothing has been read once until it has been read twelve times. Read these words. Make them your own. "Eat them up," as the ancients said. But with all the reading and thought, get understanding. The intellect can reach no more than its limits of reason and logic. The New Covenant this book speaks of is lodged deeply within yourself already. Your Heart will take you there. I assure you, this book heralds Something Wonderful.

SPECIAL NOTE

One of the grandest gifts I could give the reader is to introduce *two small volumes: THE GOSPEL AC-CORDING TO THOMAS* and LaoTse's *TAO TE CHING.* You may be familiar with them already. If not, you will enjoy them mightily.

The Thomas "sayings of Jesus" came into my studies around 1958 when they were first published in English. They came ringing a Hallelujah Chorus of bells within me, confirming my own insights and intuitions of many years, just as the *TAO TE CHING* had done earlier. Now, these years later, the authenticity and antiquity of "Thomas" is an established fact recognized by scholars the world around, and I am not the only one to deduce that both men are making essentially the same subjective statement—and addressing the innocent, guiltless Child within us all.

These two books require a reading from a "subjective" point of view wherein they make a consistent metaphysics. Neither book can be comprehended by the Western set of mind that views "things" as separate objects "out there" in the world.

If the reader should find unfamiliar quotations from Jesus as he reads this book, he can find them in *THE GOSPEL ACCORDING TO THOMAS.*

It might be well to note that LaoTse preceded Jesus in history by about five centuries. The scholar can follow the Gnostic Idea from East to West to its birth as a doctrine of Love in the first century A.D.—only to have all but traces of its original subjectivism removed from worldly view within the first 500 years of its history. Interestingly, this is what both Jesus and LaoTse said would happen—and the prophets before them. However, both men say, in nearly identical terms, that in the final days of linear time "There is nothing hidden that shall not be revealed, and there is nothing covered that shall remain without being uncovered."

BOOK ONE

CHAPTER ONE

MANKIND'S SEARCH FOR TRUTH

Da Shan, Mythical Mountain of Seeking and Finding

THE INFANTRY SOLDIER OVERTONE

In the book *A Guide to Awareness and Tranquillity,* I wrote briefly of my time in warfare and one of the grand lessons about judgmentalism it afforded me. Over the years people have said how much that story meant to them, perhaps more than all the stories I have written. To the Western set of mind there is a certain incongruity about an old soldier being one to whom a measure of Light has been revealed. I can understand that.

Many singular events that I have never written about occurred during those days. I was, after all, a captain of infantry in two long wars. I lived with Chinese infantry troops in the field for nearly three years—subsisting with them, nearly starving with them. The few American soldiers in China had very little support from the United States during World War II. We were at the end of the world's longest supply line, and anything that reached us from home had been flown over Jap-

15

anese occupied countries, over the great Himalayan Mountains into Kunming, thence to be trucked and packed in by animals to us, wherever we might be. I didn't live very well during those years. My last year in China, as the great war came to an end, I joined Chinese troops who were actively engaged against the Japanese and fought in the battles that recaptured Ishan, Liuchow and Kwelin.

In Korea, less than ten years later, I commanded King Company, 279th Infantry Regiment, 45th Division, during the final months of that awful war. I also commanded Heavy Mortar Company, 279th Infantry Regiment. Things were much harder for me in Korea's combat than in the long, strange war in China. Being older didn't help me in Korea, nor did I have wise old Mr. Shieh at Korea's great Sandbag Castle or at Vulture's Roost on the 38th Parallel.

It is interesting that I've never written about those days, even though I've told of the learning events to seekers who have come to visit here in Alabama. I especially relished telling such tales to the metaphysical "absolutists" or to the young zealot idealists who arrived expecting only gentle words of peace from a Godly teacher. Since stories of strife, warfare and suffering are the last thing those people expect to hear from a "metaphysician," that's often what they got. Show me a revelation and I'll show you a traumatic event from which that Light emerged. Show me a true vision of heaven and I'll show you a descent into the anguish of hell wherein that vision was tried, tested and found faithful. "Prove me now herewith, saith the Lord. . . ." "Put all things to the test," Paul echoed.

And now, having written nearly everything necessary for the final book, I sit me down on yet another Memorial Day to remember my soldiers who fought with me in many battles. Let me write a Glimpse or two from those days.

First, harking back to China, Mr. Shieh and I, with five American teammates, were being pursued by a Japanese combat patrol. We were "retrograding," bringing up the rear of our little patrol, trying to get back to the safety of friendly lines. We were close to being captured. In those days, neither the Japanese nor Chinese "gave quarter." That is, we took no prisoners. I knew that if I were taken by the pursuing Japanese, it meant certain death. On the other hand, Mr. Shieh might successfully pass himself off as a Chinese peasant.

Oh, I cannot write this story! At this minute it is enough to remember Mr. Shieh seeing and pointing out the beauty of those purple blooms on the distant mountain we had yet to climb. I marveled at a man who could see beauty under such oppressive circumstances. I marvel more that he helped me learn to do it.

During the Korean War, an artillery round burst among my men on the left flank. Several bodies were hurled about and I ran to see the extent of the damage and whether the platoon leader was still effective. Sick to my stomach at the sight, I sat down among three of the bodies sprawled along the slope. I became aware of a visual "Presence" hovering beside them. A misty, blue-white light of sorts. A different kind of light, primal, persuasive and powerful. I could not explain what I saw then, nor can I now, but with the sight, and *because* of the sight, I was absolutely certain within myself I was being shown evidence of the deathlessness of Life—the survival of the Child, the Soul of men. I felt a marvelous sense of relief, almost *gratitude*, concerning those men and everything happening that day.

Within a few minutes of that incident, my regiment, and my part of the line in particular, was hit by an enormous wave of shell fire and oncoming Chinese troops. Hell erupted in a manner that no one can sufficiently describe or picture for another. One simply must experience something like that to fully understand.

But, to the ongoing Glimpse I'd like to write here if I can. In the early moments of that terrible onslaught wherein everything that moved was slaughtered ten times over—advancing troops, men, women, children, dogs and chickens and every moving creature caught at that place at that time—I was suddenly unable to hear. My world went silent and I was enveloped in an immeasurable calm. In the midst of that horrendous din of exploding bodies and shells, I could hear nothing but my own voice. In some marvelous way, I was caught up in a quiet, tranquil dimension, separate, but attached to the carnage at hand. I had not been wounded. I felt as well as one could be expected to feel under such circumstances. I could hear my own voice and even my breathing quite clearly. I went from gun position to gun position and heard myself giving calm encouragement to my troops. I could see their mouths move in reply and gratitude—and terror—but I couldn't hear them. I heard myself but couldn't hear the shells bursting in my face. I was beset with a wonderful enwrapping calm that let me move fearlessly to do whatever the moment asked me to do, as hideous as those moments were.

Perhaps a man can so detest a situation that his body produces the chemicals which, in turn, erect a barricade between himself and the galling situation. But as this was happening for me on that long day in Korea, there was a clear perception that a superlative Reality stood just behind the events; that there is another Scene just above this one, surrounding it; that Reality was bursting through that corridor of chaos into my own conscious recognition. I walked with a detached courage, as if the mortal body couldn't be and wouldn't be hurt. I ran from soldier to soldier, gun to gun. I was knocked down, spun around and stung with rocks and earth, feeling nothing but a calm, clear sense of Life's dominion over the sights and sounds of the world; as though, with the Presence I had sensed and seen moments earlier among the first bodies felled, I was SEEING and FEELING Life's eternal Nature, *even in the face of death.* Perhaps this was the beneficent calm Mr. Shieh had felt those years earlier when he saw the blossoms on the distant mountain.

That particular hellfire and damnation in Korea lasted four nights and three days without sleep for my troops and me. I have never forgotten the different time frame and the enwrapping inner peace nor how I was held and supported during that time—or non-time. More significant, that Peace has not forsaken me since those days, at least not when I was mindful of It nor when the chips were down and I called for It. How do I call for It? I bring forth the Child of Me.

Why I write this now after all these years, I really don't

know, but on this Memorial Day when I feel everything necessary for the book has been written, I sit me down and write something that might tell others, like Janice and Bill, that there are times when the anguish of the lesson is absolutely necessary—that leaving the anguish may not be the answer. Now, with absolute assurance, I can tell people, old and young, their lessons can be learned under the most difficult and trying circumstances. Better that we leave our nets after we've learned their lessons. Better that we call on the Child because the Child knows what to do. The Child and the Presence are the same one Presence and It is right here where we are, transcending this world's time and space.

The final tone in this Overtone: The day I moved King Company onto line in Korea, I was given the Order of Battle of the "enemy" opposing me just across the valley on the next mountain. Facing my regiment, and me in particular, was the Chinese 6oth Army, *the same troops I had lived with and trained for two years in China*. We met again, eight years later, in a terrible and senseless slaughter.

In the apparent world, our friends and enemies are the same—and, sometimes, needlessly, insanely, we try to destroy one another, thence to find that Life is eternal. Like Arjuna, in awful combat, I was instructed in certain of the Mysteries and learned the sense of senselessness.

Memorial Day, 1985

Making sense of this world of appearances has much to do with understanding the nature of Light/light, space, energy and time. Especially time.

TIME AND COSMOLOGY

"A new clock is soon to be turned on in the world of time and space," said old Han, talking to the group at the pond. "There is something that must be understood about time. The metaphysician's insistence that matter isn't what it seems to be and that time isn't real is only half right. I think that time is to be understood very soon."

A JOURNAL MUSING

Godhead existed before time and space. The Ineffable still exists, infinite and eternal.

Then what are time and space about?

They exist for an essential purpose: that mortals might eventually come to understand and know the scope of the Ineffable source of themselves. When space has been traversed and the mysteries of time calculated, man will find he has touched only the edges of Ineffability. He will find himself like one who has counted all the grains of sand that cover the earth, measured all the leaves in all the forests of his dreams, and then awakens to find he knows nothing of the Dreamer as whom he exists.

HAN, MASTER OF KWANGSE PROVINCE

Talking to the little group assembled at the mountain pond, Han said, "When the Ineffable asked 'What am I?' the tangible world came into being. When the Ineffable asked 'Who am I?' life appeared."

"What the hell does that mean?" the soldier asked, impatiently.

"Very simply, the tangible world is God's knowledge of What God is," the old man answered. "Life is God's knowledge of *Who* God is. The Child within that sparks the life of each of us is God's own Self-awareness in the process of happening. That spark is God's Self-image. The arrogant and frightened ego that surrounds the spark is the husk of man-made nothingness standing like a veil between Godhead and Its Self-Image. The Who includes the What and there is no division between Awareness and the images that appear within it here."

"And what does *that* mean?" the soldier asked, shaking his head in frustration.

There is a clear relationship between science, religion, metaphysics and time's cosmology. There is also a clear relationship between the awareness that reads these words and Everyman's appearance in the physical world of time and space. In this part of the book, let us set out to understand these relationships.

DA SHAN, THE MIGHTY MOUNTAIN

Listen to the story of Da Shan. Out of the flat plains of Kwangse Province rises the mythical mountain Da Shan, tall and majestic, reaching up through the clouds. Its peak is enshrouded in a different light, powerful and penetrating, for which the ordinary light of the slopes below is a limited and finite copy.

Da Shan is a granite mountain, almost pyramidal, with four faces, steep and tortured, ascending to a perfect pinnacle where the climber who reaches the top may stand balanced on one foot—not unlike a man balancing precariously atop the great pyramid of Egypt.

In Kwangse Province, the mythical Da Shan is "The Mountain of Seeking and Finding." It is said that all of us in the world are on its slopes, whether we know it or not. Han, the old sage of Kwangse, says the purpose of the human experience is to reach Da Shan's peak, thence to find one's original and final home that transcends time. There, he perceives his genuine identity and begins his promised reign of dominion over his own subjective world.

Among the sayings of Jesus found in the ancient Gnostic library at Nag Hammadi is this: "Blessed is He who was before he came into being." That is, blessed is the Identity that preexisted this body of things; blessed is the True Identity, the perfect image of Godhead, for which this body and experience in linear time are retroactive *confirmation*. Atop Da Shan we meet the One who existed before this tangible view of things came into finite being.

Our real Identity already stands atop that peak, exchanging light with Light and Light with light. The struggle for understanding may seem long and difficult, but it is retrospective in time, actually CONFIRMING the fact of Wisdom which is already the nature of the true Identity.

This knowledge *UNDERSTOOD* permits our daily living here in the world, the ascent of Da Shan, to happen smoothly and rapidly, as it was ordained as a birthright for every man who searches for the Truth.

When these discoveries are made, Han says, the climber discovers the penultimate marvel: that the Real of himself has been atop Da Shan all the while, unbound and untouched by time and space. "Yes," Han tells us, "One finds he has always stood above Da Shan's tangibility, the whole world under his foot." Then, the old Master of Kwangse said, "The balanced View at the peak of intellectualism discloses the final limits of human wisdom; thence, a troubling wonder of wonders: *that the objective and subjective human experience in the world has always been retrospective Self-examination, appearing to the climber as a forward movement in world-time.*"

Ah so. Don't struggle with this now, reader. We will proceed to examine this deepest of Mysteries *because it has to do with matter, time and space,* a mystery you and I and human science will solve momentarily.

IS DA SHAN REAL, UNREAL, NEITHER OR BOTH?

We are building an analogy. Its purpose is to enable us to understand the simplicity of religion and metaphysics and their place in pure science. The mythical mountain Da Shan faces all directions. The mountain is not separate from the earth, so when we speak of Da Shan, we are talking about matter, the world's tangibility. In this sense, the top of Da Shan is the top of the physical world and represents the place in time and space where the Intangible becomes tangible and where the tangible reverts to Intangibility.

Is there such a place in reality? Of course there is. There is a *point* at which something flows from nothing. There is a time in time when time began and matter exploded into form, even as there is a time in time when the purpose of time will be understood, and, perhaps, no longer exist. In one view, that approaching time appears confirmed (and seems inevitable) as each individual's physical demise. The leading edge of the intellectual world isn't far from that comprehension now, before death. There are those in the world who already understand the nature of (and temporal need for) time, space and tangibility.

HUMAN LIFE

Myriad forms of life appear to live on the mythical mountain. People are walking on the face of Da Shan, going uphill or downhill to one degree or another, or in circles, getting nowhere at all. Those of us doing nothing to discern Truth—most are doing nothing—sink more deeply into the density and darkness of Da Shan.

On the human scale of things, we enter the tangible scene of time and space somewhere on the mountain and leave it physically somewhere else—hopefully nearer the top. There are those like the Buddhists who say we leave the mountain when we've reached its uppermost limit and have done what we are here to do. Then, in total nothingness of husk-self, it is said we become the understanding Self of Something, to do God's bidding. *That* work is the real work which has barely begun in time.

Da Shan the world, mythical or not, is *finite*. Our search for the truth begins in time and ends in time. Like sand pouring through an hour glass, the sands of time begin and end. Time isn't what it seems to be, and there isn't much of that mythical stuff remaining in which to find ourselves balanced atop the mountain of understanding. Time's hold on us, our hold on it, is not eternal. The tangible tree of life *as it appears in the world* is not eternal either.

THE HOLE IN THE WALL

Han told this story:

Once in Kwangse Province there stood a great wall so high it blocked the sun and nothing grew in that place. During the Third Dynasty, a certain stranger came down from Da Shan. He stood beside the wall, made himself into nothing and vanished. He vanished so completely, the story goes, that a part of the wall vanished with him. Where he had stood, an opening in the wall appeared, like a door, through which people could come and go from one side of the wall to the other. The morning light streamed through that doorway and, where the light touched the ground, the first flowers grew in Kwangse. People were attracted to the new garden of flowers and light. They became the people of the original Community.

Han looked at his friends and said, "The Stranger who made himself nothing was praised for creating the Community and became the object of much worship. But it was not the Stranger who grew the garden that attracted the people; it was the Light. It was the Light," Han said again. "Light builds the community, not we ourselves. At the peak of Da Shan, we become nothing, no place, no thing; then we become the empty doorway, the Way, between light and darkness."

Who is Han? Han is the Child within myself. Han is the Child-I-am.

SPECIAL NOTE TO THE READER:

THE TRUTH IS NOT DIFFICULT TO UNDERSTAND

It will be immediately rewarding if the reader will let go the popular belief that "metaphysics" or "subjectivism" is a difficult subject to understand. It is NOT. We shall prove that in the pages ahead.

The idea that the deepest "Truth" is abstruse and difficult is a myth unintentionally projected by fine people who, for the most part, have had undiscerning teachers or inadequate, incomplete textbooks written before the Truth had been fully revealed to and confirmed by their authors. For centuries we've heard the Truth misstated or adulterated by well-intentioned teachers who didn't have the least idea what they were really talking about and whose unsupported, unproven commentary *couldn't* be comprehended, much less put to the test. For years we've studied or tried to study inconsistent philosophies that do not hold up under reasoned, rational analysis. I doubt that the Almighty can make sense of much that is written and shouted in the name of Truth. But metaphysics, as it actually is, is not a difficult concept to understand. Our capacity to understand subjectivism is growing in each of us daily. It is a clock turning on within us whose time has come.

Just as school children hear about the supposed horrors of geometry or Shakespeare, thence to avoid those subjects if they possibly can, exactly so mankind through the ages has avoided in-depth studies of science, religion, philosophy, metaphysics or Truth, afraid he couldn't understand them and unwilling to make the effort he believed *necessary* to comprehend. It has been such fear of theology that has kept so many from a study of it. It is the *misinformation* concerning metaphysics that keeps scientists and religionists from examining the worth of subjectivism. And certainly the distorted "junque" one finds in metaphysical works keeps students who *are* searching from arriving at the green fields of simplicity *just ABOVE* theology and metaphysics where the Goals of all our studies are met.

Throughout my life I have delighted in pointing to the underlying essences of religion and philosophy so they could be understood. I have made the intricacies of metaphysics perfectly plain to those who have come to study with me. Not one has failed to comprehend whatever was necessary to resolve his questions and wonderment of the moment. It will be the same for the reader of this book. Truth is not trying to evade our search. It discloses itself to a willing heart. We ask and are given the answers. We seek and find.

We are all natural philosophers, effortlessly *living* a divine philosophy which is intermingled with our own ideas—and we are doing this every minute of the day. We are all natural *subjectivists* as certainly as *objectivists*, and we are being both of them simultaneously to one degree or another. For instance, I look across Woodsong's meadow and see a tree. That tree is an object in my view. Simply observing it and being one who believes in God, I am an objective religionist. Ah, but listen, listen: aware that the tree is "beautiful" and "alive" and of a certain dignity and grace—or anything else concerning the essences of that tree—I am simultaneously thinking and observing *subjectively*. Hence, I am also a natural philosopher and metaphysician living my subjectivism. So is the reader thinking about these words. The forthright fact is that none of us with the least spiritual inclination can look at or think about anything *without being a philosopher, a metaphysician, whether we have ever read a single spiritual book or not.* As quickly as you and I define our terms herein, we will be walking in the same meadow of mind. It will be helpful for the reader to substitute his own words for those of mine which may seem unfamiliar at first.

The study of metaphysics as a *science* may seem a complex subject to grasp *intellectually*—that depending on whose version of Truth it is—*but to understand and live as a natural philosopher-metaphysican and MORE is not only easy but unavoidable.* Furthermore, it is essential. The world, as it is, is soon to erupt in our faces. A new mode of mentation is on the way.

Reader, do not wonder whether or not you are spiritual enough or *intelligent* enough—or have enough faith—to *understand* the Truth. You will understand it. You were meant to understand the Truth from the beginning of time, whether you consider yourself religious or not, intelligent or not. Does a flower have enough intelligence to bloom? Actually, you understand already. There is something deep within all of us that knows *already.* Yes, there is Something Wonderful in the midst of us that *understands* the discipline of the world and the important issues of life it includes. That knowing is ready to spring up and break out into our daily affairs and make life rich and meaningful *again.* This volume is intended to prove that.

Woodsong on the Hill, 1986

THE THREE SIMULTANEOUS POSITIONS

There is a little understood Zen saying that goes "First, it is a mountain; then, it is not a mountain; and then, finally, it is a mountain again."

Our perception of the Truth moves forward continually at those three basic "levels." Actually, they are happening simultaneously within each of us, with emphasis on one or the other at each moment in time, depending on our experiences and mode of mind. The three positions are rarely in balance, but our ongoingness in time slowly develops the balance. Events in the years ahead will bring many of us to the balance, thence, to see the *final* position clearly—the "it is a mountain *again.*" When we see the mountain again, *this time we will know what we are looking at.* We will also understand why we lost sight of reality for a time.

The first, "It is a mountain," is the objective level of things. We begin as children observing an objective world, learning about people, places and things. Our training and schooling come to us from the objective position: I am here, identified as this body; the mountain is over there. The mountain is real. The world is real. The body is real. Space and time are real. Sin, sickness, and death are not only real, but inevitable. One is prone to stop at this position and stay there. One can see that St. Doxy and Calvinopolis are two very large cities on Da Shan.

Somewhere, for the evolving and fortunate, and usually out of some trauma along the way, one learns of idealism, of metaphysics and its subjectivism. (As it seems, however, many more hear about the subjective idea than get it straight.) At this level of discernment—the metaphysical—we experience (and hear about) proof after proof that "matter" is not what it appears to be, but is "mental," that "things" are within awareness, that matter and its space and time are not real, that we are not actually identified as the body but *as the Awareness that observes the body*, and so on. At this point in our ongoingness, and as the Zen Master put it very well, "The mountain *is not* a mountain." One is especially prone to stop at this position and stay there—and to this day, nearly everyone in Metadelphia has done just that. A relatively small town on Da Shan, Metadelphia has high walls around it.

Let me emphasize that *both* the objective and subjective perspectives are happening in all of us simultaneously, here a little, there a little. The purest objectivist who has never read the first metaphysical statement has, nonetheless, at some place in his experience—maybe when terribly ill, drunk, full of drugs, or in the midst of a fearful, passionate episode in combat—become momentarily aware, if only subliminally, that there is more to the world than appears to the ordinary senses. The religionist who is still worshiping objectively has had many moments when the subjective feelings of Spirit came through and he knew without question that the mountain is more than (or less than) a mountain.

The metaphysician who hasn't actually understood his subjectivism, and put it to work, might be declaring with all his intellectual might that "God is All and there is no matter," but the religionist who has no conscious knowledge of metaphysics *and has felt the "Spirit" while reading his Bible or looking at a flower* may very well be more conscious of Truth than THAT metaphysician. The step from objectivism to subjectivism is claimed long before it is taken.

Finally, there is the third level of awakening of which we are capable, every one of us, metaphysician and religionist alike: *Rediscovery* of Identity, the Child within. This is the sublime level of perception, and it doesn't take a metaphysical education (or any other kind) to get there. The Child within has been with us since our time began in tangible space. The inner Child has a perfectly balanced View from atop Da Shan and knows how to act subjectively in an objective world.

No, the Child within us doesn't throw away its metaphysics as the metaphysician has mistakenly thrown away "old theology." The Child teaches us correctly about the ephemeral nature of matter and the allness of God. The Child doesn't insist that we leave our wonderful subjectivity (or objective world either), but shows us how to LIVE a perfect balance all the way to the end of the temporal span.

Nor does the Child throw out every old concept of religion, especially mankind's love of humanity. Rather, the Child of us comes to discover religion again, this time with a knowledge of what it is and what it was *originally*—and why it appears on the scene as a confusing melange of doctrines. The Child teaches us how to live subjectively in an objective world and in so doing, shows us that "It is a mountain *again*," a tangible world that doesn't fool us and that we *understand.*

The Child within leads us to the Balance, and the Balance allows us to begin the dominion and "reign," the heritage of those who understand. The Child takes us quickly to the top of the mountain right here in the world. The Child of us is the real of us. Reader, there is a way to *find that Child,* and this book is about that.

THE TOP-DOWN VIEW AS OPPOSED TO THE ORDINARY VIEW

"The top-down view," the subjective view, is a way to think, a mode of mind. The top-down view "begins" its thoughts (about anything and everything) with Ineffability, God. Then, from THAT position, one reasons his way toward the scene at hand. The top-down mode of mentation begins with God as all in all, pure and perfect. The awareness of the reader presently reading these words is God's Self-awareness in the process of comprehension. This mode of thinking is the very foundation of subjectivism, though few metaphysicians seem aware of that. The top-down mode of mentation finally becomes *essential for our every thought and calculation*. The top-down view knows the "real" of us is the Life of us—and is the very Awareness that perceives these words. This awareness was never born. It doesn't wither and die. It was never born into matter and can't go out of matter—rather, matter exists as the knowing, the wisdom, of God. The "real" of us knows in some marvelous way that only GOD is going on. The "real" of us knows that the *reality* of this human experience is God's activity.

WALKING WITH MICHELE

"Awakening" is a little like seeing the first star
in the evening sky.
Suddenly, there it is,
alone and faint
—but clearly there.
We stop for a moment and say "This is the first star I see to-
night" and maybe smile inside.
Under our breath, we say the little verse about Star Light, Star
Bright, first star I see tonight. . .
The Light of Life, the Joy, first comes as something just that
faint and small, hardly noticeable, yet something that has hap-
pened every night of our lives and gone unnoticed
—until one morning or afternoon or evening we SEE it—really
see it
and stop for the first time to savor the event
and appreciate it
and give thanks for the wonder of it.
Something wonderful happens within the heart of us.

*It is a small moment, but for the first time we recognize it to be
within the Awareness we are
—and we know—we know it is Part of Something Grand
and wonderful
and true.
Something Holy,
something extraordinary.
We finally know it isn't happenstance, nor luck nor accident.
We recognize it (whatever it is) as Something mysterious
—a holy moment.
Like the first star, we finally NOTICE
and savor
and give great thanks for it.*

Especially give thanks.

*I am the beauty I see. I am the joy I see. I am the excitement and
enthusiasm of EVERYTHING I see—because, I can't recognize
something unless I AM it! It is Me! It is I! It is this holy Awareness of God I am.*

WHAT ARE THE ADVANTAGES OF SUBJECTIVISM?

When the subjective idea dawns, one's views become quantum; one's religion becomes quantum; one's experience becomes quantum; one's knowledge begins to multiply until it
becomes quantum.

What is meant by this? When the subjective idea dawns, one
begins to realize that *the entire world is unfolding within himself*. It begins to dawn that the appearance of mankind "out
there" is one's "objective" view in total—one's own "possibilities" carried to near infinity.

In the pre-subjective state, one was merely one among millions; in the subjective mode, millions are within oneself. In
the objective state, there is just me and my pathetic little view
of things; in the subjective state, there is this divine Awareness
(which God is being) and it includes all views within itself, infinite possibilities.

In the pre-subjective state, time is linear and sequential. In
the subjective state, time is less linear and not necessarily se-

quential. In the subjective state, time may move in both directions or not exist at all.

Einstein's equation came from a subjective state of mind. See what that little subjective idea has done within the objective world! In magnitude, subjectivism can do for the individual what quantum mechanics has done for science—and more. But, without the Child within, even subjectivism is dead in the water.

SUBJECTIVISM AND RELIGION

To the objective view, there is God and a sinful mankind struggling to return to God's grace. To the subjective view, there is God and God's Self-Awareness appearing as all possible individual states. The "return" is leaving the bonds of objectivism to re-embrace the Original Child, the subjective "Mind of God"—to let that Awareness be us which is also the Christ Truth. *Then*, if we are willing to continue, we find and live the balance. Here, the objective world is *understood*, not denied. The balance is a step beyond subjectivism, just as the subjective idea is a step beyond the objective view of things. But, listen, listen: *The Child within can be found anywhere along the line at any moment!* When the Child is found, we go quickly to the balance of things.

SUBJECTIVISM AND THE BIBLE

The blind caterpillar has one opinion about a particular leaf on which it walks. But how much more expansive that view becomes when the caterpillar is a sighted butterfly! Exactly so, the subjectivist has an expanded view of the Bible, considerably *beyond* the confining, restricting, legalistic interpretation given it by fundamentalist, objective churchdom. The winging butterfly's statements and actions relative to the Bible-leaf may seem an abomination to the caterpillars still digesting the letter of the leaf. Just as quantum mechanics seems to make a mockery of objective physics (but doesn't, really), exactly so, dawning subjectivism seems an insane mockery of religion to some religionists, especially those who think they are seeing and interpreting the Bible with the only possible view.

But just as the subjective states of mind seem superior to the limited views of objectivism, so does the view of the rediscovered and resurrected Child within (This is the third position, the "It is a mountain *again"* position) come as an infinitely superior view to those held by the churchman, scientist or metaphysician!

My metaphysical friends have always been nonplussed by the thought that there could be a position beyond the GOD IS ALL position. Indeed, there is. God is beyond all concepts and all "positions." Later, we will cover this ground in detail. Meanwhile we remember that there is the third position, quite beyond metaphysics as it presently appears in the world. "Finally, it is a mountain *again.*" Here we know what to DO concerning the mountains of life—and find ourselves capable of moving them.

LETTER TO AN OLD FRIEND

(A summary)

Dear Mary who writes of her search for Truth,

Yes! You have been there all the while—standing on the very peak of the mountain of recognition! Since before Abraham was, Identity has been right here. Now you know for yourself that the "climb" to the mountain top of Understanding, Intelligence, Wisdom and Identity is actually *confirmation.* Human events are happening in reverse, so to speak, CONFIRMING the Fact of perfect Alreadyness. Those events happen "precept upon precept, here a little, there a little."

Yes, exactly as your letter states, "Our fastest way to the top of the mountain of nearly endless seeking is to understand that Identity is there in Truth ALREADY" ("The only Way there is to BE there!"), and then our human experience begins to CONFIRM that fact. Our confirmation is *inverse* and comes sequentially, step by step. We see things marvelous in a twinkle, but it may take a lifetime to confirm them.

On the human scene where time holds sway, this confirmation seems like the ascent of a mountain, the flow of the river to the sea, the growth of a tree from seed to seed and a return to our Original freedom. The Authority of God is *confirmed* for us, "line upon line," just as you write. Originally, this is what "confirmation" meant in the eyes of the enlightened.

Mary, I delight in your letter, remembering all the times you growled at the absurdity of the world, its injustices and enigmas. Now, it is good to know you understand some of them for yourself and "have returned to the non-self atop Da Shan." You didn't need to remind me of your "incredulous disbelief" of those early days—nor of your "endless arguments." How could I forget them? But, as you have seen, your Self-discovery was *inevitable*. "At last I see It for mySelf," you write. "Self-discovery *in time* is inevitable because it has already happened in timelessness." Exactly. You state the sequence precisely. The wonder is that we could have overlooked the obvious for so long. But it didn't seem obvious at first, did it? Now we find ourselves wondering exactly as Jesus did, why the spiritual leaders and metaphysicians of the world are the last to see this mystery rather than the first.

Mary, now that the things I told you have proven themselves to be true, please listen carefully once more. Your work has just begun! There is much for you to DO in this world of appearances! For every person I have helped around the bends of the river or along the slopes of Da Shan, you will help a thousand. Inasmuch as "those other people" are within THIS consciousness of sequentiality (time), we have arrived at the ability and *obligation* to address them ALL and tell them of their birthright. We *do* it now that we know it. We help others find it and do it, now that we can. We don't stop until everyone within us has had the opportunity to walk through the Door we find ourselves to be.

You will be given "yours" who will hear your Voice, and you will be faithful to them, giving them your Glimpses and substance, and they to you, even as you have been faithful to me and I to you. This is what we are here for, Mary, lady of the New Covenant within.

I love you!

Mary has found a measure of herself, called "Identity." It didn't happen as she expected. It didn't happen because she did the things outlined in the textbooks and teachings of the churches and philosophic schools. Nor did Mary do it *alone* as seekers are wont to believe is necessary.

CHAPTER TWO

DEVELOPMENT OF COSMOLOGY

Da Shan and the Mist

Every theology that has grown out of Light contains a mountain illustration. Judaism and Christianity have Sinai where Moses talked to God and from which Moses descended, bringing the Commandments to those on the slopes below. The childlike founder of Christianity was taken to a mountain to be tempted. He delivered one of the great sermons of the world from the slopes of a mountain. The Indians of the American Southeast have a holy mountain in their cosmology and tell stories remarkably similar to those in the Bible—myths developed long before they knew of the Bible. Buddhists, Hindus, Taoists, Moslems and many others have their mountains of Light and Life. All of them use river, tree and seed analogies as well.

There is good reason for this telling of a mythical mountain which mankind is climbing. *The analogy will bring us to a breakout into a meadow of green grass and simplicity.* Just a little more about Da Shan, the world.

THE METAPHYSICAL INVERSION OR REVERSAL

The retro-nature of "the climb"—this human experience—is an important dimension of the cosmology to be comprehended if the "metaphysical inversion" that so mystifies the world (especially metaphysicians) is to be understood and lived intelligently. Certain states of mind know nothing about this inversion or "reversal" in the nature of things and care nothing about it. Others have heard of "the divine reversal," or whatever else it might be called, and accept its validity, but they simply cannot understand it. Still another group understands the reversal intellectually but can't find its application in the world. Finally, there are those to whom this mystery has been fully revealed *and who are charged with its telling*—but face the world's intransigence and incredulity in doing so.

When "the reversal" is understood, the wheat and tares mentioned in the Bible are understood as well. So are the *reasons* for religion in the world and for the appearances of sin, sickness and death. Further, those who know this mystery are able to distinguish the honest message from the misleading one or from the intentional lie. The Da Shan illustration will lay the groundwork to enable the credulous, the simple and childlike—*no matter how intellectually astute they are or are NOT*—to perceive this essential unfoldment of "metaphysics" and, finally, *to get beyond that maze of boggling erudition and move onward!* There is more to Truth than metaphysics alone, my friend, but we do well to understand "the reversal" and its "contradistinctions." They will become crystal clear as you read this book. That is a promise I make to the persistent. Some schools of thought say those who understand the inversion are enlightened!

DA SHAN IS AN IMAGE OF AN IMAGE

In *The Gospel According to Thomas* we find these remarkable words: *Jesus said: If they say to you: "From where have you originated?," say to them: "We have come from the Light, where the Light has originated through itself. It stood and revealed itself in their image." If they say to you: "Who are you?," say: "We are His sons and we are the elect of the Living Father." If they ask you:*

"What is the sign of your Father in you?," say to them: "It is a movement and a rest."

That in mind, imagine still *another* mighty mountain beyond Da Shan. It is an unseeable Infinite Mountain of Reality, preexisting Da Shan in exquisite Simplicity. *That* mountain transcends all names. It can't be seen directly by those who are climbing Da Shan, but when one reaches the tangible mountain's peak and stands balanced there, he begins to perceive the Mountain Beyond Name, mysteriously inverted, its peak touching the peak of Da Shan. It is a Mighty Universe so vast that even Da Shan is but a granule within its heart.

In a twinkling, the balanced Child, but ONLY the balanced Child, sees that Da Shan is an *image* of the Mountain Beyond Name. More, he sees that Da Shan, the image of the real, is an infinite *quantity of images of images* of the Mountain Beyond Name—all spiraling inward—and because Da Shan is so many images, and images of images, compacted inward, Da Shan (the world) appears opaque and solid to the climber, his own body a physical microcosm of Da Shan.

The Child perceives, further, that the light which is the substance of Da Shan is only an image of the Light of the Real Mountain Beyond Name. The limited light of Da Shan is in motion; the illimitable Light of Mountain Beyond Name is at rest. Da Shan appears one way in its own limited light, quite another way in the timeless Light at rest.

Standing atop Da Shan, one also finds that the physical body has a Twin for which the climber's self-image is a poor inversion. Indeed, the real Identity stands within the very center of the Ineffable Mountain Beyond Name and atop DaShan simultaneously. More than that, The Child is everywhere on Da Shan at once, as well as at the Heart of things. This "other" Identity has a Name—the Child, the Christ-Light, the Guide, the Original One-I-AM, the Comforter, Messiah which has never left the State of Grace of Mountain Beyond Name and has never been bound by the world's time and space, *even while appearing there.*

Atop Da Shan, the balanced View, *the Child's* view begins to comprehend that everything under its feet is imaged confirmation (to infinity) of the REAL; that everything beneath the balanced foot exists in time's inward spiral—present to confirm eternal Timelessness and infinite spacelessness.

Ah so, as the good people in Kwangse often say, what does this mean? For starters, it means that at each moment of time on the face of Da Shan, the unbound, unconfined Child within us is available to guide our way to Da Shan's peak wherein time ends and Timelessness exists already.

What does the Christ Child, the Heart within, tell us that helps our ascent? That in Truth, the Real of us is victorious already—and in proportion to our belief that those words are true, THIS tangible experience in the world of people, places and things *progressively moves to CONFIRM that Fact,* proving the Light of the Eternal—appearing in our experience as another step toward the Truth, another Glimpse.

How? As a perfect balance maintained against all worldly odds; as inward scenes of beauty; as feelings of joy and well-being beyond human comprehension, all rushing to confirm the Real—the veritable "proof of God" the world (Da Shan) is looking for.

WHAT ELSE DOES THE CHILD WITHIN TELL US?

It tells us intimately of "The Equation" without which no one tangibly reaches the pinnacle of understanding.

What is the Equation? It is the mysterious Balance—the perfect balance actually lived *in the world of appearances.* This will become clear in the pages ahead.

THE PATHWAYS

Da Shan has four long known and studied pathways to the top and a fifth pathway not so apparent. Love, devotion, service, wisdom and then the Child's Way. Five avenues in all—like five approaches, five balances, "five trees" as early Christians spoke of them. The Child's top-down view reveals the bottom-up pathways, each a perfect balance. Therefore, we look out into the world from wherever we seem to be and find ways that lead irrevocably to ultimate comprehension. The fifth and last is a composite of the others and is the most direct route of all. That is the way that has been shown to me. It is the pathway one Child wide. It is the Child's Way.

Many of us travel more than one pathway during our lives and some of us none at all. At the end of our span of time, the pathways plainly merge, and, as the fingers of the hand come together at a common arm leading to the heart, all the ways are understood and appreciated in the heart of us. From the slopes, each way is singular, none necessarily better than another. The fifth way, the unseen way, is the Child's way, the New Way, the straight and open way to Godhead. This work discusses that pathway in detail.

When one arrives at the peak of understanding, he finds he has not climbed a real mountain at all. Rather, the climb in tangible time and space *confirms* the Eternal Identity residing already in the heart of Godhead—Mountain Beyond Name. Or, to say this obversely (which is the way the world appears to us): At Da Shan's top, one finds he has climbed the mountain an infinite number of times and every mortal's search is his own, appearing as all possibilities happening simultaneously.

At the peak, one finds that the Child's Equation is the Key for every climber—*and he announces this Equation to his world!*

WE STUDY WITH A GENTLE TOUCH

"Sam, I have been searching for Truth with all my strength, *but. . ."*

Excessive struggle to understand is damning. Too much effort can be as much anathema to Truth as too little. The very one who strives with might and main to crash the gates of comprehension is the one least likely to find the Feast within.

Crumbs, maybe. A glimpse here and a glimmer there, but never enough to suit him. Never Wisdom ITSELF. Never Realization ITSELF. The one who climbs toward the Truth will ever be the climber. The one who struggles will ever be the struggler. Reading for information is an effort but reading for confirmation is a joy. The one who grits his teeth and juts his jaw is the metaphysical masochist who beats his head against a wall he builds himself by insisting he is the ignorant one. The climber and the mountain he struggles to climb are one climber.

Listen softly. Listen gently. Consider the difference between *measuring* a tree and *being* a tree. Identified as a rootlet, a twig, a leaf or a limb measuring the tree, the leaf reaches outside that sense of identity and measures the near infinity of Self and wonders how it can be done. Identified as the tree, the tree IS the measure, and the looking is confirming joy.

Whatever wig-wagging gyrations the leaf on a tree may perform, it is the tree living the leaf, and the leaf is nothing of itself. The tree is the leaf and the leaf needs naught but to be itself—which it is being already in fact, through no prowess of its own.

Listen again: the bud on the tree, closed within itself in darkness, may think it is an identity capable of independent action. It may feel it is blooming itself through its own great effort, but when the bud opens into the light of day, it looks roundabout with new amazement and declares, "TREE am I, not bud. TREE is being all I am. Tree is me and all I see. TREE is being this IDENTITY, not bud at all, not Bill, not Rachel, not Janice. Tree is being all I am. As a bud I am nothing of myself at all, at all! Tree am I, neither suffering nor afraid."

Wisdom atop the mountain of knowledge am I, not a climber, not a climber.

Reader, do you see this? Do you see the wisdom of letting go? Do you see the stifling, self-perpetuating *arrogance* of viewing oneself as an anguished climber still struggling to make a breakthrough? If one must struggle, then let him struggle to confirm the Wisdom he already is in Truth. The effort to lift ignorance up to Wisdom merely perpetuates the belief of an identity in need of an uplift. We let go excessive effort to put off the old identification. We sit easy. We rest in Already. We claim the Child within to be the real Identity— *then read our books and do our work to confirm that fact.* We claim that one whom God is in charge of.

My quest for Truth has taken me many places in the world, and I have studied at the feet of many enlightened teachers. Each in his own way said, "Perfection is *already* spread over he face of the land but men perceive it not." "I have sought Truth all my life, but lo, that which I seek, I am!" "Not with a mighty effort, but with gentleness and grace." "Not by might nor by power, but by my spirit, saith the Lord of hosts." My studies went from searching to confirming. The two efforts look the same, but the results are very different.

The Truth we seek to confirm is closer than fingers and toes, not leagues nor years away. A supernal Harmony is already in command of the AWARENESS that reads these words. Godhead is being this life "we" are, this Awareness-I-am; not you, not me, not us. GODHEAD is life—and responsible for it.

We begin the break with "mortal mind," the misidentification, the "old man," "the liar from the beginning," when we admit to the empty nothingness of an ego struggling to climb the mountain of comprehension. Rather we acknowledge the allness of GODHEAD and Its Self-awareness. There is nothing unenlightened about the awareness looking at these words—though we may long hold to the old belief that we are ignorant of Truth. Ignorance resides in the role we play as a taskmaster to God, trying to make God do the taskmaster's bidding. Only the taskmaster needs a "breakthrough." TREE OF LIFE am I, and as tree tends its blossom, so Godhead tends me.

Everyone who has studied with me knows we suggest that our study be done with a tender touch. When the symbols of symbols get heavy—and they do, over and over—we put them down for a time to look at the symbol directly. It is nice to read a book about trees, another thing to walk among them. The walk makes the reading easier, and, without the walk, the reading remains incomplete.

A grand Wisdom is being the consciousness that reads these words and looks outside the window at the trees standing silently there. We are prone to become profound with a book in our hand, but how much more profound one can be while touching a tree in the wildwood or tending the needs of stranger! What is this business of analyzing, comparing and judging everything endlessly? Why the excessive flood of words to get at Truth when Truth existed before words came into being? Words are an essential tool, yes, yes—and Da Shan is better because of them—but there is a marvelous balance between the book and the trees, between the study of words of Truth and the living of them.

Reader, is this too simple and naive? Intellectualism thinks so, but intellectualism without the heart has failed to bring

Peace. This simple act of naivete, this inane and childish bit of stillness will soothe the troubled breast, and open the doors of the Heart to arenas the intellect knows nothing about.

Let me take you there.

FIRST MENTION OF THE DIVINE EQUATION

In Kwangse the group sat talking.

"With all my travel and study I've never heard of the equation," the soldier groused.

"I haven't either," said the minister. Neither had Lee nor Mary.

Han said, "One who doesn't live the Divine Equation simply doesn't know it. To know it without living it is to be dead. To know it is to live it. Personally, I do not see how one can know he knows it without living it, but I don't know everything."

"But friend Han," shouted the soldier, "you just told us that the real Identity of each of us is Omniscience itself! How can one be that and still not know everything?"

Han said, "God knows everything, but I don't. I am merely the *knowing* of God, so I certainly don't know everything."

"That doesn't make a damned bit of sense," the soldier said. "I call that circular reasoning," he added, leaving the room.

KNOWER, KNOWING, KNOWN

Knower, knowing, known. These three are one. The Knower is the known. The Knower is the knowing. Yes, yes, but the knowing is not the Knower. Western metaphysics, as it is mistakenly interpreted, leads one to equate himself with Knower. Then to attempt to BE the Knower.

The awareness reading these words is the knowing of Life/God/Godhead—but God is greater than God's Self-perception. "My Father and I are one, but my Father is greater than I am." (Jesus)

"How can I be God's knowing going on and still not know what to do or which way to turn or whom to believe?" the soldier asked.

Han answered: Learn the Divine Equation.

"How in heaven or hell can I be God's knowing and still not

know the Divine Equation? I've never even heard of the damned thing."

Han answered: Live the Equation and you will know.

"Malarky! How can I live it if I don't know it, you son of a sick horse?"

Han answered: Ask.

"Who? You? You just said that if you told me I wouldn't be able to hear it or understand what I think I hear. This is insane! You are crazy."

"Perhaps," said Han, "but I know the Equation."

DA SHAN AND THE MIST

But there went up a mist from the earth and watered the whole face of the ground. And the Lord God formed man of the dust of the ground, and breathed into his nostrils the breath of life; and man became a living soul. (Genesis)

If one draws a great X on a sheet of paper and visualizes the top half (to infinity) as representing the invisible Godhead, let him understand that the bottom half represents the entire tangible universe—Da Shan, emerging out of Ineffability at its peak, even while being embraced by that Godhead simultaneously, not unlike the manner in which a sphere embraces the points, lines and planes within itself.

Then let one understand that the lower "half" is the mirrored image of the Ineffable above it, below it, surrounding and permeating it simultaneously. One sees then that Da Shan, matter, is at once *image* of Image and is immersed within the Center of Godhead, "Great Mountain beyond Name."

Next we perceive that the ideal state to recognize in the human condition is that our Original Identity is unbound by time or space and stands atop Da Shan; that the limited view of ourselves (image of Image) struggling along the slopes of the mountain can *call upon the Original*, the twin, to carry it quickly to Da Shan's Peak in conscious here-and-now spatial, sequential fact. The fact is, the Original Identity, like the photon, is everywhere in time and space, constantly—there being no human condition we can get into that the Child-Image doesn't know the way out of.

Atop Da Shan, we find ourselves the very Center of Being,

the non-spatial point at which Ineffability flows into image below—and where image below flows back to Godhead. The
"real of us" (Child, Identity, Image of God) is "located" at the
very middle of the "X" I asked you to imagine. Where does
your world begin, reader, if not right here where your eyes
read these words?

This illustration, when understood, shows one at a glance (1)
the picture of the world and why it isn't "real," (2) human experience in time and space, and (3) our sequential journey
that comes to an end in time even though it exists forever in
timelessness. We can understand that all above Da Shan is
Light and all "below" on the slopes merely *images* of that Light
(called "limited light"), making an inward, downward spiral
into immeasurable multiplicity, finiteness and stolid darkness.
Beneath the peak of the world, tangibility is bathed in the limited, imaged light of Light, finite and in motion, a holographic
duplication of the Real. The lord of that duplication is the theological Lucifer, angel of limited light, once chief angel, "fallen
from grace" for trying to be God and duplicate His universe.
Later we will see that nothing has fallen from grace REALLY,
despite theology's sundry interpretations of Holy Writ.

The Glimpses that come to us in our human struggle on the
slopes of the world are the ever-present Child of Light-beyond-
light breaking through, disclosing an unsuspected wonder of
Reality. In truth, *these Glimpses are all that's really important in
the human experience*, all else being the contradistinctory lessons that LEAD to them.

Our prayers, meditations, yearnings, longings, and spiritual
leadings are ever directed by Godhead through the Child of
Us, the Original of Us who resides atop Da Shan in the bosom
of God. That Child, like the photon, is everywhere at once in
space and time—available instantly to guide us through the
necessary "ascent from tangibility."

"Necessary? The descent isn't *real*. It never happened!" says
the metaphysician only half-correctly. More about this in later
pages.

Even now the Child of Us stands atop Da Shan in the very
heart of Godhead, the entire world under his foot, free of the
imbalances of the slope, free of the human conditions that
propel us in one direction or another on the face of Da Shan.

The Child is ever the Christ Light, Soul of OurSelf, capable of hearing our every needful desire along the slopes and absolutely willing to help us make the upward propelling decision and movement on the slopes of Da Shan, unavoidable image world of *The Discipline*. The "discipline of the world" continues until we are atop the mountain in living fact, not mystical or metaphysical profession.

Understand, from the center of the great X where the two mountains touch, downward, there is another light of the world, the limited light of tangibility (appearing to be) claiming to be the reality for the tangibile scene. This appearance of limited light is spoken of as the Mist that arose to deceive. That deception is not without God's perfect purpose, as you will perceive for yourself. The limited light we are writing about here is the same light that science says is moving at 186,300 miles per second and illuminates this page as you read.

Even the body that walks the slopes of Da Shan is but a microcosm of Identity, *image* of the Child-Image of God. The Child is a microcosm of the Real. The physical body of the present reader is quite *capable* of reaching the top of the mountain of understanding within its lifespan, no matter its age or condition, and in doing so brings attention ever more to the Child-Real, and ever less to the body of flesh. More, we find the physical body's purpose in the tangible world is to do the "will of Godhead." There are things for the Self-realized to do in the days ahead, and quickly.

For those who attain the peak during this discipline, this lifetime, there comes a moment in time to speak of the Equation—Life's flow into life, Intangibility's flow into the imaged forms of Tangibility and back again. For a time the Child of us speaks to the entire world, and the world, having become the *subjective world of our attainments and learnings,* has also become our imaged Selfhood.

Atop Da Shan in living fact, not querulous metaphysical abstraction and profession, we have shrunk egoistically from nothingness to nothingness to *consciously* be again the Son of God, the Logos to Life. We have ended our descent into the images of tangibility as though they were the reality of Life. Finally, our vision transcends the world's mist and we have realized our Original State, never fallen from grace, never guilty of human atrocities and sin.

Line upon line, precept upon precept, here a little, there a little, we have come to comprehend all the events of our linear lives in time as the Good necessary to bring us consciously into the fullness of the Godhead, bodily.

Does this writer claim to stand atop the mighty mountain of illusion? Dear God, I make no such claim, having no idea the extent of Limitlessness's Image, but write as I have been taken and proven.

EVERY ASCENT OF THE MOUNTAIN IS LEGITIMATE AND GOOD

Philosophy is the moribund approach. Its enemies are intellectualism and self. Theology or Religion, the pathway of faith, is brilliantly straight and true insofar as it keeps us *mindful of God, simple and childlike, honest and helpful to mankind.* Its enemies are the objective bias and leaders who worship themselves before they have turned to God. Metaphysics and psychology make a direct approach, albeit with many devastating sidetrails and entrapments. Its enemies are arrogance and self, leaders who turn to God before turning from self, or teachings that attempt to make the self into God. Service and Love are the wonderful way wherein the Equation is lived without stint and without thought, enwrapping everything in equality and tenderness. Condemnation, envy and jealousy are the enemies of service. Love, its hope in childlikeness and mercy, has no enemies who can touch it—but lust would try.

Now, for the tumultuous days ahead when the false foundations of the world will be shaken apart, comes the final pathway—the hidden Way of the Child and Its Equation.

Everyone who can see the Child of himself still acting in any of his ways, will be capable of running quickly to the final blossom of Life, calling to the Christ Light of Himself for unfailing help and respite. That one is carried aloft, up and out of the darkness of shattering icons and selfness. The old nature, finally recognized and understood, is left behind.

The Child of us has knowledge of the center Ground of religion, philosophy, metaphysics and science—already knowing all *that needs to be known to make it through time.* The Child will lift the willing of us to the High Place and there we reign over our own overcoming.

CHAPTER THREE

UNDERSTANDING THE HUMAN EXPERIENCE

Transcending Dualism

HUMAN EXPERIENCE IS RETROSPECTIVE CONFIRMATION

The human experience is not IT, but is the confirmation of IT. The human experience is the linear unfoldment, running backward in time so to speak, *confirming* the Real. The world experience is present as CONFIRMATION of Ineffability, searched for, expected, perceived and understood. Not the ship, but the wake of the ship. Or, as so many in history have put it, the tangible experience is the shadow of the real.

That shadow is overspread with many shadows, infinite possibilities happening simultaneously, but each unfolding is forward moving in time. The central figure among the shadows is this one we call ourself, enshrouded in self-centeredness, selfishness and ignorance. Its obligation is to become a passerby and walk gently through the many shades of meaning, discerning the Real Confirmation of Godhead and resting therein, content that Godhead is indeed the All of all. Because Godhead is Already, our physical discernment is actually retrospective and appears sequentially—forward going and progressive in space and time.

As everyone who has perceived this remarkable *simplicity* knows full well, it is nearly impossible to express it in writing. Why? How can one speak fully of multidimensional Allness while using words which are, after all, mere symbols of symbols, man-made, sequential and locked into the habitual mode of thought that regards one's struggle to be from ignorance at the bottom to light at the top, while believing time and space to be the final dimension?

Surely a first step in discerning the Real is the perception that all the shadow events are appearing within one's own head, so to speak. This inner nature of comprehension is central to everything. Lo, *subjectivism* is born. Subjectivism is the second plateau along the apparent climb upward, the intellectual, self-centered time, the arrogant and superior time. Remember, Identity exists already, so the "climb," the "progress" and "pathway," and all things else in time and space, are ***retrospective to and from the true Nature of Being***.

The "pathway" from ignorance to Light (as it seems) is like one daydreaming aboard a Ship, looking at the wake in the far distance, then following that wake backwards toward the ship where one is; thence, "finally" in time, awakening to the Presence of Ship whereon one sits and learns of the qualities and attributes of Ship. Aboard the Ship, one looks back at the wake and sees everything there CONFIRMING the Fact of Ship, his experience seeming like a long swim to reach the knowledge that Identity is perfectly birthed—and berthed— within the Ineffable.

This analogy is not precise in all ways, but we will straighten every imprecise point before many more pages. Remember, reader with whirling head, we are moving through the thickets of cosmology and theology quickly. There is a breakout into a remarkable comprehension along the way. Be patient just a little longer. After all, time and space have puzzled thinkers for ten thousand years—and we are soon to understand them both!

The pathway from the trailing edges of the wake back to the ship is often likened to climbing a mountain. At the peak one discovers the true nature of Identity which Life (awareness) has been all the while. The human experience is all mountain climb—none of it real, but all of it necessary retrospective confirmation of the Real. It is important that the reader understand these metaphysical points if he is to get his intellectual itch scratched. This inverse order of events is seldom understood in metaphysical teaching and few who call themselves students of Truth have their subjectivism straight. But hear this: In Truth, it makes no difference whether anyone understands Godhead or not. Godhead is SELF-UNDERSTANDING, happening in timelessness. Life is that "happening" in progress. But to UNDERSTAND God's allness is to be able to make it through this repeating human experience and FIND the Child-Identity made in the Image of God. It is also *to learn the grand Equation,* live it, and assist our own subjective view of "others" in making the climb successfully and "returning" to Source. "We" came from that timelessness and we are going there again, to paraphrase the words of Jesus.

The author doesn't claim to have reached the final peak of understanding, not knowing how many other mountains may remain to climb, but I have been shown the Equation which is the pearl, the Key to overcoming in "this world." To say that another way, I am not at all times *consciously* aboard the ship, but I am holding the boarding ladder, reaching out for "others" swimming my way. I stand atop Da Shan, one arm reaching up, holding the One; one arm reaching down to assist those on the slopes of the world. The *true* Identity of the reader is in exactly the same place.

Metaphysics suggests that a knowledge of images leads to a knowledge of What stands behind images. This has been precisely true in my experience. Specifically, a knowledge of the electromagnetic energies called "light" have led me straight to a greater knowledge of Light, for which the limited light of the world is an image. My use of the term "photon" as a particle of light in some of the essays following does not cover the whole range of science's meanings for light, but it suffices to explain a most meaningful parallel in our rediscovery of Identity. Just as light appears to behave in two ways, so we appear to have two identities— one of them limited and finite, the other quite infinite; one of them located as a point in time and space, the other virtually omnipresent, existing on both sides of time.

WHY THE DUAL APPEARING OF IDENTITY?

Why does Identity appear dual in nature? That is, why the "real" Identity and the facsimile who struggles with ego and the like? Why the Real and the one in the world that fools us so? Why the one atop Da Shan and the other on the slopes? If God is All in all and omnipotent, why not one identity to start with, pure, perfect, made in the image of God? Why the second man, made of the elements of the earth? Religion stopped trying to answer this question in the first century of Christianity. Metaphysics has given no practical answer whatever. The body of this book will answer that ancient enigma to the satisfaction of scientist and philosopher alike.

First, understand that the Genuine Identity, the Soul of us, the Child of us, is that one atop the Mountain, unbound by time and space, residing in the heart of Godhead beyond Name and, simultaneously, everywhere on Da Shan—not unlike the simple photon which, moving at the speed of light, is virtually everywhere in space nearly simultaneously. That is the genuine (and only) Identity (Image of God-Self) as God made it.

Our time on Da Shan, perhaps many linear lifetimes—certainly nearly eleven thousand years in the present experience—is our "descent into matter" or "into hell" as it is spoken of theologically. That is, it is the time of learning via contradistinction. It is the accumulation of *conscious* knowledge wherein the experiences on Da Shan allow one to comprehend and fully appreciate the wonders of Ineffability and the *rediscovery* of the Original Identity. This embodied, human struggler is the "second" identity, the one apparently bound to time and space, destined to measure tangibility to its limits in his quest for the Original. The second identity, arising after the mist, is man's tendency to forget his birthright, moving away from God toward selfness—into ego and multiplicity. As the Tree of Life prepares to bloom and seed, there will be a universal reversal of this tendency. We find the Child still alive and untouched within us. We begin the conscious return to the Father's house, Light beyond light.

Our difficult times on Da Shan bring our appeals to Ineffability, God, for deliverance and salvation. Who doesn't turn to

God when he's starving or when his life is threatened? The Entity, the "angel" nearest us—beside the Ineffable Itself—always present, ever listening to us and knowing our condition and thoughts, is the Original Child of Us, *awaiting that call*, eager to answer, capable of taking us through the monstrous metaphysical mazes of our own making. Our experiences on Da Shan are exactly what is necessary to bring us Knowledge, thence to exchange the personal sense, the climber's role, for the Child. Every step we make consciously *up* the mountain, we are less the climber and more the Child, until, atop Da Shan with the world under our feet, we have *consciously* "returned" to the Child of God, this time KNOWING our heritage. There, which is right here where the struggler reads these words, we encompass all the world at once (subjectively) and become the NO-PLACE, NO-THING where the Ineffable flows through to tangibilty and becomes our new, subjective world; and where the world's tangible essences return to Ineffability. We become the NO-Place, NO-Thing, Way, the DOOR between Ineffability and the world. This is what Pure Life has always been, the exchange point, the midpoint between Above and Below, Outside and Inside, First and Last, Male and Female, Spirit and Matter.

It is metaphysical folly to lay claim to Identity who isn't a climber without *making* the paradoxical climb in linear time.

THE ILLUSTRATION OF THE ARTIST

A wondrous artist sits down and says, "Let me make a mighty work of art. It will be a perfect image and likeness of myself. I shall make this image so perfectly it will even know itself in its fullness. And it will know that I made it."

The consummate artist proceeds to make an image of himself that comes alive. Well now, consider. What would this image fully *know* about itself? What would it know about its joy and dominion, qualities of its maker? What would it know about eternity and infinity? Or any of the attributes of itself? Thinking about this, we might ask ourselves what we knew about the joys of the child when we were child-children. Nothing really. We had to leave childhood before we knew what we left behind. As a child, what did we know about those carefree days? Of security and dominion? What did we know about who we really are and who we are not? Nothing—until we were exposed to adulthood, the life that *is not* the child. With adulthood (and for quantum mankind in general), and having walked the roads of the world (some of us through religion into subjectivism) with those roads apparently leading nowhere, we finally hear of the Child again and *find* it. *This* time we know what the Child IS.

Finally after eleven thousand world years of human history we have a simple, understandable statement that explains precisely WHY the appearances of evil exist in the world, and those charged with instructing others are not interested, as if it were not important.

The terrors of the world are the chrysalis of Self-discovery. We emerge from the necessary far country of ignorance and its anguish, to rediscover the Child within and "return" to the Father's house.

KNOWING IS NOT BEING

Han said, "Let the illustration of Da Shan make your religion, philosophy and science clear. It can if you let it. Sometimes it is easier to see a parallel pathway than the crowded one we are walking.

"The ruler of Da Shan ('the prince of this world') is the belief that the world of matter is the final reality. It is also the belief that the body one calls his own is one's identity. These are most powerful and persuasive beliefs, particularly the latter one.

"Yet, if we examine these beliefs we see that they are temporary and necessary mistakes—the mistake of KNOWING temporarily accepted as BEING. This mistake, which is no mistake at all in the final sense, lasts only for the 'duration' of the body's 'time.' The mistaken acceptance is rejected (involuntarily?) in the 'death' of the body."

The little group sat pondering. They didn't understand. "Let me say that another way," said the teacher. "Being includes knowing, but knowing cannot include all of Being. If one is to fully understand himself to be God's Self-knowing, *let him know what he is not, then he will fully know what he is.* The child is the Child, but doesn't realize it until he has lived the adult—and then, when the Child is uncovered, that one *knows* the Child. Awareness is the knowing of the Real God. The god of Da Shan would have us make the personal identity into a god—and we try with terrible futility."

THE ILLUSTRATION OF THE SYMPHONY

Once upon a time a weary old near-sighted mule was confined to a small barbed-wire enclosed pasture filled with brambles. One day the mule unwittingly backed into the briars. In surprised pain, it leaped over the fence to find itself in a pasture infinitely lusher than the one before.

Question: Should the mule condemn the brambles for their thorns, or thank them for being the instrument to a greater sense of freedom?

Thank them, certainly. But humanity as a whole doesn't do that. Why not? The answer isn't as obvious as it seems, and the question deserves a careful answer. Subjectivism offers an answer which will also serve as a primer for answering many metaphysical questions that arise in our study of Truth. Here is the answer, delineated backward, as metaphysics often does things. I call it the Illustration of the Symphony.

A knowledge of the Symphony begins as a knowledge of the individual or personal notes that delineate the Symphony. One cannot separate the Symphony from the notes that delineate it—but the "power" (authority) lies with the Symphony which is *being* the notes. The notes "live, move and have their being" *because* the Symphony, Godhead exists. The Symphony is eternal and so are the notes that make it plain. But the notes are finite and tangible while the Symphony is infinite and intangible.

How so? Because *infinite* means "whole, all, complete, all-inclusive" and one note is not the whole Symphony. Since that note is not infinite, it is finite, measurable, possesses form and is concerned with sequence or time.

Every musician knows that as the *notes* are seen, understood and heard, the Symphony "behind" them begins to come to *conscious* attention—and once the intangible Symphony is memorized, *our dependence on the tangible, finite notes has lessened,* but the notes still exist because the Symphony is eternally Self-known, Self-delineated. That is, the Symphony will forever know itself in its wholeness and in its detail.

Likewise, as with the Symphony, our knowledge of the infinite IDENTITY begins as a knowledge of the individual, "finite" people, places and things within awareness. Who can deny that the tangible universe appears as the delineation of ISNESS, the INEFFABLE? One cannot separate images from the Isness-being-images that delineate It—but the power lies with Isness *being* the sights, sounds and images of awareness. People, places and things have their being *because* Isness (Symphony) is.

Godhead is eternal, and so is the *essence* of "matter" (form) as today's grade school student knows. But Godhead is infinite and intangible, while the images of awareness are apparently finite and tangible. How so? Again, because not one "thing," nor all of them together, can be *all* there is to Godhead, any more than all the notes on the entire score of the symphony (Symphony) can be all there is to the symphony *sounded, heard, lived!*

As with the Symphony, when the sights, sounds and feelings of the "world" are seen and *understood,* Godhead comes more to conscious, tangible attention, and line upon line, precept upon precept we find our dependence on "things" has also lessened. This includes our dependence on liquor, drugs, lawyers, wheelchairs and hospitals—not to mention the need to attack other images or to suffer confusion about how to defend the Child-Self from situations that delineate our immutability.

MORE ABOUT THE SYMPHONY

Consider an INFINITE and LIVING Symphony. Living means awareness, life. Awareness means *knowing.* Our Symphony *knows* Itself. *That* is what "delineation" is all about in the first place. That is why the measurable, finite notes on the paper, why the appearance of a finite world of interrelated people, places, things and combinations thereof. The Symphony knows Itself in its intangible wholeness, and this means (listen, listen) **that the Symphony also knows what KNOW-ING is.**

If the Symphony knows all it is, doesn't it know what "knowing" is as well? Of course. Therefore, since "knowing" is not all there is to Symphony, the Symphony not only knows itself in its wholeness, it knows itself in its parts, in its infinite variety, in its individual notes that delineate itself to Itself—Itself to itself. Consequently, the Symphony knows finite form, time and sequence as well as Intangibility. Furthermore, It *knows* it knows!

Patient reader, no illustration is perfect in every detail. They can all be picked to pieces. Ponder this one gently and find the Glimpse it discloses. Follow it with the heart, not the intellect that insists on a limit.

Because our analogy is presuming an *infinite* Symphonic Godhead, we perceive that "knowing" is the only real knowing going on. An infinite symphony knows that its knowing is without limit, restriction or boundary, yet that knowing is not all there is to Godhead.

At this point we are able to ask the intellect a question the Heart can answer already: Does an infinitely wise Symphony know what it is NOT and could never actually BE? Yes. It would also know its "is *nots*" were fictitious IMPOSSIBLES— the delineators that allow wisdom (knowing) to be *infinitely* wise. Of course it would, else its knowing would not be unlimited knowing, hence not OMNISCIENCE at all.

And finally, to the awakening "point of difference" here: Would not our omniscient Symphony perceive (without fear or confusion) that a sharp or flat note was but an obverse delineation of the correct note? And would not the wise Symphony perceive that the fiction, no matter how it sounded, was naught but a marker of the *real*? Yes! Yes! Such a Symphony would know exactly what delineates (identifies) itself to Itself in *its* detail to infinity.

Consequently, for each "note" there is a knowledge of fictitious, but seemingly real "is-nots" to outline it—wheat and tares—and the Symphony knows the IS from the hypothetical *is-nots* necessary to define itself to infinity. Reader, let us be very simple here. This isn't as difficult or as twisting as it sounds. It is the knowledge that our hand is *not* yon bird, mountain, meadow and all else that renders the *total* knowledge of the form called "hand."

When we speak of Symphony and its multitude of notes, we are not talking "duality" or "multiplicity," but referring to *one* Symphony *in the action of knowing itself.* Mind and its Self-awareness are one Mind being all knowing. Omniscient means infinite knowing. Infinite means without limit. Knowing, limited to only what IS, is limited knowing. To unlimitedly know what IS is, means to automatically know what is not and could never be—and within the arena of *tangibility* (which is what "knowing" IS), the latter appears just as tangible as the "real," *yet it is a "holographic" fiction;* LIMITED light attempting to outline Light.

So it is, our CONSCIOUS experience, so much concerned with finite images of perception, is like looking out upon a vast Symphony of that which, in our wisdom, we can examine in its wholeness, or sprig by sprig—and this gleaming field of wheat is the WHAT Identity knows Identity to be. Even as we know what the field is, we know what it is not and could never be—the appearance of tares strewn throughout, tares outlining every sprig, and even *the tares* pointing to the REAL, exactly as poverty delineates Sufficiency; as hatred delineates LOVE; as fear clarifies confidence and trust; as death points to LIFE!

Heretofore, the old objective teachings had us busily pulling up the brambles and tares, rooting them out, trying to heal them, change or destroy them, in the name of God, good, of course. Now we see them as the powerless delineations of the REAL—and remain untouched by them. We finally understand the strange admonition to leave the tares alone until the harvest. The apparent dualism is ended. *It is no longer light and darkness; it is every bit Light and its infinite Self-distinction.* It is no longer Life and death; it is all LIFE and the powerless delineation of all that Life knows it is *not* and could never be. It is no longer a matter of "peace beyond understanding" and an unremitting warfare against terrorism, disease, agony, principalities and powers, sin, sickness and death; it is all the Childlike Peace we eternally are—and "the world," which is everything that makes that Peace fully KNOWN. Finally "the two are become a single one" as Jesus put it—and, great God, what a day this realization is!

ONE MULE IN A THOUSAND

Now we see why only one mule in a thousand, two in ten thousand, see their anguish to be their blessing. The rest write indignant letters to the board of bramble directors, lower the boom on them with uprooting criticism and wail in anguish at the sound the thorns make in their organizations. All the while it is the mule's wind whistling through the thicket.

One leper returned to thank the carpenter for his healing work, this illustration suggesting that for every clear chord delineating the Symphony there are nine times nine sour notes outlining *that* chord. This is why we find in the early literature of all schools, that not everyone who appears to be living is necessarily alive.

A LITTLE MORE ABOUT DA SHAN

Birth and death on the face of Da Shan are the ongoingness of Eternity, appearing in time. Beyond the body that is alive and dead is Awareness which is eternal. Awareness is the balance between movement and rest, birth and death. Awareness is Life, whereas the living body is only the *image* of Awareness.

Male and female on the face of Da Shan are the first outpicturing of the WHOLE Identity—but still image. *Genderless* Being is the balance, whereas the gendered form is image of Image.

Above and below on the face of Da Shan are the ongoingness of Ineffability. We surrender the image's self-importance to the Image, the Child of God—who leads us to "all Truth."

It is true, the peak of Da Shan is an intangible *nothingness* wherein all image-importance is surrendered to the Child-Image of God who leads us consciously to Godhead. Even the Son of God makes himself nothing before the Father, Ineffable One of All.

"CONFIRMATION" DEFINED

Godhead is the Eternal Fact; the universe of tangibility is Its Self-confirmation *following* in time.

God is Infinite and Eternal; space and time exist in the arena of Self-confirmation, wherein events are sequential.

Identity is Singular Godhead; the appearance of multitudes is Its confirmation to all possibilities following in time and space.

Godhead's Life is omnipresent and the forms of life are Its confirmation following, in all degrees.

Enlightenment is Godhead's Self-knowing; our glimpses and glimmers are Its inevitable confirmation.

One Already is the Fact; near infinite numbers of possibilities are Its confirmation following.

Godhead is One Already, and all objectivity and subjectivity in their many dimensions are God's confirmation following.

Science is the leading edge of intellectualism, the inevitable confirmation of Godhead.

Nothing is going on but God. All that's going on "here" in time and space is layer upon layer of confirming appearances, limited light's inward spiral. The appearances have no God "in" or "within" them, yet the appearances exist within Godhead. Confirmations—majestic as they are—are neither real nor unreal, but they exist with Godhead and are God's Self-knowledge happening eternally.

The awareness that reads these words and seems to write them is God's *knowing* happening—and that "happening" is confirmation of the ONE. The confirmation is not Godhead, but exists for Its Self-certification and joy.

Now, our subjectivism straight, the reading will be easier.

CHAPTER FOUR

OUR REAL IDENTITY

The Child Guide

THE CHILD GUIDE

The Da Shan analogy suggests that we are to get off our soft sofas and get up the mountain of understanding. That is, we are to get going here in the world to *understand* the nature of things, "the world," life and its lessons. It is one thing to rest on our objective/subjective laurels and talk about the all-ness of God and quite another to actually *"know what is in thy sight, and what is hidden from thee will be revealed to thee."*

To understand what is before our eyes is to understand appearances. It isn't enough to call matter unreal, illusion, dream. It isn't correct to call matter Spirit either—unless one can make himself understood so that others see the Substance he sees. What *is* matter? What is light? What is government *really?* What is the reason for the appearances of warfare, suffering and pain? What is the *reason* for the presence of the physical sciences, mathematics, medicine, religion, metaphysics and so on? To hang in with theology's view or philosophy's view isn't enough. What is *our* view? Do we know *why* dualism "seems" to appear so consistently despite the metaphysician's denial of it? Do we know *why* life appears to exist in finite, aging, struggling bodies? To be able to *answer* these questions is what is meant by climbing the mountain of understanding. Science is doing a much better job of that, at the moment, than either religion or metaphysics. The astronomer and physicist may be leaving God out of their equations, but they are coming up with answers concerning *time and space* while metaphysicians are still denying their existence.

To climb the mountain is to KNOW the answers to everything pertaining to the scene at hand. It is to "Know what is before your eyes. . . ." I suspect that that particular saying of Jesus was inadvertently omitted from the forming canon because organizing theologians were not willing to have neophytes perceive what binding, confining "doctrines" were being promulgated, as much out of self-interest as out of a love for Truth.

"William, if the world is a mortal myth, why should I waste my time trying to understand it?"

Who is the one who has time to waste, if time isn't real? If time isn't real, what is there to waste? Do you understand WHY the myth hangs on so tenaciously, despite the thousands of years it has been spoken of as a shadow on the wall of a cave? Physical scientists who make no mention whatever of Godhead in their theorems are measuring those shadows and finding themselves touching down on Godhead, almost as if they had backed into It. If one measures the shadow long enough, he finds the tree it leads to. But he finds it in living fact, not metaphysical theory.

"Modern science is only now reaching the place the Hindu mystic reached four thousand years ago, William."

Yes, yes. But where are *you?* The mystic climbed the mountain. He didn't merely profess to. He knew why the myth seems real. Science is climbing the mountain, and we know it because what they are finding is becoming applicable to quantum mankind. Here we are at Woodsong using their discoveries to record our voices. I know from my own experience that when the metaphysician does what he should—when he climbs the mountain of understanding beyond religious profession and metaphysical theory—his work also appears as a quantum benefit for all mankind, right here in the mythical world.

So, how do we get going? How do we climb the mountain in actual fact, even when we know *about* the metaphysical statement that there is no mountain to climb? We search for and FIND the genuine nature of ourselves, the Child. The Child within us will confirm Who and What we are. That is what the mystics did to allow themselves to know about the myth of matter. Those mystics, in a marvelous way, changed the world. But there is no way to climb the mountain to its peak without the Child, and there is nothing in churchdom, metaphysics or science about the Child. The Child is within us—the very Awareness that perceives the nature of Godself, Itself.

The Child and Its guidance are essential in our search. If one thinks his religion, his philosophy, or his theology is the means to finding the FINAL Answer, he is mistaken. The Child of Light and Love is the pathfinder, the guide, the way-shower up the mighty mountain in Kwangse Province. Science, religion and philosophy can take us a great distance, but the Child takes us to Dominion. It is absolutely essential that we actually get in touch with that eternal Child. How do we do that? Now we are coming to the reason for this book.

At some point along the slopes of Da Shan, we realize we can't make it to peak alone, even with the help of our studies, computers and linear accelerators. We are not even sure which path to take, with so many books and people shouting that their way is the only Way. Our religion has failed to make the Guide sufficiently real to us so that we can actually *feel* it, find it, confirm and follow it. Our metaphysics has done no better—with all its protestations of Identity, Self, Allness and God's Absoluteness and those interesting ideas along the hem of things.

In some agony and much frustration, often painfully, we finally come face to face with a glimpse of Something that tells us about the Child within. In desperation, longing or suffering, we find that intuitive light, wherever we are in the world along the slopes of Da Shan—and when the first feeble glimmer arrives, we have the intuitive feeling that It has been with us all the while, awaiting our recognition and call. Of course it has. It has come to us from the Child within, the Christ Light of us.

I had to find the Child on my own, as you must too, but I

can be of considerable help as you will presently see for your-self. Those who think they have found the Child because they have found a religion or a subjective study they are content with, are mistaken. When we find the Child, things become new. The entire world is seen in a new light.

In the mind's eye, we can equate "Child" with PHOTON which is also, like the Child within us, everywhere in space at once. The Child is everywhere in our experience, not only available to assist our learning, but leading us into and out of experiences in order that we may more fully comprehend the nature of Reality.

THE FOLLOWING: A CONVERSATION FROM SOME YEARS AGO. I was speaking with a group of theologians and metaphysicians who were hearing of the Child within for the first time, as may be the case with the reader. The talk was in-tended to put a finger precisely on WHAT the Child is. My guests did not know that. I have often thought of this as the "incredulous group" because they were so astonished to hear what followed. One gentleman in particular was angered that he had come so far to listen to such "nonsense." The essence of that talk is printed here in some detail because everyone present eventually *found* the Child and the marvel that comes with it. Now, years later, I know that such agreement doesn't always occur so quickly. Perhaps this particular choice of words had something to do with it.

We were sitting outside under the loblolly pines of Alabama. Present were a physicist, a mathematician, a Christian Science practitioner, a venerable Roman Catholic nun with a scholar's knowledge of Christianity's origins, a young Buddhist monk and a Rabbi newly moved to this country from Europe. I was delighted to have such a diverse group, and not a little amazed that they had heard of this one hidden in the backwoods of the Southland.

The talk begins:

Good morning, everyone. This morning, if we can, let's put aside all our studies of Truth. Let's put down our theology, doctrine and metaphysics for a time. There is something much simpler and more important I'd like to talk about; something much more basic; something that is absolutely fundamental if we are to go all the way with our spiritual comprehension.

All right? Have we put aside "religion" for the moment? Science? Physics? Our over-concern with those complex things causes us—at least it caused me—to overlook Something Wonderful. That Something Wonderful brings us to understand new things about *time and space; to see* that we aren't as bound by time as we thought. Are you ready?

Listen gently. There is a Child inside us. It lives. Vigorously. It is as youthful as ever and it hasn't lost a thing to time. What's more, that Child is capable of resurrection and emergence right out here into this world of trials, tribulations, space and time.

Let me say something about this. We all know how much the world wants to know of this wonder—the Child within—unable to find very much said or written about it. The Bible has something to say about "the Child," but the churches don't. The subjective groups don't mention it at all. But the Child I'm talking about is not solely a religious or theological child, but the very kid-we-are that is still deep within each of us, just as it was when we were child-children.

Yes, there *is* a Child still living in each of us. We've heard this before, but no one has gone into much detail. No one has written the really helpful things. For instance, who has told us that the Child is all that is *real* about us? Who has told us that all this grown-up, grown-old and grown-tired-of-the-world business isn't *true* and isn't the way things really are, and that the CHILD within *is* the way things are? Most mention of this mystical marvel is poetic fluff and stuff that rings true in the heart but isn't sufficiently explained to grasp intellectually and practically. Ah, that's it. The intellect of us doesn't understand about the heart and the Child, so it relegates them to another world.

Well, since no one seems willing or able to tell of the Child within to the grown-up, grown-sophisticated and grown-old leaders of the world, I will. I have found the Child-I-am and I know what it is. Actually, so does everyone, deep within. But the trick is to *reach* that "deep within" and get to the Child so we feel it and *know* what it is.

(Pause) Hear this mystery: We are the Child first, then we

are the not-child and then we are the Child again.

(Pause) We were Child-children first. Those were the days we dimly remember when fairy tales were real and Aesop's fables had their place in our thoughts of animals and forests, cabbages and kings, princesses, knights and frogs and first stars to make our wishes on. Do you remember how you felt when you were a child-child? Would it suprise you to know you can feel that way again? Well, you can!

(Interruption) Dr. Scott, you needn't look so surprised and shocked. You've come all this distance from your university to hear what I've found, so you may just as well relax and hear this old soldier out. You've listened for two minutes, and the look on your face suggests you know everything to follow. That's the way the intellect of us works in the world. We run our projections along a line and expect them to unfold that way. But, doctor, are you quite sure there might not be something new to come out of this? I think you will see there is.

Back to our youth in time. That was the time of our closest encounter with the Original Child. We were Child-children then, and the inmost Child of us was happy even if the human view of childhood was miserable. The human view at this now-moment includes a nearly infinite number of possibilities, and we are not stuck to just one line of unfoldment in time and space as most of us think. The Original Child's view may seem lost to us today, but it isn't.

"William, we all know of the advantages of childlikeness and the foolishness of childishness."

Please hear this: I am not talking about childlikeness. I am talking about the Child itself. I am certainly not talking about childishness—this is the furthest thing from that. The Child we are speaking of right now is the inner Child when we were young, lived by the outer child, by this husk of flesh. Now we are to *find* that inner part of ourself again because it plays the final, integral part in our search for the Real. At the moment, just take my word for that. We are not searching for childlikeness and humility. We are looking for the Child itself. That Child *is* the Real of us and is capable of taking us consciously back to Reality. Nothing else can. Nothing else will.

Subjectively speaking, I've found that the inner Child includes this body, this outer old bastard, within it—for good and perfect reason. We will talk about that later.

TALK OF THE CHILD CONTINUES

Now listen gently. As children we heard about adulthood and learned the advantages that growing up and growing old were supposed to proffer. Like everyone in the world since the beginning of time, we bought that bill of goods. We longed to be big children because they could stay up late and go places and do things little folks couldn't. Furthermore, the thing called "time" assured us, we believed, that the adult would come and the child pass away. So, quite by divine plan, we locked ourselves into a sequential, unfolding world "time," and the burying process began. With shovel after shovel of adulthood and adultery, we buried the real Child under a mountain of worldly sophistication, education, judgmentalism, self-importance, guilt, age, debility and thoughts of approaching death.

Now, here we sit under the loblollies and look around. We groan, rub the stiff joints and wonder where the years have gone. Whatever happened to that little child's view of things? It has gone, we think, without our really finding the Truth, without having done much in the world, and without even thinking there might be Something Else besides the relentless march of time that buried the Child in the first place.

We seem to think the Child we were lives only in memory, don't we? Oh, but the wonder is, Dr. Scott, the ageless Child still lives within us, untouched by the world's trouble and the passage of time; untouched by those accumulated experiences and pains along the slopes of Da Shan, great mountain of seeking and finding. The Child doesn't give two hoots in hell about physics, metaphysics, theology, cosmology and the various schools of whatever the world gives us to study in and about. The Child is untouched by guilt or by the suffering of age. He hasn't lost his memory. She hasn't lost either her grace or energy. There are no years lost to the locust and that original little boy and girl of us is untouched by time. The Child within us lives, by God. Lives!

Doctor, you are watching my old friend Abraham wipe tears

from his eyes. Do you wonder if perhaps the Rabbi, with all his years and scholarly knowledge of the Talmud, isn't hearing and feeling Something deep within himself this moment?

Listen, listen: *Where do those tender feelings come from?* Can you guess? It is the Child that brings tears of insightfulness to our eyes. The Rabbi feels the Child! THAT Child we feel within us is our faithful Guide up the final worldly slopes of Da Shan's peak. That Child brought us together today to hear of Himself. But the Child of us must be recognized, acknowledged as living, and *called for* if we are to feel its presence returning within us.

Some of the goop heaped on our human backsides is guilt. Most is the anguish of time and what time is believed capable of doing—and expected to do. Much of our consternation has to do with lack or lost faculties—the dimming vision, slow reflexes, empty pocketbook, failing memory and zip; but all of *that* is the great pile of lessons learned which we have allowed—via Divine Plan—to hide the Original Child whom we have been deluded into believing we left behind years ago in time! Yet it is that same Child within that gives us the *lessons* of time and space and makes them bearable. The injuries of those lessons aren't real in the absolute sense of non-time. It is the CHILD that is real—and the Child is miraculously untouched. What's more, and what's important here—the very purpose of our gathering—*the Child can return! It can make a comeback! We give it a hand and lift it up and put it back where it was before the burying began. The Child lives and is still present to live US and walk with us through the events of the world— straight home to full Self-discovery.*

Ah, yes. What seems so interesting is that the simple, the troubled and uneducated are going to find the Child and believe It before the sophisticated and religious folks do, before the metaphysicians do.

DREAM STUFF?

My friends, this isn't dream stuff we are talking here. At this late stage in the world, too much is at stake for metaphysical word games, philosophical and religious half-truths and psychological upsmanship. We haven't much linear time left to stand atop Da Shan in conscious living fact. So we are talking absolute reality now. Truth. Fact. More than that, we are saying something that everyone is going to find is true for himself, all alone, if only when this physical body stops responding to his every whim and is put aside in the experience the world calls death.

I'm here this day to declare for a fact that *one doesn't have to await the death of the body to find the Child-heart within himself, lift it up from the distant past and out of the binds of time, and become that one again.* This gentle Child within is quite willing to reanimate and revitalize the present body we seem to think we are struggling and dying in—and bring the Child's wisdom and knowledge of Reality back to our conscious recognition once more.

LISTEN to me carefully. We are still quite capable of seeing and feeling with all the unencumbered joy and delight we felt as children. Absolutely! Still. Right here in the world. No matter how old and how lost we think we are.

SWEET NAIVE POLLYANNA!

Pollyanna must come to mind as one hears words such as these, as if this were her final stand in our affairs. This time let's grab her. If she's the Child, catch her quickly. "The wise man will not hesitate to ask a small child seven days old about the place of life. . . ." Those were the words of Jesus. Isaiah told of the Child; Jesus identified *as* the Child he found himself to be. We are to do the same.

(Pause) I doubt that many will want to understand these things until their enchantment with self-importance and adulthood has passed. Just as a soldier who has thrown grenades and fended bayonets understands what fear is and what peace is, youth doesn't understand the Child until it has put it aside, buried it and lost all trace of it for a time—thence to miss it and need it—then, fortuitously, at a moment like *this,* come home to it again. Do you hear that? Come home to it again! Indeed, this is the purpose of adulthood, the struggling human experience and irrevocable move toward death in time.

It's like the old man who went back to his home in the hills of Tennessee after working in a mill town during the hard days of the war. When he returned to the mountains, he knew what blue sky *really* is and what a frisky thing a squirrel is and what beauty actually is. When he got back to his clean, unspoiled hills, his "was beautiful" of memory turned into an "is beautiful" *now* again, and he began living the beauty that had gone unrecognized until he lived the ugliness of war.

Well now, listen closely again. We've lived our adulthood to total frustration for nearly eleven thousand years of human time, time and time again, to no avail. So now, finally, we look within, find the Child still alive, uncover it, listen to it, follow it—and that Eternal Child of God within, the Christ of us, takes us straight up the mythical mountain to the peak *where we become that Child beyond time, in living fact for all our world to see and understand and do likewise.*

No. This is no Pollyanna tale being told here. This is a truth for everyone, old and young. These words sound one way to the intellect, but they feel quite another way to the listening, non-judgmental heart within us—and then, sooner or later, perhaps this day, the feelings come to confirm that it's true and to make it alive and real, despite our sophistication and human importance, despite the gnarled fingers, stiff joints, dimming vision and painful memories. *Despite* them and despite the world of time and space. Ah, then—a miracle for some of us who choose—*instead* of them.

You see, religion has missed the mark ever so slightly. It has us awaiting a linear Christ *in time,* but the Christ Light is *closer* than that. It is not only within us. It *is* us. (Pause) Did you hear that? It IS us. When we find that out, we comprehend clearly that the linear Christ of time *CONFIRMS the Child we are.*

Metaphysics has said nothing about the Child whatever, has it? Subjectivism, for all its looking within, misses the Child entirely—and the Child's Equation. There is a good reason for this, as we shall see later.

THE HUMAN EXPERIENCE

A recent coversation at Woodsong follows:

The human experience is essentially the awareness of people, places and things—specifically, our own. Experience is here and now. In the most absolute sense, our present experience is God's Self-awareness, God's Self-witness, Self-acknowledgement, Self-appraisal, Self-utilization and Self-enjoyment. It seems to be "ours," but it belongs to God.

Overspreading this Self-perception is God's knowledge of the contraries—what God is *not*, making what God is, fully understood. To whom? To God's perfect Self-Image, the Child we are.

As we get this straight and begin to see the subjective idea—"I am perceiving/perception happening; I am Awareness itself, perceiving naught but my own perceptions"—the correct identification becomes more and more the basis for our thoughts and actions. At this point our experience begins to undergo greater changes.

"But, Sam, this is the whole question. How do we go about making the proper identification *become* the basis for thought and action?"

Good question. How do we do this? By the conscious acknowledgement (knowledge acted on) that the Ineffable, the Supernal One, Isness, Reality, Godhead, is the only possible Identity that actually exists and is, therefore, *being* this Awareness-I-am here and now. Hanging onto this realization, we slowly let go the old sense of self. Who is the old one who says MY mind? We let that one go "line upon line" and the greater Identity confirms Itself "precept upon precept, here a little, there a little."

This is the first step toward the "rebirth" spoken of by those who know what they're talking about. When the Child within (The God Identity) is *really* acknowledged, It comes alive. We feel it. With this Child, that we actually *feel* within, comes a simultaneous refutation of the old bastard's view of things—and, blessedly, a natural forsaking of them. We also let go the thoughts and actions that supported the "old man's" position. Suspicion, doubt, judgment of the motives of "others" and many forms of judgmentalism simply vanish.

"Would you say this experience is essentially God's experience rather than mine?"

In reality, of course—and not just essentially, but totally. But at the same time, the world experience is the time we are still saying, "This is my experience and that is yours." It is also the time we're saying, "This is good" and "That is bad." From the peak of the mountain—Identity discovered and proven—things under our feet are, for the most part, understood. At this high place, one looks in retrospect to see without *doubt* that nothing but God has ever gone on. We understand without equivocation that the world experience is our own step by step, line upon line *discovery and confirmation of that fact of God's allness.*

Yet, the Child within us (which is the Christ of us!) allows us to suspect this a long time before we're atop the mountain in conscious fact. Inwardly we're claiming that no Identity exists but God, and doing this, sometimes, against great odds; outwardly, we're slowly beginning to live judgelessly and to see good, God, in everything. Do you see?

(Pause) "Hey, I'm starting to understand! Yes, yes!"

THE CLIMBER DISAPPEARS

"Here is something mysterious," Han began. "There is no way for the climber to stand atop Da Shan. Do you know why this is so?"

A smile brightened Ho's face but he said nothing. Lee gave him a poke, whispering, "You can answer that."

"This is for you to answer," Ho said.

Lee began hesitantly, "To reach the top of the mountain is to no longer be the climber."

"Yes!" said Han, clapping his hands like a child. "Exactly. Now tell me, when will you stop identifying as the climber?"

"When I reach the top," Lee answered.

"Oh, more quickly than that," Han said softly.

"One is never the climber, really," Mary said. "The climber and the old man are the same."

"Then who are you, if you aren't Mary?" asked the soldier.

"I am the Child, the guide who takes me where It is."

"You answer when I call you Mary," the soldier snorted.

"Yes," the lady replied. "That's the name of this body, but it is not my name. This body is not all I am. I am so much more, and so is everyone. I know the Child lives atop Da Shan with one foot on the granite peak and one on Greater Mountain of No-name. It was Mary's anguish that started my search, but the Child led me beyond the limits of myself. The closer

I came to the conscious top of the mountain, the less I was Mary and the more consciously I became the Child. Yet, had I not hailed the Child from down the slopes, Mary would have never been understood and put off."

"Ah so," Han clapped his hands again. "You have found the Child."

"Maybe she's found the Child," the soldier muttered, "but she still answers when I call her Mary."

LETTER TO LAUREL

Dear Laurel,

Yes, the Child is the Guide—ever available, closer than fingers and toes, our very Selfhood.

But all of us are humbled first. We are MADE to bow our arrogance and human dreams before Something Unseen. THEN, the Child comes alive, pulling us, pushing us, kicking us up the mountain, past every human mess, past all the old temptations, through the most amazing, intricate, narrow pathway which is one Child wide. You are on your way, Laurel! The Christ Child of your very Selfhood will NEVER leave you nor forsake you—and it is a Mystery of Mysteries.

There is Something Marvelous, *and it all has to do with our WILLINGNESS to surrender the me-sense to God—and to accept SELF as subservient to Godhead.*

I know why this perception comes so slowly to metaphysicians—and with such reluctant surprise: Because of the built-in metaphysical insistence that we, as the *"real* Identity," ARE God. Not so, not so, simply not so. We would like for that to be so, and we rationalize that it is in the name of GOD AS ALL IN ALL. But exactly as the Carpenter said time and again, only God is God, and we are the Children of God. "My Father is greater than I." Yet, "My Father and I are one."

The Child is pure and perfect
without sore knees or high blood pressure
without a tribulation
without a battle with age/time/space/world that It doesn't UNDERSTAND as GOOD going on—and then see confirmation of that good.

Ever since the "beginning," the human problem has wavered

between the same two ridiculous extremes: The attempt to be a separate selfhood apart from God and the attempt to BE God. Both end in the prolongation of the Discipline, the world not understood.

"Lest ye become as children," said the One who had it straight. It is hidden from the wise but revealed to the simple and childlike.

Laurel, along the way I found the Absolute which called God ALL. Then I worked very hard to *make* God all. Then I tried even harder to make *Bill* God. Then, brought to my knees, I found how NOTHING in ITSELF Bill (and Bill's world) is—but how marvelous LIFE is. Then I learned that Life, Awareness, belongs to God—and that Awareness, Life ITSELF, is the CHILD, the Image of God! With the Child's help, I somehow managed to let go the me-sense who was trying so hard to understand God, and found myself *already living as the Child of God,* holding God's hand every step of the rugged discipline's way. Suddenly—or precept upon precept, here a little, there a little—the "world" was revealed for what the world IS—and I consciously became less Bill and more Child.

The absolute position of metaphysics is a step along the way—our most arrogant time. But the demand has ever been, to learn LIFE'S lessons and let go the imposter who believes he OWNS Life and its bodies. That word "surrender" is in all the holy books of the world, and it is an accurate word in my own experience which is all I can really tell about.

Yes, as you said, we can let our human arrogance go, our pride of accomplishment, our human attainments, even the pride *in our lessons learned,* and do it ON THIS SIDE OF "THE GRAVE" if we really want to. But it takes the doing. In actual fact. More than profession. It takes a real "turn around" and *return to the Child Heart within us*—"in dust and ashes" humility. You've DONE that, my gentle Laurel. LOVE takes in a Stranger. The Stranger is the very Child of God we are.

In the tangible sense of limit/world/measure/time and space, we (as a measuring mortal) are all brought to zero in this world or the next.

The surrender is traumatic **but it is worth it!**

Upon the surrender to the Ineffable Unknowable Beyond

time and space, we are shown a marvel of marvels and given a subjective world to reign over.

Every word of this is TRUE, as you are slowly and PER-FECTLY learning, Laurel. You've learned it just as I did. We loose and unbind our world, DOING for it as we can. That *doing* is essential.

You will have the strength, the means and the ability to do what you are intended to do here in the linear world of time's unfolding. But we're brought to bow before God first—most of us in our extremity, and most of us unwillingly. This is true especially for those who have heard a different drummer and have hewn their own pathway in the world. **Even that is as nothing before God.** But, becoming "nothing before God" becomes ALL POWER in the new world. You will see. It is amazing and wonderful.

A JOURNAL ENTRY

It goes a little like this, Father: We write in our journal one day, "Hey, come alive, Child inside of me!" and then, one day we find ourselves writing, "The child LIVES and is ALIVE inside me!" Finally, somewhere along the line we write, "Hey, by damn! I AM the Child!" and we perceive the fictitious nature of the 'me' who thinks the Child is inside a physical body! THAT one was the deceiver and is nothing! Then, still later, as time goes to the not-child—and when the Child has been proven a reliable, honest Guide up the mountain of searching, confirming that EVERY-THING is God—we hear ourselves saying to those with ears to hear, "Hey, there's a Child within who can explain things to you and save you from your anguish. Find it! Live it! It will lead you to the Original One, the Christ Light of Godhead!"

CHAPTER FIVE

OUR REAL IDENTITY, BEYOND THEORY

Recognizing and Feeling the Child Within

"William, you say I'm to find the Child within myself. How do I actually do that beyond dreaming about it?"

First—and absolutely essential to the process—*we affirm the Child's existence and presence.* Like God, the Child doesn't seem present to the old nature's eye; there are no intellectual proofs immediately at hand. We accept its existence and presence on faith just as we accept the presence of God on faith. Before long, the Child will stir within and prove it is very much alive and present.

"What will I feel?"

Oh, goodness, Mary. The Child within is actually the child we *were, still here,* a child. It laughs for us, it sings in our heart, it remembers. It is interested. It is curious, thoughtful, full of love, excited sometimes, just as we felt as a child. These very feelings begin to return inside us. In small ways at first, like remembering how the freshly cut grass smelled when we were children. It may be the sound of frosty ground crunch-

77

ing under our feet. We hear it and remember hearing it that way on our way to school. We hear those sounds again just as we did as children. We feel certain feelings again, some of them most remarkable. But, listen, listen: *this time*—now that you have been here to hear these strange words—we will *know* it is the Child within—and that knowing is essential. Identity is hoving back into view! This time we know it is the Original Child coming back to consciousness, stirring and renewing itself. This time we know it is the *real* of us coming again to reprove the nature of Reality. It is coming to enliven us and we are glad.

"That sounds wonderful, William. What do I do first?"

Mary, we just said. We *affirm* the Child's presence within us. We *admit* wholly, fully, faithfully that the Child still lives right here, right now where we are. We determine to let it up and out, to bring it forth from the stultifying sophistication and guilt of adulthood and time. You see, the Child of God IS here—our real Identity, our Original Identity. It is that part of us that will survive when the finite body falls away. It is the soul of us that existed before this tangible body came into being. Before Abraham was, the Child of God is. We are IT.

"This child is still in us, you say. Is this the soul that religion speaks of?"

Yes! Precisely that. And isn't it wonderful to finally know what that mysterious and nebulous concept is all about? To know *what* it is and *where* it is and *how it is felt* and that it *lives in such a tender and wonderful manner?* And especially, that it is still filled with enthusiasm and joy? And that its *re-discovery brings renewal right here in the world?*

"This certainly puts the notion of the immortal soul in another light, doesn't it? (thoughtful pause) It clarifies the doctrinal and theological statement, doesn't it?"

Yes. But much more, Mary. We are finally doing what we are supposed to be doing. "Lest ye become as children you will in no wise enter the kingdom of heaven." And remember another statement as well, ". . .a Child shall lead them."

"If the Child comes alive again, as you say, what does that do for me here in the flesh?"

So many things I can't count them all. A twinkle in the eye comes back. Fear falls away. We aren't so concerned about time, the body and its affairs. We know the Child is us. We trust the Child to lead us straight to a knowledge of truth. As a matter of fact, the Child is the God of us.

"The child is God?"

No, the other way around. God is being the Child. The Child within is the perfect Image of the Ineffable, the first identity made in the image of God as the Bible relates. It lives and moves and has Its being in God. It has never been sick. It has never suffered nor made a mistake. It isn't vaunted up nor bowed down. It isn't guilty. It is not bound by temporality or space, and It understands what time and space are all about.

"The bubbling I feel inside at this minute is my real identity?"

Yes!

"What about this awareness right here, as I look at you and listen to you?"

This Awareness is the Light of life and belongs to God. Awareness is the Child I am. Awareness becomes US as we have a change of heart, let go the old man and return to the Child within. This present awareness becomes sharper and clearer because it has things to do in the world. It bubbles a lot more, Mary.

"Well, for goodness sake, I don't know what to make of this. . ."

You don't know what?

"It sounds so good—and *feels* wonderful—but I don't know. . ."

The doubts and distrust don't belong to the Child, Mary, but to the illegitimate old bastard of us. What do you have to lose? Must I argue for what I've found, when, in your inner disquiet, you asked to come here to see what I have found? Why do you doubt me? Doubting, distrusting and forgetting the Child Identity has backed us against the wall, struggling in the world, bowed down with grief, depression, fear, guilt and age. All the while, the Child is in here, waiting to get up again. The Child leads us in the time and space world to this one or that one—and the Child within has brought you and me together just to hear these words. Why doubt that? Did you come here looking for things to approve or disapprove first? Are you sampling wines until you find one you like?

"I'm here out of curiosity, William, to see if you are genuine."

Mary, you have found more than that. You have found the keys to the Kingdom and to your very life, provided you can bring yourself to believe what you are hearing, *put the words to the test* and go where the Child of yourself leads.

"William, on the one hand it sounds so easy—maybe too much like the things I've heard in church. They use other words, of course. Soul instead of Child. And that's the rub here, I think. I don't like things theological or religious. At the root, yours is a new theology or a restatement of old theology—I don't know quite which. What happened to all that absolute metaphysics you wrote for so many years?"

Nothing has happened to it, Mary. The subjective message is entirely intact. It was and is correct as far as subjectivism goes, but metaphysics is only a part of the Grand Mystery. One eventually breaks through subjectivism and its metaphysics into the green field of simplicity again, *finally knowing what the complexity was for and about.* The bottom line of it all is this magnificent Simplicity of Identity we are talking about this morning here under the Alabama pines. The Child has dominion. The Child is the place of exchange—within and without, above and below, first and last, male and female, tangible and intangible. The Child leads us consciously to all Truth; we find the Child within ourselves. This is no new theology. This is not a new religious view or new doctrine. It is the secret Fact that doesn't miss the mark as religion and metaphysics have missed it.

"I am baffled, William. I just don't know."

Well, think about it, Mary. You've heard it straight and true. The Child is you. It is up to you, yourself and God.

WHERE DOES THE OLD NATURE FIT?

Unfortunately, as it seems, we manage to insert an imposter between the Child and Godhead (inside) and between the Child and the world (outside). We surround the Child with that shell of identity, the old man, who has *his* ideas about things, and that is where our trouble lies. To try to get rid of the old nature first, as religion and metaphysical instruction has us doing, is to enter a void without vision of the Child. We find the Child first, then the old nature falls away as the morning mist along the river vanishes in the sunshine of a new day. To find the Child is to end the domination of the old man—and there is no other way.

Ah, but the world-finding is soon to begin. Man has grown in time's field, the original seed forgotten. Now the new seed is forming inside the bolls and it is nearly time for the Awakening harvest.

KNOW WHAT IS BEFORE YOUR EYES

Along the slopes of Da Shan, we identify as a mortal, an ego, and are faced with all the problems inherent in that limited belief. On the world's slopes, we struggle with opposites assailing us from all directions. Atop Da Shan, where the Child takes us (and becomes us) quickly, we stand with the entire world under our feet, having dominion over every "thing" we understand. Our way to that promised dominion is to let the Eternal Child, which is there, and *everywhere* in time and space already, *come to us, confirm* our rightful Identity and *prove* that we are, indeed, the Child of God, atop the Mountain.

That confirmation appears to the old nature of us as a speeding up of the climb to understanding, even as you may sense already as you read these words. Then it comes as wonder upon wonder happening in our affairs, *not all of them easy,* until the old nature vanishes like the nothing it is, leaving us atop Da Shan, our head in Reality, our feet upon Reality's *confirmation.*

CAN YOU REMEMBER?

The Child has a special way to act in the world. Can you remember? There was no worry about where the next meal was coming from. There was no worry about the heat or cold. There was no concern for the body. There was constant *expectancy!* There was constant looking and examining and enjoying every new thing! All of this is a way we can feel and act again—because the Child within brings us back to life.

Truly, the whole secret very nearly lies couched in the simple wonder of *childlike expectancy!* That is IT. Expectancy, expectancy. Of what? GOOD. Just that. Not good as one personally believes it *should* be; not good as anyone has outlined it to mean; not good in any prescribed personal determination— but good *however* it appears.

Does good appear just because the child expects it? It appears whether we expect it or not, but the expectation *allows us to see it*—because we are looking for it around every turn and over every hill. When we sit down to rest, there It is, in front of our nose!

A LETTER

Dear Mr. Samuel,

I send these words to you because I know you will understand them.

There is a wonderful feeling here in the far west and IT is getting into my soul. That is, the Child I used to be is coming back for me again. It has started happening again during the past few days. It is happening right now as a matter of fact.

How to describe this feeling? It can't be written, except by comparison with the crappy feelings I have had so often since those days long ago when I first found it, or it found me, but I couldn't believe it.

It is like this, as nearly as I can write it: I found Something years ago but I wasn't ready then; there was more living to do and more abuse to experience—plain old suffering to learn what really is real. So, with God's mysterious way, I built a great wall around myself to inhibit it all until I could REALLY do with it as I should. Now, it has started coming back again. It is coming back again and I am full of joy because now I know what It is!

Lying still on the bed a short time ago, I went back in my mind to the days when I felt this way before. I heard someone sawing a board and remembered when I was sawing boards for my Spring Street house. I feel that Something now as I did then. Through and through. I am hearing sounds as I heard them then. I am feeling in the Heart of me as I felt then. Even the air smells the way it did when I was a young man in time.

It is coming back! It hasn't gone as I thought. I am feeling the Child inside myself again! You said I would.

Yesterday, as Sue and I drove with Margery down to the beach, I felt it for a moment and said, "I'm feeling the California feeling," but no one knew what I meant and I couldn't tell them. Then again, later, as we walked around the block. Just for a few seconds. Now again, this afternoon—and it is lingering longer. It is staying! It is coming back, thank God, it is coming back!

How can I ever tell anyone what it means to move backward and forward in time like this? People will think I am insane. But the Child I am is coming back!—and this is what I meant when I told Sue and Margery that, "If I could feel like this all the time I just might live forever."

Something Wonderful is happening. The Feeling of Yore—like love—is coming back, full fledged, shaken together and running over! This time I will RUN with it, as you said, Bill, and let it take me to the top of the mountain.

Bill Samuel, as you write in your journal so often, so now I write in mine, "Thank you, Father. Thank you, Lord of Light and Life." This is indeed mysterious and marvelous!

P.S. It is months since the above was written. I have hesitated sending such a crazy, mixed up letter. Dear Lord, I feel the Child STILL, even now as I read the words above and as I write these. It has happened exactly as you said, Bill. The Child is alive and kicking. Oh, yes, he has come out from the world's burial and I am alive again!

The feeling within, the Child my friend is finding, is the Guide to Life. It is the Christos, Gnosis—and when accepted as one's Identity—the Logos Itself.

ANOTHER LETTER

Dear William,

Today is my 80th birthday and I'm spending part of it writing this letter to you. As everyone always says, it doesn't seem possible that so much time has passed since those first days I remember in the little crib with the Mother Goose characters on the headboard. Time flies so swiftly, but that doesn't matter anymore because now I *know* that time is not real.

And I will have this known: The old body may be pushing eighty years, but the Spirit of me is the eternal, ageless Child. The fingers are stiff and the muscles weak, but that spirit is as frisky as ever. As a matter of fact, that Child inside is better than it used to be. It has had half a century of rest, buried under the world's trash pile and guilt.

Thank you for helping me rediscover the little girl still here and leading me to new heights of insight.

Joyfully, I am,

IT IS POSSIBLE TO SEE GOD'S GOOD IN EVERYTHING

Everything pertaining to the Mystery has to do with looking for good everywhere. The ability to do this is all so very simple and childlike that the old nature of us doesn't want to believe it is even possible. What a wonderful Mystery it is—hidden all these years in simplicity and clothed with childlikeness.

The child looks out to the world for its instruction. The adult turns within and struggles there until, when the Child is found, he looks outward again in new and constant *anticipation* of GOOD.

It is a strange demand, the intellect insists, to look for good when there is so little good to be seen anywhere. "The world is about to explode. Civilization teeters on the brink of annihilation. Where is good in any of this? I look about and see horror, not good. Look at the newspapers and the newscasts on television. Is there any good there?"

There is that wonderful statement of Jesus found in *The Gospel According To Thomas* where he speaks to the ANTICI-PATION of good. "The angels and the prophets will come to you and they will give you what is yours." At first thought, the metaphysician or theologian might argue that the *anticipation* of good is to deny its presence right before our eyes. It is just the opposite of such denial. It is to look at *everything* and search for the grand good there. That good is sometimes obvious. We see it quickly in the long-lost gold ring lying in the garden. It isn't as easy to see it in the gray stone we've just bumped our foot on. The pitfalls and stumbling blocks—the angry politicians, the shouting demonstrators and terrorists— occlude the perception of good there. Or so it seems at first— until we make the breakthrough. After a time of looking for good in the world, we begin to see it everywhere, everywhere. Good comes to confirm itself for those who look for it and seek the wisdom in God's creation roundabout.

Haven't we been proclaiming all these years that God/good is *everywhere?* And hasn't the mystic been whispering that God is all? All means what it says. If God is all and God is good, there is good in everything—and there is, there is! Make me prove it. I have very nearly found it in everything.

THE ANTICIPATION OF GOOD!

This experience "I" am living has grown into something quite beyond words. No hyperbole here. Exactly the way it is. Simply an explosion of inner Joy and a continuing confirmation of that Joy beyond anything I had ever known except for the briefest moments. Oh, how to say this? And why? I answer the "why" quickly: I write as a marker for my "others" who dream of such joy. It is true! It happens! It isn't just a "dream of desire along the way." I do not know how lasting in the world's time it will seem to be, but "my" life has been made full.

The other evening at a lovely lady's house one of the guests spoke of going to a concert and suddenly getting caught up in a glorious tingling thrill of joy and delight. Her eyes sparkled as she told of it. Everyone could see her tears of reminiscence and knew what a genuine joy she spoke of. Then she fell silent, her eyes closed, and I heard myself saying, "That's it! That is the joy of the experience everyone calls enlightenment." Some speak of it as illumination—sparks from the Child within. First we recognize those fleeting moments and *acknowledge* them for being the Light of Life they are. In so acknowledging them, we are faithful to the pennies of such moments and eventually find ourselves trusted with the dollars of them. Greater moments come. And greater. We look around one day to find we are living in the continual *confirmation* of the Joy we have faithfully *anticipated.*

These words are true and faithful. They tell of a great Joy beyond words. What must surely be one of the wonders of wonders: I have not seen a person who cannot prove the honesty of these concepts for himself and begin to live a New Life and a new marvelous experience.

"The joy of that moment at the concert will expand and expand," I told the lady, "so that the 'thrill' continues."

"I don't know if I could stand that!" she said.

JOY IS OUR HERITAGE, OUR BIRTHRIGHT

We are the children of GOD, so joy is our heritage! Why should we deprive ourselves of the Inheritance by thinking one must perish in the flesh before God's Kingdom becomes God's Kingdom? "And God saw *everything* he had made and, behold, it was very good"! That good is right here, right now—even as I struggle to write *about* it. Good is ours for the anticipation! But that's not the end of the matter; the anticipation and receipt of Truth is only half the joy. There is much to be done with that Truth once we've received it. That is the subject we'll be into soon.

WALKING WITH THE CHILD

Dear Rebecca,

Sit easy as you read this.

Clearly you are a lovely lady. Clean and decent and pure. "Worthy of my secrets."

*I cannot wave a wand and make all pain and anguish go away—**but they will go away!** Line upon line, precept upon precept, here a little, there a little.*

If anyone has ever attained to the Secret of the Child within without human anguish, I have never seen or heard of him. "Blessed is the man who has suffered, he has found the life." Rebecca, be assured that your inner turmoil is not in vain; it is not

for nothing; it is not anything you are guilty for. Rather, it has been as necessary for you as it was for me—as it is to every small and large creature emerging from its self-spun darkness.
Here is a mystery:
The little girl of yourself is still present within you.
In the world's belief, the child of us gives way to adulthood with all the anguish of growing up, growing older, marriage (or non marriage), family, and all rest of the world's tribulation. But the little girl of you is still very much alive, Rebecca. I ask you to DO the following which will prove it:
If you will take a quiet walk this evening, the Child of you will go with you. If you let her, she will see the pathway, the grass, the trees and mountains for you, just as you remember her seeing them when you were an absolutely carefree child. Anticipate that as you go for your walk.
If you walk quietly tonight, mindful of the Child of yourself, she will let you hear the distant sounds and smell the evening fragrances exactly as she let you hear them and enjoy them when you were that wonderful seven years old.
Gentle Rebecca, that little girl you were doesn't feel the anguish of the world nor anything wayward. The pure, simple, credulous pristine Child of us doesn't give two hoots about religion or mysticism or human problems. She holds God's hand eternally, fearlessly, joyfully, calmly, filled with awe and wonder, excitement and surging love.
*That is the Child I send this letter to. That is the Child I know you were Originally—and are now. That is the Child YOU know you are as well. She is the one I saw from the first time I met you those years ago. She hasn't gone anywhere. She hasn't been destroyed by time, guilt, mistakes, age nor anything else. The Child of us seems to leave us in human time. It is supposed to—hidden for a long time in time—**thence to be re-discovered** and reborn right out here in time's sequential unfolding. She is the Original Christ Child of us, closer than fingers and toes, closer than breathing, waiting to be reacknowledged, called forth and rediscovered.*
*Walk with her tonight, Rebecca. Look at the stars **as you did those years ago.** Be still and patient. Something will stir within. You will feel Something deep within yourself. That greater than sensual marvel stirring within is the Christ Child of Yourself telling you that you are coming alive again and coming home again;*

*that your longings can be fulfilled; that you have important things
to do here in this arena of time and space.*

*Hear me once again, Rebecca with the strawberry hair: Your
own Child Selfhood is still alive! You will be looking at the world
through those True Eyes again. I promise you that because I know
what I have found for myself. The Child of you is the Child of me
is the Child of Everyman. "Lest we become as children. . . ." it is
said.*

*Tonight, in the quiet of your walk, feel that grand Marvel
within yourself—nothing less than the kingdom of Heaven itself.
That marvel we feel can grow into Something a hundred times
more marvelous than anything we have ever imagined before. You
and I are holding hands there, Becky. We are One with God and
with all children. We joy uninhibitedly with a holy delight within.*

*Religion knows a little about the Child, but has rather misdi-
rected attention to a figure "out there" in linear history. Metaphysics knows nothing of the Child at all! Isn't that interesting?
But, don't misunderstand; metaphysics is subjectively correct. It is
a PART of the Mystery. Religion's misdirection is correctly part of
the Mystery, too.*

*I have more to tell you as you find the Child! Your time will
come, lady who laughs and cries and worries about her children.
The first Child to concern yourself with is the one within.* **That
one takes care of the others.**

*Walk through the Door tonight, Rebecca. Walk on beyond your
fears. See how very much alive you are still. Something Wonderful
will walk with you tonight. Watch and see.*

*Love from Woodsong on a misty morning, birds singing extra
special for you and me—and everyone.*

OLD HAN, MASTER OF KWANGSE PROVINCE

From the soldier's notebook:

The teacher was in a mystical mood the day the important
metaphysician arrived. I recorded the words carefully and
write them here.

Han said:

"There is a Flame within us. It burns bright at times and we
feel it mightily. When it burns we are warmed through and
through.

"There is a Child within us. When it stirs we are brought alive.

"There is a bright Light within. It comes ever closer as we get closer to the Child, bringing a power with it that makes everything new.

"Between the Flame and the Child and the very bright Light, nothing else is so real. The world falls away from them—line upon line, precept upon precept, here a little, there a little.

"I marvel at the Wonderful Plan that made me out of these three. We stand as a solitary, these two and I. I am become the Child and I reign as witness over my subjective view of things. I am given Dominion here.

"Now hear this, all my old friends of Kwangse Province, all that is true for me is true for you. The Child within us proves it true."

A loud voice came from the court yard. It was the important priest and metaphysician. "Oh yes, Master Han," he shouted so everyone could hear, "That sounds marvelously mystical and inspiring, but if it is true, why do you sit there eating porridge, looking more feeble than anyone? You don't look like one who has learned the Mystery of Life to me. You don't look like a teacher of Truth is supposed to look."

Han finished the last spoon of porridge, stretched himself on the cot and emitted an enormous belch. "The holy man you are looking for is inside you, my friend. The honest teacher tells you that." Soon Han was sleeping. The stranger left quickly to find another teacher.

CHAPTER SIX

THE LIGHT OF TRUTH BREAKING THROUGH

Glimpses and Glimmers

PERSONAL JOURNAL ENTRY

I have been given a secret of secrets, surely the most valuable thing in my world. It is said that kings would give their kingdoms to know it, but they can neither find it nor discover anyone to tell them what it is. Dear God, It has found me, of all the people in the world! Thank you, Father of Light and Life.

The body was ailing, yet, at exactly the right time this morning, Laurel called bringing a Glimpse onto the scene. The glimpse is an elixir of God. It did the good work! If ever I have wondered about proclaiming the power of our "glimpses and glimmers," that wonder was dispelled for the ten thousandth time this morning when that gentle lady spoke of her new insights into this and that. The "this and that" was just what this "body" needed. It responded immediately and I heard myself laughing with Laurel.

Yes, yes. It is a marvel of marvels. I take the Child's secret of the Glimpse and, without regret, throw the lesser things away. "Let him who has ears to hear. . . ."

EVENING TALK ON THE RIVER BANK

(Middle of a conversation by the campfire. Samuel speaking.)

A marvel happens in our affairs—a healing, say. Haven't you wondered what does the good work? Haven't you wondered *exactly* what happened or what caused it? Oh, we know that God is the source of all such good things, but exactly *how?* If we knew precisely what to look for, wouldn't that be a help? Of course. But we are usually looking for the specific healing, the answer to our perceived need of the moment, and if THAT need is met, we feel we've been successful in our study and prayer. It comes as a surprise to all of us, but the healing isn't the point.

Listen, listen. It is the Glimpse that does the work. I don't know why that fact dawns on us so slowly. We seem to take forever to understand that the glimpses of Light *inevitably come with healing on their wings.* It is the glimpse itself that does the work in this space-time sense of things. More, the Glimpse *is* the work! It doesn't come merely to do for us, but to *be* us.

Why are we seekers of Truth so slow to put our finger directly on the *agent?* We know God does the good work, but the specific agent, the specific event, goes unnoticed until something special happens. This very moment in our experience is a "something special" happening, so keep listening carefully.

For years I worked and struggled, pondered and pined to "know the truth." I read voraciously to catch the glimpses and glimmers, but the vital *connection* that was absolutely essential eluded me. That is, I didn't understand it was the Glimpse *itself* that came through as Godhead's own Truth entering this scene I am, to brighten and enliven it.

Once upon a time I wanted the glimpse to bring information to this old sense of myself and work a wonder for it. Hear this softly now: The Glimpse doesn't just *bring* the truth like a messenger; the Glimpse *is* the Truth; the Glimpse *is* the Light; the Glimpse is our genuine Selfhood *emerging!*

The value of the Glimpse *itself* eludes everyone until precept upon precept, here a little, there a little, slowly it dawns. Many *never* make the connection—not even ministers and practitioners who are working to teach and heal their worlds. Most remain unaware that it is the Glimpse of Light that matters and does the work in the phenomenal world.

So what is the big deal here? We have intuitively known something good happens as we search and study our Bibles and books. That's why we study so expectantly. Yet, somehow, a veil hangs between the Glimpse and the inner knowledge that it is the Glimpse *itself* that matters and has come to us for a specific, healing purpose *of its own.*

"What are you saying, Bill? All day we have been talking about the Child within. Now you seem to have changed course."

We haven't left the Child at all. Tonight we are examining the Child in even more detail. Let me try again. The GLIMPSE of Light does the work; the glimpse has the value, and nothing else in all this human experience is half so real as that instant of insight. That's what I mean here. That Glimpse is the Light of Godhead breaking into this consciousness of tangibility, into this awareness of space and time. The Glimpse is the Child stirring within. The Glimpse doesn't merely come from the Child, it *is* the Child of us.

Perhaps my initial inability to fully understand this had to do with the methods of instruction in my school days—or the way I was taught to comprehend things sequentially in a three-dimensional world. Maybe it was the way intellectual comprehension follows spiritual revelation, the way revelation precedes understanding. The Glimpse of Light precedes the tangible scene even though we are not conscious of that. Most definitely my inability to understand had much to do with my linear sense of time.

People often say they have some sense of the Truth "intellectually straight" but haven't felt it in their hearts yet. This usually means that they are, as I was then, trying to catch a Glimpse *along some specific line* of the heart's desire of the moment—about money or health or something. Well, I don't know that we can determine exactly what the Glimpse is to be *about,* but I am absolutely certain the Glimpse itself is the Real breaking into this limited dimension of human thought—*and here in this tangible sense of things we need a continuing flow of Glimpses.* Never mind whether they concern one's current questions or clear up intellectual points about religion and metaphysics or "heal" a problem of the moment. Never mind *that!* Go for the Glimpse! The Glimpse is the Child of ourself coming through! The Child comes with feelings, yes, but as insights of Light we can confirm in the world.

Yes, the Glimpse is the REAL coming into our affairs and it is the Glimpse that counts, not our human experience.

(Pause to stir the fire and watch the sparks fly upward.)

"Yes, I'm seeing and hearing something!"

Good. Now listen gently. What *needs are to be met by* the Glimpse or what *happens to us because of the Glimpse* is not as important as the Glimpse itself. **The Glimpse is IT. It is the Child Identity coming through.** Light comes as infinitely more than human thinking imagines.

THE DUAL NATURE OF LIGHT AND ITS GLIMPSES

Next, I would like to explain that our Glimpses "come to us" (a concession to words) from two directions just as the tree's sustenance comes from two directions. One Glimpse comes directly from light, like sunshine touching the leaves of the tree; the other Glimpse comes from the world, just as the tree draws nourishment through its roots. The food arriving at the roots is essentially indirect or "delayed" light. Let me say this better.

Once the wonder of Glimpses is understood, it isn't long until we've examined them carefully enough to see that they come from two seemingly separate sources. First, there is the direct Glimpse, as when we're writing in our journal or when an answer comes out of the blue from NOT thinking. Then, there are the *indirect* Glimpses as when we see the beauty of a galloping horse or the grace of a new rose in the garden or the tender smile of a stranger. One Glimpse is direct, the other indirect, as if delayed in the world's time while it developed for the receptive awareness to see it.

I am not able to make a distinction between the *values* of these differing sources of Light. The Glimpses of insight are wonderful no matter how they come. They do their good thing every time. They bring health and unseen blessings each time they arrive. Those that are triggered from the sights and sounds of the earth are like sunlight dappling the surface of a crystal lake. These are the ones the artist and the sensitive see. We grow accustomed to looking for these Insights from the earth but are not so conscious of those that come directly, without the delay of time. However, Glimpses arrive in both ways, and their Origin is the Same Light beyond ordinary light. This is in part what Jesus meant when he said that the stones would minister unto us. "Cleave a piece of wood, I am there; lift up the stone and you will find Me there." Yes, there is Light beyond light; there is a significance in everything, quite beyond the values given by men.

To make this still clearer, let me mention how these two sources of light become apparent quickly when we write. Journal tending, like any meditative or contemplative activity, essentially frees the head from the ordinary sensory input which can be overwhelming in the world these days. Attention reduced to words (or non-words) alone, allows the *direct* Glimpse to tiptoe in—sometimes thunder in— so we can be *conscious* of it. Very often it comes with information completely unrelated to the material we're writing about in the journal. It may be the answer to a question we had asked ourselves ten years earlier, about another matter entirely. Or, It can come directly, as the Answer to no question we had asked at all. But in this writing mode, Light also comes indirectly, as the simple consequence of singlemindedly following a line of thought or searching for the right word to use. This indirect light becomes plainly apparent as we write, because later we can go back to examine those words and can't believe we have written them.

For me, writing induced a state of mind that nothing else did. Meditation or contemplation were too inactive for me, too passive, too much an escape, too little an involvement with *understanding* the tangible scene. The meditative or contemplative state seemed a little like the child letting go the hands of his mother and father in a crowd, to try to go it alone. We will talk about this tomorrow.

Now, I have learned that the two apparent sources of the Glimpse—one direct, non-moving; the other, delayed in time— are a single source: Light of the Ineffable. Science's discovery of holography came to me as a wonderfully brilliant confirmation of this insight about light. I knew of this before I knew anything about "holography," or that tangibility was holographic in nature.

What "happens" in a moment of "illumination" involves moving back in time, beyond the delayed light of the mountain, the tree, the river, the scene, to the non-moving, direct Light behind it. One would like for this directness to be the mode of perception all the time, but that would be too much to bear for very long in linear time. And listen, listen: It is self-defeating to make such seeing the *goal* of our pursuit of Truth. Rather, it is enough just to know beyond doubt that Light beyond light exists as the source of everything, and that we are not bound to a finite time or to a limited point in space to perceive it. I was waylaid much too long striving to have the mystical experience, as though that were an accomplishment to be attained before the Truth was true. Better to *let go* the sense of an identity who *can't* see the Light, and accept the fact that Awareness, life, IS the Light of Life, God's knowledge *happening* in linear time.

As one lets go, it becomes natural to have more Glimpses. They come with greater strength and regularity—*provided we know what to do with them when they arrive.* Ah, that's the subject the seekers and teachers of truth know so little about. It takes "time" to learn that. Among many things I do with my Glimpses is to look for their *confirmation* out in the tangible world of people, places and things. Direct glimpses are precursors of knowledge breaking into the community of mankind. Presently my Glimpses tell me that a new clock is soon to begin ticking in the guts of people everywhere—a sound that can't be turned off, a grind that won't go away, an itch that can't be scratched by ordinary means. I anticipate *seeing* these insights *confirmed as Good* in the affairs of men.

Yes, there is a time to withdraw from the world and think of other things, but there is a time to come back and see the mountain *again*—and *commence to do* on the mountain what that seeing commands.

SIMPLICITY COMES

From out of the complexity of pure science and absolute metaphysics come the most marvelous SIMPLICITIES. For me, metaphysical absoluteness was apparently necessary to break out into Knowing. I don't know if it is necessary for my "others" to struggle as I did, but others don't need to suffer in those same areas if they will BELIEVE the Simplicities I've found and then make them their own; that is, if they will put them to the test and live them for themselves.

Those Glimpses that come with contemplation, meditation, study—or on the gentle evening breeze—are the Spirit of the Unknowable. They are the Word that "proceedeth from the mouth of the Lord," as it is put in Biblical language. They are essential for our inner growth and awakening. Whatever we actually need in this human scheme of things *begins with those blips of inner light.* Not the glimpses other people have, but the ones we have for ourselves. Those Glimpses "come from" the Center of Ourself, from the Child, the real Identity of us, "he who was before he came into being."

ABOUT OUR NEEDS IN THE WORLD

Suppose the country rose thinks it needs a certain chemical. It meditates and prays and listens to the revivalists on the wind, but when the sun breaks through, the sunshine brings what is necessary to help the plant absorb all needed chemicals—and do all things else for the plant's ongoingness—things of which the plant has no conscious knowledge.

Let us get this straight. The Glimpses of Truth are the most meaningful things in our affairs. They come with whatever we actually need for the long haul in time and space, if not for the moment—and they come with whatever the physical body of us needs whether we are conscious of the need or not. When the Glimpse comes, *"healing" that we aren't yet capable of recognizing is happening,* albeit not necessarily the healing we *humanly want.*

Now, hear this too. We don't sit about and wait until we need the Light before we act in this human scene of things. That's pretty much the way the world does it. Rather, we keep doing those things necessary to see the Light of Life in our affairs; we keep at the work of living the simple Equation (Truth) as a gardener keeps at his work—and our garden prospers in the Light.

Not long ago, a lady was here and I asked if she felt she had made spiritual progress during the past year. She said, "Definitely not. I've made no progress at all, spiritual or otherwise. My life is falling apart and that's why I'm here." She said she couldn't remember the last time she had had a moment of insight.

The world's disintegration has already set in if we're not regularly catching more Glimpses of Truth. If we haven't perceived one in recent days, we're headed for human trouble.

But to have glimpses of Truth regularly does not mean that one lives forever without an apparent decline of the body in the passage of years. If the Glimpses are still coming, we are laying up Treasures where moth doth not corrupt and our worldly affairs do not turn into an anchor around our necks. If new insights are *not* coming, we're headed in the wrong direction. If they are coming, we savor them, examine them and remember them in the greatest possible detail. That's why we keep the journal. The Light of the Glimpse is bringing so much MORE than we think we need.

ANOTHER NIGHT AROUND THE CAMPFIRE

What heals? The glimpse of Light. What does the good work? The Light. No difference between glimpses and glimmers and no matter if they are spelled with a capital or not. What do I do when someone comes to me for help? I give him one of my glimpses and tell him to give one of his to someone else. *If he HEARS mine and gives one of his own, he moves toward tangible health that moment, and both of us soon have more glimpses to give! That* is a significant part of the grand Equation—a Simplicity beyond words. And it WORKS wonders greater than I can tell. It does MORE than simply "heal" this or that. It benefits the entire WORLD.

How is it possible for a glimpse of Truth here on the river bank to do such an enormous thing as help all mankind? It is possible because the world and all mankind are subjective, WITHIN this Awareness we are. We are given dominion over that subjective world that we have come to understand, find guiltless, loose and let go. This world is ours to TEND as surely as a gardener tends his flowers. Our garden needs a continuing flow of Light and that Light comes as our inflowing bits and pieces of insight. We are to GIVE those Glimpses to our world as we receive them, live them, comprehend and confirm them. This is part of the Mystery of the Equation.

No one in metaphysics has written of the Child yet, or the Equation and its Balance. I may never publish these words, but at the moment it appears that task has been given me to do—just because, finally, humanity is on the edge of a willingness to understand what lies beyond intellectualism. Mankind really wants to know how to live his intellectualism intelligently without destroying civilization in the process. Metaphysicians have nothing in their literature about the Child or the Equation. Metaphysics includes the Child's way to think—subjectively—but very little about the Child's way to live and act for mankind. In these final days of our human experience, it is essential that we get acquainted with the rest of these three marvels.

THERE IS A TRUE MEASURE OF PROGRESS AND SUCCESS

The only measure of real success in all the world is whether or not one is coming to perceive more truth. No one knows this better than we do—each of us individually—and we know whether or not we've had new light in recent days. No one else can tell us more about this personal progress than we can tell ourselves. It is our own inmost business. But, if we haven't been seeing ever more light, we haven't been making progress, and we are sinking into the quagmire of Da Shan.

Once we've recognized a Glimpse for what it is, the Child within knows there are more glimpses to be seen, experienced, lived and celebrated. More, we know those Glimpses offer new perspectives of old views. They tell us more nearly how things really are. They brighten and enliven our affairs. *But most of all, those Glimpses come with healing on their wings*, reviving the Child within.

With each bit of Light we are more the Child and less the climber.

Gentle listener, this is what you have come here for. *There is something one can do to begin having those wonderful glimpses of*

Truth again! We will talk about that around tomorrow's campfire.

PERSONAL JOURNAL ENTRY

In helplessness
I try mightily to shake the gates of heaven and am finally brought one way or another to stop and give up.
In helplessness, I am forced to stop everything and just be. I am forced to stop trying to get the answers and just be.
Then, the more I be, the more the answers come to be understood, thence to be questions no more, nor answers. And then I know what to do with the answers, those blessed glimpses and glimmers.
At first this seems to be another paradox, but it isn't. Getting still lets the water settle and then one begins to see things that he couldn't see when the water was ruffled by trying so hard to catch an answer.
I get still and the answers come.
I get still, and this awareness is perceived to be the knowing of God.
But I am so slow getting still because the knowing wants to be the Knower, as though it had a mind of its own. The known is within the knowing, but the immanent Knower transcends it. And I am so slow being humble enough to admit that. I keep the water stirred trying to be the Knower, and to know what the Knower knows.
Listen, heart o' Me:
I have faced awful situations from which there was no apparent escape. I shook and pounded the gates of Heaven lamenting the hopelessness of Life, wondering why I was born and what life was about. The more I wagged my head, the worse I felt until the anguish forced me to sit down in helplessness and throw myself on the mercy of Something. THAT was when I put myself where I have always been, back into the capable hands of the One I am.
Oh, you say I don't understand that Life is not threatened and cannot be intimidated? That I don't see the Absolute Fact that God/Life is ALL in ALL or, if I did, I wouldn't even speak of the appearance of Life being threatened?

Oh yes, I DO see that God is all in all. I am not less certain about THAT than in the first days of my first discovery; I am only less adamant in my choice of words. Why? To be understood. By whom? Everyone, who is myself.

ANOTHER PERSONAL JOURNAL ENTRY

The end of the year is a time to stop and take stock of the year just past and see if any real progress has taken place. If we have seen more TRUTH during the year and have seen evidence that Truth is at work in our affairs, we know very well "progress" has taken place. We answer affirmatively even if other things have fallen apart. More, we know from whence that progress has come.

With all my heart, I want those who may read the words of this old journal to receive a tangible measure of hope—a Glimpse of the Child's Light. If so, they will be on their way. They will surely be on their way!

Once the Light has found us, it doesn't let us go until it has blessed us fully.

CHAPTER SEVEN

∽∾

THE CHILD LIVED
IN THE WORLD

Interface and Journal Tending

THE POINT OF INTERFACE

We all want more Light. We all need and want the flow of
Light for our Truth to be new, fresh and effective. In this regard, Jesus said, "If you bring forth that within yourselves,
that which you have will save you." So what do we do? It is
confoundingly simple. We reach out to the Child within us. *We
talk to the Child we know is there.* We do this initially by means
of our journal and later by writing and talking to the "rest of
ourself"—the Child "out there" in time and space.

We write to the Child-I-Am with simple words in our private
journal, *exactly as we would talk to God.* The Child of us IS the
God of us and is our connection, our interface, with Godhead,
Mountain Beyond Name. The Child is also our interface with
the entire tangible universe—Da Shan. It is as if the Real of
us, the Child, holds God's hand with one hand and holds the
world's hand with the other. We stand precisely in the middle
between these two that are One, Godhead and Man. The
Child is the Third—Logos. These three are one.

LISTEN GENTLY ABOUT THE PLACE OF INTERFACE

When one plays the piano, the point of interface between the player and the sounded music is exactly where his fingers touch the keys. The surface of the keys is the place where the inner music of the soul becomes the outer melody in the living room or concert hall. There is no space between the fingers and the keys, just as there is no space between the Child-of-us and our fingers as we write. The Child-Soul of us is where the melody is first heard.

If one is a composer, the point of interface between the melody heard within and the melody the world hears "without," is also at the tips of the composer's fingers—as he plays and as he writes those notes onto a piece of paper.

So, the INTERFACE is WHERE the "inside becomes outside" and where, as we listen, the outside becomes inside. In the Thomas book, we hear Jesus say, "When you make the two one, and when you make the inner as the outer and the outer as the inner . . . then shall you enter the Kingdom."

When one writes a letter or a book, the point of INTERFACE between the reader and writer is the tip of the writer's fingers and his heart, and the eyes that read and the reader's heart. There is no real space between the eyes, the Heart and the tips of the fingers. When the writer gets the fingers to state the Child-heart's feeling, the interface is completed, heart to heart.

As I sit here writing these words at Woodsong's study desk piled high with books, papers and letters, the point of interface between the Child-Heart-I-am and the entire world of time's tangibility is the keyboard of the good Rabbi Moses Goldberg—the typewriter. The Child-Heart of me touches God on the one side, the world of time on the other. Reading these words, the reader goes straight to the writer's Heart—and to his own, simultaneously. As you will see very plainly in the days ahead, there is only one HEART, one Child, one God. It is the same for all of us.

DISNEY WORLD

I visit Disneyland at every opportunity. It is a wonderful

place to go. There is no questioning the delight and enchantment there. Few enter the Magic Kingdom without feeling the Child-Heart within.

I think my favorite time of day at Disneyland is in the evening when California's golden sun has set and the street lights of the village are beginning to twinkle and sparkle everywhere. I've learned the best place to sit at that time of day is at the Mainstreet Railroad Station. From the big wooden benches that overlook the city square, one looks down on the magic. Tired and happy people are strolling below, looking, laughing, smiling and heading reluctantly for the gates. Viewing all that wonder and happiness, I am reminded that it all began when a man took a pencil in hand and let an image inside flow outside onto the paper—the image of a mouse he named Mickey. If ever one wanted to see the tangible outside become like the inside, let him look and see the child heart of Walt Disney *made tangible* so everyone can see it and exult. The dream began in the heart of the Child-man, but the tangible Disneyland in time and space began at the point of a pencil.

As I write this, I am there. Such is the magic within us.

THE DIRECT ROUTE TO THE CHILD WITHIN

Certainly, the most direct route to the Child of us is to pay attention to our words and thoughts. We do that best by actually looking at some of those thoughts we have written. Just as there is magic when the audience LISTENS to the sounds in the concert hall (the Child's interface with the world), so there is tremendous magic (listen, carefully!) as we turn the process around to *discover* the Child and *its interface with REALITY.*

Metaphysics and religion, as they have developed in the world, have been woefully inadequate in showing us HOW to make this turn around. There is as much a DOING in this inner reversal as in its outer expression.

WING AND THE MUSIC OF THE RHOMBOIDS

Han told the story of Wing, the famous musician of

Da Shan. Wing's music was known throughout the world. To reward him, God allowed Wing to hear the sacred music of the rhomboids for three entire evenings—a melody so enchanting it brought the fields and meadows alive and caused the trees to dance.

But Wing didn't write the melody while he still remembered it. He felt certain he could never forget such a wonderful song. But before Wing could write the song onto parchment, it had flown from his head. When the king asked why he had not written it before it was forgotten, Wing replied, "Everything is in my head. The whole world is within this Awareness I am, so it really isn't necessary to write anything."

The king had Wing's head chopped off. The cynics said, "The world was in Wing's head and now Wing's head is in the world."

"If Wing had made the effort to write the Insight, it could have been heard by everyone," said Han.

Yes, we write our insights before they are forgotten. Then we live them. Then we tell them to others who see us living them.

WHY JOURNAL TENDING?

"I don't like to write, Sam. It is difficult for me. I write rotten letters and don't have the time to try to write well. I'd rather read. Why do you stress journal tending so?"

One doesn't have to write well to keep a journal of his thoughts, of his glimpses and glimmers; no one is going to read it but the journal tender himself. When one understands the secret of spiritual input and output, and few do, he realizes that writing *well* isn't important, but the mode of mentation that writing requires IS important—and once one is comfortable with the "mode," he can maintain it whether he is writing or not.

Journal tending is fundamental. Writing is a discipline that engages and utilizes the FLOW of life. It is the FLOW from the INEFFABLE, through consciousness, OUT into tangible WORDS that does the good work for us *in the world*, not necessarily WHAT is written. The FLOW is the thing we want to get going again. *The flow completes the interface, top to bottom, inside to outside.* The FLOW is interrupted when one stops living the Equation. The flow IS the interfacing Equation in operation. We are LIVING while we are completing the FLOW; we are dying when we are not living the flow. We interrupt the FLOW of Energy (individually and in quantum) and there is a corresponding increase of stored, deadly energy to CONFIRM the interruption. One doesn't have to look far to find the negative confirmation of his own indolence. We interrupt the FLOW of LIGHT and LIFE (the divine Energy) and we see a confirming accumulation of fat, poverty, cells gone amuck, fear, starvation in the world and all else appearing negatively in our affairs. We become CONSCIOUS of the FLOW again—LIVING it to the best of our ability—and the Flow gives us the most wonderful things to SEE, FEEL and write about. Writing our Glimpses of Good is a sure, certain *action* that sparks the Flow of Light and Life in our subjective world.

INSIDE/OUTSIDE, OUTSIDE/INSIDE, THE CHILD'S INTERFACE

Nothing, absolutely nothing, is more important than the following: In all existence, there is a *"flow"* involved. Be gentle with yourself and remember the flow of old. What was it? When we were children we interfaced with God and the world freely. Our imagination *flowed* without restraint *into the world of people, places and things.* By the same token, the world of people and things flowed freely *into the child.* We saw a frog (outside) and, presto, the imagination was off and running. Or, we thought of kings and queens (inside), and immediately the people walking up the street (outside) became part of the royal court (BOTH sides).

Adulthood has woven a veil that hangs between the Childheart and the world. The world outside has become the adult's reality, bound in time. The free-flowing exchange from inside to outside, outside to inside, has been interrupted and insulated by the unconscionable bastard we insist on being in linear time.

Just as a stopped-up kitchen sink needs to flow again, it is necessary for us to regain the flow—outside /inside, inside/outside— moving freely again. **Examining one's own thoughts is the necessary first step**—and make no mistake, *it is necessary.* The Child thinks differently than the old man, as you are feeling already while the Child comes alive in your experience. Of course, writing is not the only way to examine one's thoughts (and thinking), *but it is the most immediate way to do it by oneself.*

In human history, the "breakthroughs" to greater dimensions have inevitably occurred with writing playing a major part in the process—from the ancient forest wanderers to these final days of this civilization, as physicists sit pondering their equations. The historic Jesus may have written only in the sand, but who can dispute he caused much to be written? So, we do this writing for ourself alone—without an intermediary between ourself and God. Who stands between the thinking and the thought but our Self? In the end, all the words being spoken and written in the name of Truth are as nothing compared to our OWN experienced interface with Reality—inside and outside.

The instant a word of our own is written on the paper before us, our tangible scene has been altered—moved toward darkness or light, for better or worse, by that written (and spoken) word. If we keep the flow passing between the heart and the fingers that touch the world, the old bastard's barrier becomes less opaque and our experience in the world starts improving. As the Child of us shows us our birthright atop Da Shan (and we're quickly on our way the moment we take pen in hand), the climbing adult diminishes, the Child increases in consciousness, more and more—until, atop the mighty mountain of Kwangse, naught remains but the True Identity, the Child I am.

Despite all you have heard elsewhere, there is no way "There" short of finding and living the Child that IS there and everywhere. There are no shortcuts. No church can take us there. No doctrine can do it for us. We may lay metaphysical claim to our heritage until the jade eggs of Da Shan hatch, but we don't *receive* that heritage until we BECOME the Child in conscious, living action. Intellectualism has its place, but it doesn't take us home. The Child's conscious "return" to the peak of the mountain is accomplished *in living fact* before one gets off the temporal world's wheel of trials, tribulations, beginnings and endings, time and rebirth.

LETTER TO A FRIEND

Thank you for the call, dear friend, Zeke.

Jeremiah spoke of the Mystery as arriving "Line upon line," a reference to the last letter of the old Hebrew alphabet, which came to be believed to have special power. He added "precept upon precept." It has come that way for me, Zeke. I do not believe it comes to anyone otherwise. There may be "road to Damascus" enlightenments, but those events are not UNDERSTOOD or CONFIRMED quickly. Understanding comes "precept upon precept." Yours will come more quickly now because you are willing to get the veil out of the way—and to DO what you will be given to do.

Listen carefully: Get yourself a notebook and begin a journal. **There is a "flow" from the Ineffable Beyond Name into our conscious/unconscious awareness, and from there into tangibility. We move into that flow as we clothe our Glimpse with words.** That Flow is continual, constant, ever-flowing—from Non-Movement into tangibility and the world's movement.

The purpose of the journal is to consciously become **the very point** where the Ineffable becomes tangible in the world, that is, to unblock the Flow and allow it to move through our CONSCIOUS awareness again—*just as it did when we were children.*

This is not a religious approach, Zeke, because the flow of Glimpses from Godhead pertains to EVERYTHING good, true and wonderful. Beauty, wonder, form, color, tenderness, the fragrances of flowers, the beauty of children and mountains and June bugs, excitement, enthusiasm, FEELINGS of love and awe, and especially memories of the grand events of our lives are all part of the Flow.

Mark a section of your journal "GLIMPSES" and begin making a list of the notable Glimpses you have had in your life.

Glimpses of what? Nothing complex here. Just THINK BACK and remember the joyful, moving, significant moments.

When you first fell in love. When you got your first bicycle. Any of the special, meaningful events you remember. LIST them. It isn't necessary to write in detail about them. At this time, just LIST THEM. Such as (some of mine):
1. Military school and homesickness.
2. The little girl, Barbara.
3. The picnic and the cow's soulful eyes.
4. The man screaming in the church.
5. Walking to meet Mom in the evening.

Go back to your childhood, Zeke, and recall all the events that stick in your mind for ANY reason, painful or otherwise, because their sticking in memory is evidence *they taught you something.* You may omit the most painful ones if you like, but be certain to list the GOOD ones. What they taught isn't important right now. You are just making a list of the powerful MOMENTS in your earlier days.

At the moment, it seems I'm asking you to to recall memories, and in a way, I am, but we'll call them GLIMPSES later, as you will see. This is a meaningful exercise, Zeke. Just do it. Pay particular attention to the sensations, feelings, moods and memories that come, AND KNOW THIS: As those things "come into consciousness," *Something very healing to the BODY is coming with them.*

Will you do this, Zeke? Set up a specific time, early in the morning and again in the afternoon or evening, each day. Not long. You set the time. Ten or fifteen minutes MINIMUM. Some days, when the Flow is really coming, STAY WITH IT. In a year or two (for you, how about a month or two?) you will be surprised and delighted to find that the Flow is CONSTANT and that you can actually do what the prophet said: "Whatsoever things are good and true . . . think on these things."

You have just begun. I assure you, that Child LIVES, Zeke. Everything you felt as a kid, you can and WILL feel again! "Prove me now, herewith. . .!" The Child within will lead you to all things else. Then, you will have the opportunity to do the same for many others, even as now I do for you.

Hang in there, man. We have a lot to do for our world!

THE MODE

I can't remember when or why I began using the term "journal tending" because it really isn't that. It is more a jotting down of thoughts as they come or an examination of one's own thinking. It is very often a conversation between the me-sense and the Self within. For many years my journal was a shirt pocket and a dresser drawer; whatever words, phrases or sentences came were jotted onto whatever was handy—old envelopes, receipts, grocery bags. These bits and pieces were emptied into a drawer each day, and it was many years before the activity was even half organized.

The reader, however, is not being asked to do an effortless thing either. It *does* take time and a small effort to sit down and ask God a question—and then to be still and listen for an answer. When we talk to friends, some slight momentary attention is necessary to select the right words to describe the antics of our dog romping in the autumn leaves just raked. But we do that almost effortlessly. No more effort than this is required for keeping a "journal" as I propose doing it. Just remember, it isn't what we write that matters half so much as the MODE we put ourselves into as we write. Writing may be a "discipline" most of us don't enjoy because we can't write as easily as we can talk—and we are afraid to look at our results—but writing is invaluable because of the receptiveness it engenders.

But, my friend, if you will take my word for it at the moment, you will quickly find yourself with a remarkable *"something to do"* that will lead you straight to the Child Heart of yourself!

Through the years many have told me that writing was the last thing they would ever do. On my desk this moment there is a letter saying, ". . .if writing is required to discover the Truth, I'll never know the Truth." Yet, I've seen those very people become living lights in the world, some of them publishing books. Not everyone who keeps a journal will write to the world, yet not a single one who writes a word—even one word on the back of an old envelope—can keep from changing his experience by that very word. There is a mystical truth in the saying about the "web of interrelatedness": When a leaf falls to the earth, the universe is shaken. Just so, when one writes a single word, the universe is shaken. That is a fact which I will "prove" momentarily.

To this point in the book, we have talked about (1) the Child within, (2) the power of Glimpses and (3) journal tending. The journal has been introduced early because we will use it to get BACK to the essential Child and Its Glimpses, without which one is not living. Let me repeat, the power of the journal doesn't lie in the words written in it *but in the MODE OF CON-SCIOUSNESS one falls into as he writes!* That "mode of mentation" takes us to the Child and the Child brings us GLIMPSES!

WE SMASH THE BARRIER BETWEEN THE OLD MAN AND THE CHILD

It is essential that we make a *conscious* connection with the Child. Why? Because the Child interfaces with God. Imperceptibly we let go the "we" and become the Child—to the utter amazement of ourself. Bit by bit, we let go the ego-climber and its fictitious interface with God and world. This doesn't happen overnight, but once we know we are looking for the very Child of ourself, the pace quickens dramatically.

There isn't a person in the world who can't begin this marvelous transformation at once. We come face to face with the Child and are transfigured, never mind what seems to be going on with the physical body—its age and condition. The transformation is a marvel not unlike the butterfly's emergence into the light of day after its dark night in the binding cocoon. The Child's interface with the real world is no less dramatic than the butterfly's view transcending the blind worm on the quaking leaf; it is infinitely more beautiful and fulfilling than the old man's counterfeit connection with his world. The material world is seen for the insubstantial image of Image it is. The material world is also perceived for the purpose it serves—to confirm God's allness. When the Child is finally found again, we become aware for the first time in our lives that the interruption wasn't and isn't "bad," no matter how terrible the human picture, and we find that the human saga is a wonderful, *necessary* part of the Plan. Nothing about the human experience has been happenstance or outside the perfect Plan of the One.

ABOUT THE UNREAL NATURE OF MATTER

Strangely, for all our professing the unreality of matter, seekers of Truth are often the last to understand this tangible world which is subjectively within us, flowing out of us, so to speak. Religious objectivism, metaphysical subjectivism, and human science would shake the gates of heaven to understand *why* "matter" seems so persistently real despite its holographic nature. But without the Child within, no one can solve this problem. The Child's mysterious balance, the Equation, allows us to understand.

There is a parable of a woman carrying a jar of meal on her back, and when she gets home, the meal has leaked away and the jar is empty—meaning, the weight of the world, the monkey on the back, the human values, have imperceptibly slipped away to be replaced with KNOWING.

ACTION, NOT STUDY

We start our journal and begin the *conscious* interface with the Child immediately. We don't read about Truth forever as though it is perceived intellectually by sitting with a book in our hand. The return to the Child, *to feel the Child*, is an actual doing which we can and must experience for ourselves.

Our correspondence with one who has found a measure of that Child of Himself can be marvelously helpful.

The words of this book must now go beyond the discovery of Identity *to the Child's declarations and revelations themselves*, but the reader should understand that all that follows from this point (in this book and in one's life) necessarily has TWO SETS OF INTERPRETATIONS. The first is made by the old nature of us, the climber struggling to find Identity. The second is the interpretation and meaning the CHILD/HEART of us WITHIN hears and responds to. That interpretation, *LIVED in the world*, whisks us up the mountain. Often the Heart hears first, followed by the old nature's intrusion trying to "understand" and, when it can't, strewing doubt and confusion, frequently with a battery of intellectual obfuscations. For this reason, multiple readings have always been necessary with literature that speaks to the Real of us.

As we comprehend the Child and ITS instruction, we are making REAL progress for the first time since our discovery of Truth.

INCREASING SENSIBILITIES AND A WARNING

Finally, there is another matter the reader must understand concerning the discovery of the Child. As the Child's leadership becomes real to us, there comes a remarkable, sometimes astonishing return of *sensitivity*. Line upon line, precept upon precept, we begin to FEEL again and, for many of us, it will be the first time in years we've felt so clearly and strongly about anything. You are likely feeling some of the increase already.

An important word of caution here: The delights of this returning sensitivity can be *(and will try to be)* as heady and misleading as were our involvements with the world. Many years ago, I knew a lady who found the Child of herself. She mistook her new sensitivity to be an increasing libido and went charging down the world's road with that tiger by the tail. At this stage of our search we shouldn't need to be told how powerful, broad and deceiving THAT trip of sensualism is. We must not be swept aside or off the mountain's edge because of the grand increases of feeling that come with the Child and Its new vista—not just sensual feelings, but all the sensations of unbound youth.

The Equation, about which we are writing (a little here and a little there), allows us to hold the body's sensualism in perspective, so that we are no longer led by the nose of unchecked passion. Without the Equation LIVED, this heightened sensitivity can carry the *climber* in the wrong direction.

Further, let it be understood that we cannot live the Child's Equation for the purpose of increasing sensualism—that is, to gratify the senses with the pleasures of the world. That attempt meets with utter failure and brings us to a rude comeuppance. *What selfish human intention gains, that same intention destroys, and more;* what the old nature gains by selfish design is taken from it. Nothing from nothing, a state more miserable than before. The old nature is *surrendered and given up* as the Child leads to the High View. We surrender it willingly before the Child puts us atop Da Shan.

Those who persist in their search for Truth will find the New Vistas infinitely more wonderful than all that has been surrendered along the way.

There must be no misunderstanding here: There is no way to hold to the human pleasures of the old man's linear world while acquiring those of the Child's. Strangely, it takes metaphysicians longer to understand this than it takes ordinary folks. The Child's new world includes the lesser worlds to infinity. In the end we have lost nothing but illusion and its deceit, but we have found Identity and gained dominion. Therefore, we don't hold back in the human scheme of things. Unlike Ananias and Sapphira, we are willing to let go everything concerning the old nature. What comes with the higher view is infinitely more.

A WEIGHTY PUFF

"He talks about a growing sensitivity," said Mary.

"Yes," Lee replied. "Our sensitivity returns."

"But I'm too sensitive now. I'm not sure I want that."

"Oh, he means the good things," Lee said, touching her hand. "We settle into a balance first, where the old sensitivities go away—our fears and dreads, our dislikes and terrors leaving us. Then, out of the balance comes a return of the feelings we held as children before we were programmed and desensitized."

Mary sat pensively. "What kind of feelings return?" she asked hesitantly.

"Little things we've forgotten about." A smile covered Lee's face. "I began to smell the grass again as I did when I was a boy. Very little things began to excite me again—like the sight

of a deer at the forest's edge or a butterfly circling my head.
Even my holly berries became red again."
"And you found joy in those things?" the troubled lady
asked incredulously.
"Yes, yes! And you will too. Watch and see."
"Dear God, I hope so," Mary sighed.

A JOURNAL ENTRY

A jay crying in the cold.
*There is something new to see every day, something to be
learned—and, sometimes, it can be very wonderful. Awareness
exploring the infinity of life, as old friend Alfred used to say.
There is no end to this exploration of infinite Being or to the
Joy it brings.*

*A jay came to the feeder in the holly bush a few minutes ago
on this very cold January morning atop the hill. He let out his
piercing screech to warn away others who would dare intrude
on his private stash of mid-winter goodies. "Screech! Squawk!"
he shrieked, not ten feet from the keyboard of my typewriter
tucked warmly behind the study window overlooking the holly
bush. I looked up, as who wouldn't, just in time to see a back-
lit, top-knotted jay's head discharge its noise. With each squawk
came a big puff of steam! Now, in all these years of bird loving
and watching, I've never seen their tiny breath. Somehow, the
thought of it never came to mind, or I didn't notice, believing
their breathing was such a small affair it couldn't or wouldn't
be seen by anyone but the bird. This morning I've learned that
a jaybird can huff and puff billows of steam on a cold morning
with the best of them. And one can see it plain as day if he is
situated just right, sun behind a holly bush and sunflower seed
in the feeder.*
*Well now, who would have thought the sight of a tiny puff of
breath would elicit a paragraph in my journal, filled as it is
with weighty matters? That puff of steam is the weighty matter
for THIS day! That was a rare sight, I'll tell you! Like one
more tiny, hand-crafted arrowhead for my collection of memories. Precept upon precept our insights come, breath upon
breath, in an endless line of blessings.*

Thank you, Angels, for this breath of another day!

Woodsong on the Hill

HOW QUICKLY DO WE FIND THE CHILD?

How to write this with the gravity necessary? Let the heart hear this. The very MOMENT we become conscious we ARE the Child in actuality, that MOMENT we are in touch with the Divine. *The CONSCIOUS interface has begun.* The Child speaks to us of HIGH things immediately and we become conscious of them. We write as we go along, examining our thoughts.

CHAPTER EIGHT

❧

INCREASING THE FLOW OF LIGHT

Sharing Glimpses and Glimmers

FROM THE JOURNAL

REBIRTH OF THE CHILD

*Now and then in the affairs of men
there comes a moment of reflection when
the old bastard in us sits down with his pipe and the Child
stands up to watch him light it.*

*Ah yes. The Child within us stands up and we rediscover
him. We find he hasn't perished over the years but is very much
alive and kicking.*

*But then, for most of us, attention goes flying back to the old
man, his pipe and his troubles. As the last bit of smoke curls
upward, flattens against the ceiling and disappears, the little
boy is cast aside, relegated to the shadow of humanhood and all
but forgotten again.*

*We think of these light moments as a memory from childhood
returning briefly, never dreaming it is the Child Itself stirring
and never in our wildest dreams believing we ARE that Child
still, just as we were as children and can come alive again and*

BE that childlike Child in living, conscious FACT!

Sad how we treat the Child, isn't it? Oh, but isn't it a marvel how that little One endures and how, at any moment, that innocent view springs to mind again with no intervening years eaten by the locusts! Isn't that a marvel of marvels? Yes. Hell, yes! That is a marvel of marvels.

The Child sits right here and writes these words and laughs and laughs. The Child's re-emergence and re-birth are a marvel even to the Child.

But what matters most and needs never to be forgotten: the Child within is alive! It is lighthearted and well! It is awaiting my willingness to let It out. The Child lives in Light and sends it to me bountifully!

ONE OF THE PROBLEMS

Our study of the truth brings us Light. No question about that. Books, classes, meditation, discussions, yes, but those sudden moments of Light and Love come at unexpected times and places as well. Who doesn't remember?

However, a serious problem rarely admitted in religious and metaphysical circles and *seldom* mentioned in science, is that those moments of insight, so common when we first begin to study in earnest, have a way of becoming less frequent. For most seekers of Truth/truth, the light doesn't keep coming with the same impact and excitement of those first days. For many too many, enthusiasm wanes. Even Einstein and Edison spoke of this. I think everyone experiences the dry times, wondering what has happened to his faith and trust, his enthusiasm, interest and clarity. Our perception of the light diminishes *because we haven't done with the light what we are supposed to do with it.*
"In what measure you give it shall be measured unto you again."

LETTER TO LORETTA

Dear lady with the bright eyes,

I give you this parting gift "such as I have." It is about Glimpses and Glimmers. They are tiny seeds.

You have decided to begin a simple journal and examine your inmost thoughts. Grand! Right in the front of your notebook, mark a section for GLIMPSES. The words you write there will become very special as you will see.

Sit still for a time and think back in your life to recall a special moment. Record what you can of it—when that special moment happened; where; whatever is remembered and, if you can, what you learned. For some of us, only a time or two from a lifetime may come to mind. I don't remember much about the Glimpses from my early youth. But if we can remember ONE instance in our life, *that is enough* to begin discovering the Secret of Secrets. That Glimpse is a seed which will still germinate just as did the ancient seed found in the tombs of the Egyptians and Romans.

When we write about our Glimpses of Light, we are preparing ourselves for ANOTHER glimpse. *If we want another, we write and tell of those we've had.* There is no better way to get them, no magic study that will continue to bring them forever; no book will produce another half so well as *the telling of those we've already had.* Listen carefully: We TELL the old ones; we receive NEW ones.

The journal entry—even if only a single word that reminds us of that long ago Glimpse—does something wonderful and mysterious, indeed. It prepares the way for someone to enter our experience, someone to whom we can tell that Glimpse! Don't ask me why. I only know it DOES—magically. You can see for yourself as quickly as you try it. I don't know the psychological and metaphysical factors involved, but I know our experience is SUBJECTIVE, and when I write my Glimpse, I (1) *prepare the way for someone to come into this tangible experience to hear it,* and (2) *when I tell it,* I get more Glimpses.

Jesus said that the man old in years will not hesitate to ask a child of seven days about his place in heaven. When we find the Child within, we begin receiving Glimpses again, and slowly, line upon line, we ourselves become that "Child of seven days" to whom our entire subjective world will one day turn. Those Glimpses we've had, prove to us that we are the Child of God. The man we tell them to is our own subjective selfhood-in-time. When we share the Glimpse we have come to understand and confirm, we have done a portion of what we are on the green earth to do—to proclaim the REAL, the GOOD and the TRUE. This is what completing the interface is all about.

Loretta, when the Glimpse comes, it comes with healing on its wings! It is the medicine we need most, the elixir of youth. It comes with the strength and power of an eagle to lift us and carry us aloft on wings of fire. It comes with REAL power that heals the sick and binds up the broken hearted—not just for ourselves and those we know, but *for all to whom we give it.* But we must GIVE it, Loretta; we must COMPLETE THE IN-TERFACE. You know how seldom I use that word "must," but we must *follow through* with the transaction and clap our hands in the cathedral. If we don't, then the little we've been given is taken from us, exactly as Jesus and the prophets said.

Well, little lady who gave Rachel and me a port in the storm, here is the explanation of what I did that worked for me. These words are the instruction that finally arrives in our ex-perience to be seen and understood when we are ready—say-ing *exactly* what we and EVERYONE can do. They are words that have come from the fire of life and living—refined, tested and proven. Anyone can put these words to the TEST and see for himself whether or not Samuel is writing nonsense. No one will know until he has tried them and tested them, will he? Try me, Loretta. Find me out. "Prove me now herewith!"

I look at our Harry and know it isn't too late, even for him lying there in that hospital, tied to tubes and bags. He lies there *telling others of his Light!*

His children listen and are amazed. They think he is pass-ing along his wisdom to educate them, to help them, but Harry is doing that for HIMSELF because, with the telling, comes more Light to be seen and shared. The Glimpses bring SPIRITUAL TREASURE and "another world" where time isn't what it seems to be. It is the "more to see" that brings healing and health, well-being, spiritual riches and all the things that are TAKEN WITH US when we finally understand and let go temporality in this human condition.

I don't know the end of this matter, Lady Loretta of the bright eyes, but what sings in my heart, day after day, is that these GLIMPSES are the spiritual treasure we take Wherever we "go." They are all that's really real of this tangible experience in time. They are the "treasure laid up in (timeless) Heaven."

Why and how do I believe this so? Because, from Glimmer to Glimmer no *time* intervenes. In the midst of Light there is no passage of time from one glimpse to the next. All the human events between are forgotten—dream stuff that slips away. My Harry is learning how REAL the Glimpses of Truth and how *insubstantial* the rest of the human experience except to *confirm* the Nature of Deity.

Even as I was writing this, two calls came from the few who know Rachel and I are here. They told of WONDERS and EXCITEMENT in their experience as the consequence of the last NOTES. Those notes were Me "telling my Glimpses" to me. The calls were the responses coming back as more Light and Life. The tangible calls came because *the tangible effort was made* to give the Glimpse. This is part of the Equation. We make no effort, we get no response.

So, right here at this sweet little cottage, you've seen these ideas lived and practiced. You've watched them produce MORE Light that has enlivened everyone.

FROM THE HAN DISCOURSES

The small lady sat quietly, deep in thought. They had been talking about the Glimpse and the importance of passing it along. At last Mary said, "I don't have the opportunity to talk of Truth to anyone. No one I know is interested in these things. What am I to do?"

Han smiled and touched her hand. "All we must do is *want* to tell someone, then *be willing* to tell someone. Inevitably, a way appears to do it. The Heart of us that received the Light directs the subjective World to whom we give the Light."

"I haven't the least idea what you are talking about," Mary said wistfully. "But, oh, I remember how much the Truth of old meant to my mother and me," she continued. "We were so sweetly innocent then. I remember how we looked forward to Sunday and going to church. That's where it began for us. We had no horse and carriage or automobile in those days. The Church was two miles away and we walked there so eagerly. I recall the times when it was raining—storming even—and we walked through gales of wind and rain. Those days were so wonderful for me." She stopped talking, closed her eyes and smiled.

"Listen to me!" said Han happily. "You've just done it! You've just completed the interface! That story did it. That's all there is to passing a Glimpse along. You see, Mary, there is nothing difficult or demanding about it. Nothing religious or metaphysical must be said. Yet, we pass along something of the Light. The Light is the 'talent' that we musn't bury. You have just dug it up and handed it to me, Mary. You have given me a Glimpse of Light."

Mary was startled.

"You see, you didn't have to make a great spiritual or metaphysical statement, did you?" Han laughed. "You just passed a Glimpse to me, and, having done it, you can expect to get another! It is most amazing what those Glimpses are and what they do."

CONVERSATION AT WOODSONG

"That's too damned simple, Sam." George was ever the pragmatist, never satisfied. "There has to be more to it than that."

Who says the final things to understand are difficult, occult, religious, mystical, metaphysical, absolute? How complex was Einstein's equation? Five characters. We finally break out of theological and metaphysical complexity to rediscover the Child and his simple Light. The Child catches the Light because the Child is the Light.

MORE ABOUT THE INTERFACE

The Divine Interface with the external world, the linear world of time and space, requires *clear, understandable and honest words* from the internal Child-heart of us to the external Child-heart of us! This interface is the "rest of the transaction" and constitutes a great portion of what is meant by "Give to God that which is God's," a major part of the Equation of Life. The Equation, remember, is the Child's way to live in this apparent world, and is something that metaphysics hasn't had much to say about, concerned as it is with the way to *think*.

I know a lady who has seen much Light, but has withdrawn from the world into metaphysical or mystical seclusion. She is terribly depressed, wondering what has happened to the Truth that meant so much to her in earlier years. She has struggled for the Truth so earnestly. The lady's friends have tried to prevail on her to tell others of her insights, but she is deeply engrossed in a listening attitude, searching the heart of herself for new ideas and more light—nothing comes as it did before and she wonders why.

The glimpses the lady has been blessed to receive *stop* right at the edge of tangibility and go no further. Her Light is ready to break out onto the tangible world scene like an electric idea, but her silence is deadening. Now she wonders why her experience is going as it is, filled with anxiety, stress and depression. She writes to me, "How can this be? Is this justice? I have devoted my entire life to the study of Truth, and for all appearances and feelings in me, it is as if the Truth were dead."

Our transaction in the tangible world isn't finished until we have given our Glimpses to the subjective world in our hands. These Glimpses are the "talent" that must not be left buried but put to work in the world of images upon images, "lest the little we have is taken from us." This is a large part of the simple and wonderful Equation. What was the parable of the talents if not a statement that the Light is to be put to work in the world?

WE PASS THE LIGHT ALONG WITH OUR WORDS

Certainly it is marvelous to sit back and bask in the Light; often it seems an interruption to complete the *transaction* by taking the time to tell of it to an acquaintance or a new friend. Furthermore, articulating the Truth isn't always easy. We quickly learn that even the best statement is not the Truth *itself*. But listen: Words are our *primary* interface with "people." This is why our spiritual development isn't finished in "time" until we pass along the Light that has already come to us— which is to tell others of our own hard-earned insights in honest, simple terms. Isn't this what was *originally* meant by "taking the gospel to all the world"?

If we are to see our world come to perceive the Truth, we commence jotting our insights onto the backs of envelopes until we are able to put them into a simple, helpful comment that can be understood by others. We are not finished with the bits and glimmers of Light until we've done this. We "tell," clearly and simply—even if with no more than a clap of the hands in gladness or a smile to a stranger. *Then* we are able to "look out" and see the response in the external world, and the world is blessed. That response is often the very demonstration of God's love the seeker is looking for.

THE JOURNAL AGAIN

At first, most of us may not like the idea of "completing the interface." It sounds hard—but it isn't. It is as easy as patting our foot to the Symphony. We do it first in a few words in our journal. There, in the aloneness that words demand, we are able to select the best word or illustration that suits the scene we're writing about at the moment. Then, we wait expectantly for someone to come into our experience to tell it to. They come! The subjective Self-I-Am brings them to me.

Before the discovery of the Child within, we've primarily been repeating the "Truth-words" of spiritual authorities, or our mouths have been clicking off half-truths. Now, with the journal's help, we begin to work loving wonders in our world by completing the Interface and telling our *own* Glimpses. The Light sparkles "from" us and passes on to "the rest of ourself."

AN EXCHANGE OF LETTERS *(Abbreviated here)*

Dear George,
WE DON'T KEEP GETTING GLIMPSES UNLESS WE KEEP TELLING THEM! You might ask the Sufi mystics about the Truth of this.

Dear Bill,
You are right about the Sufis. They tell the same stories over and over. Each man has his own stories, of course, but they overlap. Essentially Sufis speak of the Light they have seen,

saying their views are peculiar to themselves and, therefore, they are responsible for telling them because no one else can can tell them as well.

CHURCH WORK AND BIBLE STUDY

Many religionists and metaphysicians believe that their participation in church or their private study is the way to Light and Life. Some believe this is enough. But it is not enough, not even nearly—if one wishes to move on to the ultimate recognition of Self.

A transcending moment occurs when the seeker finally comes to comprehend the *subjective* nature of tangibility—of all things and events as within himself. "Ah ha! The church is in *me!*" he shouts joyfully. Well and good, but there is still an apparent world, filled with struggling people who live and move and have their appearances within the subjective awareness that perceives them. When we took Awareness to be the Identity of us, we took the entire universe into that Awareness—every man, woman and child in all existence. We have a responsibility to do as we've been told—for all mankind.

What do most of us do with the Glimpse of Truth? We study earnestly in every spare moment to have the briefest glimpse of Light—which now we see to be an *original* idea, and which the Child within brings into conscious recognition. It allows us, for an instant, to see and feel *something* in new light. Well, that is grand, but unfortunately, that's where it ends with most of us. The transaction isn't completed.

THE FLOW OF THE BUILDING

Suppose you have an idea for a beautiful building. You dream something new and unique. The idea just "comes" from Somewhere—from the Child within. You don't stop with the light of the idea, but you put the dream into gear when, via your *action*, the inner idea is slowly committed to symbols, words and paper, placed into the hearts, heads and hands of others in "the world," on the tangible scene of this present Awareness. Ultimately, the inner idea finds its expression as a completed work of art and, listen, listen, it then communicates to *everyone* who sees it, saint and sinner alike, with no further effort on your part. Notice the flow, the linear transaction from above to below, inside to outside.

Of what use is the simplest idea if there is no *application* of it in the tangible arena? At this point we might remember the spiritual admonition to "make the inside and the outside into a single one." The inside *is* the outside. The outside confirms the inside. We carry the inner idea to the outer scene, and the outer wisdom perceived in "things" into the Heart within. Unless we take those Glimpses and turn them into seed-ideas which become usable in the world, we simply stop having more of them. Oh, we have more Glimpses, yes, but ever fewer and fewer, until somewhere along the line we wonder, like my lady friend mentioned earlier, what has happened to the Truth that once worked so well for us. We fall into the slough of despondency; we wither, shrivel, and expire, leaving our friends to wonder why the Truth didn't work as so many of its spokesmen claim it does.

There is much to consider if one wishes to go all the way to Da Shan's peak and be convinced *he has never been away.* Clearly something has been missing in the usual objective/subjective approaches, else the world would have *listened* and learned. In the past, most have left their studies too early—before the full Idea of the Child, Giving, Supply, The Divine Interface, the Equation, and so much more could be Self-disclosed and truly understood.

There is something most remarkable in these words, reader. If you will stay with them, examine them *and determine their validity for yourself,* you will find it. This statement is startling, new and very odd to the scientific and metaphysical schools especially—but it isn't new to the Real of us, to the heart of us, to the Child of us. The Child will read these words and understand in a twinkling *that what is said here concerning Light is correct.*

We complete the transaction! We make the interface! We give God what is God's and we give man what is man's.

NOW WE KNOW WHAT TO DO

Isn't it grand to finally find out *what we are to do to get mov-*

ing again? Over the years, so many have told me they would do whatever God asked them to do if they only knew what it was. Or, they have said they would do anything at all to be able to catch another glimpse of the Real, and *feel* the joy of the Child. *Now you know!* Whether you are new to the religious scene or an old metaphysician for whom the universe came into being, the Equation is the same for everyone. To live it is to LIVE. To withhold it is to die. For metaphysicians, I amend the last line: to withhold it, is to "pass on" and have it all to do again.

This chapter is intended to make the point that we have not finished with the Light of Truth until it has been absorbed, lived, proven and passed on (reflected). Then, when it has been so given, we are introduced to the Fire from whence it came.

At this point, we begin thinking of the importance of communicating to ourselves clearly—for which writing is the best possible discipline.

THE BRIDGE

In a recent exchange of letters, a European gentleman and I discussed the importance of thinking cosmologically, of starting at the top, with Ineffable-being-this-Awareness, then working "down" to the situation at hand. This included not just the immediate situation, but the situation as it pertains to Everyman. After all, the cosmological Child atop Dominion holds God's hand above and Everyman's hand below.

Since that manner of thought enables us to make the "link," I should explain exactly how this link is made. I use an example from the only experience I can speak of with authority, my own—indicating how "top-down thinking" evolved in time and has thrown light on the scene for me and others. Specifically, I tell how, concerned about the well-being of my home, I solved a problem for myself and for others afterwards. It went like this.

Certainly, at the beginning, I had a human concern about my home, my place, my residence. That concern turned me, as always, to God. At my journal, I began my consideration of "God" as the total and absolute all of all. This is the nature of top-down thinking as opposed to the usual way of beginning with the problem and trying to drag it up to God for a "fixing." That is, I brought my concept of the grand Ineffable to mind, knowing that It, whatever It is, is the fount and source of all that actually is. More, I considered this "Ineffable" to be pure, perfect, without problems or "anything that works a lie."

That carefully in mind—*and having written something to that effect into my journal*—I brought myself to the "next" step. That step, for me in those years, was to equate Godhead with Mind—a good equation. *I wrote something about that in my journal* also—and then sat there at my desk considering Mind.

The consideration of Godhead as Overmind (Mind) brought me inevitably to the next step: Mind's *function*. What IS the function of Mind? To be aware. Ah ha, I had come to this present Awareness right here, right now putting these words into my journal. I could see at that time (though it had taken me many years to come to perceive this) that this very life-I-am IS that Awareness of Mind. *And so I wrote.*

Then, there was still another "step" to take, another question in this ongoing and top-down process that always begins with the Ineffable: Awareness is aware, but aware of WHAT? Again, having learned line upon line, precept upon precept, that awareness is forever looking at "qualities and attributes" of Mind, I wrote something pertaining to that into my journal for the umpteenth time. Ah, but *this* time something wonderful happened. The intuitive "leap of understanding" arrived from Godhead straight into the Identity-I-am—as which I sat there writing, as which I was functioning. Suddenly, I thought about the PLACE, the LOCATION, the RESIDENCE of *Awareness in Mind.* In a twinkling it became apparent that Awareness-I *had no tangible location*; that it-as-THIS-awareness *was everywhere Mind was;* that it-as-I didn't have to worry about fending for a place—and I could see there was no *real* location problem with this Life-I-am. I mulled this over and wrote what I could; marvel after marvel came to mind even as I was writing.

Reader, do you see what I am pointing toward here? It is a multileveled marvel indeed, but this is not the end. This is such a subtle action, this matter of consciousness *bridging the gap* from darkness to Light. For the first time that I can remember, I perceived my human LOCATION of *place, residence, home,* to be the tangible evidence of the unassailable "location" of Mind's Awareness within Itself. There is no problem THERE. THERE is HERE. And, although mere words fail to depict what is being said to the heart of us, the reader will certainly understand how the *feeling* that arrived in the twinkling of an eye was one of grand relief, joy and understanding—a GLIMPSE of Light. With THAT feeling, I knew there would be "confirmation" on the tangible scene to prove the validity of the new Light. And, of course, there was— much more quickly than anyone imagined possible.

Still not the end, my friend. There is more. Listen softly. Here is the BRIDGE from Intangibility to tangibility: With the new Glimpse in conscious hand, I wrote, as quickly as I could, exactly what I COULD write of the insight itself. Then, as always, I wrote what the new Light presently allowed me to understand *that I couldn't understand a few moments before.* And, as I have learned to do, following that *I wrote of the OLD views that were superceded by the new.* These three actions constitute what I call THE BRIDGE. This is what is meant by bridging the gap. These bridges become invaluable later as we continue the flow (top-down) and begin our interface with our world of "others." It is a bridge that others may walk upon as we have done.

Next, I wrote of the certainty I felt that the new view would be confirmed, and, as I said, it was. A most wonderful home came into my experience, more valuable than any I could pay for at the time, but given to me at a price I *could* pay. Many have heard this story, *but not in relation to "the bridge" or as I am presenting it here, relating it sequentially to the journal we tend.*

This is still not the end! There is the matter of putting these things to the test. I found that my own confirmation was a wonderful thing, but would such top-down thinking do the same for others? Many who heard of my new home came to see for themselves, and the ensuing conversations quickly allowed me to share my Glimpse. That sharing carefully used "the bridge" of words from my journal, carrying my others from one side of the river to the other—from the same darkness into the same conscious Light of Life. Those who took it upon themselves to really listen to those words, put them to the test and then "go and do likewise," soon found themselves with a "demonstration" of God's constant care of God's same Self-awareness; and since those years, numerous others have done the same.

Still not the end, but getting close. Now, these many years later, I publish all the bridges I've crossed and give them to my unseen selfhood whose hand I hold, thereby completing the TOTAL interface—Ineffable, through Awareness, outward to all tangibility. Had I not written the pre-view and post-view into my journal, I'd likely not have remembered the specifics nor have been able to put the clear cutting edges to these words.

JILL AND MATT

Many years ago, a minister and his new wife came to visit aboard my houseboat, Lollygog. They were concerned about a place to live in an area of California where there simply weren't many affordable places. Matt had found a dream home, high on a hill overlooking the Pacific playground of Southern California. He felt, however, it would be inordinately hard to pay the asking price. I told this lovely couple about Awareness's "location" within Mind and of its effortless confirmation we could expect to see in the world. They went back to California and were greeted almost immediately with the news that they had their new home and that his church was going to assist in his purchase of it. The home was located literally on "Bounty Lane." God is bountiful in God's Self-care. Why not? My "bridge" of understanding had been put to the test and proved again. To this day when someone asks my help concerning his place in the world, I walk that same bridge back and forth and take him with me into the light of a new day.

CHAPTER NINE

THE BALANCE BETWEEN ACTION AND NON-ACTION

Living Subjectively in an Objective World

FLOW, INTERFACE AND HEALING

One sits quietly in prayer or, using another analogy, one sits in the great cathedral thinking of a Symphony. No healing is necessary in that inner space between the Symphony and the thought of the Symphony, is there? No imperfection there. Inevitably, the healing *appears* necessary "out there" in the body, the concert hall or cathedral—in the people, places and things world of linear time. Something "out there," usually this body or that one, needs something to come to it or go from it; health to come, discomfort or insufficiency to go away.

Well now, if we are agreed that healing has to do with the "out there" (even when we believe we understand that "out there" is really "within this awareness," and that the feelings of joy and well being are always "here" within awareness), then we are ready to understand something more about "healing."

THE CATHEDRAL ILLUSTRATION

Reader, imagine a lovely cathedral, ancient and awesome.

You and I sit alone in the middle of it, long slanting rays of light from the great windows cutting through the darkness inside. Everything is bathed in mysterious color and silence. Not a sound or motion do we notice anywhere. But if we had the eyes of an eagle or a barn owl, we would see many little church mice scurrying to and fro, scampering silently into and out of the hidden places of the great cathedral. Unseen by us, some mice have discovered the picnic basket we left by the door.

Our illnesses and anguishes are like those church mice. They come into our affairs uninvited and unwelcome. They eat their fill of our treasured picnic cake and go scampering on their way. Sometimes they do *not* go on their way, but linger as an ache or pain—or fear—deep in our sense of things. Some of those aches and pains are progressive and terminal, we are told. *Those* are the most odious church mice of them all.

And there is more. Outside stalk the great rats of starvation and poverty in the world. Another huge rat of violence and war comes and goes from view. Alongside runs a rat pack of disharmony, dissension and distrust joined with those of guilt, age and loneliness. Perhaps as hateful as any are the great rats of confusion and suspicion, fed by the ever-growing, all-encompassing glut of untested information and opinion. The cathedral, the body that sits in it, and the grounds just outside are our own subjective world, you see. It is a subjective world within the Awareness we are.

Now, imagine sitting there in that lovely cathedral, unmindful of the church mice, mind filled with naught but the grand Music of the Spheres, or, mind filled with thoughts of Godhead and Its allness. Prayer, meditation and contemplative practices are intended to end our thoughts about the body, the mice, the cathedral and its gardens, and they do—but, at best, those activities are temporary palliatives.

Now, suppose I ask what Godhead and its allness have to do with church mice and rats? In our metaphysical phase of ongoingness, we proclaim in all earnestness that there are no REAL church mice or rats in all existence. In the perfection of All, there isn't a single real evil. God is all and only, we say. There can't be God and something else, despite the fact that there still *appears* to be God and all those rats and mice of evil as well—which, of course, other people believe, but we, as enlightened students of Truth, do not.

Ah so. Then what is the ache or pain? "Unreal," you say.

Yes, and because it's unreal it should go away, right?

"Yes, it should go away."

"But it *persists*," you say. "Not enough love in my affairs, not enough understanding, not enough faith. I haven't demonstrated it yet."

Oh? Then there *are* church mice in the choir loft?

"There just *appear* to be. They are part of the *seeming*."

Then you want a part of the SEEMING to go away?

"Oh, yes, I want all of the seeming to go away; I want a healing. I confess I want a healing because I am tired of this appearance. I am physically tired of the constant picture of time's relentless march toward decay. I am tired of growing old and tired of wondering why it is happening even when I know that time isn't real and I have been *denying* it for so long."

Denying the reality of appearances hasn't done the least bit of QUANTUM good in the tangible world as far as appearances go. A demonstration here or there, a saint here or there who has done something in a small circle in a small pond, but the world outside continues its acid rain and terrorism. Why, why, why?

Objectivism says the world is full of church mice who need to be told about God. Subjectivism says the church mice do not exist, that they are unreal. Objectivism carried to its extreme has us running all over the cathedral, mesmerized by the mice and accomplishing nothing but a scattering of them. Subjectivism carried to its extreme has us sitting quietly in the middle of the cathedral, meditating, praying, mind-blanking and so God-mindful we never notice the mice. But while we deny their seeming, they seem to go right on eating our tangible picnic. The Zen-like absolutist may disclaim the reality of the mice and perhaps seldom be bothered by them, but at the end of the long day he, too, must stir himself from his reveries, leave the quiet of the cathedral and go outside into the darkness where the rats are larger than the mice. We find that our best efforts at God-mindedness and all of our proclamations of the indivisible allness and onlyness of Godhead taken all the way to the limits of absolutism, are not enough to *preclude* our having to go to the bathroom, feed ourselves or tend to our own appearances of age and debility. One can be a hundred years old and still not know the Answer to the primary question, *why the appearances* of sin, sickness and death if God is good and God is all.

In those days when time becomes heavy again—or precious—who will say the world's objectivism was any worse than our grand metaphysical subjectivism? Or that subjectivism is *further along* than (what seems to be) its opposite? Metaphysicians will not like the following observation, but it is *objectively* true. In the heavy years of age, more anguish is lived in the metaphysical community than in the religious and scientific community. Why? Neither the religionist nor the scientist feels *guilty* for not knowing enough about God to heal himself.

SOLUTION?

The Balance. The divine Balance. Here is yet another "mystery": Between the two (objective/subjective) is ONE, greater than either separately, and the Source of both.

The Child within us has known this all the while. Between the central idea of subjectivism and the central idea of objective religion, is the balanced activity of the Child. The Child runs up tangibility's Da Shan in perfect balance, *living his subjective Idea in the objective world.*

FROM THE HAN DISCOURSES

"Damnit, Han. Those are just words!" the soldier thundered. "What am I supposed to DO in the cathedral? Be practical, man. Tell me what to do to get rid of this great rat grind of fear in my belly! What is the balance I am to live in the world? Tell me directly so I can understand and have my healing."

"Ah so," Han sighed. "Ah so."

"Ah so, my foot. Tell me, if you *can.*"

Han smiled, understanding such exasperation and its honesty. "Ah so," he said again. Then he added, "The balance we all need is attained when we complete the interface."

At the evening fire, the soldier grumbled. "He didn't say a damned thing. He made another mystery. 'Complete the interface,' he said. What in hell do those words do for my gut? He said nothing new."

"Oh, but he did," said Mary. "You should have stayed to listen."

The following week Han said, "We are impatient. We leave our nets too soon. We throw our books away before we know what they say. We leave our schools before we know what they teach. The old nature of us is fooled by words. The Child of us understands words and their importance."

Yes, we are impatient, especially in the Western world. We want the fruit before the tree has grown. We want the Truth right now before we've lived it because we've been told by subjectivism that we are the Truth already. The problem lies in the fact that subjectivism *alone* does not speak to the balance. It *knows* nothing of the divine Balance. However, even *that* is exactly as it should be here in the objective world. During the time we examine subjectivism, we *turn away* from objective reality as we are supposed to. Subjectivism is the study of the subjective Idea or Image and is, itself, half the balance. It can't be expected to address the objective half beyond saying it isn't as important as it seems to be or claims to be.

Ah, but how do we come to *know* Balance, and know we know it? How else but by living the imbalance of either religion or metaphysics? Or both. How else can one really know about *balance*? In the line of things, one learns what is beyond the point by passing the point. Can one pass the point without being there first? We pass the imbalance of subjectivism exactly as we passed the imbalance of objectivism. By *moving on* to the Balance of Everything.

If we do not topple off the narrow ledge of things, the imbalance of religion and metaphysics leads us straight to Balance. It seemed a big "if" in my own affairs, but I finally found It, or It found me. Now, having found it and lived it, I can tell of it. But what has this to do with healing? Let us return to the cathedral.

BEETHOVEN AND THE CHURCH MICE

Imagine how much stir we make in the silent cathedral as we sit there *thinking* of Beethoven's Fifth Symphony. We sit and think of the crashing cymbals and pounding drums, and not a church mouse runs away. If one did, we'd be surprised. Don't we make a great to-do when prayer is answered? Why would we do so if it weren't unusual to us?

But what happens if, while thinking the rhythm of the Symphony, we begin drumming our fingers and tapping our foot to the rhythm? The change is enormous. *The whole place echoes with the drumming. We have bridged the gap between the melody inside and the tangible scene outside.* We have completed the external interface. The worldly scene in time and space takes note *and the church mice scurry to cover.*

Why does the religionist—especially the metaphysician—believe his tangible scene at hand will respond as he sits reading his book, silently *thinking* Beethoven's Symphony? "God hears in silence and rewards openly," you say. God hears the silent meditations of our heart, no question about that, but God gives us a way to *clap our hands to the Divine Rhythm* so that the tangible scene responds quickly—and would one even be thinking about "healing" unless something were amiss in the tangible scene to turn our thoughts to God and the Truth?

To expect a healing or an improvement in our daily affairs just because we pray as the world prays and read a lot is about as effective as pulling the lanyard on a mental cannon and expecting the crows to squawk and fly. We think God, and as we do, the Equation flows outward through our fingers *into the tangible scene where the crows are.* We think God and the Equation flows, telling us what to DO about the church mice and the corn in the field.

Silent prayer or any other kind of meditation and contemplation *without action in the world* is like asking God to end our thirst without our drinking water. Metaphysicians are grandly insistent that the Truth will work in their affairs, but inevitably, *they give God a personal condition to meet.* I want God to do it provided it doesn't happen through the efforts of a doctor, materia medica or any action beyond prayer. That is, we'll happily accept Infinite Godhead's intervention provided God does it the way we think it should be done. Spiritual medicine, *o.k.,* but not material medicine. Please, God, take care of my lumbago, but do it my way. God, heal my cancer, but without the help of men. God, end my hunger, but without my having to eat the food in front of me. God, help me understand the Truth, but do it in thus and such a manner. God, let me demonstrate my church full of interested people again, but without my having to invite anyone to attend. You see, God, I don't want to hear a single dualistic term because I've been told how dualism is the cause of all problems, and I want the words of Truth to come to me just the way I want them—*gently*, very gently. Reveal the truth to me, Lord, but it must come through the pages of the Bible. If it isn't in the Bible, it isn't the Truth. Help me, God, but do it so I don't have to do anything more for my world. The body isn't real, but please heal this chunk of unreality, God. End my thralldom with drunkenness, Lord, but I'm really not enthralled with it, I don't think, so let me drink a little wine to prove it.

Poor God. What fools we mortals and metaphysicians be.

THERE ARE SUBJECTIVISTS and SUBJECTIVISTS

There are those who make a start in religion and metaphysics and then there are the really earnest people who don't stop overlong in the comfortable corners *but keep going.* The religious subjectivist—the metaphysician and philosopher—who doesn't complete the interface from Mind to tangibility, and from tangibility *back to Mind*, is walking in a void of voids, allowing judgmentalism to destroy his inmost happiness while disclaiming the reality of matter. Moreover, he finds himself unable to do anything about the inescapable "unreality" that sticks to him like glue. These are the good but misled people who have stopped in Absoluty. In the absolute mode, one wears blinders to his knees. The disclaimer of matter's reality is not the *final* subjectivism we are called to understand and live. Matter is not what it seems, but what it is, is to be *understood* and not denied.

The real subjectivists are those who have found the simple Child of themselves. These are the metaphysicians who enjoy the inclusive vistas of Metadelphia but aren't trapped there. The Child with his journal leads us straight through the heart of Calvinopolis, St. Doxy and Metadelphia—even through the prisons of absoluteness itself—through every closed door and through the thick walls of religion and metaphysics. The Child within takes us on to a BALANCE which we maintain as we hurry up the mountain, *LIVING our subjectivism objectively in the world.*

That balanced walk takes us along the narrow pathway of confirmation where we *see* the high ideal beginning to be perceived and lived in the world of men.

Somewhere near the peak, we and the Child become one in actual living fact, not just in metaphysical profession. We are given CONFIRMATION. In a new name, we reign over the All in all that exists within. That reign isn't a passive sitting back to enjoy the "fruits" of nirvanic bliss or subjective joy, but an active WORK in the world that elevates, heals, cleanses, inspires, and dissipates guilt, and in so doing, explains and *answers* the paradoxes of life. More, it puts wings on our feet and on the feet of those who see our Light. Atop Da Shan, one looks at the world and sees it again as did the Zen master who beheld the mountain "again" from the perspective of no mountain. This time we stop our endless denial of matter's reality or existence and see matter for the *confirmation of God it represents.* We stop chattering like monkeys about the inability of words to speak of Wordless Ineffability and begin *saying* it. We begin to understand the paradoxes of human living and, perhaps for the first time in our experience, we know what to do about them. More, *we find ourselves with the ability and means to do something for our entire world—and we get off our butts and begin DOING it.*

The journal we tend may seem to be only the smallest stirring in the cathedral. After all, how many mice scramble at the wiggle of a pencil? But soon we are drumming our fingers on the arm rail. Soon the sounds of our feet are rhyming the rhythm of the Child's celestial sounds and are *doing* something in the Cathedral and its gardens of Mind. *We are in this world to do something good for all mankind.*

The Child of us holds the hand of all mankind, and as the world responds, the Child knows it. The Child, as you surely know by now, holds the hand of Godhead—and God knows exactly what we have perceived in the cathedral. The Flow of the Child's Light pours from God through the tips of our fingers and from the words we speak. That flow is reflected back to us, delayed by time it seems, thence to return to Source, bearing evidence of our effort. Either we live this Equation or we don't. If we live it, we are alive. If we don't, we are yet sleeping in the Light and little time is left for us to awaken.

The journal has been the means by which the me-sense of me has been aligned with the Child of Self, thence to be displaced by it. My journal has been my interface with God and man. Even now, those words are these words—and it can be exactly the same for the reader. All you must do is begin. See for yourself whether or not your own inmost thoughts don't begin to do wonderful things in your affairs.

They will. They will. No longer must the scholar, the psychologist, the minister or the practitioner do the stirring vicariously for you. You will do it for yourself. This matter of our saving grace is not up to the government or the church, the philosophy or system. It is a matter that takes place between ourself alone and God.

A FIVE-NOTE CHORD THAT OVERCOMES
THE DISCORD OF INERTIA
The first note: THE SEARCH FOR BALANCE (Han and Mary)

Han said, "The old schools say our fall from grace is obvious. They teach that we are on the physical mountain, born into time and space, not one of us exempt. The new schools say the opposite. Time and space are unreal, they teach. Matter is unreal. Da Shan's experience is only a dream."

"The second group is correct," the soldier said. "Matter isn't real."

"What *is* real?" Han asked.

"A spiritual world. God's perfect world. Perfect God, perfect man, in his sinless, unfallen state," the soldier answered confidently.

"Ah so," said Han. "How do you explain this moment as we sit talking around the evening fire? A moth just flew into the flame."

"We are discussing God's Reality, not the unreality of a moth," the soldier answered.

Han mused. In a moment he asked, "Why do we discuss truth rather than something else?"

The soldier answered quickly. "We learn there is no satisfaction in talking about the world's difficulties. Such talk turns to vanity and becomes a futile exercise."

Han closed his eyes. He spoke softly. "Then right here as we discuss truth, Reality, we have a choice to do this or go the world's way, talking of sin and its evil, advocating, as religionists, that one climb the mountain to return to his birthright?"

The soldier nodded. "That's essentially what the old schools do."

"Or," Han continued, "we can talk of our uprightness and sinlessness as the subjectivists do?"

"Yes," the soldier said.

"Ah, yes," the old teacher smiled, eyes aglow, "and where do we make this choice to go one way or the other?"

"Here and now, in front of the fire," the soldier answered, beginning to wonder where Han was leading him. "As you have said so many times, Master Han, this moment has nothing to do with mortality and matter."

"Yet we all sit here before the evening fire."

"Yes," the soldier agreed. "Without thought of matter or sin at all."

The village minister entered the conversation. "I sit here in front of the same fire and despite all the talk of oneness and allness, I still see a world born in sin and degradation from which it must repent. We have a difference of views here, not two worlds."

"Ah, yes," said Han. "Two views and many possible courses of action or non-action between. One view, looking at shadows, calls for repentance. Another view, looking beyond appearances, speaks of guiltlessness, claims dominion and calls itself the son of God. Both views are here before the evening fire. But there is still another view, isn't there?"

The soldier and minister looked at one another, puzzled.

"There is an Answer that transcends these two views." Han looked at the smallest image before the fire. "Mary knows what it is," he said.

The little lady spoke softly. "Yes. The world has many views and countless actions. They are poles apart. The Heart of us sees the middle ground above them all."

"You are a heathen Buddhist!" the minister shouted angrily.

"You don't understand your subjectivism!" the soldier accused.

"Yes!" laughed Mary, clapping her hands. "I am everyone and I am the entire mountain." With a bright smile she added, "I am even more than that!"

Han said, "Awareness includes all the possibilities. Our actions in the world are those that bind us together in harmony. Action is not intended to divide us into right and left, objective and subjective, truth and error, real and unreal, prophet and false prophet. The fundamentalist who insists on the literal interpretation of his books must surely hold to that view because his house is built on literalism. One who sees the Spirit behind the letter is closer to the unifying Spirit which brings men together in love and understanding. Truth is not a divider in the end."

THE SECOND NOTE (Enter Sue)

"Sue, you speak of standing atop the mountain with the world under your feet."

"Yes," said Sue. "That's what you have taught me."

"Do you really stand there?"

"In Truth, yes."

"Then why do you cry, Sue? Why do you tell me of your insecurity and of the anguishes of living?"

"You are my confessor," the lady laughed.

"Your confessions are statements that you don't stand atop Da Shan yet."

"In the *world,* I don't seem to, but in *reality. . . .*"

"Da Shan *is* the world, Sue, so why do you speak of standing atop the mountain with the world under your feet, claiming a dominion you haven't confirmed?"

"I told you. That's what you've taught me to do."

"If I taught you that, dear lady, I lied."

"But that's what I THOUGHT you said. Am I not the pure and perfect Child of God, even this instant?" asked Sue.

"You are, indeed, but the conscious mind and body is still crying and suffering on the face of the mountain, a mighty distance from the peak of confirmation."

The fire crackled and a band of pond frogs began their evening song.

"I don't understand. I simply don't understand," Sue's voice wavered, her eyes brimming with tears. "I'm confused. I'm terribly confused and I don't understand why my world doesn't conform to my knowledge."

"When we understand, we have the feel of Da Shan under our feet," the old teacher said.

"What am I supposed to *do?*" Sue asked angrily. "Dear God, what am I supposed to DO!"

"Climb the mountain, as the old schools say. Claim your heritage, as the new schools say. Do *both. DO both!*"

The frogs started another chorus. The fire crackled.

After a time Han continued. "We do MORE than the old schools require. We do MORE than the new churches require. It is not enough to *turn from* the old ways in relief as we did when we first found subjectivism. We discover the Balance above and beyond the two poles of view. There is a Child in us who lives the balance. The balance *includes* the parts but is greater than their sum. This synergism takes us to Da Shan's peak *in fact,* not profession. In fact, not in a 'seeming.' It takes us to *understanding,* and, listen lady Sue, *then* we stand with the feel of the world under our feet. What good has our professing done? None at all. None at all. Listen: We *live* our subjectivism on this objective scene!"

The night sky shone bright; the stars twinkled. Sue began to smile.

THE THIRD NOTE

The obvious truth that the exclusive idealist is so reluctant to admit is that he sits before the same campfire as the minister.

The obvious truth that the minister is so reluctant to admit is that he can't escape the subjective nastiness he calls a sin and condemns. Most unpalatable of all to him is the thought that there are not *separate* entities outside himself in need of redemption.

As far apart as these extremes seem, they are the same view observed from opposite ends.

"What is the answer to this dilemma?" the soldier wanted to know.

The Answer the Child gives is supremely simple. We claim our heritage right at the campfire and then get up, get moving, and start CLIMBING the mountain for as long as it appears we are on it. We climb it and know we are making progress when our "understanding" grows and our human condition begins to confirm that growth. It is wonderful to claim, "We *are* there already!" *provided we are taking the enlightened, objective footsteps that GET US THERE in conscious, tangible fact.*

Then we give that "understanding"—to which we have attained in actual living fact on the rugged mountain—to those following who are able to hear us.

We have then struck the Balance, the transcending middle ground between the old view and the new, subjectivism and objectivism, inside and outside, first and last, male and female, above and below. We slow our mouth down by writing in our journals until we have the words STRAIGHT. When we get them straight, we LIVE them around the campfire, not talk about them endlessly.

Then, the old teacher said, "I don't believe one has the slightest knowledge of that 'middle ground' until he has *mentally* fled the confinements of St. Doxy, Calvinopolis and Metadelphia, climbed their confining, deadening walls and, taking a balance of these with him, has run alone and naked into the meadow beyond. There, the Child comes to us in our aloneness. The Christ Child of ourself leads us by the hand to a new Dominion *right in the physical world decried by realists and denied by idealists.* It is senseless to CLAIM that dominion until it has HAPPENED! The dominion of the Child, unlike the orthodox or liberal view's claim, transcends OBJECTIVE/SUBJECTIVE. It is BEYOND the purest religion and most absolute metaphysics. BEYOND it by leagues and leagues, to infinity and back again!"

Metaphysicians claim a knowledge of It and don't DO anything. Churchmen do EVERYTHING a man can do on the face of the Mountain, but they claim no knowledge of IT, **AS IT.**

There is a balance, a middle Ground, gentle Sue. The CHILD takes us there *quickly, but only if we DO what the Child asks us to do.*

THE CHRISTIAN SCIENCE INDIANS

The story goes like this: One Wednesday evening, a group of Christian Science Indians were sitting around a campfire giving testimonies. One of them fell asleep and toppled into the fire. Immediately, everyone began "knowing the Truth" while the Indian in the fire went up in smoke. He passed on.

Across the campground, a group of Baptist Indians were sitting around their campfire, "witnessing." One of them fell alseep and toppled into the fire. Immediately, everyone sprang into action, grabbed the unfortunate from all directions and pulled him apart. He died also.

Moral: *Somewhere between knowing the Truth and doing nothing, and knowing nothing of subjectivism (or very little) and doing everything, there is a transcending Action to take—LIVING our subjectivism openly in the world.*

METAPHYSICS AND YOUTH

Young people hear of the wonders of subjective ALREADY-NESS and it appeals to them. They want their dominion

NOW, but for the most part are not willing to do what is necessary for realizing it. They talk much, but they surrender nothing. Subjectivism, half-taught, half-understood, caters to their greed by telling them they can have whatever they wish.

METAPHYSICS AND THE ELDERS

The old people hear of the wonders of Alreadyness and are willing to do anything to attain it—provided that action meets the standards of their belief system and includes a separate Savior outside themselves. They talk much, *but they surrender nothing*. Objectivism caters to their belief of personality and separation.

Solution? We live the subjective Truth on the objective mountain. We surrender the old ways FIRST and take on the New Ways as the Child gives them to us. We find the BALANCE of the middle ground.

The BEING of the subjectivist and the DOING of the objectivist are not two separate entities. It is ONE ACTION, LIFE AUTHENTICATING ITSELF. It is BEING *appearing as BECOMING*. Which equals: 1. Sue coming to understand. 2. Sue seeing the Child Self. 3. Sue sitting before the campfire and tending the fire *just like everyone else sitting before the fire*. It is Sue being in the world but not of it. It is Sue doing something for her world.

As the Awareness of Mind, I see my Sue as Me, living her Childlikeness. As William in the world, I *confidently anticipate* the CONFIRMATION of that singleness and see it, my subjective Selfhood, lifted up.

THE FOURTH NOTE OF THE CHORD, THE FINE DISTINCTION

If one isn't faithful to the appearing, then that appearing never appears as BECOMING—that is, as our getting farther up the mountain. The seeker who turns his back on the appearing, disclaiming its reality, is half right, but the part that's half wrong diminishes it all.

If one is faithful to the appearing as if it were the only Reality, that appearing never appears as a BECOMING. The religionist who never disclaims the power and reality of matter, is half wrong, and the part that's half wrong diminishes the rest.

Solution? We find the balance between the inside and outside and live that balance wherever we seem to be so long as we seem to be there. That balance takes one beyond his metaphysics and religion, *yet he never has to leave them to live the Balance.* He doesn't have to leave his job or his world. He doesn't have to claim a dominion he hasn't earned. He doesn't have to leave the world's warfare to be untouched by it. He doesn't have to do anything BUT BE FAITHFUL TO THE APPEARING. Faithful to the appearing, he finds the appearing's anguish leaving him bit by bit *and leaving the world as well.*

I am faithful to the appearing when I deny its apparent authority—because nothing has real authority but Good. (Why doesn't the religionist see this? It is a mystery.)

I am faithful to the appearing when I *do* for the appearing WHATEVER seems to be the best course of action for the GOOD of mankind. Why do I act so? Because, so long as it "seems" I'm in the world, I strive to help my world. (Why doesn't the subjectivist see this? It is a mystery.)

When I have acted in such a way here in the world of people, places and events, I have been given a course of action that blesses all mankind.

When I have acted and been victorious here in the world of appearances, and *told of my victory to those who wanted to know of it,* I have been given greater victories. I conclude, therefore, that I am not finished with the living of Balance until I've ACTED in the world by helping my others find it equally.

THE FIFTH NOTE

Intellectualism gets very close to the truth of things, but doesn't quite make it without the heart.

The heart gets very close to the truth of things, but doesn't quite make it in the world without the intellect—as anyone knows who, upon the discovery of the Child-heart, has tried to throw intellectualism out the window. Intellectualism's inadequacy is evident. Civilization "out there" nears gridlock and death.

Yet, clearly the only way the heart can accept intellectualism—the world in ridiculous argument before the campfire—is with love. So, as the Apostle wrote, without love everything is lost.

Here we come again to the importance of love—non-rejection. We stop *rejecting* the scene at hand. There is no escaping it for any length of time as long as it appears. We do as we were admonished—watch it, understand it, and tend it faithfully. "Be a faithful witness." We do that to the best of our ability until the end of our days in front of the fire. Metadelphians know precious little about this, just as religionists know precious less about subjectivism.

If we remain faithful to this limited scene of contradistinction and argument, *what wonder might be in store for us where the illimitable Light doesn't waver or cast a shadow?*

Unfaithful to it, we find our suffering goes on.

PERSONAL JOURNAL ENTRY

There is a river down the road of time and I will be there soon. After the long trek through the hard, dry places, the river is welcome. I put down my burdens at the river of Life and rest a while from the tribulations of the worrisome world.

In the mind's eye, I go to my river often. Along its peaceful banks are special places where memories are soft and embracing. My heart floats lightly on that river, oblivious to the cares of the dry world, mindful of nothing but the beauty at hand, no heaviness anywhere. Now, far away in an alien land, I think of the river and take myself there. At this moment the thinking of it is as grand as the presence of it because I can leave out the anguished world's bittersweet—the fear, the sounds of quarreling.

What do I take with me as I return? I take my world because it exists here within the consciousness of me. As this Moment of timeless Being, I have just the tender world without the heat and anguish of time's learning. Every good and decent thing within me rises and stands as a solitary. Kindness and love fill my river to overflowing and bathe my world in joy.

It is the same for Everyman.

CHAPTER TEN

THE SECRET OF SUPPLY

Giving and Receiving, Two That Are One

"Let me tell you a paradox," Han said to the soldier. "The world in which we awaken each morning is not the Real World. It is an image of the Real. But those who know the world is an image of the Real, wake up in the Real World every day. This is a paradox and it is the truth."

POUNDING THE STICK IN THE DUST

Rebecca is here and she is a lovely lady. She and her husband are having problems meeting their financial obligations. It is difficult raising a family these days, as expensive as everything is. This brings to mind the story about pounding the stick in the dust when I was having such problems.

It was about this time of year. Two men came to me wanting contributions to the Heart Fund and the Community Chest. I turned them down, as usual, with the old metaphysical response, (aloud) "I give in my own way," while silently I thought, "Why should I contribute to research for illusory diseases that don't really exist?" I also recalled that just a week earlier a young man had come to me wanting something to eat. When I asked him to help me work for half an hour until

151

supper was ready, he walked away saying, "I'm hungry, man. Don't you understand?" No, I didn't understand. I watched him stop at my neighbor's where the lady of the house gave him something to eat. I stayed awake half the night justifying my action, concluding that no one gets anything for nothing in this world and that I had done the right thing asking him to work just a little for a meal.

The seekers of Truth I knew in those days, especially metaphysicians, were not much for giving to causes such as the Heart Fund or medical research or starving Africans.

Anyway, the next morning I went to the woods, as I often did, to resolve my own "supply" problems, but this time there was no resolution. Nothing happened under the trees. I was as blank coming out of the woods as I was going in. Almost back home, I sat myself down under a tree one final time, hating to walk that last half mile back into the world. "What am I doing wrong, God?" I asked once again. "How is it that I can help people with *their* problems but I can't help myself with mine?" I asked the question, and then it happened.

The answer came as clearly as if a voice had spoken. The words flew into my head. "You don't do enough giving, Bill," they said. Immediately I became angry and defensive. "What do you mean, I don't do enough giving? If I didn't give so much of my time to everyone, I wouldn't be in this difficulty." Again, the Inner Voice said, "Bill, you don't give enough."

I pounded my stick on the ground and saw a cloud of dust rise. It was a hot, dry day in August. "Damnit, all I do is give, to anybody and everybody who comes my way asking for the Truth. I never say no or ask for anything in return." I pounded the stick and the dust flew again. (Incidentally, that stick is in the back of my car to this day, still used when I walk through the woods or hunt arrowheads along the river.) As the dust settled, I heard it again. "You have read it many times, Bill: Give to God what is God's and give to Caesar what is Caesar's."

"I GIVE God what is God's, as best I can, and you KNOW that!" The soldier Bill pounded the stick again.

"But you don't give Caesar what is Caesar's."

This inner argument remains vivid to this day, as surely as the memory of the overwhelming Inner Joy in South Carolina one summer when I was a kid; as surely as the memory of the Light experienced in San Francisco last summer. "Give Caesar what is Caesar's?" I yelled incredulously. "Give to CAESAR? Why should I give to Caesar? Caesar is the BELIEF. Caesar is the illusion. That's the UNREAL. Why give to the ILLUSION, the BELIEF of life in matter?" And I pounded the stick again in that grand arrogance known only to people who have discovered subjectivism and the unreality of the world.

There was silence. I had my conscience backed into its own corner. "Give to Caesar, my foot!" Then this Whatever that pops into one's head asked a question of me. "Tell me something, Bill. Where do you need money and help? In God's world or in Caesar's world?"

Dear God! In the twinkling of an eye a Glimpse had arrived and I understood something new and wonderful. As usual, it seemed at first that I had *always* known this (something one thinks he has always understood fully—but, somehow, *this time* that something was different). This was New beyond new. *It was plainly the point of my weakness in the world.* I thought about the young man who was hungry and the two who had wanted support for the Community Chest and the Heart Fund. Even while the dust was settling from the flailing stick, I realized that I had NOT been giving to Caesar's world. No. I had been withholding, storing agony for myself. I had not been completing the Interface.

Quick as a flash I saw what to do in the world. Isn't it always a grand relief to suddenly know what to do when one has been suffering? But, just as that wonderful knowledge arrived, there came the realization that I had very little of the world's goods left to give. Everything with my business was attached, awaiting payment of a big business indebtedness to a supplier. Just before heading for the woods, I had scolded my little boys for wearing out their shoes so quickly, wondering where the money to buy new ones would come from. If I was to give to Caesar's world, what could I give?

Across the dusty road a patch of bright brown-eyed Susans bloomed along the fence. I picked a bouquet and took it to my neighbor down the street. From that day to this, I have understood the admonition about giving TO THE WORLD OF APPEARANCES if I expected that world to give back to me.

Most surely, we give our spiritual gifts, but we give the sack of beans, too. I met the business obligation to the supplier and all my worldly goods were released to me again.

Why had no one in metaphysics told me about this requirement to give to Caesar? Because subjectivism without the Child simply doesn't include this requirement. If it did, it would have found the Child's Equation long ago to include in the subjective textbooks. If it did, those organizations would be prospering today, not drying on the vine.

For every supply problem, the admonition is loud and clear, simple and elegant: Give God what is God's and give Caesar what is Caesar's. That statement is not a parable. It is a simple statement about how one is to conduct himself in the world if he wants things to go well in his world. As a metaphysician I had been good enough about giving God what is God's, but I used my subjectivism as a selfish excuse to withhold from the world—all in the name of my grand metaphysical absoluteness and knowledge. Today, look at what mankind has stored away for itself by *not* living the Equation—enough useful energy to pound the entire earth to dust.

From that day at the edge of the woods, to this, I have made it a point to give to my world—something beyond the ordinary, every day of my life. The Ineffable, in turn, has given back to me in countless ways beyond the ordinary, including knowledge of the Equation.

As I sit writing this today for what may be my last gift to my unseen selfhood, I can be certain that ninety-nine percent of those who read these hard words will take note of them one way or the other, positively or negatively. They will contemplate them and their hearts will respond, suggesting that a simple and tender Truth beyond ordinary comprehension is being stated here. Then, like me, they will one day test these truths to see for themselves, and their affairs in the world will begin to bloom immediately. But only one metaphysician in a thousand will think to thank God or thank anyone for writing the human words. Not seeing the necessity for THAT is another of those blind spots, or bends in the river, within the subjective view; it will remain so until the time one begins to put his subjectivism to work in the world. This is understandable. Our subjective search-time is our within-time, not our interface-with-the-world time. During much of our subjective unfolding, we haven't yet learned that the outside *is* the inside. We've been too busy denying the outside's reality.

Let one find the Child within himself first. Then he can learn the lessons of Interface without having to deny the reality of the world. When one discovers what the world is about, he learns what to do in the world *and begins doing it*. We ACT. Perhaps "completing the interface" is part of a lesson that cannot be learned until one has stopped making that interface, thence to rediscover it, even as the Child is lost in order to be rediscovered and LIVED.

The meal the young man was too hungry to work and wait half an hour for was a huge bowl of homemade bean soup, a speciality I loved during those lean years. The bouquet of flowers I brought from the woods a few days later and gave to my neighbor, resulted in an invitation to come into her home and have a warm bowl of soup. I watched my bouquet of flowers turn into a tangible bowl of bean soup. This time I learned the lesson.

ABOUT THE JEREMIAH PAPERS

The Child hears the hard teachings and knows they are true; the old man of us rails in discomfort. The more uncomfortable the old nature, the more likely the Child to be delivered from the ashes of adulthood.

It is the Child who stirs within us in the light of the glorious glimpses. It is the Child who, having stirred, revives us, and then we become the Child. The Child and the Heart are the same. The Child is in touch with the Eternal, our absolute interface with the Ineffable, the One, the Mountain Beyond Name.

So, we are not disheartened by the prophet's hard words. He comes to us in the final days, tangibly or intangibly to take us by the shoulders and shake us out of our ruts. We may rail at his pronouncements and dislike his effrontery. We may not like having our sophisticated and cultivated facade torn away, our carefully hidden nastiness exposed. But beneath our discomfort and behind our inclination to turn away, the Child of us, the heart of us, knows his hard words are true.

The nations who dismissed their prophets have been destroyed, their inhabitants dispersed. We hear their words and the Child comes alive again. A new nation is born.

The prophets have, nearly every one, spoken of a mysterious Child and childlikeness to prevail in the end days of linear time. *For unto us a child is born, unto us a son is given: and the government shall be upon his shoulder; and his name shall be called Wonderful, Counsellor, The mighty God, the everlasting Father, The Prince of Peace. (Isaiah)*

ABOUT THE SECRETS OF SUPPLY

Dear William,
   If you know so damned much, why aren't you rich?
                     Love,
                        George
P.S. I ask respectfully, but I am serious.

Dear George,
   I presume you mean money since I am wealthy beyond belief in other ways.

Dear William,
   I mean exactly what I wrote. Why aren't you rich? If the truth is worth attaining, it should certainly bring a monetary reward. If you are merely surviving without the sweet amenities of abundance, as I hear, why should I pay any attention to your words?

Dear George,
   It is not my words that matter, but your own. However, your question deserves a good, clear answer—especially since so many in the world believe that personal wealth and possessions are an indication of success. But when I write that answer in full, it will be written for my world. Please be patient with me while I sort out the words to speak to "supply" more clearly than I have ever done before.

> Reader, please note: All that follows in the book [except for the Related Papers Section] is predicated on the knowledge of specific points that have been made in the earlier chapters. I am writing overtones now. Overtones upon overtones follow.

SUPPLY

Dear George,

Now to answer that question you asked me twelve years ago. I appreciate your long wait.

Certain esoteric "secrets" are self-guarded. Those bits of wisdom are the ones that come from the inside first, not necessarily related to the sights and sounds one gets on the outside. In some instances, understanding comes to the inside, but only when the secret is lived consciously or unconsciously in the world.

The wonder of such a marvelous secret is that we can be told of it by those who know it, and, trusting the teller, we do as he suggests. *Then* comes our "reward," the secret, quite beyond intellectualism, words or anything the wealth of the world can buy. Without trust, we seldom do anything that is required.

Such a secret is the Child's mighty Equation. When people who have not managed to put the "me-sense" behind them for a time come to study here (and many don't even know a sense of self is to be understood and let go), they sometimes try to write down the words I say, as if that would capture the secrets those words seem to contain. They believe they have caught the Secret in their linear words or mine. But regarding the Equation, unless they are living that Mystery, they have only the narrowest idea about what is being said as we talk of it—or, sometimes they don't even hear the words! But if someone trusts and believes me, it is a different matter.

HAN AND THE PEDDLER

"The old peddler has a house as neat as a pin," said Han.

"Yes," Ho answered, "because he doesn't accumulate things but offers them to the world."

Dear George, "prostrate in depression,"

You say you have no light to give your world. Well, if that's how it seems to you, you can now take the first step in lifting yourself from that bed of anguish. Get up, get out and give someone a gift. Take some of the tangible wealth that you do have and give a bit of that to someone who needs it. Make this gift today, George, even if you merely walk down the street with an old sweater in your hand and give it to the first man who looks as if he needs it. It is not easy to take this first step toward real wealth, but do it. Just trust me and do it.

I tell you this remarkable wonder because your letter tells me you are in need of it. I have lived this "process" and know it is true: We give a portion of our substance to the world and, as the consequence of that tangible giving, we soon receive a Glimpse of Light! That Glimpse is manna from heaven—the REAL reward of giving to Caesar's world. The Glimpse that comes shortly after the warm glow of doing something for another person (outside one's own family) is the Light, the Spirit, the Word that "proceeds out of the mouth of the Lord." It is the spirit of life that comes with healing on its wings.

Do this for yourself *today,* dear friend George, and watch what happens!

Let the student of Truth who feels he has no light to give, give something of his *substance,* however little he has, and soon he will *have* an infusion of Light, a Glimpse of Truth, to give as well. To whom? To anyone who seems to need it or deserve it.

One cannot know this is a marvel to do until he has done it and *lived* it so. This is a Self-protected secret.

THE ILLUSTRATION OF THE SEED

George, dear old friend, I'm glad the depression is over.

Your new bother isn't new to me either. I suspect you've fallen into the same trap that held me a victim for so long. As you can see, when you gave your "big favorite sweater" to the "old man down the hall," you perked yourself up sufficiently to write this bombastic letter about my "blindness to dualism." This is a point at which a *little* knowledge of metaphysics can be deadly, hence the many cautions against beginning the search without a willingness to go all the way.

George, in the name of denying what I THOUGHT was "dualism," I nearly destroyed myself. In an astounding ignorance of "Oneness," I denied the nature of all twoness—as if one song couldn't have two renditions, or a form, two uses. A single bottle has an inside and outside, a top and bottom. Is that dualistic? In the metaphysical proclivity toward the insanity of denying every dual appearance, I failed to see the REAL Truth behind the ACTION of still another dualism: (1) giving and receiving, (2) receiving and giving. Giving and receiving are not TWO; they are one flowing Process to which we, as metaphysicians, awaken more slowly than most. Could it be that you are laboring in the same darkness? If so, the words that follow will be a blessed light to walk by.

Listen gently: We plant a small seed in our garden and let nature do its work. If the seed is to survive *in this world*, it begins giving immediately. But—here we come to the natural, built-in blindness of subjective thinking—note that the seed gives (acts) *twice*. Once to the earth and once to the sky. One shoot goes out as a rootlet, another goes up as the stem; one is a gift to the earth, the other a gift to the Light of Life.

This process is so in all nature. It is before our eyes everywhere. Every living thing shows us this simple principle, "dual" as the words make it sound. All one has to do to see that this is so, is to look for himself. Show me a tree that isn't living this principle, and I will show you a dying or dead tree.

Now, we see that the seed *receives* twice. Here we go again, George. Another disdainful dualism that the tree had better not try to avoid. It receives *twice*: once from the earth and again from the air. In all nature, this is true, my friend, even if all nature is just a dream that isn't happening.

Then, for those who continue to search for the Secret with persistence, we observe that the nutrition the seed receives from the earth is passed along the stem to the sky, the plant keeping only what is necessary for growth, and that growth enabling it to give yet *more* to the earth with greater roots and *more* to the Light with greater branches.

Likewise, the wonders the tree receives from the light of the sun (and beyond) are passed on quickly in a marvelous flow downward into the earth, the tree withholding only what is necessary to grow and bear fruit after its kind. In all nature, this is so.

Finally, we observe that wherever this flowing "process" of giving to Caesar and giving to God is stopped—or even interrupted for long—the plant languishes and gradually perishes. In all nature this is so. How do I know? By looking and observing.

George, wherever mankind recognizes this Process within himself and lives in harmony with it, he prospers beyond his wildest imagination. Wherever the principle is broken, he withers, without luster in his life *and without any contribution to his experience or to his world.* To see that this is so, look around yourself! Those who withhold grow heavy and depressed in spirit. Their mental houses are stuffed with trivial things.

As a metaphysician, I was good enough about giving God what is God's, but I was woefully inadequate about giving to the world beyond those things I *had* to give. "Why should I give to an illusion?" I asked, just as your letter asked me in no small wonderment; yet, in the old days, I wondered why I had so little of the world's riches to pay my utility bills when they came due. *I had nothing of the world's value because I had given little or nothing of the world's value to the world—beyond* the mandatory taxes and prices I paid for the things I needed!

The Christly admonition is plain: Give to the world (external) the things that are the world's.

Orthodox churchdom is consistently good about that kind of giving. Its members give tangible things to the tangible world. They give to Caesar what belongs to Caesar. And religion generally prospers in material ways as a consequence. Look at their sprawling megaplexes. More, the prospering churches do all kinds of charitable things in the world and bring their members to make substantial gifts toward those activities. Metaphysicians like to point out that churches are unaware of the complete principle of supply, but those sweet church people, to whom the metaphysician feels superior, give to their world and flourish thereby in worldly goods. What is more, the whole earth is blessed by those people. It is the metaphysician himself who often knows little of the whole story of supply. One must look long and hard to find a school for charity's children sponsored by a metaphysical group. Show me a home sponsored by metaphysicians for the aged children of the world who haven't the money to take care of themselves, George.

"There are many who are first who shall be last," said the Christ Light of genuine Love.

All right, George. I've written these words again, for whatever purpose they may serve. You may have to put them in your pipe and smoke them a few more weeks, months or years, but one day you'll come to understand a wonderful Principle, just as I did. The Christ of history spoke of this principle two thousand years ago, and so did Abraham before him. Instead of writing about "the dualism" that "entraps" you, give some attention to how and why you have recovered from the "awful depression," that old/new disease of the affluent society.

TWO KINDS OF GIVING

Certainly as far as time and space go, there are two kinds of giving and two kinds of receiving—to and from the world, to and from Spirit. It is the "flow" again, the inside and outside, the outside and inside.

Our metaphysical training, as it has come to us from the present textbooks, leaves us absolutely blind to this. Most of the subjectivists I have known had no idea about REAL giving whatever—and that's sad, considering the glut of words written in the name of "supply." As the earnest metaphysician, I overlooked the essential relationship between these "two" because I thought any such idea was dualistic. And, for thirty years, I've found the same blindness in others at the metaphysical bend of the river—*especially* those who withdrew from their organizations before they learned what was there to learn. Oh, but there is much, much more to learn about the Equation. If you are looking for the secrets of supply, read on.

This chapter has been part of the "hard teachings." It seems for a brief time to heap guilt on the heads of those, like me, who didn't know about giving. Though I needed to hear these things long years ago, I only want to rehear them gently now, because the Equation is not an easy point for the world to hear. Unless this is comprehended in clarity, it is a place for the old nature to scream obscenities.

SEQUENTIALITY *or* WHY EXPLANATIONS ARE DIFFICULT

When something significant happens in our affairs—nearly any kind of event—it happens as a series of sequential events that are nearly instantaneous. It is considered impossible to explain the totality of this series in one telling. For this reason many of our experiences are not understood immediately. Even when they are, it seems impossible to explain to others so they can grasp them with the clarity we would like.

Let me explain the mysterious series idea. One pulls the trigger of a loaded shotgun. There follows, almost at the same time, an explosion, a jolt against the shoulder and a great splash in the water where the target bottle floated a second before. Following that, we hear the echoes of the gunshot resounding from the hills. The physicist is concerned with (or attuned to) the trigger pull and the jolt against the shoulder. The musician most notices the sharp sounds and the echoes along the river bank. The artist sees the splash of water and the circling waves coming to shore through the haze of burned gunpowder. The event is viewed through a multi-mist of emotions: surprise, fear, hatred, disgust, excitement, on and on to a near infinity. It is also viewed through the preferences of the viewer. The artist sees what he wants to see. The physicist thinks in his own preferred terms. How does one speak clearly to these different viewpoints at once? Or, even in the same book? It seems impossible, but it can be done. We are doing it in this book.

Well now, what has this to do with the matter of supply? Consider: When one nears the peak of Da Shan—and one is nearing it, or he wouldn't be reading this kind of material—

the circling trip around the mountain to the top takes ever less time. The scenes below repeat themselves, each time from a different perspective, slightly altered. We don't get the next view until we have been willing to leave the present view and move on. Then, at the peak, we are able to look wherever we wish and all the views appear simultaneously. The final view, compared with the first view when we began our climb, is overwhelming, to say the least.

At the lower slopes, our dispatches to those behind us were easy enough to write, but what we wrote along the way wasn't the final view of things. At first we thought the old scenes were left behind forever and we had no way of knowing how often they would be back to be seen again, and yet again, from the circling positions above. During our study of subjectivism, we have special difficulty coming to grips with the fact that nothing, absolutely nothing, has been *overcome* until it is *understood* fully and that as long as one is breathing the air of the world, there remains something to be understood about the Light of Life and the world it creates. The absolute position (subjectivism without the Child) fails in the final analysis, the metaphysician as helpless as anyone before the appearances of the body's death, all the years of study, meditation, contemplation and devotion notwithstanding.

As Awareness itself, we are Everyman. We are all the onlookers—physicist, artist, musician, seeker and finder. One time we read or see through the artist's eyes; at another reading we hear through the musician's ears; at another, we are the physicist, the mathematician, the astronomer. The occluding hazes of preferences or separateness cannot be let go in the objective mode of thought, but they can be surrendered in the subjective mode when the Child begins stirring and is found! We are not through until that happens.

There even remains something to do when one stands atop the mountain *understanding* the scene, living as the Child of God. *We are charged to do something before the Movement ends and the Rest begins.* What? *Free* our subjective view from the ties that bind therein. What is bound on earth is bound in heaven and what is freed on earth is freed in heaven, just as Scripture says. Before we leave the mortal coil, we are charged to make peace with it—understand it—every bit of it, line upon line, precept upon precept, until that work is finished. How do we know when that is done? I am still being instructed and these words are that instruction previously received, listened to, followed, confirmed and (finally) written to mySelf. Only God knows when it is finished.

THE WOODSONG BOY

The little boy in me likes to go to the woodland
and walk
and camp
and look for arrowheads.
The little boy loves to taste the sunshine and listen to the blue sky. That's where I've been. I found a handful of arrowheads today and they are beautiful.
I heard the blue of the sky
and listened to the green of the grass
and felt a blossom explode into a wine of fragrance.

Tangibility is the product of the Intangible,
therefore the body of us will find itself cared for
as certainly as the oak and willow,
as surely as the laurel and lily.
By whom or What?
By the same Ineffable for whom the body of humanity blossoms.
How do I know this is so?
Because I have lived it so,
am living it so NOW
and
KNOW
it is so.
Science and I will confirm it so.
Watch and see.
The Mother of Tangibility hovers o'er Me
and I am without desire, satisfied.

None who have come to Woodsong
have left without hearing the melody that tells of the Presence—
Father—to whom tangibility is wed like notes to a Symphony.
  Those who listen,
really listen to the rustling pines overhead,
will know
in their hearts
that tangibility is the delineation of Infinity
just as surely as the notes that sound the Symphony's melody are
sounding it perfectly.

Woodsong, 1970

"Ah so," said Han. "I am very tired. Who knows what a battle it is to say these things? Sharp Edge, stay with Me a little time longer. Amen."

CHAPTER ELEVEN

PROFOUND SIMPLICITY

The Child and the Child's Equation

GIVING GOES IN TWO DIRECTIONS

We have noted that the two aspects of giving are like the seed giving its roots to the earth (Caesar) and its limbs to the air (Spirit). What is the equivalent in one's human experience? Giving to the earth is giving a part of one's tangible substance to someone who needs it. As certainly as a seed must give part of its actual inner substance to the earth—literally and actually—so the victorious man must give some of his worldly substance. The man who gives little or nothing to the earth is certain to receive little or nothing from the earth *and must resort to taking what he needs from others.*

GIVING TO GOD WHAT IS GOD'S

The question now becomes: *How* does one give to God what

167

is God's? There needs to be no doubt or argument about how one is to do this. We do it exactly as the Christ Light lived and taught. "To Caesar and to God." Ministers give the spiritual bread of life to the congregation. The metaphysician who talks to his or her friends about the wonders of Truth in his personal affairs is doing the same—in different words and in a different context, but these two actions, the minister's and the metaphysician's, are the same.

Such giving is precisely what Jesus meant. He *lived* this activity with a ministry everyone is familiar with. Then, that Light of Life told those who could hear his voice to go and do as he had done: to tell the Story and "heal the sick."

The objectivist churchman gives freely of his tangible wealth, but often he doesn't give so freely of his own inner glimmers. *In the world there is a great reluctance to talk about things so personal and meaningful.* If there is talk at all, it is usually expressed in the words of some respected spiritual authority or quoted as scripture until one becomes little more than a walking anthology for the words of other people. This is hardly being a spokesman for one's own gift of Light. One's own Light is left unwritten, unstated and sadly unreflected. As a matter of fact, the churchman often has little he *can* say about the "sweet glimmering joys of the inner Gift" because those sparks come primarily from *giving* them.

The orthodox schools are more likely to make moral, psychological and ethical gift-statements to others or statements from scriptures that support an organizational view of salvation. These statements, from object to object about objective experiences, are the first step. Ah, but when the subjective idea dawns and we realize that the world lives within the Awareness that sees it, *our gifts to the world become quantum in their power.* It may appear we are giving to one needy man or woman, but we are giving subjectively to the universe of Man.

On the other hand, having heard of Oneness and having experienced some intimation of the power of subjectivism in his affairs, the student of Truth is more likely to give *that* aspect of Truth to his acquaintances; but Glimpses do not continue to come from that activity either, *unless one is giving his substance to the world as well*—and here we have the strange blind bind of Metadelphia and its extreme position in Absoluty.

Nothing in metaphysical literature to this point in time tells of the Child or the Child's Equation. The whole wonder of "giving" becomes most remarkable when one does *both kinds of giving and receiving.* A divine synergism develops, as one quickly finds when he puts this double-barrelled action to the test.

ABSOLUTE BOSH AND NONSENSE, SAMUEL!

This is a difficult concept for students of the Truth, especially those who are hanging tightly to the absolute position that decries the reality of matter in all of its appearances. The metaphysician within myself was certain the charities for human ailments and disasters headed the list of illusions that weren't happening and *shouldn't* be supported.

The absolute position insists that broken hearts and cancer are not real and do not exist. The paradox is, they don't *actually,* but that is not the point here. They *seem* to exist and we are all dealing with the seeming, however absolute and isolated we think we've become. The consciousness of need appears in the same "seeming" world the metaphysician denies and ignores. Wherever one has been able to move beyond this peculiar-to-metaphysics barrier sufficiently to get up, get out and give to a charity or needy family anyway, *that one begins to receive in ways he never thought possible!*

Still, that much giving is only the *first part* of it. There remains the other part—and even that is only a bit of the Equation.

I liken the second kind of giving to the seed's inexplicable *gift to the sunlight.* It shoots a tiny stem up into sheer nothingness—and when it does, the entire universe gives back to the seed. Even so for the seeker *when he finishes the transaction* and gives to God what is God's. In this arena, the objective view of things surrenders before the least Glimpse of subjectivism.

Nothing is more basic than the following "spiritual" truth. Giving the spiritual truth *is the door-opener to Light,* just as giving one's substance is the door-opener to worldly riches. I do not believe one receives the real glimmers of Truth until that one has given of his storehouse to others—and, most certainly, he doesn't continue to receive them unless he does.

BEYOND THEORY AND SPECULATION

These exchanges must be made in actual fact, not merely thought about and considered and judgmentally debated as to their merits. The gift goes "out" from our tangible bodily hand into the hand of someone else "out there," in Caesar's world. And our own words of stories and events wherein the Light of Life has done something in our affairs is spoken out of our present body and listened to by someone at hand to receive the essences, the spiritual light, which, essentially, is giving God what is God's! The interface with Light/light is not *complete* until this is done in actual fact. Oh, but when we have done it, we feel it and know it is right!

The "gift to God" is most quickly accomplished *with words to men,* written or spoken. But both gifts are made and both exchanges are completed right here by oneself, out of his own wealth (external) and his own Glimpse, himself (internal).

THE METAPHYSICAL IN-HOUSE PERFORMANCE IS NOT ENOUGH

In the early years, metaphysicians were good about giving the spiritual truths. Their testimonials were attended by outsiders who had come to hear what subjectivism was all about. Today, those exchanges have become a closed performance, from student to student, who, for the most part question the correctness and sincerity of the words they are listening to.

Recently, Rachel and I visited with a lady practitioner who said, "I don't believe those testimonials anymore. Those people don't know what they are talking about because they are so dualistic." Such words hardly come from one who is running with the subjective Child of himself. In Metadelphia, that in-house exchange has become as productive as hugging one's own photograph. The spiritual glimpses the metaphysician once received regularly *are not arriving as they did—and his church is like a dying tree.*

One more point that will ring a bell with many readers. The Equation has to do with the *flow* of Truth, inside to outside, above to below, and then, *the other way* simultaneously. We learn to receive, too. Have you noticed how hard it is to give things to some people? Metaphysicians are prone to be that way at certain bends of the river. But to accept the gift proffered is to allow the other man to be a giver. We learn to receive as well.

PATTING THE FOOT IN THE CATHEDRAL

Even more apparent, we see many who have withdrawn from their organizations, where at least they gave a little to Caesar's world, and they are drying up spiritually like prunes, wondering what has happened to their Truth. Nothing has happened to their Truth. They have stopped sharing it with the rest of themself.

I recall how wonderfully the Truth came to me back in those early days of my subjective discovery when, in grand enthusiasm and naivete, I shared it with everyone who would listen. Ah, but how the glimpses came in those days! Reader, how long has it been since you spoke to a neighbor or a friend about anything the subjective Light of Life has done for you? How long since you have spoken of subjectivism to anyone outside your little circle of friends? Or, how long has it been since you took a needy family under your wing and gave them some of the physical and tangible things they needed? Vaunted churchman and metaphysician, listen: The little backwoods Baptist lady with hardly enough to feed her family has very likely done more of the merciful gift-giving necessary to the world than has the metaphysician secluded in his mental tower.

Do words like these seem unduly brutal? Look for yourself and see how many subjectivists stand in the soup lines serving homeless street people. See how many orphanages and homes for the elderly of all denominations have been built by the metaphysicians of the world. Compared to the works of the "old theology" subjectivists (and scientists) disdain so, their work for the world has been little indeed.

WHILE I AM STILL IN THE WORLD, LET MY INTERFACE BE COMPLETE

Interface seems to be at the surface with people, but it is deep in the Heart of God.

You and I come together at the intellectual level of words and conversation, but that level is deep in the Child's Heart. The Child of you and the Child of me is the same One, deep in the heart of God.

Whether I say anything to you or not—whether we even meet or not—we are already One in the Child-Heart of things. When or if it appears we must talk to one another for any reason, I will strive to bring my Heart and my mouth to say the same thing. Therein we will understand each other in harmony. Therefore, I tell you now above all things else, I will endeavor to speak of the Child-Heart of Myself. In so doing, we will be in total harmony, like two old friends who have known each other forever. Why not, old shoe, why not?

The Lights of the World have discovered the Child. Those who run with the Child have found the Equation. Those who have found the Equation live it because it is like death not to. To live the Equation is to look round about and see wonder everywhere in everything, despite the appearing, despite the world's antics.

Ah, then, the world sees our seeing and comes to ask about it that it might see the same. If we are persistent, if we are honest and speak of the Heart, if we don't stop until the world has discovered the Child and its Equation, we will see our world come to confirm our Heaven at hand.

When will we know we have been persistent enough? When the world ends its warfare and struggle to understand. That is when the Final Covenant begins to be lived in the "external" world, confirming our own living of the Covenant. As the Bible states, that last covenant is already written in our heart. There is no intermediary between us and it. There is no intermediary between God and us. Therefore, nothing exists between this Awareness I am, this Child of All, and Godhead Itself. Our work isn't finished until we look up and out, roundabout, and see our subjective selfhood at peace.

WE COMPLETE THE TRANSACTION

The Light thrives and *comes in abundance* when Light's grand transaction is completed—only when one interfaces with the rest of his world (inside/outside) and stops holding his precious Light (and substance) within himself as if no one existed "out there" who appears to need the Truth. *These are the ones whom Jesus warned that if they did not give of the little they had, even the little they had would be taken from them.* He said that if they did not bring forth that which is within themselves, they would lose it!

"Within a man of Light there is light, and he lights the whole world." How can he do such a thing? His world is subjective!

BACK TO THE JOURNAL AGAIN

One wonders why these things are not being told and taught in the world. The simple answer is that this fuller revelation of giving and receiving hasn't dawned within either the objective or subjective schools as yet—and it won't until we tell *our* Glimpses and Glimmers in just the way we are doing it here. We get out our notebooks and begin.

Well now, here we come again, yet again, to the place of importance our words occupy—and why we write in our journals as we do. We have found writing to be the most powerful of all disciplines short of the Equation itself. It is the natural accompaniment to the Discipline into which we all come for a divine purpose, and which we leave when finally we succeed in unbinding our own subjective view of things.

Writing allows one to create the best possible INTERFACE for giving God's gift to God.

A PAINFUL MEDLEY OF JOY OVERTONE

"Who are the awakened?"

"Those who have found the Child."

"But they haven't attained the top of the mountain when they first find the Child, have they?"

"No. The Child within leads them there, showing them how to live the Equation!"

THE MINISTER

A minister was invited to visit the Second Master of Kwangse. When he arrived at the Second Master's house, the minister said, "Your words have been meaningful to me and I have long wanted to meet you face to face. I have given your words to many in the Province."

"Yes, I know," said the Master, "That is commendable and is the reason I have invited you. I want to give a gift of gratitude to you in return for your telling others of me." Then, the Master said The Secret Words for the Equation. As quickly as the words were uttered, they were followed by a flash of lightning on the mountain. When the thunder stopped echoing through the hills, the Master said, "I will explain the words to you if you wish. They will allow you to enter the Province Treasury and give whatever you like to your world."

The minister, busy thinking what he was going to say next to impress the Master, didn't hear the words of the Equation or the offer to explain them. The host repeated the offer. When the thunder stopped shaking the mountains, the promise to explain was made once more, but the minister's much thinking still didn't let him hear. The tired old teacher told the Word and made the promise for the third time, saying it differently in order to make himself understood. The minister neither heard nor asked. "I have appointments to keep and I must not take too much of your time," he told the Second Master in feigned humility, and hurried away.

The Second Master of Kwangse told Han about his visitor who was too busy to either see or understand the magnitude of the proffered Gift. "Why are you surprised?" asked Han. "The Master of Galilee prepared a feast and invited the business men and merchants. They were more anxious to keep their schedules than eat the Food. That simple man denounced the business men and told his servants to let anyone come to the feast who wished. Now, my friend, why should you be surprised that your invited guest hurried on his way, more interested in his bondage than in the Way to freedom?"

Truth seekers are eager to free themselves of pain, but seem unaware they are to resolve the world's pain as well. Subjectivism makes it possible to help the universe entire.

We open our doors to those who find us. We talk of the Equation to those who are living the Equation because they are worthy of it. Even that is no indication they will drink the Water at our cistern, but if the Truth is important to them, they will come asking questions and we answer honestly, exactly as we would have them answer ours.

WHO ARE THE LEAST SIMPLE?

"Who are the least simple and childlike people in the world?" Mary wondered.

"I think ministers," Lee said, after a moment of thought, "because they are so serious."

"Soldiers," said the soldier. "If they get childlike, they get dead."

"Young adults," said Ho. "They want so much to be adults they hurry to leave the child behind."

"But they are close to the Child," said Lee. "Ministers are often so somber, so sanctified and self-righteous. They take everything seriously as if the world was hinged on the front door of their particular building."

"Isn't it?" asked the soldier, looking for an argument.

"Never mind," laughed Mary. "We are asking who are the *least* childlike among men."

That night at the campfire, they asked Han.

"Who are the least childlike?" the old man puzzled. "Wouldn't it be best to know who is most childlike?"

"You are," Lee said quickly.

"Then why do you ask a child such a question?"

"Because you can answer it," said Lee.

"Then, my friends, can you see that the way to know the man who is least childlike in the world is to become the Child yourself?"

The fireflies sparkled that evening.

"Why did the Carpenter say to pray without letting others

hear them? Isn't prayer on the street better than no prayer at all?"

"Oh yes," said Mary, "but I imagine he was talking about the secret Equation."

"How so, Mary?"

"If one is accustomed to giving, he doesn't say anything about his gift. He just gives. He acts without regard or regret. If one is not accustomed to acting so, he says, 'I left something for you on the table.' That is better than not giving at all, of course, but it is not as one acts from the Heart. To act from the Heart is to give the gift without expecting something from that one in return."

"That's ridiculous!" the soldier shouted. "There are those of us who have grown up with nothing. We have had to work hard for the things we have. We can't be faulted because we place a high value on the things that have come to us so slowly. We part with our possessions more carefully than those who have much, but I am not guilty because I don't want my gift overlooked or lost!"

"There, you make my point," the little lady with the bright eyes smiled. "It is the matter of Value that we are talking about. If an unseeable Reality is the real Value, then our material things have less value—or none at all. Isn't it strange to call matter unreal and then clutch it so tightly, hesitant to let it go out and help others?"

"Well, I need a little of that unimportant material stuff to buy food and feed my family," the soldier from the far country growled.

"We all do," Mary replied, "but it is our giving that is the value to us, not our gift."

"Why do you and Han and the preacher talk so damned much about giving?" the soldier asked with anger.

"Because it bothers you so," said Han from out of the shadows. "When it stops bothering you, we will be able to move beyond the things you cherish most to Something to be cherished more."

TOUCHING THE TENDER PLACES

Han said, "The role of the honest Teacher, like that of the

prophet of old, is to touch our tender places. What is pain but
the push to find Something Beyond? Somewhere along the
line, we learn this slowly. If we are fortunate, we find someone
with the courage to tell us directly and honestly in words we
can understand, in words that punch their way through our
crust of selfishness and fear. The Teacher within does not give
us the smooth stone or the soft sound. The Truth is not always
gentle."

"You lure one here with the soft sound, you know," the soldier said, still growling. "Then, when he gets here, you nail
him with hard teachings."

"The man who leaves here is not the man who came here.
One day he will see what he left behind while he was here."
Han stirred the fire. Everyone sat thinking. In a moment the
old teacher said, "Tell me something, soldier. Tell me your
most vivid memory and what it has taught you about
yourself?"

"The battlefield," the soldier answered quickly, beginning to
catch a glimpse. "You needn't ask if that was painful. It was.
It surely was."

A hush fell across the meadow. Even the fire stopped crac-
kling. Barely above a whisper the soldier said, "Why must I
learn things so slowly and painfully?"

"Find what purpose pain and pleasure serve, my young
friend, not so much how to avoid pain and how to get pleasure. When one knows their purpose, he knows to avoid their
extremes."

"Have you avoided them, Master?" the subdued soldier
asked.

"No. I have learned their lessons."

"All of them?"

"I don't know. I don't know."

Unabashed, the soldier wrote home, "I'm glad to know
there's something the old bastard doesn't know." The slow
seed had been planted, however. It would take years, but the
seed would grow apace and the soldier would find it one day.

Friend reader, this has been a bell-clanging and pounding

chapter. It can be invaluable to the student who is willing to go all the way to the top of confirmation's mountain. My experience tells me that many will feel uncomfortable with these pages, no matter how much the words are softened. But when half the apparent world is starving and the other half accumulating and gorging itself in sensual gratification, accumulating and storing enough energy to destroy the earth in the process—someone must tell of the Equation again. The sincere of myself will grow to appreciate what has been written here when, in the search for happiness, all else has been tried and has failed.

CHAPTER TWELVE

ILLUMINATION

"Line upon line, precept upon precept..."

AFTER THE POND EXPERIENCE

Dear Bill,

I have finally reached the place where I desire only for Christ to take this life and live it.

My knowledge of the Christ is on the surface. I want to feel and realize Christ as what I really am. I long to have a transforming experience. So far, understanding has come drop by drop, although I must admit it is coming faster now, almost a tiny stream.

Didn't you have a spiritual experience at the pond?

Love, Linda

Dear Linda of the soft voice,

Are you ready to read this?

Trusting the heart, we'll begin. Listen carefully: The Truth comes to us line upon line, precept upon precept, here a little, there a little. It is supposed to unfold that way and no other way! The Road to Damascus experience has become a fanciful dream. "But when you see your images which came into existence before you, (which) neither die nor are manifested, how

179

much will you bear!" Jesus, the Christ of history, asked his disciples. (*Gospel According to Thomas*, Nag Hammadi Library) We do not *desire* a "pond experience." We need, rather, to go about it another way. Wonderful as the metaphysical messages have been, they have been poorly written *when they lead one into desire.*

The Light is happening around us constantly to be recognized in small ways. When we are faithful to the small Glimpse, we get more. We are honest to the smallest glimpse first, tested with it, tried with it, examined with it—and then we get another.

As you write your Glimpses in your journal, you are taking the first step toward getting (giving) MORE Glimpses. Be FAITHFUL to that, a little each day. In our next communication we'll take that to its next step and write about Glimpses themselves.

WHAT I LEARNED AT THE POND

The Melody of the Woodcutter and the King is the story of the day I first learned about the plasticity of tangibility. That was the day I really saw the dominion I could lay claim to right here in the world. That account is familiar to those who have read it, but not many know *the rest of the story* unless they have been here asking specifically about illumination.

The "pond experience" was my first conscious insight into "contradistinction," though I didn't understand that at the time. One doesn't know much about subjectivism until he has perceived the matter of "contradistinction" and gotten it straight. We really have to get it straight before we can get further along.

The pond experience was certainly what the religionist or psychologist would call a "peak experience." Those experiences are often explained away as psychological quirks—or fleeting dyspepsia. Nonetheless, they happen frequently, awaiting our recognition. That morning, after I bent myself down to drink the cold water, I stood up and saw a new and different world. I saw "a new heaven and a new earth" spread over everything, and while I don't always see the new one now, I have never had the same view of the old.

CONTRADISTINCTION

That morning, those years ago, when I looked around at the new view, everything was dancing with light. In particular, I remember standing transfixed. The pond was blinding. The black man plowing the field beside the little lake glistened with light. So did the mule pulling the plow. And the birds following behind, pecking in the new turned earth, were little darts of feathered light, flashing from place to place. The man's sweat ran down the reins, a river of pure light that dripped little orbs of fire onto the ground. I looked at the new scene and the wonder of it without any feel of the earth under my feet.

Very slowly, and in ongoing amazement, I continued my journey through the field to the mountain beyond—another half a dozen miles with a hard climb at the end. A strangely effortless event. I seemed to walk without walking. I went slowly and stopped often but can remember very little of events along the way except for a brief conversation. I stopped to talk to an old man who sat on his porch, leaning back in a cane bottomed chair, his feet on the porch rail. He was carving something with a pocket knife. He looked at me strangely, as though he wasn't sure who I was—and I remember thinking he certainly *WAS* looking at a new person, one he had never seen in all his life. From that country house, the climb up Double Oak Mountain began.

But, hear this, Linda. There is a point here which seems most important to those looking for the experience of "illumination." While the pond event was happening for me, I saw clearly that such an event hadn't happened sooner *only because I had carefully excluded it from my experience.* How? By limiting expectation to something *spectacular.* By yearning for Paul's experience of being blinded on his way to Damascus. Either my studies had been deceiving, or I had allowed myself to read the need for such an experience into them.

As I walked up the mountain that day, I marveled again and again *that all this had been available from the very beginning if I had simply acknowledged it when it had happened in the many small ways before.* I knew then: I had ignorantly blocked the Flow of Light. This experience was the breaking of the dam. Instinctively, I knew my entire life would have been further along if I had only acknowledged the Light of Life in the many ways it had already appeared!

The absence of my conscious recognition and acknowledgement had deprived me of so much. What I'm trying to write here is that *the experience of "illumination" is happening all the time in small ways, to be seen and appreciated.* The traumatic events like Paul's may be more a matter of our awful ignorance of God's grace than our achievement or attainment of wisdom.

Well now, my wonderment at the time was enormous. I floated, it seemed, to the top of Double Oak Mountain and began setting up camp. I remember gathering firewood for the evening warmth and preparing a place to sleep. Then, as the sun went down, the unexpected "lesson" began. I was nudged by the "equal and opposite" of the human day's experience.

Elation slowly gave way to a strange, unexpected and growing sense of hopelessness. (Where has It gone!?) I found myself with an inability to DO anything. (What's to DO?) I watched the sunset, arms around my knees, and saw the stars emerge one by one. I didn't move. Finally, I couldn't move. The evening chill descended and I wondered why the hell I didn't light the fire. Try as I might, it seemed senseless to try or even move. I couldn't bring myself to bend down and light the wood that would have warmed the evening. (Dear God, where has the Joy gone?)

By midnight, cold and shaken, I was thinking of the hopelessness of "mortal life" and thought it would be better to hurl myself from the mountain than see the world again as I had seen it before the experience at the pond. By early morning, in complete anguish, I was quoting to myself that the darkest hour is just before the dawn—and noting, for the first time I can consciously recall, that if it weren't for the stygian darkness all around, I wouldn't be conscious of the stars. With that, some relief came, and in a few minutes the dawn was breaking. Never had a morning been more welcome. I was still sitting with my arms around my knees—frozen into place by now—but this time I *knew* another morning was on its way. I was grateful for even the hope of it. I think this was a time I really understood what the ancient sunrise ceremonies were about—and Easter's rebirthing!

A new world had been revealed in the morning of a spring day. The chimerical nature of the old world was seen in the afternoon. That night, in the cold and dark of a human night, only a meager memory of the Light at the pond remained. In the place of Joy, desolation and depression had descended. My confidence in the old world had been smashed during the day; yet, in the dark of night, there was only a fading memory of Something Wonderful to take its place, and, as I looked at the stars, I was aware of my human nothingness and emptiness. Though I didn't know it then, I was coming to discover the nature of learning.

As all this was happening, I knew the reasons for it perfectly well—the reasons that Light must come to each of us "line upon line, precept upon precept, here a little, there a little." My friend Linda, it is important that we acknowledge the smallest blessings and are faithful to those pennies of Truth, first. Remember the verse in the Bible about being faithful to pennies so we can be trusted with dollars?

Our excessive yearning after a grand illumination is a self-defeating exercise that occludes a view of the constant blessings going on around us all the time. Now I know—and tell my others—that we are faithful in the small ways if we are to be trusted with the grand View from the peak of Da Shan, the world. Even then, when we have been tested and proven and carried aloft "on the wings of Love" to that High View, that View's *confirmation in the world* still comes "line upon line, precept upon precept, here a little, there a little."

Linda, if you can find another who has had the View, ask him if these words are true! Better still, live the pennies and see for yourself!

WHAT DID I LEARN AT THE POND AND ON THE MOUNTAIN THAT NIGHT?

I learned that the ebbing, flowing light of this world is tributary to a greater Light that doesn't move. Perhaps the photon is an IMAGE of True Light, but the True Light, changeless and unmoving, is the "Light of the Father." The image is just an image of an image of an image.

I learned that the human experience is a holy Lesson going on and one is to learn it, one way or another.

I learned that I live and relive experiences until I see the good in them. When I learn to thank God for the lesson learned, I am taken to yet another View on the mountain.

Thus, I began to learn the principle of contradistinction which suggests that everything but the Light of Life itself is an image, positive or negative, of Something Greater. That everything points first to its contrary, thence to the Balance between, thence to the Something Beyond, transcendent and immanent simultaneously.

I began to learn the meaning of emptiness—the old self, the me-sense, naughted. Beyond this, there is the new Self to be!

You are very much loved,

ILLUMINATION IS NOT A MYTH

Illumination is a Fact. We have, however, grown accustomed to thinking it must always be the other fellow, the saint or the avatar, who experiences it, not ourself. Then, we wonder why those who have awakened have gone from the scene. We think of their withdrawal to lofty ivory towers where they sit in lonely solitude.

"Illumination," like all things sublime, creeps into the conscious awareness of the willing and childlike. It enters on kitten's feet, unannounced. It comes as the prophet said, ". . .here a little, there a little."

"But how do we know when we KNOW?"

We find ourselves with the Answer.

"What is the Answer?"

The answers to the problems that perplex us—and others.

"Do you know the answers?"

Those that, by God's grace, I have been shown, come to know, have proven and am finally given the courage to tell about.

"How can I know you know?"

You can look for yourself at the words that are written. You can ask and see if the answer you get is applicable in your affairs—and works in your heart.

If the religionist's religion isn't doing all it has promised to do, that one hasn't found the Light behind religion. If the subjectivist's metaphysics isn't working in his affairs, that one hasn't found the Light that underlies his subjective studies. The fact is, in Western metaphysic's subjective textbooks, there is no general inclusion of the subject of Illumination at all. Why? The answer is painful.

Certain perspectives that can't be seen otherwise come into view with the Light of Illumination. When we make the *confirming trip,* our view of the world-game is enlarged, and we see the importance of the hit, the run, and reaching home base in actual fact, *beyond theory and speculation.* Most people are playing games with their spiritual studies, their science and their metaphysics. They are tripping along the comfortable edges, talking a lot. With knowing comes *doing.*

GUIDEPOSTS

Certain guideposts indicate the changed perspectives that come with enlightenment:

There comes an *undreampt* comprehension of the REASONS for Light/light, time and space, past, present and future. Neither teachers nor books discuss this yet—but some good physicists and mathematicians are getting close. They have only to discover subjectivism's Child within themselves and to recognize the totality of consciousness.

The meanings of (and reasons for) other special things arrive also—such as beginnings and endings, above and below, first and last, inside and outside, essence and image, male and female, overtones, bridges and time, balance, contradistinction, synergism. Quite beyond expectation, beyond words, it seems presently, but not for much longer.

A marvelous childlikeness and simplicity arrive.

We have unexpected insights into the reasons for religion and philosophy; we begin to understand the reasons standing *behind* the three stages taken intuitively toward wisdom and understanding; we see not only the reasons for the appearances of evil in the world, but also the Reason beyond that.

There is a new awareness of HONESTY and an equal aversion to deception. One becomes aware of the incredible quantity of horsefeathers and bologna presented to the world in the name of Truth, from authorities who are no authorities at all. We see the fraudulence and deception inherent in certain practices and eschew them. We can see why and how people in the world claim a knowledge of Truth long before they are living it.

There comes an enwrapping, protecting Power of another kind, most amazing.

The sticking places in religion and subjective studies become transparent—and we see the good reasons for them.

Especially this: the natural and simple ability to see good in everything develops beyond every expectation! And with this come a grand generosity of spirit and a willingness to 'help the world.

Finally, possibly grandest of all because it is the reason for living, comes the DISCOVERY of the Child within—and the Child's way to live, the Equation!

The Original of us is ATTAINABLE, right here in the tangible world where hell and its terror seem ubiquitous and inescapable to others.

Oh, there is more to this attainment of the Child than TALKING about it—but talking is necessary. Most of mysticism, religion and metaphysics addresses unimportant issues. Science is working with effects, without the Child's guidance. Organizational metaphysics doesn't have the essentials straight, and the protectors of dogma (with their concern for numbers) refuse to see the subjective Truth as anything but a threat to the status quo, even when that Truth is spelled out before them—no different now than in the days of the prophets or when Jesus called religious leaders dogs in the manger who would neither eat the oats nor let the cattle eat them.

There are other guideposts—cosmological, hierarchical, ascending and descending—none of which is to the least degree mystical or difficult to apprehend by the Child of us. All of it is revealed intuitively on the wings of Light, without hard study. We find ourselves knowing without effort. None of this is what one expects, whether he is a churchman, metaphysician, scientist or mystic.

There is a mighty reversal and a return to the Beginning in the end, completely unexpected; not a turning back, as words make it sound, but an ONGOING into wonder after wonder inexplicable to the unattained and arrogant nature of us.

It comes as God's grace—glimpse upon glimpse, precept upon precept, bringing a new recognition of the value of the Enlightened among us whose wisdom we seek out. My own religious and metaphysical studies were misleading in this area especially. I see my metaphysical friends stagnating at the plateau where everything is perceived "within" themselves. Just as I did before them, they stand there, ignoring the outside of the cup, even denying its reality, while trying to heal the inside. The religionist washes both sides of the cup but defends his personal dogma and accuses others of heresy without knowing anything about the subjectivism he is condemning. The scientist peers at the faint glimpses of light in his microscope and telescope, using the very science and essence of subjectivism, but, as yet, is unaware of the guiding Child within himself.

Who will get these three things straight? The reader first, then the world following. Why is this the order? Because the world exists within Awareness and is following in time. Beneath the increasing confusion and complexity of this world is the original little boy or girl we once were, still there, awaiting our recogntion and call.

MORE ABOUT THE INTERNAL CLOCK IN HUMANITY

A marvelous new Event is about to begin for mankind, if it hasn't already. That Event will be, in part, the "discovery" of another force in nature, the edge of a greater dimension that, when understood, will put everything relative to life, space, time, matter and our human society into new and unexpected perspective. Our physical sciences stand at the edge of this discovery already—and where science stands presently, mankind is sure to follow because the world trusts its pragmatic provers. This Event has already broken through to touch individuals here and there. Its power and new dimension have been quietly proven and put to work in the world. Science will shortly confirm this, but lo, human sciences, by their very nature, will be unable to show us how to use this inner Event. Science gave us nuclear power but was unable to prevent our destructive use of it.

Well now. This is the sort of finding of a greater dimension one would have expected to emerge from the ongoing religions, from the new metaphysicians or the avant garde. Rather, it will come from the particle physicist, the mathematician, the astronomer, the new cosmologist and the childlike dreamer, precisely for the reason that their thinking *is* ongoing and not so bound by the creeds, dogmas and solidified interpretations of scriptures which bind the Hindu, the priest, the Zen student, the rabbi, metaphysician and minister—and, especially, the ordinary churchman.

The two dimensional caterpillar is just one dimension away—one internal effort *of its own*—from another stage in its own development. When it emerges from its inner writhing within the cocoon, it has entered the next dimension of its affairs and, lo, the old order of blindness has passed away. The caterpillar has become sighted and everything around him is amazing and wonderful to his new eyes. Limited before to the strides a caterpillar can make with its little legs, now the new creature—butterfly—has wings to fly through fields undreampt before.

Similarly, the cicada, living in the darkness of the earth for most of its life, feeding on the roots of trees, begins to feel a stirring within himself which is so dramatic it causes him to let go the familiar source of food and begin pushing against the black earth surrounding him. Like the caterpillar, he wriggles and writhes his way into another dimension of light, color, expanded dimensions and new freedom.

Consider the remarkable clock that brings the cicada to do this. Some of these creatures are on a seventeen-year cycle. Here in Alabama they go from alpha to omega in thirteen years. After that long span in the blackness of the earth, something within them causes a stirring, so accurately timed that the bug emerges at precisely the moment necessary to evade his foe and survive—like a quartz clock of solar precision fashioned by an angel physicist. The clock waits thirteen years, seventeen years, and suddenly clicks on at precisely the right moment in time.

Well, just such a clock has been switched on in quantum mankind. Friend-reader, there is another entire dimension of existence for each of us and it is just an instant away—a minute internal "awakening" away. That dimension has already begun to call our attention to itself, whether we want it so or not. Men here and there are beginning to act differently. The attuned eye can see it. The sensitive heart can feel it. There are many in the world who know intuitively and undeniably that something spectacular is already happening—and they are right. It happened to me more than forty years ago, though I didn't know just what it was then—and twenty years were to pass before I *really knew* what it was. It changed my life in a most marvelous way, and since that time I have been made aware that nearly identical experiences have happened to hundreds more.

THE CLOCK IN QUANTUM MAN

An inner Light tells me that people have clocks within them as certainly as the rest of the creatures in nature. We know something of this already. Puberty kicks in at a certain stage, then the mating and homing urges, et al, throughout our human span. But, listen, listen, something new and marvelous is presently happening to QUANTUM MANKIND. A new, worldwide "urge" has begun. To this time in time, only a few have been made fully aware of this mystifying insight. A strange *new* disquiet and discontent. New urgings that have no rational explanation because they have never been felt by mankind at large, nor written of in words easily understood. We are seeing signs of this Divine Clock already in the bizarre behavior of this group and that. We've been blaming "civilization" or television or something else for the strange twists and turns mankind has begun to perform internally and respond to externally. Recently we have taken to calling it anxiety, stress, informational overload and so forth. Something deeper is on the edge of exploding. The Divine Discontent that some of us have struggled with all our lives is soon to stir all humanity, bewildering all but those who know what it is and what is happening. Those who know are those who have had early access to these urgings and have responded in small ways.

While all of us suspect there is more to life than the human scene, a universal recognition is sure to come that INDEED there IS Something Else—another dimension spread over the human experience. As we said, it is likely that science will confirm it first.

THE CENTURY PLANT ILLUSTRATION

Imagine a plant that has lived in the desert for nearly a century, then finally prepares to bloom, seed and die, its seed to begin another century of time. Imagine, also, that this plant has a winter's rest each year and new growth each spring— and has been doing this for ninety-nine years. Then, via a clock that has been inside that plant from the very seed it sprang from, it slowly—or suddenly—begins the epic event. It starts to grow a stem and a bud thereon.

Can you imagine how the fragmented plant must be self-shaken by all this strange, new happening, so unaccustomed it is to blooming? The roots must wonder where they are supposed to send their nutrition NOW. The limbs wonder where the new growth is going—and why. The roots and leaves all send their substance into the new growth and finally to the flower itself. The leaves must complain that they are not receiving from the roots as before and the roots must wonder why the leaves are not giving to them as they have for ninety-nine years. "Tradition is being destroyed! We must stop this foolishness and return to the old values!" This preparation of the bud is a shakingly new activity that embraces the plant now. The inner clock, dormant for ninety-nine years, has sprung into action and the century plant finally blooms, to seed and expire.

The *real* bloom, for which the plant was originally intended, forms, blooms and carries the plant's essences and imprints into its seed-self. All the other spring "bloomings," the other cycles, the other events through the ninety-nine years have become as nothing compared to this final great blossoming which has been the purpose of the plant from the beginning—to prepare its seed for another field.

What has happened for some of us individually is soon to happen for all mankind. There are two views we mortals contain—the individual view and the quantum overview; the man-with-a-name's view and the holistic view. From the standpoint of a View I have been blessed to live, I see clear indication that a new world clock has been turned on in the SPECIES—in Quantum Man, exactly as God turned it on in what appears the individual "me" forty years ago. Just as the century plant makes a final flowering at the end of its span, so the Tree of Life—appearing as humanity—is soon to begin a strange behavior from an unrelenting inner urge that will result, after much internal and external turmoil without precedent, in a New Bloom, a New Community. This divine stirring, different from all that has gone before in this pulse of events for eleven thousand years, will bring mankind to re-examine his values; rethink his ideas and beliefs; retest his religions and philosophies, his governments and systems, and find them woefully inadequate; thence to turn within himself into a *subjective view* of Life, to discover the very Essence of Self-*within*—the Child of God.

These events, already begun, will become quantum—every man alive feeling and responding, flailing positively or negatively, responding in all ways, unable to find respite in the former things.

THE INNER CLOCK AND WORLD TRAVAIL

The world has begun the travail that ends in the birth of the Child within—Messiah, Redeemer, Savior!—closer than breathing, closer than fingers and toes, not far off but here all the while. What is more, we will see THEN that this Event, the "birthing," has every bit, each step of the way, been foreseen by the lights and prophets, Eastern and Western, above and below, first and last, male and female. More, all of this will be WONDERFUL—precisely what has been called for from the beginning—naught but GOOD going on—the REBIRTH of the Original Image of Godhead.

How do I know these things are true? I was shown all of this wonder forty years ago at the pond and didn't believe a bit of it—no way!—but, in the years since, having been faithful to the Vision, having been tested by it and forced to live it, its veracity PROVEN line upon line, precept upon precept, here a little, there a little; and having found confirmation for every Glimpse given, and having LIVED the Quantum of Mind as Awareness confirmed—and tested by THAT—I have been told these many years later to WRITE my findings to my inner Selfhood and "prepare the way" for the Child's rebirthing and reappearance in "the world." I have done that as best I could.

By the time this book is published, the "quantum appearing" of the divine discontent will have kicked in for the world-at-large. Not bad, but GOOD happening. The Child, the "Children of God" will survive.

BOOK TWO

TABLE OF CONTENTS

RELATED PAPERS

FOREWORD 199

1. Who Is Han? 200

2. Two Basic Questions Answered 200
   How Does An Old Soldier Dare To Write A Book
   About The Truth?

3. The Secret Of The Seed 203

4. Old Croak And The House Of Mirrors 204

5. The Secret Contains Three Slow Steps 208
   The Elements of the Secret
   A Special Letter

6. The Starting Place or If God Is All,
   Why Do I Feel So Rotten? 210

7. Child Equals Heart Equals Soul, The Overlooked
   Simplicity 211
   There is an Ageless Mystery In Our Ability To
   Find Identity
   The Historic Christ and the Child

8. The Progression Of Awakening 214

9. Letter To A Finder 215

10. The Me-Sense And The Intellect 216

11. Ego 218

12. On Having Sufficient Faith 220

13. Aunt Nelly 221

14. Letter To Elaine Overtone 222
    About Feeling Good

15. Bronze, Silver, Gold—and Diamond! 225

16. Surrender 229

17. A Journal Entry About Suffering 230

18. About Suffering And Death 231

19. Simple Scene, Ordinary Little Place 234

20. It's Raining Joy Today 235

21. Space, Time And Progression 236

22. The Crack In The Armor Of The World 238

23. The Holographic Nature Of Matter 241

24. The Elijah Illustration About Light,
      Time, Space And The Real Identity 246

25. Twin Eagles; More About Time, Space
      And Images 250

26. Wisdom Is Information Rediscovered 255
      Light Is Information

27. About Wisdom And Railroad Trestles 259

28. A Restatement Of Cosmology 261

29. Alreadyness Precedes The Tangible Experience;
      Predestination And Free Will 263
      Difficulties in Speaking of Spiritual Matters

30. The World Is After The Fact 265

31. What Do Cosmology, Science And Metaphysics
      Have To Do With Reality?
      Ka-Boom! 270
      A Millionth of a Billionth of a Second

32. A Word About Prophecy 272

33. Opening The Door To Infinite
      Possibilities 275

34. More Pertaining To Seeing Good 277
      A Journal Entry
      Righteousness and Godliness

35. About The Appearances Of Evil In The World ... 279

36. Confident Expectation 281

37. The Man Who Stole The Chewing Gum 282

38. The Lady At The Laundromat 285

39. The Angry Truck Driver 287

40. About The Sins Of The World 289

41. About Healing 292

42. The Alchemy Of Good... 298

43. Dreams Are Subjective... 298

44. The Great Glass Pyramid 301

45. About Action And "Getting Our Subjectivism
    Straight" 303
    Non-Action in the Metaphysical Community

46. A Letter Pertaining To Journal
    Tending... 306

47. The Bible In The Light Of Subjectivism.............. 308

48. The Subjective Comforter And The
    Historic Jesus 308

49. The Child-Messiah Arrives As We Get Subjectivism
    Straight.. 315

50. About Hard Teachings... 318

51. To Find Balance Is To Find Identity 319

52. One More Paper On Balance 322

53. Zen Buddhism And Western
    Absoluteness.. 327

54. Occluding States Of Mind...................................... 328

55. Being Open To The New 330

56. Pilgrimages... 330

57. The Dimensionality Of Good................................. 331

58. The Visit With The Magistrate Of
    Absoluty Town.. 332
    The Zen Trap, The Taoist Trap, The Absolutist Trap
    The World is a Perfect Vessel and Whoever Tries to Alter
    It, Spoils It

59. The Bridge 344

60. The Love Letter Overtones.................................... 345

61. Writing And The Community 350

62. About Love And The Flow.................................... 357

63. The Mysticism Of Journal Tending...................... 360

64. The Frog, The Toad And Old Dan Jones........... 363

65. About Confirmation, Or Proving Things
    To Be True.. 364

66. About Words, Thoughts, States And
    Stages.. 366

67. Journal Tending.. 368

68. Identity And The Genuine Community 373

69. "Silly Solipsism!" Shouts The Preacher................. 374

70. Textbook Thinking 381

71. The Galileo Illustration Pertaining To Textbook
    Thinking.. 382

72. The Narrowness Of Textbook Thinking (More
    Galileo) 386

Ongoingness

73. Illustration Of The Incubator............................. 389

74. The Shattered Mirror...................................... 394

BOOK CONCLUSION....................................... 397

EPILOGUE... 409

POSTSCRIPT.. 410

PUBLISHER'S WORD 412

RELATED PAPERS

FOREWORD

The following papers are the real meat of the book. They are independent of one another, each standing on its own like a single key on a piano. Each paper makes a specific point— among the thousands that might be of interest to a seeker— yet, every paper is related to a point (or points) in the preceding chapters, as well as to other related papers. Some of these relationships are obvious and immediate. Some are more indirect.

I consider these papers to be more powerful in their relationships to one another than by themselves. The entire book has been written with these *synergistic overtones* in mind, and they represent the means by which I have been able to communicate beyond the limits of intellectualism and its limiting words. The reader needs no special ability to make this synergism happen. It is automatic for all of us.

The Related Papers, like everything in the preceding chapters ("The Bones"), are taken from recent journals and correspondence, except when noted otherwise. While an effort has been made to dovetail and fit the bones into a progression similar to the progression by which one awakens to the subjective Truth, no such effort has been made with the Related Papers. They are arranged here in a nearly random order and may make very little sense if read before the preceding chapters have been read.

The earnest reader can see and feel something special through various combinations of papers and *his own experience.* The reader who becomes familiar with the material will find hundreds of enlightening relationships on his own. These insights become the reader's own immaculate Glimpses-beyond-the-limits-of-intellectualism. Such Glimpses constitute the *real* basis for learning and teaching.

Some papers together make powerful chords (overtones); others side by side make apparent discords—even contradictions. But the many messages of this book lie more in the harmonious overtones the reader will feel and know independently of the words, than in the information conveyed.

1

WHO IS HAN?

Dear Jack,

In answer to your question, "Who the hell is Han?"

The Han I write about is a mythical character representing one's own inner being, the Child. Han is the nearest one can come to his own self-discovery before consciously becoming that Self. Han is one's own pre-existing identity just before the Transfiguration at the top of the mountain of understanding, Da Shan. Han answers our questions. Han is the chief Angel among the world's tangible angels.

Han is not God and doesn't claim to be. Han even makes certain one doesn't ignorantly call the Son of God, God. Han is as close as one comes to his real Identity before consciously being that One. Yet, Han insists, that One isn't all there is to God. God is even more—existing within and beyond the limits of Awareness. Han says that Awareness is infinite, as God is infinite—but God-head exists even beyond infinity. Herein, Han and the Gnostics of old are in grand accord.

Han tells of the Three that are One and of the One who is three to infinity. Han is the balance between Godhead and Tangibility— the Logos. Han is I-Identity. Han is the Muse of my journal, and yours. Han is a good guy! O.K.?

2

TWO BASIC QUESTIONS ANSWERED

Laurel asked: "What do you mean by 'quantum mankind'?"

In these papers, by quantum mankind I mean ALL mankind. When we begin looking at the beehive as a single organism, that is the quantum view. When we start looking at all mankind as a single external organism, then we are looking at the appearance of quantum man in our own head.

Laurel also asked, ". . . and what do you mean by 'cosmology'?"

A cosmology is a creation story. Moses wrote a cosmology— the universe from Nothing—in the first chapter of Genesis. Particle physicists are examining a cosmology—something from Big Bang—as they work *back* to the beginning of matter some fifteen billion years ago. It is good to note this parallel when we are talking about retrogressive progression early in the book.

The mathematician intuits and *knows*, then the particle physicist looks into his accelerators to *confirm* the mathematician's logical knowing. Physics is a confirming activity. Math is designated the "pure science." Our individual intuitive knowing (which comes as glimpses of light) is the "pure science" and is confirmed in the tangible world as science's (and our own) discoveries. Do you see this? Now, our subjectivism allows us to lower the veil, *and we look out into the world for the confirmation of our knowing.* This is not unlike the physicist looking out to see technology following later to put his ideas to work for mankind—or, an inventor looking to see his invention manufactured. Our subjective glimpses of Truth are eventually confirmed on the objective scene.

Added thought: Cosmology explains half the metaphysical "reversal" inherent in the FIRST/LAST equation. Subjectivism, when understood, explains another part of the reversal, INSIDE/OUTSIDE. One doesn't yet really understand either of these equations until he considers them both—not necessarily simultaneously. While cosmology (and science) works on the first/last equation, heading back to Big Bang but not beyond it, the Child within brings us to consider the inside/outside *flow*— and its relationship to cosmology. When these (and the other balances) are brought together, it seems we get back "before" Big Bang, to the primal Self-Image. That is where these words are intended to take us (bring us).

HOW DOES AN OLD SOLDIER DARE TO WRITE A BOOK ABOUT THE TRUTH?

There is something incongruous about a man who fought as an infantry soldier in two wars, slashing his way from mortal combat and destruction to esoteric Self-discovery and Light, isn't there? Somehow it doesn't fit. Unless, of course, one makes the connection and intuits how human extremity leads to spiritual insight, how darkness makes the light plain and how guilt uncovers primordial guiltlessness. If one has heard of Arjuna's selection on the battlefield where the final struggle between light and darkness is waged, he might not wonder how I dare write this book.

This old soldier is presently engaged in his final struggle, warfare of the most primal kind for which he has been, not one bit less than a worthy candidate for a special Mystery, "duly, truly prepared." That preparation was not of myself but of Another. I have not made a single move that was not part of this moment as I sit here disclosing the lessons learned. Not a move to the right or left, not a word has come to me or gone out from me that was not part of a Plan, not of my own planning, but Another's. I have been carefully, painstakingly—most often against my will—brought to this moment in linear time to reveal a Mystery. As certainly as this is true for me, it is true for the reader as well.

One who reads these words has a right to question them. He should. Moreover, he should put them ·to the test, even those that seem most obviously true. I welcome your doubt. I've asked all who have studied with me over the years to question everything I talk about and believe nothing until it has been put to the test and found worthy. But reader, when Something begins stirring within you in the paragraphs and pages ahead—*an inner stirring that comes softly and unexpectedly, with unmistakable authority*—then you might be wise to touch and take note of the Idea you feel then, and note the Theme this book contains. I have been given these words to live, prove, confirm and make plain so those who read them may run.

Why me, an old soldier who has lived through the inhumanity of warfare? You will surely see one day. You will surely see.

3

THE SECRET OF THE SEED

When the seed first falls to ground, it contains its own final flowering within itself. Deep within, the seed "remembers" where it came from. It remembers the former plant and the flower that produced it. It remembers by way of an internal imprint of the original plant. One can actually see that imprint when he looks at the seed's internal structure with a powerful microscope. I am told this is literally the way it is with tree seed.

Well now, what has this to do with "secrets"? As the years go on and as the single' seed is broken down into its roots, branches and leaves, the seed's own internal secret is the knowledge that, at the end of its span in time, it will bloom and seed again. Individual man has essentially forgotten his own inmost secrets.

In civilization, there have always been those mystics who have known of the quantum human Seed's inner secret and its relationship to the beginning of time and space. These people, having found the beginning, have found the end as well. Their views of civilization seem remarkably similar—they speak of the society of mankind moving in the direction of his own quantum blossoming, thence to seed and finally rest. In every culture, the prophets have admonished the people to strive to be a conscious part of the seed which will be, most say, planted again in enigmatic time.

Listen carefully. One sees the title of an essay: *The Secret of The Seed*. He thinks the author is going to discuss some revelation that an examination of the seed will reveal to the reader. It doesn't seem to occur to most of us—or it didn't to me— that it is possible the author has written about a secret *the seed knows*, not one we will know when we examine the seed or read the essay. Such is the "secret" I have found and would disclose if I am given the subtle words to string.

One hears about a guru somewhere and thinks that teacher can reveal something wonderful to him. It hasn't occurred to him yet that *the guru is part of the consciousness observing the guru* and that the teacher "out there" may very well represent the external view of the viewer's own mystery within. "Ah so," as Han would say. Ah so. Could it be that this volume you are reading is not outside yourself, but is the expanding consciousness of the reader? Of course it is. The value is in the reading consciousness, not the book. But the book has its place in the world and is entitled to recognition and credit, if it is telling the Truth in new ways the reader can understand. We only slowly learn to give credit to our external views that point to our internal nature.

4

OLD CROAK AND THE HOUSE OF MIRRORS

A story of discontent and discernment.

Old Croak lived in a mill pond with ten thousand other frogs. Each night he sang in the chorus and their melody could be heard for miles.

Upon reaching manhood, Croak felt a disquiet grow within himself and he decided there was more to life than singing songs from lily pads. "This incessant peeping and croaking is driving me mad," he said. "What I need is quiet!" Bidding his friends goodbye one night, Croak made a gigantic leap into the darkness of Anywhere But Here.

As it happened, a carnival which had closed for the night was located in the field beside the pond. Croak's mighty leap carried him up and over the pond and through a small opening into the very center of the House of Mirrors. Not knowing where he had landed, Croak sat huddled in the inky darkness of the closed hall of mirrors, awaiting the morning light. Everything was silent and, strangely, Croak missed the chorus that evening.

"Croak," said Old Croak. His voice was louder than usual and it echoed weirdly. It was more resonant as well—but there was no reply. "That's funny," said Croak. He was alone in his silence, and for the first time, his disquiet included a sense of loneliness.

The next morning, Croak opened his eyes to find himself in the center of ten thousand frogs. His loneliness disappeared immediately.

"Aha!" he said. "You decided to follow me here. Why didn't you answer me last night when I croaked?"

Ten thousand mouths moved, but no sound came from any of them. Croak was puzzled.

"Why don't you answer me?" he asked. Ten thousand mouths moved, but there was still no answer. Croak frowned.

"What kind of silly game is this?" Ten thousand frogs frowned and moved their mouths, but there was only silence.

"Is this the kind of punishment I get for complaining about singing in the chorus every night?" he asked. Ten thousand mouths moved in silence. Croak stamped the floor in anger and threw himself into a double backward flip. Ten thousand angry frogs stamped the floor and threw themselves into double backward flips.

"What is this?" the surprised Croak wondered. "I thought I was the only one at the pond who could do a double backward flip," mumbled the humbled Croak. "They've been holding out on me," he said, sulking to the floor. Ten thousand frogs mumbled silently. Ten thousand frogs sulked to the floor.

As the days went by, Croak came to several conclusions—almost metaphysical conclusions. "I've gone deaf," he thought. "Somehow the mighty leap from the lily pad has damaged my hearing." Then, more seriously, in the way of a good thinker who thinks a lot, he thought, "I'm being punished by God or the other frogs. They are mocking every move I make." But after a few more days Croak's metaphysics turned deeper. He decided there was surely greater meaning behind the appearances than he first believed. "Aha," he croaked, "There is real metaphysical significance here! Definitely. Yes, definitely. In the first place, I notice that no one moves unless I move. That's a hint. If I hop a short distance, they hop a short distance. If I do a mighty backward double flip, they do precisely the same. It seems to me that what is being made plain here is that I am the power of this scene. Yes, yes. I am the power here. Everyone does what I do, yes. Now, there must be another step. Ah ha! Now I shall teach them to do what I SAY to do!"

"All right, you guys," said the reinvigorated Croak. "Enough of this togetherness stuff. I want to be alone; therefore, I want all of you to get the hell out of here!"

Ten thousand mouths moved, but that was all.

"O.K. Now," Croak began again, "all of you idiots pay attention to me. I am your teacher!" He had their attention. "Leave the room!" Croak ordered. Ten thousand mouths moved, but no one left the room.

"Well," thought Croak, "apparently I must lead the way and show them how to do what I say to do because I want them to do what I want them to do." He ordered them to leave the room again, and, this time, as he spoke, he jumped behind a piece of brickabrack on the floor. From behind the brickabrack, Croak could see only half the frogs in room. "Good!" he shouted. "Good! Half of you crazy croakers have left the room just as I ordered. All right now, guys, all of you that are out of the room, *stay* out, and all of you that are still in the room, leave the room like THIS." As he said this, Croak leaped from behind the brickabrack. Promptly, half the frogs jumped from Croak's view, but the other half jumped back into the room.

"Oh, come on, fellows! Come on, now!" Ten thousand frog mouths moved in insolent silence. "All right. Let's try that again," said Croak. But wherever he hopped and whatever he did, he could never get all the frogs to leave the room. At one point he leaped into a box and thought for a moment he was alone. Then, looking directly overhead, he saw ten thousand frogs peering down at him from identical boxes.

"Smart asses!" shouted Croak, leaping back into the center of the room, followed by ten thousand mocking frogs.

"I have learned to read lips and you jerks have just called me a smart ass," he moaned. "Oh, this is too much for me. I must be alone. I simply *must* get away from here!"

That night Croak sat on the floor sobbing silently. He thought of the old days when darkness was a time for singing and sunshine a time for playing. "In those days I wasn't leading the world of frogs, trying to make them do the things that were pleasing to me," he thought. "Oh my. The world does everything I do but nothing I tell it to do."

Then, in anguish he said, "I give up. I surrender. Whatever the Scheme of things in this world, it is too much for me to fathom." At that moment, through his tears, Croak beheld a shaft of moonlight streaking through a hole in the wall.

Without hesitation and with no thought whatever for the consequence, Croak mustered every ounce of strength he could find and leaped through the hole toward the moonlight above. It was a mighty, mighty leap. A backward, triple somersault, full gainer, double twist with a jackknife that put him over the House of Mirrors onto a lily pad in the middle of the pond. "Hallelujah!" thought the relieved frog.

The moonlight was very bright that night. Croak looked around and not one of the ten thousand frogs was in sight. "At last I am alone!" he rejoiced in delight—to be answered by ten thousand voices celebrating his return.

Croak was sort of glad. "They are saying what they want to say," he thought. "I'm not alone with myself anymore, or am I?"

Meanwhile, back at the house of mirrors, one mirror asked another, "Have you ever seen ten thousand frogs jump out of a room all at once, like that?"

"Goodness no," the other mirror answered. "They sure died in a hurry, didn't they?"

"They didn't die," said the first mirror. "They simply moved on to another plane of consciousness."

"Plane, schplane. What does that mean? They're dead and gone," said the corner mirror. "I saw them all leap into the fire at once."

"They're still alive," another mirror said. "Hold my hand and I'll contact them."

"Baloney. I tell you there are ten thousand dead frogs."

Overhead, the moon, hearing the argument among the mirrors, whispered in moon talk which is understandable only to mirrors, children and whoever sits in the moonlight, "There was no life in the images, my friends; therefore, life cannot leave the images. Isn't that so?"

The mirrors whispered, "Yes. That makes sense, yes, indeed." But they still didn't know there was only one frog.

On his lily pad in the pond, Old Croak heard the moon, too. He looked into the water beside his lily pad and saw the moon's reflection there. Suddenly he understood who the ten thousand frogs were. More importantly, he began to suspect who he was.

5

THE SECRET CONTAINS THREE SLOW STEPS

If someone were to come here today, and if by some marvel I could communicate so completely I could give him every Secret I knew, it would do him very little immediate good in the world. How so? Because he must first build the self-confidence that he is indeed what has been revealed to him. This happens for us precept upon precept, and it takes time in the world. When that confidence is established, he alone builds his credibility in his world—a credibility he has in hand before he can set out to do for his subjective world what he knows is finally necessary to do. I am certain this is why I was given mysteries forty years before I was told that "my time had come." It will not take so much time for those who come to me now.

THE ELEMENTS OF THE SECRET

Discovering the Child; living the Equation; subjectivism. These three constitute the living life of love.

When the Child is first discovered, one can barely believe what he has found. Then, when the Equation is disclosed, he ever so slowly gets the courage to live it. When the subjective idea finally and fully arrives and he learns that He is the Christ Itself to his own newly discovered subjective world, he is troubled mightily at the magnitude of the work; he stands in utter amazement at what he is called upon to do for everyone. But, with God's Grace, he persists—here a little, there a little.

It has been shown to me that the Child I have found is soon to be found by many more in this, my subjective world. Those who find It within themselves will strengthen one another as they communicate in love and encouragement, one to another.

They will give the necessary strength to those who have felt a measure of their findings. Then, as the Equation is lived, they will encourage others to live it also, bringing the world to bloom with a new community of Child-Children. They will have the seed of the Father within them.

A SPECIAL LETTER

There are three difficult stages for our breakout into Light:
1. It is difficult to recognize that the Child within is the same Child we were when we were child-children. That is, it seems unbelievable that the way we saw things as a six- or seven-year-old is the way we are actually capable of seeing things again, here and now, no matter what our human age, or that now we can go still further and see the infinite Original of Ourself! A necessary-for-a-time veil hangs before the eyes and the heart, which precludes the easy ability to think of the Child as anything but a fantasy, a dream of Pollyanna.
2. Equally slow and difficult is the understanding that the Child within us is the actual Christ Light of us. They are the same One and they are WE, I, Us, Identity.
3. The third area of personal difficulty comes in our moving from theory and mental speculation about the Child, to action here in the world. Understandable mountains of human intransigence and disbelief stand between our recognition within and the world outside. It is only line upon line that our actions in the world are recognized in the world. Then, one by one those around us begin to see the Child of us, and the Child of themselves. Bit by bit, here a little, there a little, our credibility grows, the wonders are seen and recognized. Finally, our entire subjective world (internal and external) responds!

Without the Child, first and foremost, the subjective view is nothing more than a personal attempt to manipulate the scene to one's advantage; without the Child, the equation can't be fully comprehended; without the Child, one is dead. Without the Child and the Child's Equation, science founders, without direction.

6

THE STARTING PLACE or IF GOD IS ALL, WHY DO I FEEL SO ROTTEN?

Dear Beth,

It is easy to pay lip service to the beautiful words of Truth while we go right on believing the lie and living it. How many of us have said, "Yes, God is the allness of all," while we continue like a weathervane, affected by every wind that blows? "God is all," we say, "and evil just a seeming"; then we cower and scrape before the "seeming" that frightens us. Does this sound familiar? Of course it does, to all of us.

The starting place is certainly the discernment that God actually IS all in all. This is the beginning for those who want to come out from the endless trials and tribulations of human experience. But this beginning leads nowhere until we act in accord with it. Appearances change when actions based upon them change. The fearful "seeming" must be faced at some point. It is powerless, and we stand up to it as powerless! We make the determination to do this and are girded by Angels from within and without. Then the nature of the threat changes; the sense of foreboding slips away, and we see it more clearly as the necessary learning experience it actually is, and was from the beginning.

This lesson is neither good nor bad. It transcends that division. It is neither a foreboding nor a beneficent reversal of the appearance, as metaphysics so often teaches. Reality is infinitely more than the intellectual divisions we make into real-unreal, spirit-matter, good-evil and the like.

But, Beth, this standing up isn't the end of our action either. We rejoice and give thanks, yes, but that is only the beginning. When we get through the difficulty, we don't return to the old routine with business as usual. There are more steps to take, more revelations to come, more strength to find—all leading us to really *discover* the Child within. Oh, great goodness, the Child shows us how to stand up to things! Yes, indeed.

The Child we are is most anxious to have us get to the top

of the mountain—and get there in more than metaphysical profession. The Child within takes us there in actual fact. There we see the whole Holy Scene and take up the subjective scepter.

There is no human situation we can get ourselves into that the Child can't show us the way out of. The Child of Light, like the photon, is everywhere on the mountain at once. That inmost Identity knows exactly what we need at the moment—and gives it to us with our help. What is our help? *The acknowledgement that the Child is still right here, right now, available to help us.*

Find the eternal Christ Child, Beth! You can. This is the first real step, and until one has done this, no matter how many years he has studied "the truth," he has done nothing toward assuming his rightful heritage and dominion.

7

CHILD EQUALS HEART EQUALS SOUL, THE OVERLOOKED SIMPLICITY

I have never talked heart to heart with a single person who hasn't admitted that the child was still there within him—struggling perhaps, or a distant dream from the past, but still there. All of us continue to dream dreams and wonder about soft things. The heart of us still goes leaping through the high places of imagination occasionally and soars with the high flying swallows to see the far side of the moon. That is the Child at work. Yes, the Child still lives.

Moreover, this inner one, the old/new Child of us, is healthy and well, absolutely all right in every way. None of Its enthusiasm has been dulled by the years. Its eyesight is as sharp as an eagle's, Its hearing keen as a puppy's, and all the feelings of youth are pounding with excitement exactly as they did when we were children-children, unencumbered by the world.

Much has been said about the "heart" of us. Great theological positions have been established around "the immortal soul." Reader, listen with that heart of yourself for a minute: *The little child of us, the heart of us and the soul of us are the*

Same One. Whatever we have come to perceive with the heart has been a recognition of that eternal Child within. And now, as I write of that One, I address the heart, the soul with which we are all concerned. Oh yes, the heart and soul of us—the Child—is still right here quite capable of confirming Itself, evidencing Itself and revitalizing our view of everything.

As the years pass and the world encroaches relentlessly, we lose sight of this Original Nature or Identity except as an old photograph or a memory etched somewhere in an inaccessible past. It comes as a surprise to hear that the Original Child and all Its feelings are still around; then it comes as a wonderment to learn first hand that they are not inaccessible at all, but still right here, closer than breathing, closer than fingers and toes.

THERE IS AN AGELESS MYSTERY IN OUR ABILITY TO FIND IDENTITY

As one reads these words about the Child, the heart knows this is the truth, a truth hidden all these years in simplicity and childlikeness that we have left behind. When we are alone, we still play the child's game. While we are walking or driving or puttering with the pots, there is some little something we do in the mind's eye exactly as we did as a child. There are ships and ports and storms at sea when we wash the dishes or take a bath. Don't tell me you don't know what I'm talking about. Deep inside, you do. You see, I am that child, too—the same Child—and I have *become* It again. I know, by God, by the grace of God, what I'm writing about here. And I know that the first step in feeling the joys of the Real (as we did as children) is to acknowledge that the Original Nature of us hasn't left us.

THE HISTORIC CHRIST AND THE CHILD

"Bill, are you saying that the early church substituted the historic Jesus for the Child?"

No. Churchdom has *limited* the Christ to the historic Jesus, and all of that has been done for a divine purpose the church seems to know little or nothing about. Everything that has happened is by God's grace. The historic Christ-in-linear-time came, as all luminaries, to confirm our own subjective Self-discovery. The historic Christ is the first begotten of the Father in world time, and the original believers had that straight. The discovery of the Child within is *confirmed* by the Bible and its accounts of the historic Christ and his role on earth. The Child I Am and You are "comes" to us as the second coming, as Messiah re-discovered within, for whom the Bible and Jesus are the first or external confirmation.

"Are you saying that the Child is the Christ also?"

Yes! Yes! Exactly that. "Closer than breathing." Exactly as the historic Christ said, He would never leave us nor forsake us. He has been here as the Child of us from the beginning. Our very Child-Selfhood—which seems to go away from us and returns to us, rediscovered.

"William, tell me if this is what I've heard you saying these past few days: the Child within is the *same* historic Christ?"

Yes. History, like all other things, is subjective. To rediscover the Child is to find what Jesus found, lived and confirmed before he began his ministry. When the historic Christ said he would be back again, he meant that each one who understood what he was saying would find the Child within and recognize THAT Self HIMSELF as the Messiah written in the heart, the "second coming," in actual fact.

"Are you also saying that when I was a child on earth, I was that Christ-Child?"

Yes, spiritually. And I'm saying that everyone can prove the truth of this for himself by finding that all the acute feelings of the Original Nature which were present in us as children are capable of returning to us again.

"You know theology isn't going to agree with that, William?"

Perhaps neither theology nor the subjective groups, but all who feel the Child within themselves will agree, because they will KNOW it is the Truth, having proven it for themselves. And when the theologians begin to perceive that this is indeed what is meant by the New Covenant "written in the heart," they will slowly, grudgingly give way, even those powerful conservatives so intent on going back to Biblical literalism. Not without argument. Not without doubt. Not without questioning those who have found the Child of themselves, and not without

persecuting them mightily. Not everyone will be taken up in
this Light. Jesus foresaw it accurately: Two are in the bed and
one is taken; two are in the field and . . . five are in the household, two against three and three against two; father against
son. Those without consciousness of the Child will not know
which of the senses to believe, nor who in the world is telling
the truth. Those who have found the Child within won't care
what the theologians or philosophers think. We leap through
Spirit's door and leave the flaming house behind.

8

THE PROGRESSION OF AWAKENING

The progression goes a little like this: One searches and
thinks he has found—and grows arrogant in that finding for
a long time, thence to be humbled.

Then, he finds again and *really* knows.

One lives this discovery and proves it.

One keeps going onward and finds the relationships between himself and the outside. Many people never reach this
point because no one has told them or convinced them there
is a relationship between the inside and the quantum outside
or that these two are a single one.

One perceives the wholeness of outside because he has
found it for himself.

One perceives the relationships between himself inside, and
the appearances outside, in their increasing detail. This has
been called the web of interrelatedness. A leaf falls to the
earth and the universe is shaken.

One comes slowly to know the marvel that will unfold outside from what has already unfolded within himself—and he
lives in continuing *expectancy* of this unfolding in the world.

One speaks to his world as seems best.

All along this progression, one is faithful to those who have
been given to him. He tells them to go and do the same and
instruct their given to do the same.

We, and those who have been given to us, become the New

Community, the flower of the tree of life. The Community grows.

This progression happens in linear time, "line upon line, precept upon precept, here a little, there a little."

It appears I have been kept in the middle of the River of Life from the beginning, but only after all these years have I learned my relationship to the world and its relationship to me. I have known what will "happen" in time because it has already happened here as I-Identity in those glimpses of timelessness. It is the same for Everyman. Everyman becomes the flower and the flower's seed. The seed survives.

9

LETTER TO A FINDER

Dear Jenna,

IT has found You.
IT has found Itself within You.
IT is yourSelf that has found You.
No man—not me, not anybody—can take credit for IT nor for That. YOU are worthy of It or It would have never taken place in your heart. You are a credit to IT or you would have no consciousness of Its presence.

What did you do? I do not know precisely, but you are childlike, trusting, humble, open, gentle, caring and altogether loving within yourself—and you love. Those are Its Qualities and Attributes. Once It has come, It never leaves us nor forsakes us unless we lose those qualities to pride or selfishness or arrogance or, like Moses, try to take credit for It.

The Secret has found you. It is GENUINE. It is REAL, but the unenlightened know nothing of It and would profane and destroy It if they could.

Don't you worry about whether or not you can handle ANY sit-

uation. IT, the Child of Yourself, and God will take care of every circumstance the human of you ever finds itself in.

It is Its own proof. Nothing can speak for It, except to praise It and herald It and declare the fact that It is.

The Child of You and the Child of Everyman who makes himself worthy of IT is the same Child. We look for the REAL in everyone even if it doesn't seem present there. We stand as solitaries in a world awash with illusion and falsity. Not everyone who says "Truth, Truth, Lord, Lord" is alive, though they seem to be worshipped and praised and become leaders of many. Many who appear to be ahead of us are behind us. Spiritual pride puts us behind those whom we think we are ahead of. Therefore, we treat everyone equally, even though many do not appreciate that nor turn to thank us—but condemn us and say that IT never happened!

You have come alive in It because It is alive in You. I am full of delight because of your Self-discovery and I love you very much—but don't give me credit that is due yourSelf and God.

It is a marvel of marvels, isn't It?

I suspect you will have the joy of being Its minister to many. With IT you can do anything good that is given to you to do for It. Watch and see!

It gets better
and closer
and more wonderful yet.
It doesn't diminish!

I thank you for your honest trust. What is Grace? YOU are.

10

THE ME-SENSE AND THE INTELLECT

I have learned that one cannot toss the intellect out the window—as so often seems the case when one first discovers the heart of himself, or metaphysics. *The intellect is NOT "the old man to be put off."* The intellect is that part of Awareness that deals with tangibility, the images of perception, the images of people, places and things which appear within/as Awareness.

The intellectual nature of us has to do with reading, writing and arithmetic—and how to cross the road without being hit by a bus. Now that I've had a chance to examine things more, I have not found anyone in all of human history who has done more than subdue the intellect and its view of things. *The ego is something else*—and the ego, like the intellect, is to be understood.

Before we found the Heart, we gave all power and authority to the intellect. With the discovery of the Heart, we tried in vain to banish the intellect, to no lasting avail. But the struggle was good and necessary, because it gave us practice in listening to the Heart. Now, we are Heart-led, and intellect-wary, making sure the intellectual evidences are seen in their application to tangibility and as the confirmation of the Heart's declarations. There is a precise balance between the heart and the intellect—inside and outside.

In Metadelphia, we hear that this is to worship two masters. Not so. The heart and intellect are "a two that are one." Just as the line and the plane are two dimensions of a greater *single* sphere, so are the heart and intellect two dimensions of Something Greater—Godhead. And just as the plane is greater than the line, so is the Heart greater than the intellect. Just as the line doesn't "understand" the plane, but the plane certainly understands the line, exactly so, the heart knows all about the intellect which knows little or nothing of the heart.

Is this clear thus far? (Remember, we haven't gotten to the old man yet. The ego, the old man, the me-sense is, like the serpent, more subtle than the intellect! We knew it had to be—especially when every attempt to get rid of it ended in failure. In my study with others, we have been diligently careful to point out exactly what "mortal mind," ego, me-sense, the old man, pretends to be.) Hence, we *subdue* the intellect, but we don't try to destroy it either in the world or within ourselves. Our most fervid anti-organizational and anti-social tendencies are present during this inner battle as we come to understand this point. Eventually we awaken to a BALANCE between heart and intellect, wherein the heart is greater.

Dear friend, in my living I have found an inner guide that I can faithfully depend on. This seems a good time to remind you of it. We are prone to overanalysis and overstudy! The intellect of us loves to study and ponder enigmas. It will make a mystery of something that is perfectly clear to the heart. So, in all things, keep to simplicity! Wherever intellectual knowledge leads to something the heart already knows, they touch at a point of utter simplicity! Therefore, I implore you to keep the Truth simple. It IS simple. It is too obvious for words like these.

"What about the me-sense?" someone asks. The me-sense, the ego, the old man, the deceiver is a *superimposition* over the heart and intellect. The me-sense says, "This is MY awareness." In truth, there is no such me to say "my." But we have all believed in this big me who says "My life, my awareness, my view of things!" As the Bible declares, there is not one of us who doesn't *seem* guilty of this. This is not a guilt, but a necessary part of ongoingness and Self-discovery. We struggle with ego in order to comprehend the nature of egolessness, God.

The me-sense is a fiction and we disavow it as quickly as we can. How? By the recognition of its very good service in our behalf. God knew what He was doing! The me-sense is the *delineation* of the Divine Identity. It is the shadow of the tree that leads straightaway to the tree. We understand the purpose ego serves and *forgive* it! Thence to need it no longer.

11

EGO

"I don't have enough faith and I don't have enough understanding," Ho said.

"Of course, you don't," Han answered. "You never have had and never *will* have. God is the faithful one! God. Not man. *And God has total faith in Himself; total trust and understanding of Himself!* God is the faithful, trusting and understanding one. God, not man!

"But what about ME? Who am I?" Ho asked.

"Our Identity is life," Han answered slowly and patiently. "The very life that asks that question is divine life, God-life.

Life is Awareness. Life is witnessing, seeing, beholding. We are the *seeing* of God, but God is the faithful one, the trusting and knowing one. We have naught to do but be the faithful witness of GOOD. We are the Good beholding Itself everywhere, because the life we are is the life divine."

"Then what is this me-sense that I superimpose and call my identity?" asked Ho.

"That is the deception, the fraud, the fatherless bastard, the liar from the beginning. Right here, right now, we are God's Self-awareness, the Awareness of GOD. The superimposition of the me-sense is nothing claiming to be something most persistently. Furthermore, this is exactly how it is supposed to be for a time (delineating Timelessness) until we emerge from the enshrouding cocoon."

"How so?"

"The me-sense is the delineation of the Divine Identity; the ego is the delineation of the egoless I. How would I know the 'real' without facing the 'false' and seeing beyond it? Could I know what light is without having stumbled in darkness? Would I know what health *is* without having known discomfort or disease? But, listen, listen, friend Ho, the Light is Real, the delineating darkness merely *degrees* between right/wrong, good/evil, inside/outside, above/below, male/female and all the rest of the delineating distinctions that obversely outline the ALL ONE."

Author's journal entry:

AWARENESS doesn't have faith; it IS faith—God's faith—in the very action of happening. Awareness doesn't have trust; it IS trust, in the act of trusting. Awareness doesn't have understanding, GOD has Self-knowledge and this awareness is that Self-knowledge HAPPENING! As Awareness, I look, I behold, I see, I rejoice, I laugh and I joy! As Awareness I do not have to understand; I do not have to have trust or to trust something else. God does that, and I am that doing happening effortlessly, here and now. Those who are ready for this move to childlikeness and simplicity are indeed ready. Those who need more of Timelessness's time to incubate will understand little that is written here. Oh, but the receptive heart will hear the Hallelujah Chorus. The Child will

hear and understand, rejoice and ACT in accordance. No more
linear time is necessary for that. The Child isn't bound by the
world's time.

12

ON HAVING SUFFICIENT FAITH

To humankind, the ultimate meaning of faith is one's total
belief in God. Men are continually wondering if they have
enough faith. The one who has recognized the subjective idea
that God is One and All, and is willing to believe that, is called
on to perceive and live quite another meaning of faith. He
perceives that since God is all in all, *there is no separate identity*
to have faith or not have faith. He sees that there is no way for
a fiction to have real faith and understanding *at all.* God is the
one who has faith in Himself, Godhead—and there is no other
faith in all the universe.

Listen: The human achiever doesn't exist in real fact. He is
a mortal myth, like "flat earth." He is the "old man" to be
understood and put off. We do not have to identify as that
one, albeit we all do until we feel something within the heart
of us whispering a song of ongoingness and newness. God
really is all in all. God's faith in Himself is sufficient for everything. It is a rare privilege to comprehend and affirm this. It
removes an awful load of human guilt from us. We are able to
end the worry about whether or not we have enough understanding or enough faith! We know we have enough because
we are God's own Self-awareness *confidently seeing God's good*
everywhere!

"But Samuel, this doesn't get down to the nuts and bolts of
the human experience. How can I take such flowery idealism
and do anything practical with it here in the real world?" Does
this sound familiar? It's a good question. We have all asked it
and it deserves a clear answer. You will see that this is a question we re-ask ourselves throughout our experience, and we
are each called to answer it again and again—from all points

of the compass until the little whisper of subjective comprehension occurs.

Somewhere along the line we look around and see that man
has *never* had enough faith or understanding. Even the greatest men are eulogized as people of *great* faith but never
enough faith, else they would have solved all the world's problems and perhaps still be here. But God has enough faith to
create the earth, the solar system, the galaxy and the whole
blinking, sparkling universe, plus this very life we are here
and now, the same life the reader is this instant.

Listen gently. This awareness-we-are is God's life. Awareness
is in the perceiving business, isn't it? We are constantly perceiving thoughts, ideas, images, things and situations to infinity. Who is doing the perceiving? God is. Not "you" or "me" or
anyone else. Oh my friends, Mary, John, Jack and all, we are
the living Mind of God—and have always been. God has sufficient faith in this Awareness else there would be no awareness. But it is *God who is faithful and knowledgeable and full of
grace. It is God who has understanding.* Do you see the gentle
wonder of this? You can, you can. Be still. Be kind to yourself.
Sit easy. Turn within and ask the Child-heart of yourself
whether or not there is merit in these words.

13

AUNT NELLY

Aunt Nelly introduced my family to metaphysics. She was a
wonderful lady with a great sense of humor and a terrible
temper. We remember her most for her insistence that everything, absolutely everything, was unreal. She was also famous
for reversing everything and getting the parts of the body
mixed up, calling her elbow a knee, her finger a toe and so
forth. Her most memorable mix-up came in answer to my
question as a little boy, "How come you're so smart, Aunt
Nelly?" She smiled sweetly, tapped her temple several times
with a long finger and said, "Kidneys, my boy. God didn't give
me these kidneys for nothing."

Aunt Nelly was also very good about giving everyone instruction on anything and everything and using big words to do it, like "supposititiously" and "instantaneously." "You mustn't say anyone died," she told everyone who would listen. "You say they have *passed on*," each word to be said with the same emphasis, "because death is supposititious, you see?" Her own passing into that supposititiousness happened as she was looking for a favorite passage in her "beloved textbook" and walked in front of a streetcar. Aunt Nelly and the streetcar were derailed simultaneously and instantaneously.

"The first inclination is to tell everyone of the Truth we have found," said Han. "But let our first inclination be to live it. Then, after we've lived it for an honest week or two, we'll know better how to talk about it."

"I agree, old man," said Ding. "Too much talking means not enough doing. I had better get home and hide the wine from my husband."

14

LETTER TO ELAINE OVERTONE

Dear Elaine,

My goodness, I shook your confidence in me, didn't I? That's good. The True Teacher is inside yourself at your very center. The honest teacher in the world tells you that in the most graphic, simple, feelable way possible—as quickly as circumstances permit.

Listen gently, Elaine: "Letter 2" led you straight to the ego that you might feel the nastiness of that nearly eternal clump of necessary ugliness. Now that you know the part of yourself that felt offended, hurt, anguished, you know what to come out and be separate from. All that reacted, that felt hurt, that wrote twenty-five pages to defend itself and explain its position is the NOT-YOU, NOT-I, the fatherless bastard without root that grows outside the Garden. *That is what we stop associating with. That is what binds us to more and ever more of the same.*

Elaine, you can try until hell freezes over, but you will never lift that one up to comprehension. You will never heal it or justify it. Its purpose is to lead You to You—thence, to dominion and peace. It has done that now. Now you can thank God, thank it and have done with it! Now you can "have to do" with God instead of your old nature.

You write, "Letter 1 was supportive." Of what? That intellectual bag of opinions you are trying to lift up to God in some sort of saintly offering? No. I support your Self-discovery. That discovery isn't made by the intellectual thinker, but the thinker loosed and let go. We finally, somewhere along the long line of birth and rebirth, surrender the attempt to be the Thinker to let the Thinker be the thinker. And "we" become the THINKING of the Thinker in wonder and awe.

Letter 2, allowed you to feel the greedy grasper, the shadow identity, the one who is offended, the one who tries to understand, the one who is hurt and who hurts others and who thunders and wonders about the evil in the world, ignoring the Wonder who is BEING the world. I was introduced to Myself in most anguishing, painful ways. *You do not have to suffer as I did,* but you seem hell-bent to do it anyway. Out of old habit, I suppose, just like the soldier me.

Now that you have met the nasty one, what will you do? Nurse her back to health or let her go?

How does one do that? In emptiness and helplessness, asking God's help and confidently expecting it because that help will be coming shortly.

Elaine, there is no Way short of making the sharp turn around, from self to Self. You have found an external revelator who tells you of the final Revelator within—but you question his integrity, his patience, his ability, his View and his authority and have no real knowledge of the anguish that permits these words to be written to you. If you can't trust one who has touched down on the Heart of yourself, someone you can see and touch, how will you trust the One in whom you Live and move and have your being, whom you CAN'T see?

As the young people say, the ball is in your court now.

P.S. There is much you can do for the world in the turmoil ahead. You can tell of the World that underlies and is intermingled with appearances. But one can't tell about the Wonder that is here until he has found it—and one doesn't find it until he looks for it. If the shadow world didn't apparently exist, one would never know the Real. It's really quite a wonderful Plan, Elaine, with nothing "cruel, insensitive and horrible" about it. An enormous LOVE is in action here. Anything that awakens the sleeper is painful *to the sleeper*. Yet sleep is the means by which I know God's wakefulness and onlyness.

Enclosed is a paper from an old journal that will be helpful.

ABOUT FEELING GOOD

There is a genuine relationship between seeing "good" and feeling "good." Who can deny that certain sights bring good feelings with them? Or that certain feelings permit the scene at hand to disclose beauty and wonderment that might not have been seen otherwise?

But there is something deeper than that. Behind good and its dualistic partner, evil, is the greater Good, their basis in being. Exactly so, behind feeling good and feeling bad is a transcendent grandness, which I don't know what to call but Love. Not love as opposed to hate, but the Source for the dualistic pair, love and hate. It is a superlative feeling that, when I am aware of it, elicits the repeated remark, "I feel so good I can hardly stand it!"

What is occurring here to be written is along this line: One can't make a separation between seeing good and feeling good, yet that separation happens in our daily affairs all the time. One sees something "good" first, and then begins to feel good about it. Or, one can anticipate Christmas like a child, and then, later in time, see the events of Christmas day.

When I look to SEE good, am I not also looking to FEEL good? Yes. That's one of the primary reasons for the search for God—in order to feel better and have a happier human experience.

And, when I anticipate good, isn't it for the same reason? Essentially yes—but I have perhaps rationalized other reasons, too. I would like to think I look for good because God is the substance of every sight, and to see the good in something is to see the God there. Likewise, the anticipation in time is the only means of acknowledging the ALREADYNESS of God-head. So, I look and anticipate, hoping to feel the superlative Love/Good beyond reason and logic.

There is no gainsaying, I have been feeling the power and authority of Something quite beyond the ordinary. What is coming into print here is the tangible, printed connection between SEEING and FEELING, the two that are ONE. What is it that so seems to separate them on the tangible scene? The passions are the things that self-evidently prevent one from seeing good. Who can see the happy cup of coffee while he's fretting over the automobile accident? Who can see anything good when looking through the eyes of greed, jealousy or envy? If one cannot SEE good in things or events during those angry, passionate moments, how can he be expected to FEEL good then? He can't.

If one denies himself the opportunity to see the cup of coffee that's right in front of himself, can he be expected to see the superlative Good BEING the cup of coffee? Clearly no, the answer seems certain. And if one seems denied the opportunity to feel simple human good feelings, can he be expected to feel the Superlative Love/Good behind Everything? It seems not again.

But God is good; His mercy is everlasting; His blessings are denied NO ONE. The peace "that passeth understanding" can happen at any time. It can break right through—and with the Child, IT DOES! This is a mystery.

15

BRONZE, SILVER, GOLD—AND DIAMOND!

Important things are frequently left unwritten. Who but a poet knows the near impossibility of capturing the evanescences of feeling and thought? Where is an enlightened soul who doesn't decry his inability to tell of light? But they try. They keep trying even though some things seem beyond anyone's ability to express in words. It is as if the visionaries of the world gird up their loins and shout at the whirlwind, knowing only God knows what they are shouting about.

I'm no better. Something happened recently and I'd have the whole world know it if there were a way to tell it. Ah, but there is a way. Subjectivism tells me that my world exists right here as my own consciousness of things. That being so, I sit right down and write myself a letter outlining this recent happening—an inner event—from which everyone-I-am can take courage. The nebulousness of words be damned. I shall speak to myself and understand.

Sounds of the Japanese national anthem filled the huge gymnasium and the television camera focused on the victor. His face was wreathed in smiles and his eyes were full of tears. A young man from Japan had won the individual gold medal event in gymnastics. An American had taken second place and he stood there also, a silver medallion around his neck, a smile of pride on his flushed and happy face. The third man, from China, wore the bronze. The three men stood motionless, their faces lifted toward the rising flags of their countries, the strains of the Japanese anthem bathing the world in a tingle of appreciation for rewards so vigorously fought for and earned.

Rachel and I had pulled for the Americans, of course, eager to have the United States win this honor for the first time. As the action proceeded, however, and we saw the unbelievable intensity the Orientals were bringing to the competition, our allegiances began to shift. I wanted China to do well. This was their strong event. But the Japanese had won nothing yet and their young man was giving his all, beyond anything one could imagine. Very soon Rachel and I were pulling for the determined men from the East. The competition was close. A few thousandths of a point separated the leaders.

As it turned out, the man from Japan man won the gold by

the merest fraction of a point. Rachel and I yelled as if he were our son. We shouted and clapped when the Chinese man won the bronze. It was the perfect ending, turning out in a finale as beautiful as anyone could have planned. Japan, the United States and China—in that order.

The Japanese victor stood choking back the tears and so did we. I'm sure I listened to his national anthem as closely as he did. My heart went out to the Chinese victor as well, knowing what long years of preparation had gone into the bronze medal that rested on his chest.

Then it happened. A strange, mystical thing just for me, just for me. Somewhere along the line of listening to the soulful music and watching the smiling winners standing tall in front of their flags, I was thunderstruck by a confirming thought. Thunderstruck.

That isn't too strong a word to use for this occasion. Nor is it the hyperbole of an old writer trying to dramatize an event. To be so jolted and awed at the same time by a sudden realization of something hidden deeply in the heart of me has happened rarely in these years of my life. It isn't likely I can fully explain the "realization," but I'm damned well determined to try. A poor mention is better than none.

But who will understand? *Really* understand? One would have had to live my life
and experience my experiences
and suffer the intensity of them,
and feel them clear through to the bloody bone
in all the anguish of the many years of anguish
in the torment of those experiences
before one could fully understand.

There are a few old soldiers out there who will have a gut feeling about some of this—men who had to fight their way through two miserable wars,
one against the Japanese
and another against the Chinese.
They may have an inkling if they came out of those wars, their insides battered and broken and trembling.

But, unless they had lived in China for a part of their lives
and had grown to love those beautiful people
and fight *with* them as a soldier

—FIGHT to the death with them—
against the proud men of Japan,
only to have turned around to war *against* those same Chinese
troops in the jagged mountains of Korea,
then come home to an insensate world that didn't, and still
doesn't, see the perpetual raw tenderness of spirit that stays
with some men like an unending dream,
only then could they have an inkling of what I suddenly awakened to feel
and realize
deep in the heart of myself
that night as I watched the Olympic ceremony.

Neither the war against Japan nor China was easy for me.
Warfare isn't easy for anyone, let alone an infantryman, but
Korea was especially hard. For five years, China or Japan was
my enemy to death, in actual linear fact. I tried to kill them.
They tried to kill me. Dear God, I can't believe myself capable
of such murderous intent now.
Yet, those five long years were the least of it.
Nearly half a century later, the deep memory of me is still raw
and tired to death of the lessons of those days.

It wasn't until the Olympic ceremony was nearly over that I
noticed the red rising sun on the Japanese flag and remembered that Japan had been my blood enemy once upon a time.
I had watched the entire event without a single thought of
those ancient animosities! And there was China, too, old friend
and old enemy, and I had to bring it to mind to recall we were
once sworn to destroy one another.

What can't be said here, or well understood, was (and still
is) the sudden, grand and nearly unbearable joy of *RELIEF
and* inner peace when I *remembered*
and then, having remembered, realized that my heart had forgiven, forgotten and *moved on!*

That is, when I remembered, (this *sounds* so petty and . . .)
I was STILL glad to the core of me that the young man from
Japan had won. When I remembered, I was still glad the
Chinese athlete had won. When I remembered, I was happy
beyond belief to see the three nations standing together in the
friendship and pride of accomplishment represented by those
young men. They were the epitome of all I had fought for and

hoped to accomplish those long years ago in the mountains of China and Korea—nations now standing together in peace—and the United States still guaranteeing freedom to its citizens.

You see, I had watched this event for the hours it had been on television—and the days before that—*without a single thought of yore.* Without one thought about the scarred soul and the weight of anguish so many old soldiers carry with them to their graves. Clearly I had *really* ended the old hatreds and forgiven my old enemies. Forgiving them, I had forgiven myself—and everyone. I had *put down* the weight of an old soldier's inner torment and moved on.

THAT'S what was awesome and thunderous to me. It was proven to me in the twinkling of an eye that I *wasn't* living the old prejudices. It was *proven* to me I had forgiven and been forgiven. More, I know that if I can do such a thing, anyone who wants to can do the same.

Oh, who can know what this means to a person whose scars are invisible to others? Allowed to see that I had honestly and certainly forgiven myself, I look down to see a medal on *my* chest, by God! It's diamond!

How many men can be so privileged? Thank you, Father of Light. In afterthought one wonders if Life metes such experiences just to let us know we're on course. Yes! Yes!

16

SURRENDER

From somewhere, we come to the place of willingness to surrender everything, even our concepts of God. Concepts are not good enough in the presence of Godhead. *Willingness* to disconnect ourselves from the comfort of the status quo and move on into the mainstream of Godhead has required, for me at least, the surrender—or the willingness to surrender—*everything* but the tangible form of life itself—and I am willing to let that go, too, because it will go in time whether I am willing or not. Somehow, I was brought to stand before an interminable void, an empty and meaningless thing in my selfness, and in those days of wretchedness—not even longing for God anymore, but only for His Peace—there came the Child within to take my hand and make me into Him. Blessed One who made Me into His image and likeness! Such love He is; and we are that.

Let me be very clear here. *I do not believe everyone must be brought to such a state of helplessness before he can perceive the Child within himself.* One can hear or read honest words about the Child by those who have rediscoverd IT for themselves— and put those words to the test for himself to find them true (or not true, in the case of pretenders)—without the anguish that was necessary for me. As it was for Abraham, a *willingness* to surrender everything is requisite.

17

A JOURNAL ENTRY ABOUT SUFFERING

The letter from the little practitioner keeps coming to mind. She is convinced that a knowledge of Truth keeps the rocks of adversity from one's pathway. She is absolutely unwilling to believe that Truth often takes one to the very difficulty that teaches one most. "Absurd!" she writes in her letter.

Spiritual growth certainly makes one's affairs easier to handle. No argument there. Spiritual growth keeps one out of many difficulties he might experience otherwise. No question there, either. The study of Truth helps keep our feet from straying, certainly, certainly—but there comes a day for every student of Truth when he finds himself with one situation or another for which his vaunted knowledge doesn't help him as he thinks it should. This is a humbling time for the mighty metaphysician's role we play. "Where is my Truth now?" we wonder then. Everyone who persists in learning the Truth is brought to this humility—correctly. The little lady will get there, too, just as I did. Everyone who persists does, and "is troubled," exactly as Jesus said—even if it is the moment in time when one lets go the body of belief. The cicada struggles to emerge. The butterfly bursts through the maze of his own making. Many students of Truth wonder at this.

Question: Does one have to suffer in order to learn?

Answer: No more than the discipline of the human experience demands. But one suffers additionally to whatever extent he insists that he is not "in Truth" already "the son of God" or must suffer in order to "become" the son of God. The Child of us is already atop the Mountain. That one takes this tangible form through time and space, confirming our Dominion atop Da Shan. Anguish puts us consciously back to the Center of Being, atop Da Shan. We never actually get away from the center and circumference where God put us—but I have been unmindful of that for much of my temporal experience, and that unmindfulness was the cause of my suffering.

18

ABOUT SUFFERING AND DEATH

Winter comes with a rush this year. From summer to winter without a fall at all. Freshly cut hickory and oak are all set to burn in Ben, the Franklin stove, tonight. The water pipes have been wrapped. Sam and Sally have their doses of anti-freeze. If it gets really cold, I may try a little anti-freeze myself.

Dear Loretta, it is the *human* sense of things that moves in circles and seasons. It is the human sense of things that watches the cycles of human existence from birth to death, from joy one moment, to suffering and anguish the next. And it is the human sense of things that insists on understanding the why, why, why of suffering, anguish and death.

Once a man came here from England and wanted me to talk about my personal suffering—apparently to better understand his own. I refused, asking him why I should tell of my suffering rather than the Light I had come to discover. "Why not talk about the positive side of the coin rather than the negative? Why not tell of what is delineated rather than the delineator?" He left unsatisfied and angry. Were he to ask me about suffering today, I would do my best to answer, albeit I'm not certain I could say much that makes sense to the human sense of us, or to our vaunted "understanding."

To this tangible human viewing, I have suffered as much as anyone. Perhaps more. It is only the human viewing that believes "enlightenment" does away with tangible anguish and suffering. There is the common belief among metaphysicians that since the Truth "heals," the advent of enlightenment must surely bring an end to suffering—even an end to death. But in the human scene, the enlightened do not suffer less, but often more. Jesus cried in anguish, asking God why He had forsaken him. His disciples, with the exception of John, suffered all the way to their own executions. Paul carried his "tormentor" with him to his appearance of death. Mrs. Eddy suffered on and ON. Aiken suffered on. Goldsmith suffered on. Watts, De-Waters, Laird. None of their enlightenment prevented the appearances, within tangibility, of bodily decline and death.

The human sense of "me" (the fiction, the belief) has had an awful (to human sense) "tormentor" most of my life. But does burning the sheet of music do anything to the *principle* of music? Does the torment we dream do anything to the dreamer on the bed except eventually awaken him?

So we find reference to pain and suffering in K's journal—again and again. But he, as I, speaks about a state of mind that is beyond feeling and thought, about meditation that is explosive in nature and sometimes accompanied by physical pain.

For me, the viewing of suffering out there with others has been my external *delineation* of Joy "here as I"— the feeling of anguish and suffering "here, as 'myself' " is the delineator of Joy supernal . . . accepted on faith alone, internally. Oh, this doesn't say it at all!

Loretta, do the flowers and grasses suffer when the first frost hits them? Do the insects that perish suffer when winter descends as it inevitably does? Do they really suffer death from the cold? Or is it like a circle, a cycle, that renews itself with the spring that is also inevitable? Holistically speaking, the grasses, the flowers, the bugs come back when the cycle turns warm again—and "death" is only a resting in time and its seasons. Holistically speaking, there is no end of human or personal life even though there appears to be a suffering decline unto death to our tangible viewing. But our tangible viewing is the action of Awareness, of Life itself, which sees the seasons repeat themselves in an endless flow of seasons, called "Eternity." How do I know this is so? Because I see the cycles repeat themselves and I see the seasons return.

When I finally heard and felt and saw the Symphony for which this physical body is the sheet of music, I became the Symphony, no longer limited as the printed page. But, listen, listen, to hear and feel the Symphony is only to *accept it on faith alone!* We merely accept the *existence* of the Symphony for which all tangibility is the sheet of music. That is all. It takes the sting from death and allows us to understand the "why" of tangibility's suffering. It says that suffering, here or there, is like the dark night that makes Light plain. The Light is real. The darkness only a seeming. Joy is real, the suffering only a seeming—albeit seeming very real. When we begin thinking holistically (solipsistically or subjectively), we stop believing ourselves to be mere leaves on the tree and begin thinking in terms of tree. The leaf falls off the tree, so what? The Tree lives. This body grows old and perishes, so what? LIFE goes right on, untouched. Life is individual, alone, all in all. It only appears divided into billions of people and countless forms of life . . . in the same way a single light appears divided into many colors when it flows through a prism.

The REAL of Bill, Loretta, Rachel and Paul is NOT suffering unto death. The real of us is LIFE, GOD-Life—and it is single, only and all. Paul and Bill may seem to suffer and decline—but that seeming, seen holistically, is not real and has no power. The seeming is an "is-not" making the IS of Reality plain to Awareness—just as darkness makes the Light plain. The Light is REAL, darkness its means of being understood.

Loretta, like you, I grow tired of words and their limitations. I am weary of trying to explain things that are purely HEART-felt and have to do with simple faith beyond thoughts and feelings. This is why I publish so little now. The overtones have said it all already, as nearly as it can be said in words.

19

SIMPLE SCENE, ORDINARY LITTLE PLACE
Journal Entry

A lady called. There was panic in her voice and she was suffering mightily. I told her what I could. She quieted. "Think back to one of your Glimpses," I told her, "and really think about it. Remember some of the events."

In a bit, I went out to get a box of tea for Rachel. It was a cool winter evening and I stopped at a little roadside restaurant to get a hamburger. I was thinking of the lady in anguish.

As I sat there eating my double beef with lettuce, tomatoes, extra mayonnaise and onions, I was suddenly, gently overcome with the joy. I looked at the ordinary little place and it had become extraordinary. The windows sparkled. The greenery was especially green, and the healthy plants hanging from giant baskets, all but conversed with one another. The little people who waited on me were accommodating. Clean, smiling, enthusiastic. I sat alone at a small table near eight or ten others in the dining room. Everyone was bright and beautiful. Soft Christmas music filled the dining room and I heard myself singing "Santa Claus is coming to town" as I went for extra catsup. The carpet was clean as a pin, the tables sparkled, a sweet-faced lady busied herself wiping them. The good taste of the designer was apparent in the subdued lighting and bright colors of the Tiffany lamps overhanging the tables. I have bumped my head on them more than once over the years. I sat there with my hamburger and felt extraordinarily HAPPY. Just plain happy and full of gratitude that my affairs still let me look on a simple scene, seeing and being all the scene was intended to be—a happy place for strangers to get something good to eat. On the way out I stopped and asked the clerks if I might speak to the manager. Their faces fell immediately. "Is anything wrong? Was everything all right?" the little order-taker asked, her smile gone. She asked again, "Was anything wrong?"

"Oh, no!" I smiled. Then I told the manager how nice things were looking and going, and his face broke into an enormous smile.

"I needed to hear that," he said.

"Yes," I said. "I know."

Well, a lot of words. What comes to mind right now is that this afternoon was spent, in part, looking at an old paper on suffering—why suffering happens and what it does for us. Most surely one of the grand things it does in spades is let someone like me, when the anguish has stopped for a time, be able to see the extraordinary beauty of small, ordinary things. Yes, yes. Tonight I looked at that ordinary little place and saw absolute perfection at every wall, in every nook and cranny and along the brass rails that gleamed like gold. The atmosphere was crisp with excitement. I felt wonderful for having been there to see it all. In the mind's eye I had taken the panicked lady with me, and she had seen the beauty of it all. I said to her, "All right, little Lady, find one of those Glimpses in the mind's Eye and consider it to be the Treasure of God. That's what it is. Nothing less. It will do its good work. It didn't appear in your affairs for nothing. Savor it, my friend, and let it bring an end to your fear. God's Glimpses do wonders for us."

I walked into Woodsong just as the phone rang. It was the lady. "The panic has gone!" she said triumphantly. "Just as quickly as I brought a glimpse of light to mind, I felt bright and sparkling inside!"

I do not know how this works. But *I know what one is to do— and why.*

20

IT'S RAINING JOY TODAY

It's raining JOY today, Father!
Thank you for all the grass
    and trees
     and little critters
  who so much enjoy the wetness.

Oh, it is wonderful today!
A wet, grey day, cool and comfortable,
    Made for gentleness and thought;
    Made for sitting still and being awareness itself.

Today I look and see God's bounty from the sky,

> Downward pouring
>> Slanting grey lines
>>> Flowing into the earth's wet openings.

I am still and thankful.
So is my green selfhood.
Fill me, Lord of Life.
Fill me full.

21

SPACE, TIME AND PROGRESSION

Time and space aren't "real"—not as inexorable and immutable as they seem to be—but they are essential in this human scheme of things. Rather than deny their existence, metaphysicians would do well to come to comprehend why they are not what they seem to be and what role they play in the human experience.

When we take subjectivism into account, time and space remain the means by which we are able to comprehend the Reality that lies specifically behind them. "Point" isn't necessarily "real" from the standpoint of sphere, but it is a specific step in the mathematical *progression* in the knowledge of sphere. One goes from point to line and from line to plane, and finally, from plane to sphere. Sphere is "real" in the absolute sense, and the point, line and plane are three lesser dimensions within it, building it, so to speak. There is a natural hierarchy here—and a cosmology. Even though our comprehension of sphere is built point to line to plane, *sphere precedes them in time and space.* Our steps of comprehension are "after the fact." Sphere "knows" all about point, line and plane, whether point, line and plane know themselves or not— and none of them, neither separately nor together, can know the whole of sphere. Sphere knows sphere.

Time is one of the steps in the comprehension of its opposite, timelessness. Space is a step toward the comprehension of its quantum state, Infinity.

The logician and philosopher—occasionally the subjectivist— want to know why the fall into time and space in the first place. "If they aren't real, why do they seem to exist?" That question asked of philosophy, religion and metaphysics is tantamount to the ancient wonderment about the origin of evil, if God is good and God made everything perfectly. Religion, philosophy and metaphysics have never answered that question to the satisfaction of logicians. The absolute metaphysical pronouncement that evil *doesn't* exist outside the belief it does still doesn't answer the more basic question of who the believer is who entertains, or seems to entertain, pictures of presidents getting cancer and terrorists taking hostages. Again, the absolute position of metaphysics—"None of this is even going on. It's all a lie and I don't have to explain a lie!"—doesn't say anything that helps anything. Similarly, the claim that "death is an illusion" has done nothing to lessen the appearances of that illusion among those who call it illusory. The proper logician wants and deserves a better answer. Theology demands one but can't make it. Metaphysics cannot evade or double-talk forever without a real answer. Philosophy can't dismiss the matter forever either. Science comes closer to answers than religion, metaphysics or philosophy, but science presents the intolerable position that refuses to take spirit, ineffability, Deity, into account. Like Zen Buddhists, particle physicists and mathematicians insist they can't get beyond the limits of the senses to speculate about the existence or non-existence of Godhead, so they refuse to talk about it. But science has reached the point at which it can no longer evade the issue of Ineffability. Scientists are getting there ahead of the metaphysicians, ministers and priests, surprising to say. One wonders if they will be as successful at hiding quantum mechanics as the theologians in hiding subjectivism, dismissing it as "silly solipsism."

Now, after all these years, I find myself able to give an answer that completely satisfies the logicians and pragmatists about the reasons for the appearance of evil in the world—provided they take the (unreal) time and make the necessary subjective proofs for themselves. I know the answer is satisfactory because I was long the pragmatic logician seeking the answer, content with nothing less than precise logic itself. What I find so interesting now is something never expected originally. Now that I *have* the Answer—able to articulate it sufficiently, such that certain states of mind can understand and agree with the same marvel of marvels—the people in the world who least want to hear the answers are those who first propounded the question so vigorously. It is a paradox of paradoxes to which many masters have alluded. Jesus said: ". . . now you do not ask." The old nature of us so hates to display its ignorance.

The physical scientists are interested, when I can catch their ear. *People* are interested. But ministers, priests, rabbis and "religious" metaphysicians seem to have no interest whatever, so those who rely on them for guidance have no interest either. Those who spend their time in study, straining to catch a bit of light here or a glimpse there, are too busy to examine the quantum GIFT that is new on the Scene.

22

THE CRACK IN THE ARMOR OF THE WORLD

Nearly everyone understands that the sound of thunder follows the flash of lightning; fewer understand that the flash we see with the eyes is also delayed in time, that the flash follows the actual bolt of lightning by a fraction of a fraction of a second. If you explode a giant firecracker on top of Double Oak Mountain, you will see the flash there before I see it here two miles away, just as you will hear the explosion before I do. Light travels at a finite speed. The flash is fast but not instantaneous.

Now, let me ask: Do you see that there is Something *prior* to your own world-view of people, places and things? That is, the image I see across the room—or even in the mirror in front of me—has Something that precedes my view of it, delayed in time by a fraction of a fraction of a second, just like the explosion on the distant hill. As you and I sit here talking to one another, you see your own hands folded in your lap before I do. Our views of your hands seem to be simultaneous, but they are not. At least, not in the space, time world. Everyone thinks, "But we see each other at virtually the same time. What difference can a billionth of a billionth of a second make?" Ask a particle physicist how much difference that amount of time can make!

Years ago when I first discovered the subjective nature of the tangible universe and realized there was Something Else standing behind everything the world calls material—I called it Principle then—I realized that this knowledge should allow me to see evidences of that prior Principle—perfection where I had been seeing sickness, life in place of death. But such evidences or "demonstrations" did not always come to me on schedule or in the manner I expected. There was no consistency. It wasn't until I discovered the "chink in the armor of matter" that I began having repeatable demonstrations, as the scientists would call their experiments. That chink has to do with space, time and the speed of light. The crack appeared when the logical mind of me could concretely understand why and how it wasn't possible to look outside myself-as-consciousness and see something there instantaneously in time, but I could look within consciousness-as-Awareness and perceive SELFHOOD immediately. Then, that knowledge in hand, I could expect the image "out there" to *confirm my Self-knowing,* "precept upon precept"—and it did. It does. It must.

Who can explain this miracle to another? There certainly seem to be those within myself who are given to understand the "subjective idea" and those who are not. I do not know why so few understand—especially metaphysicians—but I can guess with assurance that this is the reason men like Jesus have said throughout linear history, "Let him who has ears to hear, understand."

Now, we come to the wonder of wonders. Suppose I get up in the morning, look into the mirror and see that image in front of me looking like death itself? What am I to do? I know that the Awareness doing the looking *precedes* that image in world time! As Awareness, I am pure and perfect, no matter WHAT the mirror tells me—or the doctor tells me or anyone else. Identified as Awareness Itself, I exist before time and space! I precede time and space. *I precede the feelings of the body or any of its appearances.* There is an instant of an instant of a second which permits, as time and space go, the misty, ordinary light to intrude with a delineating picture of things. I do not have to accept those appearances as final—nor con-

tinue to believe the humanly expected, causal, linear relationships to unfold in space and time as the world predicts.

If I hold out my hand and see evidences of the most horrible sight there—a huge cancer, say, or an angry, sullen
mate—I know that *there is a lag between what I am and what I
see*—and that same lag permits the real Light of Truth to alter
the tangible seeing with a picture of goodness! If a mother
looks out and sees the sight of her child falling under the
wheels of a great red truck, she does not *HAVE* to see the
mangled consequences of death and destruction following in
time—because the Glimpse of healing Truth comes in that instant of an instant and is perpetually HERE to be seen when
we look for it and confidently expect it. As the physicist or
mathematician would say, the Glimpse contains "infinite possibilities" within itself.

But, my friend, I had to know why I didn't have to accept
the appearance before I could expect to look back into the
mirror again and see CONFIRMATION of the immaculate
nature of Awareness *being confirmed in time and space.* Again,
I don't know why I had to know that, but I did. Perhaps you
must, too—if you expect to see the marvelous confirmations in
your experience that I have seen in mine. (This is not the only
requirement, of course. There is still the matter of what one is
to DO with the glimpse and how one is to live the Equation of
living.)

When the physicist or astronomer begins to take the prior
consciousness of himself, the experimenter, into account—and
begins to examine the awareness which is an integral part of
every experiment (and precedes it in time), he will be able to
prove the miraculous, even as I have. Why not? The difficulty
for the scientist, as for each of us, is turning from self to Self.
The old nature of us has many vested interests and doesn't
want to be forsaken. I don't believe my world "out there" is
going to appear concerned about the perfect Child within
themselves that precedes tangibility in time and space until a
common disaster looms for all mankind. Could that be what is
turning the distant sky so dark and making all that thunder in
the far places? Perhaps, but the disaster doesn't have to *happen.* What can we do to avert it? We find the Child and live the
Child's Equation.

23

THE HOLOGRAPHIC NATURE OF MATTER

The Whole contains the parts, of course, but it isn't so well known that the Whole—Godhead—is *greater* than the sum of Its parts. Nor has it been known beyond a handful of mystics through history that every part contains information of the Whole. That is, we examine a rock and the rock contains information about the earth. We look at a tree and learn of all life. We get to know a friend and have a knowledge of Everyman. We perceive Everyman and know the Self. We know the Self and have as much knowledge of Godhead as Infinite Wisdom is capable of perceiving. Is it any wonder so many of the great philosophies have advocated "Know Thyself!"

Everything I have learned has "come to me" in the form of light—one way or another. The flower I enjoy arrives as light. The face I touch arrives as light. For all of us every sensation has ever been one or another wave length of light arriving to be examined and understood.

In recent years, science has made great strides in understanding the light of the universe. The essence of all matter is light. In an old figure of speech used by the ancients, everything is an image of an image of light. We will do well to understand something of light, because light itself is the image of Light.

For years I have used what has now come to be called "The Holographic Paradigm" as a means of explaining some of the functions of ordinary light. I use the word "ordinary" to denote what I call *limited* light—light limited to a speed of 186,300 miles per second—light in motion. Its source, the Fountainhead of light, I call by whatever name I would use to refer to Godhead. I spell *that* Light with a capital. In the mind's eye, I think of It as infinite, therefore at rest. Limited light spirals within motionless Light. Light and light are one Light. Light in motion is the movement of, the *measure* of Light. To put it another way, it is Light's Self-measure.

But notice: The awareness that reads these words can take the measure of limited light. Awareness perceives limited light within itself, yet awareness can in no wise take a *full* measure of Illimitable Light. Awareness (Life) and light are *apparently* wed to one another—another "two that are one." But note again: These "two that are one" are within *Infinite* Light. *Three* that are one. A Trinity with the very Life-I-Am smack dab in the middle!

This is only a hint of the beginning. To make sense of a *Deific* solipsism with words has taken me half a century. But there IS a Deific solipsism present as the universe within Awareness within the Ineffable! The door to it all is the very Light of Life that reads these words and the light that illumines them.

To understand the wonders of limited light is to *marvel* at the wonder of Illimitable Light, Godhead, Father of lights. Consider: the light bouncing into your eyes from this sheet of paper is not only bringing images of the printed words, but images of the entire room whether you are noticing them or not. And not just images within your line of sight, but of virtually everything in the room, behind the furniture, under the tables, on the hidden shelves. If the light that illumines the page comes from the window, there is information pouring through your eyes containing an image of every mountain, every tree, every blade of grass as far as the eye can see. *Farther*—because the eye can't see what is hidden behind that building, but the light bouncing from these words does! If this seems difficult to believe, let me make it more so. The light which is the apparent substance of this bit of paper contains knowledge of the entire earth. Solar system. Galaxy. *Universe!*

This may seem a bit mind-bending at first, but once the principle of holography is understood, one perceives a most marvelous secret which the Ancients were aware of: The part contains knowledge of the whole; *every* part of the part contains knowledge of the whole of the Whole.

Let me give an illustration of this wonder of wonders. It will be particularly meaningful now that the leading edge of science has concluded that all "matter"—be it particle or galaxy—is holographic imagery, arrested or "slowed" light!

Do you remember the old, square Brownie box camera of yore? The first ones didn't even have a lens. Just an opening that would open and close at about 1/25th of a second—and take a dandy picture.

Pretend just such a Brownie snapshot was made of you and your Uncle George way back on your fifth birthday. Uncle George had come to visit bringing some wonderful gift with him. Someone took a picture which you have cherished and kept for fifty long years because that day and that uncle were very special. There you stand, stiff and straight in your party clothes, the gift in its box tucked under your right arm. Uncle George is standing to your left, a big smile on his face, his arm holding you close. In the background someone with a big fanny is bent over, but her head was hidden behind Uncle George when the picture was snapped and you have long forgotten who it was. In the left front is an image of a foot. To whom it belonged you never did know. In fact, you have long forgotten what the gift was, but you remember it was very special. Uncle George always brought special gifts.

Well now. It is fifty years later and we are still pretending. The old snapshot has taken a battering over the years. Way back when, you took the scissors and cut the extraneous foot away since it had no business in the picture. Years later when you were away at school, the suitcase was accidentally closed on it, tearing away the entire bottom half. Finally, since only the top of your head remained alongside Uncle George, you trimmed away everything except his head and shoulders. Everything. That is all that remains now: *half* of Uncle George smiling. The beautiful scene of the park is gone. You and the gift tucked under your arm are gone. The foot and the frilly fanny have long been forgotten. Except for a small fragment of the original picture, all else is a memory of a distant childhood—and much of that has faded.

Now let us stop pretending—except for the fragment of picture. Let us discuss a relatively simple physical fact. Can you guess what will happen if we shine a certain type of split-beam laser light on our fragment? Voila! Between the projecting laser and the fragment comes a holographic image of Uncle George hovering in the air like a ghost. The laser light strikes the fragment, bounces away and reproduces an image of light.

But lo, something new has been added. Uncle George is in *three* dimensions, not just two as he appeared on the original snapshot! There he stands in depth, as well as in length and height. Pot, pudgy cheeks and smile, all in three dimensions!

Look again. There's more. ALL of Uncle George is there. Not just the head and shoulders on the fragment, but the bottom half that was lost in the suitcase caper back in 1940! Can the top half of an image reproduce the bottom half *that isn't there?* Clearly. There it is. But as the lady who inspects Hanes underwear in the TV ad says, "That's just the beginning, Kid!" Look at the holographic image again. There *you* are too, tall and straight with the box tucked under your arm and all in three dimensions. And there are the park, the trees, the flowers, the big behinnie with the frilly dress, a bird and a butterfly you had never seen before—and all in three dimensions. How in the world can such a small fragment contain so much information? But wait, there is still MUCH more! The little Brownie camera "saw" one point of view as the picture was taken years ago. Now, fifty years later, our fragment still has etched on its surface a hundred thousand *thousand* points of view, nearly to infinity—almost as if the camera were in ALL places simultaneously when the picture was snapped! Well, the camera wasn't, but the light was, and that's why we are getting three dimensions. Let me try to explain while you look at the holographic images again.

As you look full on, facing the images hovering magically in the air, you will notice they are placed like figures on a stage, so to speak, the distant trees behind you and your uncle, the frilly behind, between you and the trees, and so on. As you move to the right and left of the images, you begin to notice things that were never on the original picture at all. For instance, you lean to the left and see the head of someone attached to the frilly dress. Your mother! You never realized she was in the picture! You walk to the right side of your own image and see what is written on the box. Lincoln Logs! Now you remember that long forgotten gift. Here you are looking at "information" that was never apparent on the original picture at all, much less on the small scrap remaining. The fragment somehow contains knowledge of the whole—and much MORE than was seen by the eye fifty years ago when the picture was made. Oh yes, the foot that was mysteriously in the original picture is there, too—with a faint body attached. Your father—he was running to get in the picture, never realizing he made it.

Reader, remember that we are not speaking of high mysticism or metaphysics here. We are only touching down lightly—and, hopefully, dramatically—on just one aspect of *ordinary light*, the very light by means of which you are reading these words. This instant, the awareness of you is being flooded with information quite beyond anything you may ever have dreamed. We are not limited to one point of view as we watch the sunset or the waves breaking along the shore. ALL points of view are present, right here, right now. We are not bound to the physical limits of the eyes and ears. The scene outside the window is a fragment of the earth, isn't it? And isn't the earth a fragment of solar system, galaxy, universe? *The part contains information of the Whole.*

But there is more. More! Much more. If these things are true for limited light in motion (and they are) how much more must be true for ILLIMITABLE, OMNIPRESENT LIGHT! If limited light brings information of the entire physical (holographic) universe, what Wonder-beyond-wonder exists as the SOURCE, FOUNTAINHEAD, GODHEAD which is BEING moving light! Limited light is a portion of Light. It contains information of the All as well. The awareness that reads these words *is* Light/light; the Wisdom it IS is awesome. Awesome!

Dear Light of Life, Self of my Self, *begin* your study of Light/light. Examine light. Look at light. Enjoy light. See the light glistening on the water. See light reflected from the faces of flowers and children. See light twinkling from the stars and from the eyes of love. See light lifting in the morning and lingering in the evening. Examine the light that darkness merely delineates. Sit still and *see* the wondrous Light of Life which is the source and substance of EVERYTHING. The Galilean mystic who identified as Light Itself said ". . . these stones shall minister unto thee . . . cleave a piece of wood and I am there . . . Within a man of light there is light and he lights the whole world . . . we have come from the Light." Awareness (life) is the Light from which all things come and to which all things return even as the perfect Light of Godhead is the source and substance of Awareness. At the speed of light there is neither space nor time. At Light, Life is deathless and eternal.

There is much power in this message. *If you will, you can feel it.* How much MORE is the Life of YOU!

24

THE ELIJAH ILLUSTRATION ABOUT LIGHT, TIME, SPACE AND THE REAL IDENTITY

There is a verse in *The Gospel According to Thomas*, "If they say to you: 'From where have you originated?', say to them: 'We have come from the Light, where the Light originated through itself. . . .'" The genuine Identity of us "comes from the Light." That reality seems buried deep within us, as inaccessible to the intellect as the soul is, the very essence of being. But it is not inaccessible; it is within our reach for the asking. Let me use an analogy that will help us understand.

A big brass eagle I call Elijah sits in the middle of my living room coffee table. My son calls it "montrocious," but the eagle and I don't mind. Rachel likes it, too. Company was here recently, and since the great brass bird on the coffee table can hardly be ignored, it became an illustration about light, space and time.

There are so many wonders concerning light. One of them is the mysterious photon itself, that enigmatic bundle of mystery that does so much in the world. Tiny photon, how can you be nearly everywhere in space at once? It is that particular quality of the photon which I came to explain via the brass eagle—and this illustration also suggests how the Original Nature of us is also everywhere in space and time.

The photons that illumine this page (or appear entrapped

as the very paper itself) are bringing more information to us than could have been dreamed a few years ago. Essentially, photons *are* information. Light *is* information. When viewed subjectively, information is light.

There sits Elijah, my big brass eagle who must weigh twenty-five pounds, looking for all the world as if he's just come to rest on a brass stump that stands above the water of the glass-topped coffee table. (Son Bill expects him to go crashing through any day.) For the purpose of this illustration, I suggest that Elijah is just leaving his perch, getting ready to fly faster and faster.

Well now, how does the brass bird *look* to us as he goes faster? Smaller. And still smaller as he gets to the speed of sound and smaller yet as he flies at half the speed of light. At those speeds it takes special equipment to see him at all. Then, when he gets to "light," which is to say, the speed of light—186,300 miles per second—Elijah becomes a photon to us as we sit in the living room drinking our coffee.

Where would Elijah, the photon, be at any given moment in time? From our perspective, virtually everywhere. That's interesting, isn't it? The nature of light is such that our attempts to locate it in time are impossible because at light, it exists beyond time. Experiments suggest that the photon, the eagle at light, is everywhere in the room simultaneously. Though we can't see him with the eye, the fact that he is everywhere (as light) is the reason we are able to see the things *not* moving at the speed of light. It is the steady flow of photons that lets us see one another or read these words of print. Who knows, the photons that brighten this page may be cosmic eagles—or "angels of the Light."

So far, so good. Don't worry if the illustration isn't precisely accurate, scientifically. Now, how does this room look to Elijah as he flies faster and faster? Things seem to be rushing past him more quickly, that's for sure, faster and faster as he passes over our heads. But, for the eagle's view, something else is happening which is important to take into our thinking (or non-thinking) while we make this illustration. The room becomes smaller and smaller to Elijah as he moves faster—not unlike the way the years seem to move more quickly for us as we grow older in time. Not only does the room grow smaller to Elijah, but so does the tangible universe—smaller, smaller, going, going, and at the speed of light, gone! To the photon, there is neither time nor space. Or, to put it obversely, the photon is everywhere in tangibility at once.

Yet, listen, listen. The photon is ordinary worldly light. It is called "limited" light (by the early Christian Gnostics and me) because it seems to have a strange limit built into itself. The speed of light is calculated by present physics to be "the limiting speed" of the (material) universe—a primary, an absolute—and indeed, Einstein proved that light travels at that constant speed no matter what the rest of tangibility does. The speed of sound has the speed of the sound-maker added to or subtracted from its velocity—but not light. Light travels at the same speed whether the observer is stationary or moving a million miles an hour away from it or toward it—or so they say. Einstein's equation has been proven essentially correct, relative to the photon in our tangible universe. Our worldly experience of matter is somehow pegged to a limited light in motion.

"Ah so," as Han would say. So what? Why the limit? Philosophy and theology—and maybe even a metaphysician here or there—have calculated that infinity is *beyond* limit. Such thoughts lead to the conclusion that if God exists (God being Illimitability or Light-spelled-with-a-capital), then there must be a Light BEYOND the photon-light we can measure. The ultimate Light must be omnipresent—at rest, Light that doesn't move at all. There is something in the Bible about Light without shadow, isn't there? Welcome to the club, physicists. The Jews and Gnostics, the Hindus and forest wanderers, the Taoists and many others made that determination thousands of years ago and have gone on to use the greater Light to explain things about the lesser which human sophistication is only now beginning to confirm.

If Elijah, traveling at the speed of light, doesn't see this tangible world, what *does* he see? Another heaven and earth where light may travel at a higher speed, say the theoretical mathematicians—in strange agreement with various spiritual lights of the world. There is surely insight here. When one leaves the physical body at "death," who is to say that the Child, the Soul of us, doesn't "return to" or become Light again (if, indeed, it has ever stopped being Light)? If tangibility, as we perceive it, doesn't exist "at light" does that mean it doesn't exist? If it exists anyway, how many other universes may be perceived under different conditions?

At the speed of Light there is no more consciousness of time or space—but a new heaven and earth exist "at light" and "the old heaven and earth have passed away." Could this have been what the Carpenter and the prophets foresaw when they spoke of this world being rolled up like a scroll?—and the one above it as well? How is it that the Gnostics rightly referred to the works of this world as an unreal creation by the dispossessed angel, Lucifer, whose name means limited light? Since the material universe does seem to be the creation of photons, from which Awareness can't be separated for very long this side of "death," what relationship exists between the awareness reading these words and the satanic Lucifer? Could the Zen Buddhist and the absolutist who decry all relationships between human consciousness and Reality be right after all? Is there justification for the metaphysical insight that says human consciousness *is* the anti-Truth? Wouldn't it be a surprise to the churchman who refuses to examine subjectivism to awaken one day to learn he has been enacting the very anti-Christ himself in his refusal to accept God's totality?

Or, could it be, as it has been shown to me, and as I firmly believe, that there is Something *beyond* all this matter of correct, incorrect, right, left, liberal, conservative, male, female, objective, subjective and all the other dualisms one can perceive? Yes, there is. And something beyond the concept of single/dual as well—even beyond the concept of "beyond." There is a legitimate question as to whether Reality will be found by intellectualism at all. But it can be found by the simple and childlike. If I have found a small measure of it, I would think anyone can.

This book is an attempt to go beyond science, philosophy, religion and metaphysics—without leaving them. The mysteries of time and space have intrigued mankind from the beginning. In recent years science has gotten down to real answers in a language most of us can understand. Even more, our technology is putting some of the most esoteric math to the test and the theories indicated by quantum are working. The atomic bomb, whose enormous energy appears a threat to all living things, is a verification of theory. Another discovery, in many ways more significant, is holography and all that holography suggests.

Some of the experimental work of mathematicians using their principles of quantum allows us to examine the relative nature of time and perceive the ways we may one day soon be unbound from its limitation.

25

THE TWIN EAGLES; MORE ABOUT TIME, SPACE AND IMAGES

If they say to you: "From where have you originated?", say to them: "We have come from the Light, where the Light has originated through itself. It stood and it revealed itself in their image". If they say to you: "Who are you?", say: "We are His sons and we are the elect of the Living Father". If they ask you: "What is the sign of your Father in you?", say to them: "It is a movement and a rest." (Jesus)

Whoever knows the All but fails to know himself, lacks everything. (Jesus)

If you bring forth that within yourselves, that which you have will save you. If you do not have that within yourselves, that which you do not have within you will kill you. (Jesus)

The images are manifest to man and the Light which is within them is hidden in the Image of the Light of the Father. He will manifest himself and His Image is concealed by His Light. (Jesus)

When you see your likeness, you rejoice. But when you see your images which came into existence before you, which neither die nor are manifested, how much will you bear! (Jesus)

When you make the two one, and when you make the inner as the outer and the outer as the inner and the above as the below . . . and when you make . . . an image in the place of an image, then shall you enter the Kingdom. (Jesus)

Think with me for a few minutes while we build an illustration: Imagine infinite space, eternal time and infinite life as a dimension that lies just beyond intellectual comprehension. It *is* beyond intellectual comprehension. This dimension exists in (perhaps, as) Ineffable, infinite Life and Light which is at rest. It doesn't move, as ordinary light moves.

Imagine that this boundless Life and Light could squeeze a quantum of itself (a portion of its life, light and energy) through an aperture, or hole, *within itself* where that portion emerged into a void, and in so doing represents *this* universe where we presently sit making an illustration.

Inasmuch as the quantum of ineffable substance (Life, Light, Energy) squeezed through the hole is not *all* of the greater dimension, and since it emerges into an internal vacuum—perhaps many vacuums, like bubbles—it begins an enormous replicative expansion into time at the instant it pours through this aperture, rushing to fill the void contained subjectively within the Greater Dimension. That replication, or limited duplication, is holographic—an image of the Image, not dissimilar to the generation of a child within the womb.

The quantum of light, life and energy begins an immediate, enormous expansion of duplicating ejecta to fill the void—and expands at the speed (determined, presumably, by the quantity) of moving light, 186,300 miles per second. At the point of emission, the original five-dimensional quantum is reduced to three dimensions of interrelated space plus a dimension of ongoing time, moving (in one direction) away from the place of explosion from out of Ineffable Whatever.

Thus far, our illustration represents the expanding universe we are living in and suggests that science's ongoing search in the examination of matter and energy is tracing a movement backward in time and direction, from material things to the time and place of emissive "creation." In this movement backward, science will soon reach the Alpha-beginning, the moment of big bang (on one end) and Omega/orifice/place (black hole) on the other—the time and place of the birth of the tangible universe within the void. Just recently, as a matter of fact, the orbiting Challenger put a one-ton camera into space, above the atmosphere; that camera spent two days looking for evidences of the black hole center of this galaxy. Last year, the largest accelerator ever was used to examine the microcosm. Recently, the Fermi Accelerator yielded 1.6 trillion electron volts, taking particles "back" to a billionth of a billionth of a second from Big Bang.

The intent of the orbiting camera is to observe evidence of the black hole from which, or back into which, this galaxy appears to be moving. Emergence happened, as time goes, fifteen billion linear years ago as measured by the speed of limited light. But there is non-moving Light beyond limited light, for which moving light is an image.

Science's investigations have an inexplicable intellectual limitation in front of them. At the point of the explosion, where the mass of this galaxy began and/or is returning, the forces of the black hole become so enormous that moving light cannot escape its gravitational field. There, time stops and/or moves in the opposite direction—or (if we think of it dimensionally) is transcended. Mass becomes massless, or is transcended. Gravity moves to infinity, or is transcended. Alpha and Omega become one, and/or are transcended. What lies beyond the black hole becomes unimaginable, totally beyond comprehension, transcendent, even as the heart of us here and now transcends the limits of the intellect.

Hold everything right there a minute and let me approach the black hole from another direction: We bring the Elijah Illustration (earlier paper) into play, where the holographic (material) brass eagle's mass becomes greater as the eagle moves faster until the eagle theoretically becomes a massless photon, moving at the speed of light. (Perhaps matter, already holographic, can't quite do that, but it can get nearly to the speed of light. The Identity of us, the Child or soul of us is Light beyond light already.)

Notice how the photon of ordinary light is linked with the four dimensions of time and space, virtually everywhere in linear space simultaneously, even while being connected with the objects of time and space moving at slower speeds, illumining them, all the way down to you and me as we sit here as a physical hulk (also theoretical) and think about all this.

That is, when the eagle reaches the speed of Light, there seem to be two eagles, one the physical and holographic (as all matter is), the other a photon. They are twins of one another, one moving at Light, the other virtually at rest in time and space and "lesser" in dimension, greater in mass, than the photon image of itself, one within the other, one objective, the other subjectively within the other, not unlike the first illustration of the expansion in the womb, "holographic" tangibility coming "out of" Ineffability.

These two eagles are actually one, but they seem to be two, the photon eagle the imaged twin of the non-moving eagle here on earth. The photon eagle is *prior* to the brass eagle, even though it seems the other way around. It might be said that the photon eagle is the soul or the identity of the other. The heavy, lumbering Elijah exists a fraction of a second *behind* photon eagle.

Notice that there is no condition in which the lumbering, solid eagle finds himself that the photon eagle cannot free him from—*by being on both sides of the problem simultaneously in time*. The photons that illuminate this page are on both sides of time and have been capable of moving around the earth many times since we started reading this paragraph.

But remember, when we began with the first part of this illustration, we saw that all tangibility, like the photon eagle, has its basis on *the other side of* the black hole, existing *before* the expansionary explosion into time and space. In other words, the photon eagle (represented as this universe here and now, which includes this present awareness reading these words) is the Image of, the "soul" of, a THIRD, prior, Super-Eagle on the other side of the impenetrable black hole. Perhaps science's intuiting (and confirming) anti-matter is tantamount to that third Eagle. Certainly, it is tantamount to Godhead, for whom this Image and image of Image exist.

Now hear this, illustration in abeyance for a moment while I make a statement of personal fact for me. I have found that I have a "twin" of my own. I call that one the Original Child of myself. I know the twin of me seems to permeate all time and space in this tangible universe and it brings me whatever information is necessary, right here as I (first) labor like the brass eagle, struggling alone at my typewriter to explain the Light I have been shown and have consequently proven and lived for myself, and secondly, as I labor then to announce the Light I have discovered (or that has been shown to Me) *which I have proven* in "my" worldly affairs. I know that the Child of me, like the photon, is ahead of physical me, and behind physical me in time and space, enwrapping me and mine.

I know that this twin Image of Myself is much more nearly the Real of me than this physical image that labors with these words—but the physical image of each of us has its *purpose and its destiny in time and space,* infinitely beyond anything history or human observation can imagine.

I know that I have become more and more the Child of illimitable Light as I have allowed It to bring information to the human sense of myself—those precious Glimpses and Glimmers I have been writing about—even as this is also a Glimpse being written here and now.

Somewhere along the line of time and space, we begin to intuit this Child within and without—even as the prophets and avatars of the tangible world of history have done. Somewhere we begin to affirm the inner Child's reality, as opposed to this chunk of clay, delayed in time, that comes forth and perishes in time and space; this physical body merely a recognized or unrecognized *confirmation* of the preceding REAL, following in time a millionth of a billionth of a second. Somewhere we begin to feel the Child and to affirm its living Existence. Somewhere we begin to be enlivened by It and receive CONSCIOUS instruction from It, which becomes directly applicable to the quantum images of that Child, appearing as this body and all bodies in this tangible universe.

And then, somewhere for some of us, we run AS the Child, *doing* for our subjective world whatever seems necessary to lift it up, bind its wounds, heal the heavy hearts and bring it to sing the same song of the morning star.

Then, when one is ready (as when a seed is ready), there is an Experience of enormous human proportion where the Child of Light-I-am is brought very close to the apprehension of the Non-Moving Light of Life, the Original Image, overdwelling all, the Original One on the "other side" of the veil, the portal, through which this tangible existence springs.

Just as I call on the Child of me to lead the way in the world of time and space (which is only imagery), so the Child-I-Am calls on the Ineffable One Beyond (Godhead) to guide It. In the very simplest words I can find, it is as if the Real of me is holding God's hand, and the other hand of me is reaching

out, with these glimpses añd glimmers of the Real, to lift myself bodily (in actual confirmation) to the comprehension of
the Beginning of things, which is also the End of things. It is
as if I recognize Me to be the Seed of God—and as I do, that
Seed passes through me into the world. The Glimpses are the
Divine Seed, exploding into Me, as Me.

*My fingers have flown over the keys here. I was instructed in an
instant, came here to write these words with the accompanying illustrations and presently have no idea if the Glimpse has been conveyed at all. There is an astounding and marvelous link written
here, more expansive than any I have used heretofore. It allows me
to explain in ordinary (?) terms how it is that I am constantly "instructed" and how I draw ever closer (in time and space) to the
One who exists beyond the limited dimension of time and space,
even as It exists as the basis for matter's apparent existence and is
present "where" the tangible world is.*

I am certain there are "others" within myself (subjectively)
seeing exactly what I am seeing. We are the Same One.

26

WISDOM IS INFORMATION REDISCOVERED

Wisdom is information. Information is accumulated time.
Time, among other things, is the accumulation of information
and wiṣdom. Real information is "truth"—what is, as opposed
to illusion, belief, mythology, not-truth.

What can one tell a young child about Truth? Nothing in
the world's terms because the human child doesn't understand
the world's terms yet.

What can the child tell the adult about Truth? Much, but
not in the world's terms. The world has forgotten the child's
perceptions and has grown out of them into adulthood and
language.

Consider: A man lives a long time and learns the value of
honesty. What does the child understand of the things the
man might say about honesty and truth? Nothing in the man's
terms because the youngster doesn't understand about words

and the world yet; but the child lying in the crib is living honestly and truly—that is, living the Equation that Life is. The child lives honesty and truth, pre-world, pre-adult, pre-terminology, pre-experience.

But what does the adult tell the little boy about such adult themes? We say that the child will just have to live longer, grow up, have a few experiences, get himself around the block a time or two, and then he might be lucky enough to learn what honesty (or whatever) really is in his heart.

What does the adult tell the little girl about beauty? The same thing. And what does the adult expect the little girl to tell him about beauty? Nothing in the world's terms because she hasn't learned the world's terms yet. But the adult knows intuitively that the child is *living* "beauty" in the most honest sense of the term.

Is the adult right? Yes, as far as time goes, as far as world terminology goes, as far as language and experience go, the child must live the adult's world and suffer the contraries; then, the adult (the not-child) having slowly accumulated the information in time that constitutes wisdom and truth, *can use the world's terms to tell of "honesty" and "beauty."* But to whom is this communication made? To other <u>adults</u>, not to other children.

Inasmuch as beauty has to do with the senses and their interface with tangibility—plus the feelings and emotions that come with the sundry personal interfaces with "others" and "things"—is it not plain that the child comes into the world with clear senses, already interfacing with original (baby/child) emotions and feelings? Certainly, but we can't tell very much about that while looking on the baby as an undeveloped adult; and the baby can't use many of the adult's terms to say, "Hey, man, I'm seeing pristine spiritual beauty right here in the world."

The child asks us a primitive question about something basic, like beauty, honesty or honor, and because we know the child hasn't learned the world's responses yet, nor the world's terminology or rules, we know the child must pass through more time and space so the right glands come into play and the young adult can accumulate the time and experience necessary to understand and express the basics with which we were born into the world originally.

So, what CAN I tell a young man or woman about true wisdom? I can tell them they came into the world with it, LIVING and BEING it honestly, albeit not *conscious of it* in the world's way. I can tell them they will return to it again, because, with the passage of time tantamount to the accumulation of information, they will rediscover the pristine sensations of the original Child—if not before the death of the body, then with the body's age and death. Hence, I can say, "You have come from the pure Light of Life and you are returning there again, whether you think so or not—whether you even care or not." I can also say, "You are certain eventually to rediscover the Original Nature (Soul/Child) of yourself." Furthermore, I can explain to one willing to listen and prove my words, that the purpose of the human experience is to do just that. Just what? Discover the Self.

Inevitably, intellectualism's next question is: "Why do we have to go through all this human business of losing the Original Nature and then rediscovering it slowly, line upon line? Why, why, why? Where is the justice in that?" That is the question neither science, religion nor philosophy has answered satisfactorily—but now we can!

We are brought back to the original condition of the baby. What does it SELF-KNOW of honesty, beauty, tenderness, equality or gender? It IS those things but doesn't KNOW those things. The human experience is for the purpose of REDISCOVERY—which is to KNOW, and KNOW one knows. "With all thy wisdom, get understanding." Know thyself. Knowing what is, one knows what is NOT as well.

LIGHT IS INFORMATION

Most of the information about the distant universe has come to us via the light of the stars—at least, until recently. Most of our information about the stars comes from those little pin points of light we see at night when we look up. Some of those points of light have taken thousands of millions of years in time to travel the tangible miles of space to get here; hence the

light that impacts the eyeball at night is accumulated or compacted "time" *as well as information.*

Notice also that we have to look to the earth to confirm
whatever we have learned from our observations of the stars.
For instance, we see a planet turning on its axis: the earth
confirms that information by a similar action here. Or, we see
that certain elements are present in the spectrum of thus and
such a star and find those elements corresponding to elements
on earth, which we can examine and measure. This is *confirmation* of information, so to speak. We perceive information
(light) in the heavens and put that information to the test on
earth and confirm it. Until we have made such linkage (confirmation) of our esoteric information, we keep it in the area
of theory, rather than fact. When the linkage is found, it is no
longer theory, but a provable fact.

Science hasn't discovered the close relationship between the
universe-out-there and the body-here; not yet. Quantum mechanics moves them close. When science perceives the suprem-
acy of subjective thought, there will no longer be a gap
between pure science and philosophy, religion, psychology and
life (awareness). It is said by one of the Jewish groups that
there is no element in nature that can't be found (confirmed)
in the physical body of man. There is nothing seen in the
heavens that can't be found in the material body of humanity,
positively or negatively. Science hasn't confirmed this in anything but theory thus far, but the mystic has known, from the
beginning, that when he looked at the night sky he was looking into "the mind of God." More, the mystic has known that
the Mind of God isn't separate from the awareness of you and
me that looks into the night sky.

The ultimate confirmation is not just the body of onself, but
the Awareness of Self. Body AND Mind. The body, quite the
opposite of appearances, is within Awareness, not the other
way around.

Finally, the Child within is not theory but confirmable fact
to anyone who is willing to look for It and feel It. To put that
in religious terms, one who has felt the "holy Spirit" knows it
is real, not imaginary. Putting it in subjective terms, one who
has had a Glimpse knows the reality of that Glimpse and what
it does for him. Putting it in the Equation's terms, one knows

the Child is still alive within himself and is all that is important therein.

A meaningful equation: The "river" of thought is like the mathematical point. Objectivism is like the line. Subjectivism is like the plane. The Equation is like the Sphere wherein all the dimensions exist and time vanishes. The point is limited to the point's purview, the line to the line's, and so on. But line understands point, plane understands line and point, etc. The Child-Self precedes time and space, even while being in it and understanding why it exists.

Bottom line: We rediscover the original Child within us all and run with it. It will tell us all we need to know of religion, psychology, metaphysics and science without taking us to all the extremes therein.

27

ABOUT WISDOM AND RAILROAD TRESTLES

I think science, philosophy, government, religion and metaphysics can agree that we are to seek wisdom and understanding. I remember a lady delightfully full of searching questions who used to visit regularly at Woodsong. I've always been a question-asker myself, so I appreciate others asking questions. This lady was right in the middle of trying to get her subjectivism straight so she could live it and apply it in the world. Every minute she asked another super-serious metaphysical question, trying in vain to make my answers fit her particular textbook and beliefs.

After several days of this, in some desperation, I took her arrowhead hunting, way out in the boonies. It isn't so easy to ask metaphysical questions while walking the rows of a cotton field, looking for artifacts, but neither the long walk in the field nor the heat of an Alabama summer slowed this lady's questions. "If there is nothing but God and God is omniscient, why am I so dumb?" she asked in her way of mock humility. "Are we omniscient, too, like God?" she asked, paying no attention whatever to the answer to the previous questions. "Well then, if this life I am is God's, why can't I answer the questions I'm asking you?—or find any arrowheads?"

I had been eyeing the field on the other side of the river and the railroad trestle that would take me there. I headed for it, the lady hard on my heels. "If there is nothing but good going on, why do I see so much ugliness?" Then, without taking a breath, she asked, "Would you say that we are omniscient or omniscience itself?" She asked this, carefully sounding the words so I could hear them and determine the differences she intended. At this point we were in the middle of the railroad trestle and, suddenly, in front of us, came a thundering freight train, screeching and sounding its warning whistle. We had nowhere to go. The river was at least a hundred feet below. What to do? We held on to the outer girders of the narrow bridge, leaning precariously backwards over the muddy water below, while the train pounded past, barely four feet from our fingers and toes. That train must must have been two miles long. I'll never forget the face of the horrified engineer looking at the two old children hanging on for dear life—certainly old enough to know better than be caught on a railroad bridge. So much for *Bill's* omniscience!

The lady hasn't been back to Woodsong. She has taken up residence in Nairobi, Kenya, and has little to do with William anymore. To this day, I wonder if she still laughs at our talk about wisdom when neither of us had the sense to look down the track before we ventured onto the railroad bridge.

Ah so. We found no arrowheads in the far field either. Nothing was there but a few shards of pottery which I've kept to this day. They are appropriately labeled "Trestle pottery" and I still pucker when I see them. The memory of that lady and that day is good. She found the Child of herself—and the Child will eventually take her to the Equation.

Some day when you invite me to come your way lecturing, reader, or when you come to Alabama, remind me to tell you the other true railroad stories that have conveyed so much to me and others during the years. The discipline of life is fun, you know! We break through the heaviness of science and religion—and the super-seriousness of metaphysics—into pure joy. The Child within us laughs a lot.

28

A RESTATEMENT OF COSMOLOGY

Though they likely don't know it, the scientists who are examining ordinary light and its uses have created a cosmology remarkably like the one we find in the Bible. Moses speaks primarily to Adam's disobedience. Other prophets speak of Satan's fall from his high place and of the intellectual nature's intense desire to be gratified, knowing all that God knows. In any event, the Bible hints of an argument in heaven, a battle royal and the expulsion of Satan and his angels who are banished to dusty earth where they, in competition with God, create a world of their own and strive to win the souls of mortals, using every trickery and deceit. According to this view, this is Satan's world and he is up to no good. Essentially, the world is an evil place, under the dominion of the seven deadlies.

Another cosmology has been shown to me. It doesn't have a competition between good and evil, but a temporary competition between wisdom and ignorance wherein wisdom eventually wins *and the ignorance was never real*—but necessary for a time for Wisdom to come to know beyond the limits of intellectualism.

In this cosmology, Overmind (Godhead) declares "I am" and with that declaration "matter" is exploded into the state of chaos, undifferentiated energy. Then, Godhead declares, "I know" and perfect forms begin to emerge from chaos. Godhead declares, "I know what I am" and the perfect heaven and earth are created. Godhead declares, "I know what knowing is" and the perfect Image of knowing (the Son) is created, male and female and all of this is, as the Bible states, "very good."

Then, as Godhead declares, "Knowing what I am, I also know what I am not and could never be," the dusty nether world of satanic illusion-in-time is born. Here is the phantasmagoria of idealistic impossibilities over which there is no real ruler and in which there is no real power, authority or substance. Godhead declares, "Knowing who I am, I also know what knowing *is not* and could never be," from out of which the dust-man is born who, in that arena of time, climbs the mountain of knowledge to *rediscover his original Selfhood that precedes time.*

"The world" of time and space lies this side of the REAL Heaven, and *within it as well.* How can it do both? Imagine a diagram of the sphere, with tangibility the downward and inward spiral to matter, mass, darkness, dead-end.

The tangible world is a composite of Wisdom's Self-knowledge and Self-knowing, both what Wisdom knows Wisdom is and is not, and what Wisdom knows KNOWING is, and is not. The limited world of "matter" is diametrically opposite the "real" heaven and earth, even while including the real within it, unseen (or barely seen) and unnoticed by dual knowing.

God's knowledge of what God (Wisdom) IS, is Unmoving Light. Satan's knowledge of what God is, is limited light, the *image* of Light. Satan's duplication of the true heaven and earth is made of limited light, a consistent *copy* of the Real. This is what science has discovered, essentially, in its recognition that tangibility is holographic.

The Perfect Image is the Original Child and it is beyond mere gender. The Luciferian reversal of The Indivisible One (Godhead) must necessarily appear dimensionally divided and many. The Original Child exists within each of the divided many—and is called the soul. The soul is the Original Image, the Child within. The physical body is an image of that image. And behind every body is the Original Child awaiting the rediscovery of Itself within.

And why such a Plan in the first place? How *else* would the Child KNOW—and know it knows—its dominion?

I doubt if this is written precisely enough for the intellect, but it is seen and known rightly even while I struggle to find amenable words which will be (and must stand to be) examined under the critical microscope of intellectualism's theology. The crusty shell of the old order will defend itself. Why? The dual nature of time-man and his institutions does not want to be exposed—as if putting down an icon actually mattered! The icon is cast aside at death. All icons will be put aside as the world of time is understood, rolled up like a scroll and turned off like a hologram disappearing when the machine's power is cut off.

The phantasmagoria, the holographic material world, is certain to be rolled up and turned off. The ephemeral nature of tangibility has been proven over and over for me and many others who have chosen to understand the nature of Reality. "Subjective metaphysics" has been proving the insubstantial nature of physical stuff for generations.

It is moot whether dogmatic churchdom or the stalled subjective studies are the greatest deterrent to the perception of Godhead and Its dominion. Does it make a difference? Perhaps. Whom will we tell of the unifying and harmonizing synthesis of science, religion and metaphysics? Who will most likely listen? If I knew where to direct the Light I have seen, I'd aim it at the segment of society that is least deceiving everyone. Clearly churchdom is an anchor dragging, not sanctioning a search beyond its interpretation of the Bible or other holy books. Clearly subjectivism knows nothing of the Child, the soul, little of human love and nearly nothing of the Equation. Fewer subjectivists can understand what is spoken of here than religionists—but churchmen seem to understand nothing whatever of subjectivism—unless they have taken time away from their binding organizational restraints to learn of it. *Both* churchman and metaphysician (religious or otherwise) can understand the subjective truth if they *want to.* Isn't this a hint that we are to direct this simple restatement to the entire scene of things, physicist, theologian, metaphysician alike? Ah so. Who can do *that?* Only God. God is doing it. The cosmic clock has clicked on and Everyman has begun to stir. The synthesis is coming. A grand global harmony is just around the corner—the one the prophets spoke of wherein there is no more sighing, no more tears, no more fear nor need of temples and teachers.

29

———

ALREADYNESS PRECEDES THE TANGIBLE EXPERIENCE; PREDESTINATION AND FREE WILL

The question arises: If Godhead is already the fact of everything, does this mean we don't have the ability to change things because they are predestined? The goal is predestined, yes—but we (as seekers) are able to choose which of the infinite possibilities we move toward—or whether we are to remain lost in the hands of fate. As the Christ Light says, we may choose Life and live more abundantly, or we may choose death. Most of us inadvertently choose death.

Inasmuch as the ascent of Da Shan seems to be a continuing part of the human experience from which no one has been exempt, we get up and do what is necessary to make the tangible climb with dispatch. That is the purpose of our study. But we *make the climb,* knowing the real of us is ALREADY present and has never been away. We keep this in mind. We never let it go. To let it go is to be swamped by the world scene and to lose ourselves within its claim to importance. Religion hasn't successfully kept us from that overwhelming experience. Neither has philosophy, science nor metaphysics. But a balance between them can. Allowing the Child atop the Mountain to lead us to live the Child's Equation, we quickly find this human experience proving the Real. How? With confirmation after confirmation *that we are already there atop dominion's mountain and have never been away!*

DIFFICULTIES IN SPEAKING OF SPIRITUAL MATTERS

Han, the old Master of Kwangse Province, was talking to the little group at the pond. Present were Lee, the soldier, Ho, Lee Ann and Mary.

Han said, "The pathway up the mountain gives ascending views of the scene below. It spirals upward, first one way, then another—clockwise and otherwise. Vistas below disappear only to reappear from new perspectives. *The scene one thinks he has outgrown* comes unexpectedly into view once more in another turn around the heights, but from another perspective and a new vantage point. As we progress in the world and the climb goes upward, the familiar is left behind and the unfamiliar looms larger. Then, once more, near the peak, *all sights that were ever seen return to be seen again from that nearly highest point of view.* They appear in new, ethereal Light. The peak of Da Shan glows. One is reminded of the crystal pyramid where the top-down view *includes* every bottom-up perspective simultaneously, like one peering down from the peak above at the teeming people inside the great pyramid, all looking to the top and saying different things about it."

At another time, Han said, "At the bottom of the mountain, at the first objective or the first subjective view of things, one can walk miles in the wrong direction with little effect on his journey. As he nears the top, however, there is less latitude for misdirection. A few steps the wrong way, the least fascination with himself, and one is suddenly looking over a ledge at difficulties and isolation and could easily slip and fall. At the bottom of the mountain, or along its slopes, one can talk until jade snowballs fall from heaven, and it makes little difference to those of himself following behind. But the least misstatement of direction from near the summit, and all who follow fall in the same direction."

What are we saying here? Among other things, the closer we get to the truth, the less *familiar* everything is, and the stranger it seems to the old views. More, the closer we consciously come to the Real, the more difficult our telling what we see. Why? There are fewer familiar references to use. The man atop the mountain wants to talk of new constellations that the man in the valley can't see for the interposing mountain. Communication becomes even more difficult.

30

THE WORLD IS AFTER THE FACT
Time, Space, Sequentiality

Many of the world's stories describe the human experience as a mountain climb to light and understanding. Others allude to man's progress as a river's flow to the sea, from movement to rest. All the spiritual books of the world include some kind of tree or seed analogy. We find all of these examples in Judaism and Christianity. These analogies are types of inverted cosmologies, man's return to Godhead.

Now that science has developed the technology to look carefully at the smallest particle—and the largest—and now that we are beginning to see and understand the processes by which the microcosm and macrocosm evolve, we perceive that the cosmology outlined by Moses in the Genesis account is remarkably straight. One might wonder how a man could intuit so accurate a progression of events before a science existed capable of splitting an atom or able to peer outward to the very edges of the tangible universe.

"And God said let there be light and there was light . . ." From science's perspective, we see that the release of the free photon (moving light) happened in the first billionth of a billionth of a second after Big Bang. Other such precise parallels can be found between the Genesis account and the cosmology of Big Bang, and no doubt more will be discovered. The reader will find some of them for himself in this work.

Hoving into view in a different field of science is another cosmological parallel which the cosmologists haven't yet connected to the Genesis account—or even to their own cosmology from other scientific quarters. The scientists who are working with light (laser especially) have discovered the holographic nature of matter. Tangibility seems to be the product of "split light." Or, to put it another way, the matter we perceive with our senses has its exact opposite—anti-matter. Or, to say it more nearly as Moses did, everything that exists in this universe we walk around in, has its counterpart in a higher heaven and earth that *precedes* it. One might say, using the language of the Jewish and Christian Bible, that matter is image. Image of what? Of another image—possibly, an image of THE Image. What, precisely, is the Image? According to Moses, God's own Self-Image.

Moses used a cosmology that began with God and descended or came down to matter and humanity. Present science has reversed the order of this cosmology and is working, with its linear accelerators, its great telescopes and the mathematics that binds them together, moving in the other direction, backward from the tangible evidence of humanity and matter toward the Genesis Beginning. Science moves relentlessly back up to the moment of creation, presently called Big Bang.

Listen carefully. The cosmology I have found so meaningful in my own thinking of things is BOTH cosmologies, but with specific rules. Like this: We think TOP-down first. We begin every moment of thought with an Ineffable UNKNOWABLE which we simply presume exists, the Perfect of Perfects, God, wherein there is nothing that works or makes a lie, wherein there is nothing imperfect, no time, no space, nothing but IS-NESS BEING ALLNESS. Then, from that we bring our attention "down" from perfection to perfection's expression here as our personal situation at hand, right here in the people, places and things world where we eat and work and do all the ordinary things of living. We begin our every thought process, subliminally at least, with the consciousness of PERFECTION FIRST—we get in the habit of this—then we come gently to our present state of things in the world to see what we can see.

Next, *and simultaneously,* we look for bottom-up CONFIR-MATION of ISNESS'S GOOD in our personal experiences and in the world. Sometimes one can find this confirmation only in such places as the holy books of the world or in the marvelous discoveries of scientists as they work their cosmological way *upward* toward the Original. But, there is always local confirmation of good at hand if we persistently look for it. I say again, I ask those who study with me to think top-down, but, simultaneously, to look for confirmation of God's good in the bottom-up world at every hand—because it is here to see.

Essentially this differs from present religious metaphysical practices in the following way. Rather than constantly *deny* the reality of matter, we look for the purposes and reasons for its appearance. We see that matter is neither real nor unreal, and it *appears* in and as our experience *for good reasons to be understood.* No wonder the metaphysician is having such an unsuccessful time. It is difficult to understand something one is constantly denying—and can't escape no matter how much he declares it isn't "really happening." Science is doing better at comprehending the reasons for the appearances than the metaphysician who runs about denying them. Even the rankest absolutist is finally driven to admit he is persistently having to live in the middle of his denial. Now that we have had a hundred years of looking at it, the denial of matter has accomplished nothing in the world that elevates or helps the quantum scene. The organizations sprung from the first hopes that the denial of matter would be a saving grace are themselves dead in the water, going nowhere, doing nothing—barely taking care of their own survival. They are doing very little tangibly for their own members, much less for their unenlightened neighbors across the street. No new light has come out of the metaphysical movement of the late nineteenth century, as anyone can see. If the light were there, it would be seen. Light can't be hidden.

This work has introduced the Da Shan illustration, the ship and wake illustration and half a dozen others for the purpose of explaining how we see material substance that seems very real to us but is not the final reality. The matter we see composing the universe is the image of the real universe, not the real universe itself. For me, this world of human confusion and anguish, pollution and self-destructive terrorism, as well as this world of human love, light and hope, human courage and stamina, human strength and marvel—this entire overspreading of apparent good and evil—is like the wake of the ship, all correctly present to *confirm* the DIVINE SHIP'S passage *before*-in-time.

You see, the things we see are all "following." That is, they are all "after the Fact." The light we see is actually delayed in time and space. The divine WHAT exists *before* the image we see. At this time human eyes are apparently incapable of perceiving the WHAT—but the Heart of us CAN. Even when we look in the mirror, the image we see is after the Fact of the Awareness of Image which perceives the image in the mirror. Even when I look at the body that types these words, the fingers I see (that seem so important in writing this message) are not Me, but a "following" image of the Awareness, *within* which these words come to be written. Even the body the doctor examined and made grave pronouncements to is not the Body I am, but only the image of it. There is a split billionth of a billionth of a second between the Real I am and the images I perceive within Awareness, even "my own" body.

Go ask a cosmologist how much happens with physical particles within the first few thousandths and millionths of a second of their existence. Then ask yourself, if so much can happen in so short a time, how much can happen between my own misconception of identity and my *corrected* sense of identity? How much can happen between my REAL body and my perception of the real body in such a fraction of a second? I can tell you how much! The difference between PERFECTION and imperfection; the difference between seeing a troubled and anguished body one second and feeling a renewed and vital body a split instant later. I know this is true because I have LIVED it true. Now I strive to stay here in this fanciful world of fiction-following long enough to announce the SHIP aboard which we all sail in God's justice and dominion.

Science has nearly examined the wake of the ship right up to the stern. But science. can go no farther than that because of the limits of limited light. However, we, as LIFE, are rightfully aboard the Ship WHEN WE GIVE GOD WHAT IS GOD'S AND GIVE MAN WHAT IS MAN'S.

It is our duty to come to understand just how this is so, why it is so and how it has *always been so*. Then, we are to *tell our others* so they can perceive these things for themselves and make them their own, just as this is my attempt to tell you.

Reader, can you see this simple fact of "things following after the Fact"? If so, you have a most marvelous universe of wonder and amazement soon to open itself to you. The entire purpose of the human experience has been to bring Everyman to perceive this.

I have tried very hard to get this book written while I can. I haven't been able to keep the schedule I had hoped for, amazed at the sheer quantity of Light I expected to find words for. I've done the best I could and am confident that "others" who catch the Wisdom spoken of herein will take up where this leaves off—and carry the Equation back to the Home from which it originates.

In many ways I feel like Moses, standing right on the edge of the Promised Land, not quite able to cross the river. I have truly spent forty years in the Wilderness, trying not to make the mistakes of old, claiming no credit for myself, giving none but to God.

31

WHAT DO COSMOLOGY, SCIENCE AND METAPHYSICS HAVE TO DO WITH REALITY? Ka-BOOM

Pearl Harbor Day went Ka-BOOM and five battleships were sunk.

These years later, we understand about the delay in time that goes ka-boom and we find ourselves making the quantum return to the Child within us. It seems a strange relationship, but it has everything to do with Truth.

"Friend Han, since time is relative, time is not real. Truth is not relative. God is absolute," Ho said to the teacher.

"Oh? Why can't God be relative too? Who but the absolutists say that God can only be infinite and not be finite simultaneously? God is relative to me. God relates to me."

"Han, since time has been proven to be relative and not really real, what is your concern with it?"

"To understand it; then, understanding it, to be touched and bound by it no longer."

"We are not bound by it now," countered the absolutist.

"Are we touched by it?" Han asked his old friend.

"No. We just seem to be."

"What time is it?" Han asked.

"Half an hour before the others get here for the evening campfire."

"How did you determine that?"

"I looked at the clock standing in the corner."

"Oh? And how old are you, friend Ho?"

"You know I am eighty years old! You have known me most of those years."

"Since our gathering is not touched by time tonight, we will let you explain that. One can explain what one understands."

A MILLIONTH OF A BILLIONTH OF A SECOND

Since the most recent work at the Fermi Accelerator, scientists are able to tell us that the action which freed the photon to travel took place between a millionth of a billionth of a second and a *billionth of a billionth of a second* following Big Bang.

If so much can happen in so short a time, how much can happen between the incorrect sense of identity and the correct sense of identity? The body we see with the eyes is NOT the body that is undelayed by time.

With the discovery of the Child within, the body-in-time is benefited immediately.

Ho started the firecracker burning and let it explode. The sound echoed from the hills for half a minute. He listened intently as he trudged back to the campfire where the students sat listening to the echoes also.

Lee said, "We saw the flash, then we heard the sound. The sound did not travel as fast as the light." He poked the fire.

"Yes," said Han. "That is right. Sound travels more slowly than light. Now, let me ask if we saw the flash when it happened or was it delayed in time as the sound was?"

"It was delayed also," Lee said. "Light travels quickly, but it is limited. The flash was a micro-second delayed. We saw it nearly instantaneously, but not quite."

"Then, what we see and hear is delayed in time?" Han asked.

Everyone agreed that it was.

The old man smiled and held out his hand. "I see my hand," he said. "Is what I see also delayed in time?"

"By such a small amount it is infinitesimal," the soldier answered.

"But it is delayed?"

Everyone agreed that it was, perhaps by a billionth of a billionth of a second. Ho returned to the fire, still thinking of the echoing sounds from the firecracker.

"Did Ho hear the firecracker before we did?" Han asked.

"By the time you heard it, I was two steps on my way back," said Ho, sitting down.

Han smiled again. He said, "If I cross my eyes, I can see my nose. Is what I see delayed in time?"

Everyone agreed that it was, but less delayed to the one whose nose it was.

"Then, everything I see, hear, feel, smell and taste is delayed?"

After much discussion, all agreed it was.

"Is Awareness delayed in time?" the old teacher asked.

"How can one tell?" the soldier answered. "Awareness has no place to go. It is always here where I am."

"Then, Awareness *precedes* the images within it but is concurrent with itself?"

Everyone agreed it was.

"Ah so," smiled Han. "Then we agree that there is some distance between the physical body and the Awareness that seems to indwell the body?"

No one said anything.

"Let me say that another way," Han continued. "If Awareness precedes the images it contains, even the very body most central to it, then images are *following*. Images are after the fact, just as the wake of the ship is after the ship, as the sound of the firecracker is after the flash. Could it be that the body we see and feel is the following image of a Body we don't see?"

With delight, everyone agreed it must be.

"Then if we are agreed that this chunk of clay is after the fact, in time following, does it not make sense to find the Child Ship that *makes* the tangible universe?

32

A WORD ABOUT PROPHECY

Predicting the future goes from "now" to "then" in linear time. Prophecy goes from "now" to *confirmation*—which is to say, from "then" back to now. Let me explain.

Most pragmatic people have a healthy scepticism about Biblical prophecy where virtually anything can be, and has been, predicted in the name of the Bible's sundry revelations. False prophets, astrologers, necromancers and soothsayers have been frightening people maliciously for a long time. We have grown accustomed to lurid tabloids heralding this prophet or that one. Predicting the future is not real prophecy, however, though it is easy to confuse these two different things. Furthermore, there is a difference between comprehending what prophecy is and the role preachers, priests and rabbis play trying to convince others what the Biblical prophecies are—or what they mean.

"Samuel, why do you want to talk about prophecy at all? Subjectivism relegates everything that has to do with time to the trashbasket. I left the old church because I was so tired of all the talk of prophecy."

Subjectivism does no such thing, even if subjectivists do. There is no real comprehension of what time actually is until one discovers subjectivism. Then our subjective mode of mind allows us to understand how prophecy became so important to the Lights of the world.

It has been important for me to understand about this marvelous thing that has been a part of my life wherein I have looked for and found certain events happening precisely as I had "seen." How can one ignore or dismiss such things? For me, "prophecy," as prophecy really is, has come right down to the most marvelously simple and *provable* thing on earth. The principle is the equivalent of putting seed in the ground, certain that they will be growing apace in a few days. As my scepticism about the prophecies in the Bible lessened, my ability to see what lies *behind* the "art" grew, and the mastership of prophecy increased. Now, is it possible to write of it so that the scepticism of others will lessen? I state forthrightly: The *anticipation* of Good's appearing has everything to do with *seeing* good appear tangibly on the scene where it seems absent. THIS is what prophecy is all about.

Prophecy as it really is, goes a bit like this: I catch a Glimpse. I (slowly) connect the glimpse to my personal affairs. I look for (and see) something in the temporal world that confirms the Glimpse. Then I look for other "external" confirmation to see if anyone *else* has had the near-same insight. Often I find that Isaiah, Jeremiah, Jesus, John and others must have written or spoken about the same Glimpse, because their words describe something that has just happened in my own temporal affairs, *something I had "seen" earlier in time.* Often, I can see that certain choices of words in the Bible are virtually the only ones that could have been used. Those events add considerably to my respect for the Bible, but they don't make the Bible infallible. They make the Awareness (I-Life), to which the Glimpses come, more nearly infallible.

My grandest glimpses have had external *confirmation* in the Bible. Since the Bible has been reliable so many times, confirming my own internal Light (about events that didn't happen at the moment of insight but happened LATER in my affairs), why shouldn't the Bible continue to be reliable in the matters that haven't happened yet for me?

Looking for the *confirmation* of GLIMPSES is the only kind of prophecy I know about—the only kind that is legitimate, as far as I know. When I find a book that confirms so many of the personal events of my life, I feel I can place trust in that book. I hope the book you presently hold in your hands is doing that for you.

If one can be less sceptical of prophecy *itself,* and look for the confirmation of his own insights, all his seed will grow in his garden as *anticipated!* That is the true prophet's work. Yes, I do "anticipate" certain things correctly—and their happenings are not what the psychologist calls self-fulfilling events. They are GOOD coming to light.

The world has made such a to-do over "prophecy" that it has forgotten the simple correlation between the anticipation of Light and the arrival of the Glimpse, INSIDE, and the expectation of confirmation of that event, OUTSIDE. In like manner, the unaware man doesn't see the same Flow in the opposite direction, the way in which tangible events spark Glimpses within. These things are the foundation of The Equation. Prophecy is the continuation of that same "process." Prophecy is the connection, the bridge, between the Glimpse and the world of people and events. I have never meant more nor less than that.

Prophecy is making the outside and the inside into a single

one. Prophecy is the anticipation of confirmation. Confirmation of what? Good.

I hear it said very often by the churchman, "It seems to me the prophets in the Bible were constantly predicting dire events."

Well, they also anticipated the day when the Child would be rediscovered, when there would be no more sighing or tears. The chaos they spoke of is the reward of objectivism-without-subjectivism. The dark night of the soul is the imbalance of subjectivism without an object.

33

OPENING THE DOOR TO INFINITE POSSIBILITIES

In early Christian Science literature, there was an article entitled, "Opening the Door to Infinite Possibilities." The author used a term that has become popular in quantum physics today, seventy-five years later.

Infinite possibilities. That's what the new physics speaks of more and more. Among those many possibilites is the real probability of an infinite number of universes! Not just one, but one for every point of view. Gloryosky!

This concept isn't new. Metaphysicians have long considered the "possibility" that I-Awareness am the center of my own view of things for which I am responsible to see correctly. The solipsistic experience opens the door to this subjective view of existence—and, once this marvelously expanding concept has been discovered, the idea (and possibility) of an infinite number of universes doesn't seem far fetched. Subjectivism insists that all the other views are contained right here within *this* perspective—spheres within spheres within spheres, so to speak—and they are.

The role of the metaphysician may very well be the willingness to allow another possibility to enter his thought, besides the one that may be erroneously evidencing itself. Its entry brings another condition with it—and this appears as the healing.

Someone says, "I am sick to death," and I open the door once again to the possibility that, among the nearly infinite possibilities, I can have an experience in which that same one tells me, "I am *not* sick to death. I am well, prosperous and happy." *Opening our mental door to that possibility is half the healing.*

In such a situation, the absolute approach is to know and affirm for oneself that no possibility but perfection *exists really;* therefore, one accepts no evidence (as real) but good, God's perfection, as the all and only Fact of being, here and now.

Yet, to be honest here, that is a difficult stance and it has not stopped those situations from which emerge the words, "I am sick to death! Please help me see the sunshine!" The absolute position hasn't worked fully in this (my) experience. It hasn't stopped the scene's doleful march toward the appearances of disintegration, death and decay.

As long as this experience includes the sounds of voices asking me to help "my others"—and since this is my own subjective view of things—it seems to me the work doesn't end with the recognition of God's allness, *but ends with the tangible perception of a comforted image out there that isn't calling for help any longer.* It doesn't end until my own reflection appears to understand as I understand. Why else have I been given the insight, the words and a voice to speak? Isn't this a significant purpose of life?

In this effort, I am constantly and uncomfortably brought to remember the admonition to "Heal the sick" even while simultaneously remembering (and living) the absolute stance that there are no sick to be healed, really—and all this in the knowledge that *such a stance hasn't yet ended the appearances of suffering and death in "my" subjective world.* This isn't easy to do. It's darned near impossible.

I conclude, therefore, there is still much work for us to do and things yet to perceive. I tell this to those who ask for my help, albeit I no longer believe all of us will understand *everything* we are brought to experience. To that extent, I yield patiently to the Ineffable which brings us all (at least it brings "me") to humility and trust, in the face of death. I yielded to an Ineffable *beyond* the limits of my understanding—and stopped trying to bind God to "understanding."

The final interface between this awareness of life and God is simple, childlike *faith*—faith that a very good God is the faithful custodian of this Life which He has brought into existence. That interface has been with us from the beginning. All things *else* are removed line upon line, precept upon precept, here a little, there a little, until the interface itself is all that is left.

It seems good (to me) to understand that the "interface" (the Equation) is all that is real and all that has ever mattered from the beginning. All the events which have been superimposed, including the world of people with its suffering and appearances of death, become increasingly dreamlike and evanescent when one finally lets go his love for the superimposition and ends his mental separation between Life (Awareness) and the Ineffable Godhead for which it functions.

It isn't easy to understand the point here, but it is a significant point, written for those who are intended to reach out and help others through the days ahead.

34

MORE PERTAINING TO SEEING GOOD

A JOURNAL ENTRY

Words came in my sleep this morning. If they can be recalled, it would be a wonderful gift to my world. I still hear the gist of them and their significance.

It has to do with "right doing" and what righteousness means. It has to do with Godly action and deed. It has to do with those of us who want to do as we are supposed to do.

Oh, the words come back slowly and sluggishly. I heard a rhythm of sounds saying that we look for God/good in others and this is godly action. Looking for truth in books is good, but looking for truth in mankind is better. Looking for wisdom within ourselves is good, but seeing it in mankind is better. To search for truth in disciplines is good, but to look for it and see it in mankind is the true discipline and the reason for our sojourn on earth. God's good is reflected in the good of mankind and that good is here to be sought and seen. Man is, after all, made originally in the image and likeness of God.

The gist is so simple, really. My listening ears want to hear the music of the spheres and voices of thunder, so the simple sounds of Truth are ignored. But the secret lies in looking for good. Just that. We look for good in everything and this is good action. And there is higher action yet—to look for good in humanity, quantum man. Mankind is the child of God.

RIGHTEOUSNESS AND GODLINESS

Godlikeness is seeing GOOD. This is precisely what George Washington Carver did while he held the lowly peanut in his hand. He looked at the "thing," examined it carefully and asked God to show him uses for it beyond the ordinary. Within a few years he had a hundred good uses for that inordinately simple legume that grows in the sandy soil of the South. There is more good in the peanut than meets the eye.

We look for the good in everything. It is present to be seen and utilized. But, especially, we look for the good in our fellow man. The good we see there is the good we are here. Why? We can't see it unless we be it. We recognize the good we are. We are it first, then we see it in others. We were made in the image and likeness of God—all good. "And God saw *everything* he had made and, behold, it was very good."

When I was in China, I accepted a discipline to do. I went to the village, sat on the corner by the town well, and looked for something good in each person that went to the well for water. It was easy enough to do when a pretty lady came to the well. It wasn't so easy when a dirty, ragged, bound-footed creature struggled to draw water. But I was instructed not to stop until I could see something good there.

There is something good, for goodness sake, in everyone. Everyone has a redeeming value hidden somewhere. Somehow, that practice of looking for good in people became a habit. That was my old teacher's hope, I'm sure. In the forty-five years since, I have never failed to see it if I looked hard enough. Like Mr. Carver's examination of the peanut.

Since people are made in the image and likeness of God, to see good in them is to see God in them. To see God in everything is very nearly the reason we're present in/as this experience.

And more: There is something mysterious in this simple practice. A great power begins to accumulate around us as we do this. The person we are seeing is helped by that observation as surely as if we had taken him in our arms and washed him clean of trials and anguish. And in the process we are blessed with a strange and wonderful—I don't know what to call it—power or authority or effluvium or charisma. Whatever it is, it is something very special. It is Something mysterious. One does not have to work long at this to find it so—and most wonderful for the doing. But hear this: *it takes the doing.* Not the talking about it and speculating about it—analyzing and judging it. The *doing.* We look for the good in everyone and are blessed by the looking—even as our world is blessed by the same action.

35

ABOUT THE APPEARANCES OF EVIL IN THE WORLD

It isn't that the appearance of evil isn't real; it simply isn't what it seems to be. What the world calls evil has a Divine purpose behind it.

"Sam, does this mean that God is the author of discord, disease and death? Are you implying that God is the cause of evil? Religion says that man is the author of evil."

If evil exists at all, and if God is the first cause of all, then, somewhere behind the appearances of evil, stands God.

"Oh, do you know what terrible things you are *saying*, you devil, you?"

Let me use an analogy that has been heard throughout history. I dream an awful dream and ask who is the first author of the dream. Am I? If I am, then what of the one who created me? If I had never come into being, I'd never have created the dream for myself. But I did come into self-consciousness and the dream may be my own creation; yet, as awful as the dream seems, it has a divine purpose behind it which, in a linear way, goes all the way back to the reasons for dreaming and life.

"What in the world could the reason for evil be?"

My friend, my dreams finally tell me of dreamlessness; my dreams tell me of timelessness; my dreams tell me of wakefulness; therefore, my dreams have had a good purpose. If no more, they let me think I know when I am not dreaming.

The "great deception" has a purpose, too: to point up Deceptionless being, God Being. The world of time, space, destiny and fate is the world of deception. But the world of deception is not without its limit and restraint. The Restrainer is God, behind the illusion, behind the evil and awful of this world which is also, in its subjective wholeness, a very GOOD world. Not a single cosmology disagrees with that. There is GOOD here to be seen and acknowledged. "Whatsoever things are good and true, think on these things . . . For God so loved *the world* that he gave his only begotten son . . ." So, there is something here to love, not despise and turn our backs on as mysticism and metaphysics are wont to do, calling everything illusion, unreal, evil-not-happening.

"Sam, it is said that in the last days, there will be someone who says that evil is good and good is evil. Aren't you doing just that?"

No, I am not! I'm saying that God is good and there is none else but God. I am saying that the world of illusion contains much within it that is *not* illusion. I am saying we are here to discover the corn and the darnel and know which is which.

"Some men are evil, then, as religion says?"

Within every appearance of men, there is the image of God, the Child, the soul, the Christ Light of Life which never leaves him nor forsakes him so long as there is breath in his body—whether his personal intention be evil or good in the world. I am saying that the truth of subjectivity shows me that I am forever looking at my own versions of myself and my self-beliefs, all the way to infinity. Some of them are humanly good, some atrocious. It is for me to live and do good, not evil. It is for me to make the distinctions as best I can—but it is for God to say who is alive and who is dead. If someone comes here, living riotously and evilly, I would be prone to say he is spiritually dead, but only God knows that for certain. I am not his judge, even though I appear, subjectively in the world, to be the judge of good and evil.

36

CONFIDENT EXPECTATION

"Mr. Samuel, you write that I should look for good and confidently expect to see it. I can look for good, no problem, but to confidently expect to see it is a matter of faith, isn't it? How can I expect to see good when there is so little around?"

This comes from a letter extolling the virtue of apprehending God to be all in all! It is precisely because God IS all in all—and because God is good—that one can *confidently* expect to see good everywhere. Nothing else can be seen, in Truth, can it? Eventually we will not seem to see "not good"—albeit, some of us may have our world ripped from under us first.

"But why do I see such evil in the world?" is the logical question to wonder about. We see what is called evil-in-the-world until its reason for appearing is understood. Then, it isn't evil-in-the-world to that understanding and ceases to appear so.

A man recently related the experience of his business going under in years past. "It was awful," he said. "That is, it was awful while it was happening, but *now* I understand so many things I didn't then. It was the grandest lesson of my life. Now I appreciate things I couldn't before." His wife agreed that, in retrospect, it was the most meaningful lesson of her life as well.

What was evil-in-the-world as it happened, turned into "the grandest lesson of my life." Who can call *that* bad?

"But while these things are happening, it's so miserable, Bill. Don't you know?" Yes, I know. Our anguish, like the dark night of the soul, permits us to KNOW the Peace that is real. We wouldn't know it otherwise. The Real is eternal. The anguish, temporal and unreal. The unreal passes in time, disclosing a Real that was here all the while. Its *anticipation* speeds the process! I know.

Let us say this again because it is too simple for words, hence easily misunderstood: We look for good because God is good, and we are looking for God. We expect good because God is everywhere, hence there is good everywhere to be seen. We begin to see good because God is there to be Self-seen and because (when the pseudo-ego is understood) God is doing the looking! All that has ever been asked of "us" is that we be a faithful WITNESS of the good that is roundabout!

In *Thomas* we hear Jesus talking to his disciples about the attitude of anticipation: "Say to yourselves, 'On which day will they (the angels and prophets) come?' " That is, let one's attitude be one of *expectancy*. Why not? It does wonders for us.

37

THE MAN WHO STOLE THE CHEWING GUM

There are days to write and days to read. There are days to sit loose and free, days to dream and watch the grass grow and chase dogs out of the rose garden before they water something.

Today, I am remembering, thinking back to the time when "contradistinction" first came alive for me. One doesn't often see a thief in the act of stealing, but on this day a well-to-do friend came into the bakery and I saw him steal a package of chewing gum. Obviously he didn't know that my sons and I were watching from a table in the bakery's dining room.

I didn't like what I saw. My first inclination was to use the scene as an example for my boys. "Do you see that? That's not honest! That's stealing! We don't do things like that!" But, for some reason, I held my tongue. Perhaps for the first time in my life I managed to say nothing about a distasteful sight.

I was in the middle of my metaphysical period, the time when one has seen that "the mountain is not a mountain," but when one is beginning to wonder why some of the ugly scenes on the mountain keep reappearing. As metaphysical development goes, things were beginning to come full circle, from "not a mountain" to "It's a mountain again." Anyway, I sat at the table with my boys, silently asking, "What am I seeing? What do I really see, if God is all and God is good?" I looked on indignantly and felt abused, the grind very much in my belly.

All this happened in the twinkling of an eye, of course. "I can't afford to lose a nickel," I thought. "My employees think they are merely careless when they spill salt or sugar on the floor, but I have to pay for every granule. That so-called friend of mine doesn't realize he is taking food right out of the mouths of my boys! But," I continued to reason, "if God is really all, that allness must somehow include the sights at hand. Somehow my friend isn't guilty. What am I seeing anyway?" For once in my life, I asked God what was going on.

As quickly as I asked, the Answer came, almost as if I'd been shaken by the shoulders. The words popped into my head, *"Bill, what is dishonesty but the delineation of honesty?"*

Then I heard, "Would you know what honesty really is if you had never seen the actions that make it plain?" Would I?

Well, as simple as it sounds, that's about what I thought and, as nearly as I can remember, what came to me. I watched my friend go back to his table, slipping the block of chewing gum into his pocket on the way. That night I wrote in my journal about honesty, telling God I didn't need that kind of delineation anymore because I couldn't afford it, even a nickel's worth. All of this happened on a Sunday afternoon, after church.

The following Thursday, as I was sitting at the same table

and putting the finishing touches on some bookwork, my
friend walked in the front door and headed my way. "Uh oh,"
I said to myself. "Help me hold my tongue, Father."

Jack walked up and said, "Hello, Bill, how are you?"

"Fine," I answered, inviting him to sit down. He took a chair
beside me. "Did you see me here last Sunday, Bill?" he asked.
I admitted I had, biting my tongue. Then he began his story,
and this is what he told me. All his life he had been plagued
with the terrible burden of kleptomania. He took great sensual
delight in stealing things, small and large, valuable or otherwise—it didn't make much difference. His dresser at home
was stuffed with things he had stolen over the years. He and
his wife lived in perpetual terror that he would be found out
some day and their lives ruined. Then he asked if I had seen
him take the chewing gum Sunday, and I said, "Yes."

"I knew you had," he said.

Then (and here is the wonder) he went on to say that a
strange thing had happened since Sunday. This terrible urge
to steal was perpetual, he said. It plagued him every day at the
most unexpected times and places, and it was "stronger than
sex" and virtually irresistible. *But since the past Sunday he had
been free of it.* He had gone nearly the week without that terrible urge. "Bill," he said, "I felt that you saw me *and didn't
condemn me.* Whatever has happened to me since last Sunday
has something to do with your silent forgiveness."

Well, I *hadn't* condemned him. Rather, the night after it
happened, I sat at my journal and thanked God for making
honesty so apparent in my experience. This is the first time I
can remember actually taking a negative experience and consciously turning it around in my head to the positive side—
and then thanking *God, the event, and the man who seemed to
be the instrument* for the lesson learned. At the time that I
"called the thief by his new name," I was comforted. And with
the comfort, I found the strength to dismiss the anger and
condemnation, to forgive the scene and thank it. This "turning
around," I learned later, is what the Ancients really meant by
"repentance."

Jack went on to say that he had seen all the people who
came into the bakery's coffee shop to talk philosophy. He
didn't know what was going on or what I taught, but he

wanted to be a part of it. "Whatever it is, it is good," he said.

So Jack began a study of the Truth and became a good metaphysician along the way. He was never plagued with the terrible problem again.

Such is the power of seeing the good in a situation—that is, in calling things by their right name. Not only was I comforted, but the action was synergistic. It reached out and helped my world.

38

THE LADY AT THE LAUNDROMAT

Years ago, in a hot, steamy little southern town, I was doing my laundry in the town's only laundromat. It was a dilapidated little place with puddles of muddy water on a cluttered, sandy floor, and rickety machines making an ungodly clatter. In those days it cost fifteen cents a load for the washing machine and a nickel to use the dryer. I had just gotten my laundry underway when a country lady came in with a huge bundle of dirty clothes. She was dripping with perspiration, clearly very tired and very pregnant. She was accompanied by an obstreperous little boy tugging at her, yelling like a banshee and running off in all directions at once.

What a sight: There I was, silently declaring, "There is nothing but God going on in the world. There is nothing but good happening." And then that lady walked in with her uncontrollable, loud-mouthed little boy. Ah so. I remember watching the mother carefully pinch open her coin purse and make her calculations ever so carefully before she began her clothes. Clearly she didn't have many nickels and dimes. She didn't have many pennies either.

The little boy was into everything, yelling and shouting over the noise of the clattering machines. I was sitting there observing, trying to see something good about that busy ragamuffin full of noise who didn't seem a bit bothered by the devastating heat of an Alabama afternoon. Every few minutes the very pregnant mother shouted at the top of her voice,

"Quit that!" or "Behave yourself!" But the boy heeded nothing. The mother was terribly uncomfortable, clearly at her wits end. I sweated and observed and "knew the truth," as the old saying goes, insisting that God was in charge of this scene, too.

Well, my clothes were about finished, and the lady had just put her tub of clean wet clothes into the basket to move them to the dryer, when the little boy, still yelling and dashing everywhere, ran into her basket and dumped her clothes onto the muddy floor. Dismay and rage overtook her instantly. "Come here!" she screamed hysterically.

The boy ran to me instead of his mother and grabbed the leg of my pants. "Come here!" the distraught mother screamed again, and the little boy knew he was damned if he did and damned if he didn't. Very slowly he started her way and very quickly she lunged at him, grabbed him and began beating him unmercifully.

I am a soldier and have seen people kill one another. I know uncontrolled and senseless anger when I see it. The mother was clearly out of control. What was I actually looking at, if, as all the holy books say in one way or another, God is all in all and there is nothing happening but God? What did I see? Illusion? Mesmerism?

Immediately I asked within and the answer arrived instantly, just as it did when I watched the man stealing the chewing gum. What did I see? The *delineation* of patience and love! Negatively appearing, surely, but the negatives are "not real" and the positives they delineate are "real." So I saw the delineation of the very opposite of the appearance. What else, if God really is "all in all"? Either God is all, even the present picture a part of that allness, or else God doesn't exist and we can end our search.

"Thank you for making love and patience *plain!*" I shouted over the yelling, the pounding and the screams. "Thank you for making love and patience plain!" I yelled again.

Well now. Even the machinery had stopped before the echoes of my shout were gone. It was as if I had shaken the lady or hit her. She stood looking at me with surprise and relief in her eyes—even joy. The boy's nose was running, his eyes full of tears, but he stood there looking at me, then his mother—and his nose stopped bleeding right before my eyes.

What had I done? I had called the scene by its new name. We must eventually learn to make the turn around without that constant sop, "Unreal. Matter. Illusion. Dream. Mortal mind." The "turn around" is an absolutely necessary part of the "repentance" the holy books tell of. Disclaiming the reality of something doesn't make the turn around, but the turn around is necessary. To do such a thing is a very powerful exercise in this world of plastic imagery. You may wish to try it, but expect to be surprised at the power of it. Yes, you must try it.

A short time later as I sat in the little cafe up the street, jotting down my memories of the event before the sights and sounds and revelations could be forgotten, the mother and the little boy walked in, a look of pure love in their eyes. She stood tremulously beside a table, peering once more into her coin purse, emptying its contents onto the table. She found a nickel and enough pennies to order a piece of homemade cake and a scoop of chocolate ice cream. We watched the boy eat it as if he'd never had such a wonderful day in his life.

Looking for the good in a situation allows us to call it by its right name. Dear reader, do you know what a marvel lies hidden in these words, a marvel that you can put to the test and see for yourself before this day is over?

39

THE ANGRY TRUCK DRIVER

During the energy crunch several years ago, I passed a service station that had just received a delivery of scarce gasoline. Cars were lined up around the block waiting to get to the pumps. I drove in just as another row of pumps was being opened. Or so I thought. Rejoicing at such good fortune, I pulled right up to the pump, the way one does at the grocery store when a new register is opened. I got out and began filling my tank, most happy I didn't have to wait in that long line. Then, I saw I had made an awful mistake. A big one. A long line of trucks and cars was waiting for that row of pumps after all, and I had jumped in front of everyone.

By the time I realized this, the man who should have been putting gasoline in his vehicle had climbed out of his truck and was heading my way—a huge hulk of a man with one of those muddy, battered pickup trucks with hunting guns mounted in the back window. His fists were clenched and the veins in his neck were bulging. Behind him, people shouted and waved their arms, urging him to get up there and do something about that stupid guy—me. It seemed certain I was about to have my stuffings removed.

What to do? Bill was about to get pounded into the pavement. Certainly I had not *intended* to get ahead of anyone. I am accustomed to wonderful opportunities presenting themselves unexpectedly, so I was saying my usual "Thank you, Father," when I saw the error of my ways plus the anger coming relentlessly, inexorably towards me.

What does one do in such a situation? Why do such things happen in our innocence? If God is all in all, and if God is purely *good*—and if I am indeed the very Awareness of Perfection Itself, why does this sort of thing happen and what did I see coming my way to do me bodily damage? What was really going on?

In a twinkling, not devoid of terror, I heard myself saying loudly to the approaching man, "Thank you for making your patience and my stupidity so plain!"

The huge man stopped in his tracks as if I had hit him with a medicine ball. "What'd you say?" he asked angrily.

"Thank you for making patience so plain," I repeated, and then I quickly added what seemed at the time to make good sense. "It looked like they had just opened the pump and I didn't know anyone was waiting for it."

The man, thoroughly confused, seemed to surprise himself by saying, "I was about to make a big fool out of myself, wasn't I?"

"Here. Take the pump," I said, but he told me to go ahead since my tank was nearly full anyway. "What the hell difference does a couple more minutes make?" he asked.

I thanked him and the pump clicked off. I paid for the gas and had to drive around the block to pass the station again before getting to my road home. When I passed the station several minutes later, the truck driver was still smiling at himself and his generosity to that poor little fool who couldn't see.

Silly illustration, one might think. Coincidence. Happenstance. Dumb luck. Not so. I've been living the practice of "calling things by their new name" since this Truth was revealed to me. I've watched the power and authority of the honest sound on the world's wind. I have seen its persuasion and potency. One does not use this tactic to take advantage of people, but it is "used" as LaoTse said, "to infinity." We look at the scene, discern the REAL before our eyes, acknowledge it, thank it, and be grateful for it. Absolute wonders happen.

Just "knowing the Truth" isn't sufficient. We look at the tangible scene right here in the world and *call it* by its right Name. There is GOOD going on everywhere! Since "God is all" there is nothing *but* good going on. But what is the good of knowing this if we don't live it in the world? The contrary of *not* living it, appears as an increasing contrariness to contend with in our personal affairs.

40

ABOUT THE SINS OF THE WORLD
Overtone

Part one

When subjectivism's real meanings begin to come clear to us, there is a period when, it is said, we "take the sins of the world unto ourselves." What is meant by this? Simply that the earnest, ongoing seeker of Truth solipsistically insists there is but one Mind and begins to equate *himself* with the Awareness of that Mind. At the time it happens, this perception is essential and correct, it seems to me.

But at this point we are prone to say, "I am the author of all I see," or, "I am the author of all the *discord* I see and it is up to me to get rid of that discord." This is the time of the

Christ role, when we DO take the sins of the world unto ourselves and become a willing sacrifice for all mankind. "They
are not guilty, but I am (apparently) if I see them incorrectly."
This is not quite on target.

There comes a time when we finally tire of this impossible
battle we can't win, no matter how hard we try to play God.
Here we are prone to withdraw from our groups and go into
the Zen-like stance of absoluteness. "Illusion!" we say of the
evil in the world. "Dream! It isn't really happening!" But that
doesn't alter the holistic picture of things either. We still watch
ourselves grow old in the mirror of life and, in the end, still
find ourselves at the disposal of bedpans and hospitals no
matter how hard we've denied the reality of matter. What
good has our absolute stance done for the world at this point
in time and space? Very little or nothing. Oh, but for some
who know that somehow there is Truth hidden in all this mystery of religion, metaphysics and mysticism, comes an Answer
that allows us to find our way out of the metaphysical trap of
non-being, non-thinking and the total denial of the senses. Lo,
we move beyond the complexity of absolute metaphysics to find
the Child within us! One can find the Child within without
having read the first page of a holy book or without having
the first conscious thought of God in his life. Oh, but the
Child tells us of God quickly, so that even our most scientific
intellectualism isn't offended.

Part Two

Metaphysically, one goes through many states and stages
which, as absolutists, we deny even exist in Truth. One of those
stages is to blame oneself for creating the appearances; another is to blame oneself for not having enough knowledge of
the Truth to avert the appearances—or insufficient faith, trust,
and so on. Finally (?), at least here in the tangible world of
people, places and things, one perceives a greater truth behind
the appearances—and beyond metaphysics—*explaining* to one
degree or another why the appearance exists, and suggesting
that it is not entirely illusory, but exists for one's own Self-discovery (Self-acknowledgment). Perhaps this is the time Jesus

spoke of when he said that even the stones would minister to us.

For myself, I managed somehow *neither* to affirm nor deny the evidences of the senses. Rather, I would do something like this: I declared and affirmed (in the presence of some apparently terrible situation), "There is nothing but God and God's Self-consciousness present." Then I went beyond that metaphysical stance to ask, "How does this apparent situation I am faced with fit into such absolute perfection?" Remember, for years I had said to myself, "It *doesn't* fit into Perfection; therefore, it isn't real. It isn't really *happening*," and then I'd hang in there, trying to ignore the situation that seemed so awful. If it went away, I'd thank God and call it a demonstration of God's power. If it didn't go away, I'd blame myself for not being knowledgeable enough or consistent enough.

Only very slowly, line upon line, precept upon precept, did I learn to look at the appearing and see what it might *represent* within a great picture of perfect Godhead and perfect Self-knowledge. When I did this, I began to understand what existed behind the appearings—and the appearings resolved themselves with more regularity, much as if I didn't need them anymore. I began to call this exercise, "Calling things by their right name" or "new" name.

Religion has the ubiquitous devil, Satan, to fall back on and blame. While metaphysics rightly denies the existence of a real devil, that denial has done nothing to lessen the appearances of evil in the world. After enough honest self-examination, we are finally led to conclude (in agreement with many authorities, including the Bible, psychology and a whole range of Eastern ideas), that the devil is partly, if not entirely, our own belief of a selfhood apart (fallen) from God. That very belief is what our world experiences are educating us (individually) out of—which means that our old metaphysical notion that we might ourselves *be* the cause of our own apparent difficulties may be right. Who can deny that if I refuse to eat and drink I'll quickly suffer the discomforts of thirst and hunger? If I fail to acknowledge the Source of Self, might I not bring unwitting anguish to my sense of self? But, is it the *incorrect sense of self* that I want comforted and healed? Or, am I learning about the real Self?

The bottom line here is that it isn't enough merely to disclaim the reality of evil, as metaphysicians are so prone to do at certain stages. It is enough only when we understand the *reasons* for everything appearing in and as our daily affairs, including the appearances of evil, devil, Satan. Then we begin living that new understanding and, in *experiencing* it, we bring harmony and peace to ourselves. Even then we aren't finished until we have "published" our findings for our greater selfhood to see and understand as well.

That is not the end either! Finally we are made willing to let even THAT concept go in the face of the "Whatever" God is—for even the greatest dreams of human goodness are as nothing in the Presence of Godhead. We are called to be willing to surrender everything before It and at "death" we are forced to. But, I am convinced, the surrender can be made almost without need for that event. Eventually, if the prophets are right, we will see a "time" when death and its anguish do not stalk us relentlessly. Why not?

41

ABOUT HEALING

Reader, please sit yourself down in a quiet place before you read this paper. Read slowly. Read *expectantly*. It is altogether possible, even likely, that something wonderful can happen. Why not? None less than the enlightened Carpenter said, "What you expect, believing, you shall receive."

Thousands of books have been written about spiritual healing. Countless articles and essays attempt to throw light on one facet or another of this fascinating subject. Words can barely touch the hem of healing, but this paper can point to insights that have been especially meaningful to me and to those who have studied with me.

Metaphysics develops its own areas of difficulty. Those places are peculiar and insidious—entrapping blind spots—where those with the best intentions can walk in endless circles. This is especially true for those of us who fancy ourselves on the high road—the "God is all" road—having left our organizations (for whatever reason) before we got the rudiments of metaphysics straight. (An interesting subject by itself—how our personal arrogance [the me-sense again!] had us thinking we knew so much more than the churches were willing to teach, etc.)

One of the great stumbling blocks concerns the concept of "demonstrations" and the *need* for them as proofs of one's progress. That concept begins legitimately enough ("By their fruits ye shall know them"), but ends as a stultifying entrapment wherein one circles forever if he isn't careful, looking for one healing after another until, finally, in his last years of struggle, his metaphysics crumbles in the face of fear, frustration and guilt, as if all the years of study were in vain. "Why isn't my Truth working for me now?" is the question then.

As appearances go, most of us began our study of religious metaphysics in order to (1) enjoy a more harmonious human experience and (2) learn something about Truth along the way. The Truth simply doesn't work that way, and unfortunately, metaphysical literature doesn't try very hard to set the record straight. The *adoration of God* and *the discernment of Truth which this love allows* are our first step and only objective. The healings, demonstrations and confirmations are the "added things" along the way. Until we get this straight, we may just as well forget about healings. When the chips are finally placed on the table, as they must be for all of us, it will be the *love for God* that counts and not our ability to manipulate the human scene. "And though I could move mountains, and have not love, I am nothing," said friend Paul.

Love, and love alone, permits us to see and *know* the delicate distinction between the empty fulfillment of a human desire (sometimes called "demonstration") and the grand *confirmation* that follows the knowledge that only God/good is happening. The words here are inadequate, but your heart is understanding something, isn't it?! Read on, expectantly.

These bits and pieces will help:

The ability to manipulate the human scene from hell to breakfast is proof of nothing real—and is usually the glue that keeps one stuck to the wrong scene. Look at the wonders the hypnotist performs. Or the psychologist. How about the chemist? Hiroshima demonstrates the physicist's ability to manipulate matter, but what have all the manipulative machinations of these practitioners led to? Often only more anguish to be re-manipulated—and a greater desire to do it. On the other hand, the least confirmation of *good* in our daily affairs is a mighty declaration to (by) the PRESENCE of God-at-hand. What's more, *this* good is *felt* right here where we are—and right now.

In a recent letter, which appears to have done its good work, I wrote: "William Samuel's experience may seem miraculous to you, but that view doesn't exist because of Samuel's ability to change the scene around him. It exists entirely because of the confident EXPECTATION of GOOD (God) continually Self-confirmed as this experience. That is, I look for the Good that is present. I expect to see it and then I see it! If this is too simple, I'm sorry; it is just that easy. If one jumps into the river and expects wet, he sees wet. If one looks at God's earth and expects good, he sees it. This awareness, this life, is God's viewing. Long ago I stopped taking account of Bill's seeing anything on his own. I expect to see God confirmed everywhere—and I do." So can you.

The mysterious paradox goes something like this: Ending the ludicrous attempt to manipulate the human scene to suit the me-sense's fanciful lusts (and righteous desires!), one finds the scene revealing (confirming) the Scene—and this may very well appear to be a greater manipulation of tangibility than could have been me-dreamed or me-imagined. Not trying to manipulate so much, we suddenly know what gentle good to do for others—and do it! This is love in action! Do you see? It is difficult to write these things!

When the solipsistic (internal) nature of the universe really begins to dawn within, one becomes aware of the heady ability to alter the entire world scene—even the universe! Yes. The universe is *within* consciousness. However, as LaoTse points out, "The world is already a perfect vessel and whoever tries to improve it, spoils it." For Jesus, this came as a satanic temptation which he resisted; yet his ministry still included healing, and so does ours.

The Light of the Absolute discloses that (the human appearance of) the most direct path out of illusory need into the "demonstration" of that need fulfilled, is to affirm *and trust* the allness of Godhead here and now—thence to look roundabout with expectancy and find oneself living the confirmation that only good is going on. We, Awareness, are not separate from God's Self-confirmation. For goodness sake, we *are* that event *happening!*

The events of our daily affairs are much more malleable than most of us realize. In many respects "experience" is the following confirmation of our beliefs and dreams, fears and illusions. Like all tangibility, it flows behind, so to speak—like the wake of a ship. Tangibility is after the Fact, as the photograph follows after the image that is photographed; as sound follows explosion; as the tree we see flows behind That which is being the tree.

With this in mind, consider the following analogy: The daily world experience is no more than the wake of the REAL Ship which precedes it. The wake is CONFIRMATION that a very good Ship has passed along. Isn't it interesting how we get all caught up in the boiling, bubbling froth and foam, afraid of the waves, when all the while, the wake, in its totality, proves that a ship has passed this way? It is also a wonder that we are forever attempting to effect changes in the WAKE rather than looking to the perfect Ship that Life is.

"Mr. Samuel, my difficulty lies in the fact that I can't see the Ship, but I certainly see the wake of my daily experience. How can I see the Ship?"

The answer to this question, beyond the scope of reason and logic, lies in ending the fractured look at the world experience and seeing the totality of it. The whole arena of scientific endeavor is an attempt of the me-sense to understand what Mind knows Mind to be—and what Mind knows Awareness (life/knowing) to be. The human sense of things seems unaware that this is what science is all about. Man refuses to reckon Ineffability to be the *basis* of the matter he examines. Or, like some metaphysicians, Eastern and Western, he calls everything a dream that isn't even happening. So, unmindful of Godhead, or, God outside our calculations entirely, we weigh and measure the whirling vortexes of the Ship's *wake*, believing them to be the real and true.

Reader, *we* begin with God. That is, we begin with the Perfect Ship and, to the best of our ability, walk lightly on the waters of the wake. All that is ever happening in the world is grand and *good* CONFIRMATION that God is HERE right NOW! The heart of us, the real of us—the Child-Identity Itself—sails aboard the Ship. Indeed, some have said the Child within us, the heart, IS the Ship of State. Good/evil, right/wrong, sickness/health, poverty/wealth are the right or left dualistic extremes of the wake. But the wake in its wholeness is "very good," because it confirms the Presence of Godhead.

Hopefully, these words will suggest how the confirmation of Good is infinitely superior to the demonstration of human desire. We find Goodness confirmed at every turn of the road and are not inundated by the threatening waves we feared when we first began "knowing the truth." Our real Home is not in the tangible arena of effects from prior causes, but *ahead* of causes—on the Ship.

Reader, I well remember the many wonderful confirmations that happened for me when I first came to understand what this Ship/wake illustration suggests. Since then, my daily experience has grown into a constant expectancy of Good, confirmed again and again every day with healings and more. It will be exactly so for you. It is really very simple. Just as Jesus said, we get what we expect, and what we expect is what we get. We expect GOOD every minute because nothing but good is really going on.

There is an especial Joy awaiting those who overcome. It is something mysterious and it has no name but it is Ours; it is Us; I know it is *attainable* because It has found me. If I can see It here, after the life I have lived, *anyone* willing to pay the price will be found by It, too! Part of the price is marvelously easy—doing as much to help others as we can.

The old nature of us, caught in the swirl of its little world, moves irrevocably toward oblivion. The Child of us moves straightaway to Source and finds the mysterious Joy. The Heart, like the prophets of old, is forward looking. It antici- pates GOOD at every turning and perceives It. It *does* good for others and delights in it. Moses wrote, ". . . He is a prophet, and he shall pray for thee, and thou shalt live." We look for confirmation of Good. We find it. We are the prophet. We sing the song of Joy and extend a helping hand to our world while the spiritually blind wonder at the darkness in theirs.

The receptive Heart intuits a divine (super-sensible) inver- sion of things. Plotinus and Eckhart called it just that: The Di- vine Inversion. It is the Preface to the tangible world and it is very difficult to either write or speak of because it has no rec- ognizable frame of reference. Whatever has been said of it sounds mystical and arcane until we listen to our own heart in the matter. Then it is, for each of us, sublimely simple—a strange excitement and deep Joy. It is the goal of all honest dis- ciplines, but the most distant and undeliverable dream of charlatans. It is an immediate and expanding gift for the self- surrendered who take God to be all in all. Yes, it is a Mystery that comes with healing on its wings—and so much more!

For where the beginning is, there shall be the end. Blessed is he who shall stand at the beginning, and he shall know the end and he shall not taste death. (Jesus)

The top-down messages that begin with Godhead—and stay there—are like golden arrows pointing to the Ship. They are like the Ship's undistorted Image glimpsed now and then midst the turmoil of the world's wake. The top-down message is a small, but potent, voice in a world awash with many, many voices.

42

THE ALCHEMY OF GOOD

Looking for a fence to put around the yard, one begins to see fences everywhere.
Looking for shrubbery, one suddenly sees shrubbery everywhere.
That is the Divine Alchemy at work.
Looking for tenderness, beauty and love, one finds them everywhere.
Looking for good, one finds good.
That is the alchemy of God at work.

The mystic of yore spoke of the gold, or the value, in every "thing." In the extremes of religious fervor, this was taken *literally*, giving birth to chemical alchemy. What was meant was, that one could work the wonderful Alchemy of God, Good, in his daily affairs and at every level of awareness begin to see beauty and goodness.

The *expectation* of good is not a *manipulation* of the scene (as one is prone to believe when he parrots the words "God is all, therefore everything is good already"), but is the anticipation of a CONFIRMATION that God is all, which we allow to appear *however it may*. Without the anticipation of good, we are not so likely to see it; and without the confirmation, we don't know beyond intellectualism what good actually is.

43

DREAMS ARE SUBJECTIVE

A dream is a subjective happening. That is, it happens "inside our head," within consciousness or awareness. The *substance* of our friend in the dream is *dream*—firing neurons or whatever it is that happens when one dreams and brings a mental image to mind. It is an internal event, not happening outside the head. This is a subjective event.

From the beginning, thinkers have postulated that the walking-around-in-the-world experience is just as subjective as the dream in most ways, if not in every way. Objects may be outside the *head*, but not outside the experiencing awareness. That is, we can reach "outside" the body and touch the tree in the park, but the sight of the tree and the feel of the tree when we touch it—as well as any thought we may have about anything and everything—are still within awareness. In this way, all things in our daily round are as subjective as the dream. Whether we see a tree or dream it, it is perceived as our own neurons, not anyone else's. One might say that all things are subjective simply because we never get outside our own viewing awareness to see if the tree exists independently of the sight and feel of it. Or, better, we concede that everything that is, exists within the mind of Godhead.

This brings to mind the wonderful remark of the old Chinese Master who, addressing his students one morning, remarked that he had just had a wonderful dream in which he was a butterfly. Then, pausing a moment, he asked if it might not be possible that he was presently a butterfly dreaming he was a man.

Philosophers dismissed subjectivism in favor of the objective world long ago. It was patently absurd to view the world as mental. "We may argue that the universe is happening within subjective experience, but this is plainly not so because there *is* an objective reality as well," said one of the Important Voices of the world, just as though he could get outside his own awareness to prove his conclusion true. The thought that the plane of human consciousness might be included within a greater sphere of Godhead doesn't seem to have been argued by the philosophers yet.

First thoughts of the round earth were dismissed as "plainly not so," by another Important Voice who was wrong. The earth is approximately round, of course, and our experience is more than approximately subjective. We might ultimately be led to comprehend it as omnijective.

In apparent yes/no situations, philosophers, theologians, metaphysicians and scientists somehow box themselves into the "either/or," forgetting the other possibilities such as *both*, or sometimes, *neither.* Considering awareness to be the *action* of *illimitable* God/Mind, one had best consider all possibilities as within the capability of illimitable and all-knowing Mind. Omnipotence contains the ability to DO all that can be done, doesn't it? Awareness limited to "subjective" or "objective" is *limited* awareness—hence not illimitable Awareness at all.

All this is a little like the pronouncement of an Important Voice from certain religious views decrying the possibility of a "transcendent" God, insisting on "immanent" instead—and making long arguments to prove the point. The simple fact that the Ineffable is *both* immanent and transcendent (and more) simultaneously doesn't seem to have dawned yet.

If classical physics can be said to be analogous to objective viewing, then quantum physics is analogous to subjective viewing. When we think subjectively, we are doing quantum thinking, embracing everyone and everything in the universe. *Subjectivism will do for the world and its sciences what quantum mechanics has done for physics.*

The subjective view doesn't exclude the objective, but includes it to infinity—and goes beyond, to all possibilities. We use them both. I *think* in terms of all life, but I still *see* the individual.

One sees the pretty girl, but subjectivism lets him see the little girl in the old lady, still full of beauty. The subjective view doesn't empty my world of dark and difficult passages along frightening trails, but it permits me (us) to walk them with brighter Light—and then, to make the way easier for the rest of ourself to walk there as well.

44

THE GREAT GLASS PYRAMID

Years ago someone wrote that all the people on earth, if assembled in one place, standing side by side, would occupy a square mile of land. They would certainly cover more land than that today, but let us use that square mile for the sake of an illustration that will make a point. Imagine that all humanity is brought together into a great glass pyramid whose four corners cover a square mile of earth. The people are standing jammed together like young people at a rock concert inside the great crystal pyramid, all facing the center.

Well now, how would each person describe what he sees as he looks up? Each one would see the four quadrants of glass coming together at the top. Let us suppose they can see the stars beyond, including Polaris, the North Star, whose position remains constant, and are asked to give a description of the North Star's location. The people along the south wall of the pyramid see the star in one quadrant; those along the north wall see it in another. Those who stand in the east side of the pyramid make different measurements to plot Polaris than do those in the west. As a matter of fact, every man, woman and child would have a slightly different version of the North Star's location, relative to the great glass panels that come to a point above. Each person represents a unique point of view.

Next, suppose that certain creeds and dogmas about the star's location developed through the centuries. The East-side view of things would certainly differ from the West-side view— similar to the differing religious views in the world today. Further, most people are too busy with family and other affairs to look up and measure for themselves, so they have grown to accept whatever idea is popular in their own locales. Can't we see from this illustration how religious ideas, all pertaining to the same God but seen through the eyes of differing cultures, have developed during the centuries before worldwide communication linked us all together? Man's *personal views* of his relation to Godhead are not unlike the pyramid-people's views of their relation to the North Star. Religious ideas generally re-

fer to the Same One, but have their own sets of proofs for validity. And, in truth, every statement is valid, so far as its
measure goes. Isn't it strange that some of the world's religions can perceive this difference and allow for it, while others
stand like staunch old pines in the wind, refusing to give any
other views an inch, claiming their own perspective is the only
valid perspective of the Ineffable?

Can the reader see that all eyes pointing toward the top represent individual "points of view" and "lines of thought"? If
so, let me show in a simple way how powerful subjectivism is—
and, remember, subjective thinking is the new wave of things
to come for mankind.

One person, having learned the top-down method of thinking and comprehending—the very basis for subjectivism—is
like a person who has broken away from the masses and
climbed to the top of the pyramid. His view is like a great Eye
at the top of the pyramid looking down at everyone looking
up. The top-down view *includes all the bottom-up views within
itself almost simultaneously.* The top-down view is quantum,
whereas the bottom-up view is individual. *Such is the advantage
of subjectivism and its comprehension that the world exists within
Awareness!* Subjectivism is to human thought what quantum
mechanics has become to physics. (Today we see the leading
edge of science on the brink of discovering the "subjective
idea." They have found the experiment tied to the awareness
observing the experiment. It is a start! Science will discover the
power of subjectivism before religion does, it appears—and
even before the metaphysicians who claim to know it already,
but don't know what to do with it. We guess the scientist will
know because his arithmetic will suggest, insist and cause him
to "prove.")

Does the Eye at the top quarrel with the opposing views at
the bottom? No. It *understands* the basis for the differences of
opinion—and understands the holistic reasons for mankind's
behavior. Oh, but the top-down view would certainly object if
one of the groups along the eastern or western wall went to
war against its opposite numbers, in the name of creed,
dogma and holy book.

We discover the Child within. The Child takes us (more or
less) quickly to the top of the pyramid to the View that in-

cludes all views within Itself. Down on the sandy floor of the pyramid, extremism in the defense (or promulgation) of anyone's holy book and/or bottom-up view of the Ineffable, causes men in black to make strange utterances in the name of localized views of God and to call for holy wars that could destroy civilization. On the floor, one hopes that won't happen. From the top, one sees that something *must* happen among the warring, unloving throngs *to call attention to the Child's topdown View that understands and forgives*. The prophets have all said to look up willingly—or be forced to look up in an awful Armageddon.

Two thousand years ago, Christianity came along to say, "Let that mind be in us which is also in Christ . . ." (the subjective view of things), but see how Christianity's dogmatic creeds are warring among themselves. Whatever happened to the Child's View that Jesus and others gave their lives to tell about?

We get the top-down view and live it on the sandy floor of life, right here in the objective view of things. How? We find the Child within ourselves and run with it. We publish peace (our own knowledge of this Child within) as we have been admonished to. We finally understand the exclusivity and arrogance of unyielding creeds and dogmas that discourage the individual's climb to the top of the pyramid. We see why the objective views have labeled subjectivism "silly solipsism." And, subjectively, from the top, we see that "one with God is a majority." The world unfolds within the subjective consciousness.

45

ABOUT ACTION AND "GETTING OUR SUBJECTIVISM STRAIGHT"

In all Metadelphia there is little written that calls for people to get off their rocking chairs and soft sofas and to journey up the hill of Self-confirmation wherein their work becomes quantum, for the whole world. The honest metaphysical textbooks written to date, correctly address subjectivism, not action in the world. To really understand the inner nature of things, it is necessary, *for a time,* to turn from the usual emphasis on worldly action found in the objective studies. Metaphysics is intended to bring its students into a full consciousness of subjectivism, but this isn't happening yet. Getting one's subjectivism straight is much like learning Einstein's equation. One must learn *it*—and its precision—if he expects to go out into the world and apply it. If one hasn't understood the rudiments of subjectivism, he can't live it effectively and he simply grinds away from valley to valley.

"Sam, what do you mean by 'getting our subjectivism straight'?"

I answer: Let's say one has a flash of inspiration. He sits down and suddenly intuits something like Einstein's equation. Whammo. There is Light. I have called this the Glimpse and have spoken of that in detail.

Then what are we to do? We set out to build the understructure, the bridge from the intuited Truth to its proof in the world. I call this "getting one's subjectivism straight." It is quite one thing to catch a glimpse of the "subjective idea" (the inner nature of the world—or the world's connection to the Awareness that sees it) and quite another thing to get it all straight, clarified and understood beyond intellectualism. Einstein struggled with the proofs of arithmetic for many years before he was able to come up with all the illustrations necessary to explain his glimpse. This is part of getting one's subjectivism straight, and this is what I say religionists and metaphysicians (especially) are weak in. We want the Glimpse, but we don't know what to do with it when we get it. The ordinary scientist is most concerned with proofs.

And what next? Then we set out to LIVE our Glimpse. When we see our Glimpse's results in our own world of people, places and things, we have had our CONFIRMATION. This is comparable to Einstein having to wait twenty years before the world's technology could build something that proved his equation was ACTUALLY right in the world—the link between the Glimpse and its application. All of these things are implied when I say that metaphysicians must get their subjectivism straight if they expect to see their world lifted up. Does this answer your question?

Human stasis (getting comfortable in various bends of the river) brings the personal condition to undergo changes that hasten the individual's conscious move toward the Divine Rest. The Equation again. *We keep moving spiritually or perish in human unrest.* We keep moving onward, and the change is upward—smoothly. We stop moving, and the change forced upon us is enough to push us out of our comfortable places very uncomfortably. That is true at the individual level and equally true at the group, national and world level. The great push at the group level has already begun in the world and in its churchdom of "old theology." It is soon coming in scientific and metaphysical circles, simply because subjective studies are stuck where they are, without the Child and without the Equation.

Human conditions delineate the Divine Alreadyness, the Rest-beyond-movement. The present unrest in the world is Everyman's approaching Self-discovery of the Child within.

Just as every dream is certain to end in time, so the rediscovery of the Child is an inevitable consequence of the world's having forgotten It.

NON-ACTION IN THE METAPHYSICAL COMMUNITY

Action and non-action are not two separate, opposing ideas; they are complementary sides of the same coin. Together they delineate the Divine Rest.

Metaphysics calls attention to the non-action or rest aspect of this "two that are one" and, thereby, balances the objective view's extreme emphasis on action. But metaphysics, being a way of thinking, just as objectivism is, is subject to similar misadventures when it ignores half of its own nature. Metaphysical imbalance results in turning non-action into NO action, thus enervating the expression of metaphysics in the world, reflecting that state of affairs appearing as the individual metaphysician who does little or nothing for his world in the belief that his world is illusion to be denied. Oh, what a round-robin of hopelessness and helplessness this is! What is the answer? We *live* our subjectivism fearlessly in the objective world—and the whole world benefits.

46
_____

A LETTER PERTAINING TO JOURNAL TENDING

Hello, dear Joseph. . . .

Your letter is most insightful, fun and sincere. I can understand Rachel's joy in corresponding with you.

It is just before a spring storm here, I hope. The trees and other green things are eager for the rain. Black clouds are gathering in the west. A north wind hints of a blow and the new apple blossoms are dancing in anticipation.

Joseph, your seminary friend sounds like a genuine greatest-character-I've-ever-known person. You asked how I would "handle" such a situation as that—a man who loves dogs so much he has forty of them in his home. Are you ready for this?

I would decide to know this man better than anyone I'd ever known—as if I were going to write a paper about him to submit for publication.

Most certainly I'd not attempt to change him. Day after day I'd let him tell me exactly how he feels about dogs—and why—and where his grand love for them developed. With all my heart I'd try to get inside this man's heart—because there is something special there, very special, Joseph! I would let him become my "writing discipline" for a month or so—or longer if it takes longer to hear him open up and pour out his inmost feelings. How does he relate his spiritual ideas to his surroundings and pets?—and friends? Such inner questions would be tremendously interesting coming from one who lives as you relate, sleeping with his animals. But CHANGE him? Never. If he were to act like other people, he wouldn't be as unique, different, unusual, remarkable, distinctive, divergent, incomparable, or sweet. Would he?

Gosh, Joe, this guy is extraordinary! LEARN from him.

We all play roles, don't we? Look at the silly one I have! How did I get saddled with being a luminary or an authority on anything? EVERYONE is a luminary! Over the years so many have tried to change my way of looking at the world. Oh, how the churches tried to conventionalize and modify my insights. Suppose they had succeeded? The NOTES FROM WOOD-SONG would be relative at best—and ordinary. Charles is Charles—unique and beautiful. If Charles didn't act as he does, Charles wouldn't be Charles anymore, but only our notion of what he should be.

So, there you have it, Joseph. As you look closer into Charles's feelings and tender places, he will begin to appear different TO YOU. Right? It's sorta like taking a walk in the woods one has been afraid to walk in before. It appears different when we get INTO the place—and there are NEW things to discover there. Our first attempt is to change the whole woods into a conventional place we are accustomed to and aren't afraid of—but, when that doesn't work (and it isn't supposed to), we change ourselves by broadening our outlook. The more I think of your friend, Charles, the more I'd like to know him. To REALLY know him. The marvel is, when we know like that, the one "out there" changes right before our eyes.

An old man in the Smoky Mountains taught me what "contradistinction" means. One day I asked why he stayed in those lonely mountains. He had been retained as a caretaker by the government, but was one of the original settlers of Cades Cove. He said he stayed because it was so beautiful. Then I asked him (he was a country bumpkin to young, arrogant me) what he meant by "beauty." With great patience he told me about leaving the cove and going to work near Washington, D.C., during the war. While he was there he had unbelievable difficulty—losing his wife and son and developing a lung ailment of some sort from all the factory smoke. When the war was over, he returned to the cove alone. He said he looked around and saw the blue sky for the first time in his life. He tasted the sweet water for the first time—and watched the beauty of the changing seasons—all things he had seen and known many times before, but NOW he knew what real beauty was, having seen so much that WASN'T like his Cades Cove.

I spent many days camping there—and hours talking to that kindly old man who sold honey, fifty cents a quart jar, on the narrow, dirt road that runs through the cove. His notched-log cabin is still there in the park.

Suppose someone had changed him, Joseph? No, he

changed ME—and that's always the only place real change can honestly happen. Here as I-Identity. Never out there with people. I change Me by understanding the Divine-I more fully— and then I see people more clearly.

I hope I haven't bothered you with too many words, Joseph. I am practicing on my fancy new word processor—a little computer that some thoughtful folks knew would make my work easier. I'm learning slowly but surely. Everything gets named here at Woodsong and the computer's name is Rabbi Moses Goldberg. He's quite a guy—librarian, lexicographer, file clerk, typist, accountant, indexer, semanticist and all-round good guy, willing to work at all hours for cheap—as long as the electricity is on and it looks like it may go off at any moment as the storm approaches.

Kindest love to you, Joseph, and many thanks for your encouragement, without which I couldn't write these letters. This work at Woodsong IS YOUR WORK, TOO!
Woodsong
1984

47

THE BIBLE IN LIGHT OF SUBJECTIVISM

Objectively, the Bible is a history of revelation and prophecy. Objectively, it has served to bring the central core of mankind to love God and men. Subjectively, the Bible confirms our own inner revelations. That is, we find our Glimpses echoed in the Bible, confirming the validity of our own discovery. Objectively, the world looks for its inspirational glimpses from reading and talking about the Bible. The Bible has been the Ship's rudder.

48

THE SUBJECTIVE COMFORTER AND THE HISTORIC JESUS

People who study the Truth via subjectivism or metaphysics

tend to think of Christ as God, as Truth, but not necessarily as man—especially physical man. Stressing the Christ rather than the man, the metaphysician speaks of Christ but seldom of "Jesus." Metaphysics carried to its absolute extreme, having dismissed the mortal man, must dismiss all mortality or men— so it sublimates history and must, in consequence, think of the Biblical or historic Jesus (and all events in time) as illusion or myth. This is not peculiar to the West alone. One finds the same thing in Eastern philosophy. Let me state quickly that neither the Christ nor Jesus is a myth.

When first "the mountain" becomes "not a mountain," (our move from objectivism to the discovery of metaphysics) for a time the concept of a mortal man goes out of the Christ for most earnest metaphysicians. Well then, how does one at this level of things, before he has moved *beyond* metaphysics, describe the historic Jesus of Nazareth? When one of the good, old-timey fundamentalist churchmen collars him, how does the metaphysician respond? Not very well, clearly, or there would have been a greater interest in subjective studies. A good statement that can withstand the onslaught of bickering theology needs to be made—but to do that is tantamount to making a rock fall up.

Here is that question, recently put to me for the ten thousandth time: **"What is the significance or relationship of Jesus Christ to me, as this Awareness I am?"**

Let me try to answer that question to the satisfaction of a thinker. TRUTH is applicable at all levels of human understanding, but the metaphysician has never been able to give a satisfactory answer to the fundamentalist churchman. Not just because the churchman hasn't come to accept subjectivism yet, but because subjectivism can't make the whole statement of Truth. However, the Child of us CAN.

In reply to the question above, I must answer from the metaphysical, subjective, *middle* position so it will remain subjectively correct, but still be understood objectively by one who hasn't caught the subjective idea yet. I begin a full answer: I can speak only for myself. Subjectively, people and history unfold within my self-awareness. I have no awareness of Moses, Abraham, Jesus, Genghis Khan, Dolly Parton or anyone else

OUTSIDE this conscious/subconscious awareness that writes and reads these words. I take myself to be this *Awareness* within which all bodies appear, including this one that plunks at the keyboard, as well as the one who asks this one a question about Jesus. *Everyone,* including the one who reads these words, is within myself/yourself-as-Awareness. This is self-evidently and undeniably true for each of us, even for the theologian who dismisses it as "silly solipsism." His dismissal doesn't make it untrue.

Identified as Awareness, I look "outside" and see trees, flowers, people and history in the making—all MYSELF-AS-AWARENESS going on in an unending "now." I look out and see evidences of the past (history) and possibilities for the future. I look out and read history books and bibles. I look out and see *attracting, compelling, unifying things and ideas* which are all within this Self-awareness. I look out and, despite all the teeth-clenching metaphysical absoluteness I am capable of, I still see ("seem" to see) *distracting, repelling, dividing and destructive things,* all within Awareness. Wheat and tares.

The wheat and tares "outside" myself have an equivalent "inside." The tree and the warm glow of the setting sun evoke a sense of beauty. The unifying themes evoke a sense of harmony and joy. The distracting and divisive scenes evoke discomfort, distrust, dis-ease, and so on. The obverse of this is true as well. I feel a sense of peace within and look outside and see evidences of that peace as happy and harmonious things I might not have been aware of otherwise. (Part of the Mystery is the Christly admonition to "make the inside and the outside into a single one.")

Let us examine this solipsistic fact for a moment. The first thing I see when I look "outside" is this body-image at the typewriter, an image more sensitive to me than all the other images—from this *objective* point of view. Stick a pin in this image and I yell. Stick one in that image and I may yell, but I don't always feel the pain. "My" view seems to be limited to the purview of this first image whose name is William and who sits here at the typewriter. But it isn't. After these many years of subjective living, I have learned that Awareness isn't limited at all, *but can and should perceive from many viewpoints simultaneously,* including some views little understood by the more distant images I see within myself when I look "out"— and especially not understood by my religious selfhood, nor even by my metaphysician friends who *should* understand. For that matter, Awareness sees things undreampt by men.

The belief which "the world" proclaims and the beliefs (viewpoints) I hear spoken "out there" in the people-world are written and spoken from the position that IDENTITY is that first thing I see when I look into the mirror. *That* body-image which is so sensitive, the world says, is our (my) identity. This form and shape that sits here writing and answering your question is said to be the identity I am—an identity not unlike the form of the man who walked the hills of Galilee. But clearly (to me), the body-image is not my identity. Rather, the Awareness that "looks out" and looks in, "thinks out" from that body, is the Identity I am. The Awareness *within which all the bodies and trees and books and artifacts appear* is Identity, as nearly as I can establish at the metaphysical level. My God, if I'm naught but the body, I am a mere bucket of blood and a sack of tremulous pumps. If I am that only, I am what my mother and father made. If I am LIFE, I am what God made.

Therefore, this Awareness is the "subjective" Identity I am and think of myself AS. From *this* perspective, all tangibility, all things, thoughts, ideas, books, historic figures and all history itself are WITHIN the Awareness I AM—and this Awareness embraces every form of every thing. Clearly, Moses spoke of this identity as having dominion over every creeping thing that creepth upon the earth. He also indicated that we lost sight of it very quickly in the scheme of things.

Well now, subjectively (metaphysically), some of the things I look at are more meaningful to me at one time or another. When it seems this first image within awareness, the William body, is hungry, food is a sight to enjoy. When I look at a *unifying* idea within the world of myself, I feel more satisfaction than when looking at or listening to a destructive idea, a dividing idea, or one that creates doubt and confusion in myself and in the world.

"But what about JESUS, for Christ's sake?" my questioner thunders.

He is the most unifying Idea I have, my friend, but keep your shirt on. I am answering your question reasonably, logically, step by step, leaving nothing out, which is the way the Answer comes to us. O.K.? Your question will be answered if you will be patient.

"William Samuel, I tell you that Jesus is the blood of the Lamb! Jesus saves! Jesus is the way! Praise Jesus, Hallelujah!"

Thank you for such love, my friend. Now let me answer that part of your question about the relationship of Jesus Christ and "me as Awareness." I was saying that identified as Awareness, all my knowledge of anything and everything is WITHIN Awareness—including the knowledge of Jesus Christ. It is exactly the same for you. All the bibles of the world are knowledge that comes to us by way of Awareness. I have no consciousness of the avatars, Jesus mighty among them, except as they come to ME here, WITHIN and AS this AWARENESS. Would you agree with this?

"I'm lost."

It seems so.

"If I'm lost, why am I trying to save you?"

You are not lost really, my friend, and neither am I. Let's get back to the subjective views of Awareness. About Jesus Christ specifically, because this will answer questions for subjectivists who need to know as well. They especially need to get their metaphysics straight so they can get on with the rest of the Work given them to do.

Suppose I look outside that window of myself and suddenly, unexpectedly, see a special butterfly—a big, beautiful, flashing sparkle of ethereal light darting through the sky. I am delighted and thrilled. Something in me comes alive. I would like to know more about butterflies, and about THAT butterfly especially.

What do I do? If that spectacular butterfly passes out of my sight and goes into history, I can still turn within myself, to my expert friends, libraries and books. I find a book on butterflies and learn more than I ever believed possible because such books are filled with information, are they not? (Incidentally, those books are an *external* confirmation of the Wisdom you and I already are, internally. We may not know that consciously yet, but that is partly what the human experience is about.)

One day I find a photograph of my special butterfly on page 1212. I get right down to a knowledge of everything about that special bug, and I'm so fascinated and excited, I pack my bags and make the necessary pilgrimage to Central America to the butterbug's winter home. I visit with hundreds of those particular butterflies to learn about them first hand, eyeball to eyeball.

Now, my friend. Listen gently. The holy books of the world have come to me just like that special butterfly. I have gone to the experts and authorities and libraries of the world within myself to examine them further. The Bible *in particular* has flashed and flown through my experience countless hundreds of times—and I tell you, it is surely among the special flashing lights of my world. INSIDE that book, the story of the historic Christ, the "Son of God," is, among all the stories within myself, the most influential record within this Awareness. How so? Because Something Wonderful within me stirs and sings when I even *think* of that man's statements and parables.

So, to finally answer your questions right down to a bug's whisker, my friend, I have examined the words of many men within my holy books, but the words of Jesus and the words of LaoTse are head and shoulders above all other words within myself except for my own. How so? Because those words of Jesus, subjectively understood, told me what to do with this first image, this body that talks to that body, and they told me how to live my subjective view in an objective and apparently divided world of conflicting stories, ideas and people.

And why are my own words important to me? Because here in this world of images, they reflect what I believe. My own beliefs influence my words, and my words bring results in my own subjective arena, here and now. Whose words put those shoes on your feet? The words in the Bible or the words that came out of your own mouth? Whose words put you into your present church?

"But Jesus came to save the entire world, Mr. Samuel. In Jesus there is salvation. Have you accepted Jesus as your Lord and Savior?"

You aren't listening, are you, my new friend? Much more

than acceptance, I have become ONE with the words from the Christ's mouth. I have become ONE with THAT One. Reading and rereading his words, I have come to learn the mystery of those words and stand as one with them. I have drunk those words and eaten them and they have become me. The one who uttered them in human history *came to confirm this Identity I Am and you are,* and the two of us have become one Identity.

Furthermore, as the inner meanings of those words have come alive within "me"—this form you are looking at—my entire subjective world is being lifted up, even as I am lifted up in the honest and faithful understanding of His words. As I find God's grace via the words of the Christ—and all other ways the light of Spirit comes—my world finds it too, just as you found me to come to and ask your questions. As I am saved from the former identification, all mankind within myself can be (is) saved from that mistaken sense of things as well. As I surrender the deadly deception, I come alive as the Christ-light for my own subjectivity, my entire world! And this is exactly what the Christ of the Bible told me to do, isn't it? I am *doing* those things with all the power and authority God has given Me.

At this point, I looked at the man who had come to question me and he was sleeping softly. His wife looked at me strangely, shook her head almost imperceptibly, first one way, then another, as if she were thinking yes, then no, then yes again. She wanted to say something, but didn't or couldn't. Suddenly she burst into tears and threw her arms around me saying "Thank you! Thank you!" Her husband awoke looking most bewildered.

Sometimes I look out and see those images of myself *hearing* what I'm trying to say. Sometimes they *seem* to hear and understand. Oftentimes, it is as if I were talking to a rock wall or a mud fence, but the one of myself who hears, makes plain the one who doesn't. And the one who doesn't, tells me I am to say it *better* and more clearly still, when I can, when I can, when, with God's grand Grace, I can. In ten thousand years the world hasn't understood the subjectivist yet.

If the world knew how completely the "transfiguration" has taken place here-as-AWARENESS, the world would BE on the door steps of the subjective idea, butterfly book in hand, asking questions, prepared to hear the deep things of Selfhood. The Tree of Life is soon to blossom and seed. There isn't much time, of temporal time, remaining. Life is eternal; the mortal tree of life is not eternal. "Ask Me while you can," says the Christ Light of Love.

THE METAPHYSICIAN ASKS A QUESTION

Dear Sam,

You have answered the man's question logically. I understand how I should think of the historic Christ from the "is NOT a mountain" position. Now, will you tell me how to think of Him from the "It is a mountain AGAIN" position?

Dear friend,

The purpose of this book is to help you answer that question for yourself. No book alone will answer you fully. The answer, surrounded by the wilderness of time and space, lies within you and your own interface with God. "Thine own right hand can save thee." Perhaps you should know it took thirty years to write the paper you have just read. It will not take you so long to answer your question for yourself. Just don't throw the historic Christ of the Bible out the window as science and some versions of metaphysics try to do.

49

THE CHILD MESSIAH ARRIVES AS WE GET SUBJECTIVISM STRAIGHT

When the subjective idea is clearly in hand, one is able to complete the interface with the world. During the time the subjective idea is developing, one is curled up within himself like a caterpillar in a cocoon. He is living in the world, working in the world, but growing spirtually by leaps and bounds. That is understood. We can't complain about the stasis apparent in the religious, scientific and metaphysical community provided we finally perceive *movement and progress* on the parts of those who are getting their subjectivism straight.

I submit that, with subjectivism clearly understood, one perceives for himself how to live it effectively on the objective scene of things. He lives his subjectivism objectively and remarkably in the world and becomes a light that cannot be hidden.

Then the third step arrives. "The Mountain becomes a Mountain again." After a time of balanced living, the ongoing of us are brought to make the surrender of everything. This is part of "the time of trouble" the Messianic Avatar carefully announced.

The final Secrets are to be revealed to those few who are willing to surrender even their vaunted religion and subjectivism to know GOD, Truth, aright. This is the final surrender—and may very well already have historic as well as subjective confirmation as Judaism's choice to deny the Messiahship of the historic Jesus. History records that Christianity indeed views the tangible (and intangible) Jesus as the living son of God. Perhaps Judaism, by divine Plan, rejected the Son, opting for the Father FIRST and ONLY. There is an objective reward for such a metaphysical position when the final trump is sounded—perhaps as the first group who will accept MESSIAH *within the heart of themselves to be the Original Christ-Child of God, the New Covenant, for whom the prophet Jesus represents the historic evidence* in confirmation—the Man who *made* that surrender.

Certainly Isaiah foresaw the Child of God. Certainly Jesus identified as that Child. It fits metaphysically that the discovery of the Child within will very well represent Messiah to Judaism when the Child within Everyman is found—and may even be found by the Christian community as well. But more likely, Jewish and Christian *churchdom* will fear for their dogmas, buildings and numbers—especially worry about deceivers—and refuse to listen to the Child Itself right in the heart of them. If so, the ministry of Jesus would be confirmed positively and subjectively. The prophets, including the confirming Christ of history, would be right once more. The Child IS the savior. A Child shall lead a remnant of "children" to New Jerusalem, a new dimension.

I state as a fact of my own Self-discovery, I walked the objective ground first; I walked the subjective discovery second; I lived my subjectivism in the world, discovering the remarkable Balance about which I've written. Then I was pushed into *total* willingness of self-surrender. That surrender wasn't finished until I was willing to give up my most cherished self-beliefs, even the teachings of Jesus *seen to be subservient before Godhead*. *Then* I was given the keys to the Kingdom, the Secrets of the Child and the Equation with which I *proved* the truth of the Self-revelations and the teachings of the historic Christ.

The point here (and I repeat it endlessly) is I was given nothing of the Child and the Child's Equation until I was proven willing, after many years, to surrender even my joys of subjectivism—everything—even God, *in obeisance to Godhead*. What I have been shown since has been lived and proven, every step of the Equation *confirmed*—attesting the primacy of GOD first, not the *messenger* of God, even when that messenger is the Son of God Himself. I was finally made WILLING to surrender the Christ Idea for God, perhaps a little like Abraham—and *then* the Secret was given to me so that rather than lose that Christly Ideal I could *become* it.

Since those days, all but a few things I was shown have come to pass—and what has not happened, will, if the pattern remains as certain at its conclusion as it has been thus far in time. I see no reason it won't.

In the world, resistance to Truth is individual, then group wide, then nation wide, then worldwide. Objectively, the groups will be shattered and shaken as the individual has been—then the nation, then the world.

One does not have to be shaken if he moves ON with God—but he will be destroyed if he doesn't.

These words do not sound very metaphysical, but why do they have to? The Truth isn't bound to meet human expectations. God is still a mystery to me, but the Self-I-am, made in the perfect IMAGE of God, grows clearer every day—and those who heed these words will find what I have found. We become like the fountains we drink from. Religionists and metaphysicians drink from many fountains and have become a dilute nothing. There is a single Fountainhead, God, for whom

Jesus speaks. The words of Jesus (in *Thomas* and elsewhere) are true and faithful. Whatever I have had to say can be found in those words or in the words of LaoTse who addressed nature as himself. The man Jesus drank from the Prophet's fountain and I drink from His. Jesus came as the historic, linear confirmation of the Child within—the first willing to BE that Child of God. I announce the Same Child of God, present in the hearts of Everyman. I hail Godhead first; I hail God's Original Image—the Child within the Elect of God.

50

ABOUT HARD TEACHINGS

There are "hard teachings" that are not easy to tell or hear, but as appearances go, these things must be said. One may *believe* he values the Truth more than anything in the world, but when it comes to living the Truth by having to part with some of his old nature or the possessions he deems valuable, his belief becomes a horse of another color—one that bucks at the hard teachings. Those who call our attention to the hard teachings become burrs under the saddle blanket.

For instance, there is a long journey in world-time between (1) the first idealistic feelings that one doesn't actually part with anything he gives to his world, and (2) *the fearless living of that truth wherein he learns for a fact that he doesn't.* One of the purposes of the "hard teachings" is to bridge that gap—but woe to the one who takes such bridging information to a worldly man who loves his own opinions and his worldly possessions! With those people, we are to be as cautious as a fox, my friend, and as harmless as a dove.

This doesn't state the whole area of the hard teachings. A recent letter from Joanna puts another part of it straight. She writes that in the process of Self-discovery one finds the black side of the old nature as well as the good side. We come face to face with the dark side of ourself—the not-Self. Yes, indeed. The suspicious side, the questioning side, the doubtful side, the withholding side. We find all sides before we find no sides. Joanna writes that the "comfortable worldly man" is titillated by the Truth's insistence that he search out, find and finally surrender the old nature of himself, but he recoils at the thought that his external world *reflects the old nature's accumulations which he must surrender as well.* And, of course, that is the crux of the matter. When we reach that point in our confirming climb of the mountain, we discover firsthand whether or not we are really willing to devalue the world and actually give a tangible value to the Truth we hold dear. Most of us are not—until we are forced to—*even though the Truth can never be more valuable in our human affairs than the value we actually give it in the world.* As Jesus says in *The Gospel According to Thomas,* many are standing around the cistern, but few are drinking the water.

Nearly everyone who has come to Woodsong has heard of the Child within us, but few have fully found it—or have waited to hear of the Child's Equation. Many hang up their shingles and begin practicing the subjective Truth before they have a working knowledge of subjectivism—or any knowledge of the Equation, much less the living of it. The secret of the Equation has been well kept, but the time has come for the world to hear it again and heed. A new dimension awaits those who "overcome." "There is nothing covered that will remain uncovered; nothing hidden that will not be revealed." That time is this time—and there isn't much of it remaining.

51

TO FIND BALANCE IS TO FIND IDENTITY

To find BALANCE is to find Identity—and Identity leads the way to God.

Surely ten thousand books have been written over the centuries about identity—what it really is and how to find it. Essentially, the world's holy books are about identity, the "real man" made in the image and likeness of God.

There is little doubt among thinkers that the world view of

identity isn't the correct view, and most would agree much more is to be understood. The problem, as always, is exactly *how* one goes about discovering his true identity. "Don't tell me about Identity," a letter says, "tell me what to do to find it." What follows is a "what to do."

Just as the inner Child leads to Godhead, so balance leads to the Child. The balance is to the child what alphabet is to writing. We learn the alphabet before we write. We learn about balance and live it. Lo, the Child is discovered and the Child leads straight to Identity. Heretofore, we have really been looking for the true nature of "the old man." That one isn't identity and never will be. *We find the Child,* and then we know the Child is the real Identity. Then we set out to understand the Child of ourselves.

When one has found the balance, he has found himself. One *is* the point of balance between all "the five trees in the midst of the garden." Where is the balance between inside and outside if it isn't this very Awareness I am? The inside passes through this Awareness to the outside and returns from the outside and passes through Me again.

Where is the balance between above and below? Right here as Awareness, midway between microcosm and macrocosm. And where is the balance between male and female? Here as Awareness. Certainly not here as this body. This body appears more male than female. That body seems more female than male. But, upon careful examination, the balance IS found within the body physical, the body being both male and female but tipped *bodily* one way or the other. Between the extremes of gender lies Awareness, this consciousness of being, perfectly balanced Identity which is being all there is to both male and female.

And so it is with all imbalances. The balance is found right here as Awareness, Identity. When the ancients said one's aim in life was to "Know Thyself," they were exactly right. One finds himself, Identity, and finds he is the balance between Spirit and matter, first and last, inside and outside, above and below, objective and subjective, the macrocosm and microcosm. He will also find (slowly) that his Self, as Awareness, *precedes* all tangibility in time. Awareness is *prior* to the body we seem to be looking out of.

One finds the divinity in himself before he sees it in another—and when he has actually found it in himself, he sees
it in *all* others. But of course, we think we see it in others long
before we see it in ourselves. A letter is here from a lady who
is certain she has found God living in a commune on the West
Coast, and she would have me agree that he is God. People are
all the image of God, but not one image is God. God is God
and people are life's confirmation, life's "image" as that image
appears on the tangible scene. The godly man confirms God
more obviously than do the warrior and thief, but to the godly,
the sinner is as much the image of the Image of God as the
saint is.

Beware the man who says "I am God" or permits others to
say that of him. Perhaps the only thing more sinful than proclaiming oneself to be God is to allow others to call him God.
Certainly one of the great measures of the man Jesus was his
honesty on this score. Were Jesus on television this minute, he
would say exactly what he said two thousand years ago: "When
you see Me you see the Father, for my Father and I are one,
but My Father is *greater* than I." And, of course, people would
still call him God and good and he would say once more,
"Don't call me good. Don't call any man good. There is none
good but God. Don't don't call me master, either. I am *not*
your master."

No genuine "master" lets anyone call him master. If I were
to look up and suddenly perceive that I am, indeed, the Perfect Image Itself, the First Born of God, God's only begotten
Son Himself, I would yet be image and nothing of myself. Image is image. Image is nothing of *itself*. Image is without real
power or authority except it be given to that image by Godhead. GODHEAD is the Name, the Authority and the Power,
and not even the Son of God Himself dares claim it. Inasmuch as Jesus the man made these honest and identical statements, that image appears Christly and extremely honest to
me.

It is when we become nothing that we become the door to
Something. The best door is the empty place without an im-
pediment. The Window that allows the Light is the place
where nothing is.

52

ONE MORE PAPER ON BALANCE

We hear little on the subject of balance in our religious or metaphysical study, which is something of a surprise considering the absolute necessity of finding and maintaining it. One doesn't have to look far in the scientific, religious or metaphysical scene to find evidence of woeful imbalances among people.

We must conclude that since our return to a conscious knowledge of Identity is much like a mountain climb wherein we're busy confirming the Truth of Identity, then the climbing is integrally concerned with balance. If we lose it, we fall away from the Center of Identity into the chaos of imbalance. But there is more than *one* balance to find and maintain in our search for Truth. There are several of them, each necessary in various places in our climb to confirmation.

The first balance is the karmaic teeter totter between cause and effect, good and evil—just as much the province of science as religion. This, the first balance we really become aware of, is like walking a plank across a chasm. Living morally and honestly, one maintains his balance and doesn't topple into the reactive world of negative effects or punishment. It is the "go and sin no more" balance—and is absolutely basic. It is part of the "Do unto others as you would have them do unto you" ethic.

Beyond this linear, karmaic balance is another, "higher" on the scale of things. It is the balance we begin to maintain between the inner and outer world—the inside/outside equation. We see the "image/thing" and strike a balance between the thing and the thought or feeling, the subjective basis for the image. This is the province of metaphysics.

Prior to (or simultaneous with) the metaphysical inner/outer balance is the hierarchical or cosmological equation. This is established consciously when the "below" of human authority is surrendered, precept upon precept, to the divine Authority "above," to which is given all power and importance until such time as the Above—the Ineffable—*becomes* all in all to us and the "below" of us lives self-surrendered. When the surrender is made in actual fact, *the new balance of things eventually brings us to DO what is demanded of us.* This, the reader knows, is the discovery that Awareness is God's, not man's. It is the discovery of the real Identity—and the actions that accompany that revelation. This balance is also part of the "Golden Rule."

I hastily mention the male/female balance here. The discovery of awareness as Identity mandates the acceptance of male and female equally. Awareness is as much female as male, as much male as female. We stop thinking of ourselves in terms of gendered man or woman, but as Life, Awareness—which is being all there is to the appearances of either gender. This balance is lived in the world as an equal appreciation for men and women. The Lights of the world have been as thorough in their instruction of women as of men; it has been the organizations that followed them that began the discrimination and lower status of women.

Overspreading all these balances, and going on continually everywhere in nature, is the divine Balance and its Equation—*the very living process by which tangible life gives and receives, receives and gives, in-breathing and out-breathing, passing the Light of Life onward to those within and without—and receiving from the "outside" and allowing it to pass along to the Within.* This is the divine Balance and its Equation—spoken of with such simple eloquence by LaoTse, Buddha and Jesus, among others—and misspoken in countless words of lesser truth by half-prophets who have never heard of the mystic's Equation, nor dreamed it existed. The Equation comes with the Child, the Comforter that leads to all peace. Our living It, consciously or otherwise, is the open door to the Kingdom. The Equation lived is the forgiveness of sins (imbalances).

It is not the imbalance of *too much* action (like one who oversteps himself on the karmaic plank and falls into sin) that is half so fatal to the metaphysician as the non-action of doing nothing. Intellectual and spiritual pride evoke a catatonia, a state of non-action in the world which assails one in later life. I see old seekers hanging onto their plateaus of understanding (Absoluteness being one of the stickier wickets) where one grows thick, opaque and stubborn, unable to break free, wondering what has happened to his Truth when he needs it most. On these wickets one finds himself assailed by depression, ennui, hopelessness and/or mental imbalances capable of dragging him to his tangible, human finish. There is no escape from this deadliness by making positive affirmations or by declaring that "God is all!" The escape comes with LIVING the Equation again—the balancing Child-ACTION of GIVING and RECEIVING once more as we did when we were children and when we were new students of the Truth. We allow the Equation to work its magic in our affairs again; we pass the Glimpses along to others (giving God what's God's)—to receive therefrom. We give our tangible goods to those who need them (giving the world whatever we can give of our substance) to receive therefrom.

The Balance and its Equation have been in operation from the first breath we've drawn on earth. It is the Real. It is where Identity has always been in Fact—standing atop Da Shan, Kwangse's mighty mountain, the entire world under its (our) feet. The Balance is the point of exchange between inside and outside, above and below, objective and subjective, male and female, God and man. It is, so far as I have been shown, the final Balance. In this world of images I have seen no one get to the Balance of things without LIVING the Equation. Here, the metaphysician is last. This tangible echo in the world—this material body and its affairs—doesn't get to the top of the mountain by merely claiming that Balance for himself, as metaphysics poorly expressed leads one to believe he can. Yes, it is true that a divine, perfect Balance is the eternal fact of Being—but here in the world of holographic imagery, we LIVE the balance with our "others," and this experience ultimately CONFIRMS the Fact of Balance in our comings and goings, right here among the nuts and bolts of the tangible scene.

The idea grows so quickly (and devilishly) that, as seekers of truth, we know something that others don't. Just as quickly comes the vainglorious idea that there is no one with whom we can discuss these ideas. El poo poo! The match struck in the dark corner of Da Shan's face has sufficient darkness to dispel. How the darkness is dissipated dawns slowly for us until we find one who has been given the Equation, along with the means and courage to tell us of it. These living persons are rare, but there is a written record of many of them.

Listen, listen. WE ARE ADMONISHED TO PASS ALONG THE LIGHT we've grown to perceive *TO OUR ENTIRE SUBJECTIVE SELFHOOD!* ("Preach ye the gospel to all the world!" said the One.) Our work isn't finished until we do. "When you make the two one . . . the inner as the outer and the outer as the inner . . . then shall you enter the Kingdom," has been the admonition from the first. We LIVE the Primal Balance consciously in our daily affairs and see it tangibly reestablished (for our confirmation) in our personal experience, the world. This is to see "Thy will be done on earth as it is in heaven."

Of all people within this experience-I-am, my metaphysical selfhood appears to understand *least* of the great responsibility that comes with the Truth. We have a mighty work to accomplish before we are done with the human drama and leave the slopes of Da Shan. These ideas haven't been given to us for nothing. Everyone who reads these words is capable of living The Equation.

Not everyone will write a book about the Truth, but everyone is "THE Book" to himself and can help make certain that one is written—an honest representation of his own. Those who helped Paul write to the early churches are surely participants with him now, and he couldn't have written without their help. Most metaphysicians who have withdrawn from their organizations in the belief they have a singular new track to follow appear to be doing from very little to absolutely nothing to help their Pauls and Johns, their Marys and Marthas. But, to help is to live the Equation and *participate*. As we do, we find the Truth as valuable in our affairs *as we have been willing to give it an actual value in our own experience of the world.* That is how the Equation works. If the Truth isn't working in our affairs, we have stopped giving to it. If the world is giving us nothing, we have stopped giving to the world. Many who have withdrawn from their organizations hear these words and are aghast and angered. Why? See how little they have given to their world.

Surely, the primary reason I have spoken directly of "the Equation" only to those who were living it when they came to study here (and not one word about it unless they were) was to avoid the stigma so quickly given to all who speak of "giving and receiving"—no matter how honest their reason. No doubt there were those who must have thought the twelve baskets of food collected after the Sermon on the Mount was the selfish intent of the Preacher. Our intellectual period (metaphysics) is the labeling time in our affairs when we're so prone to divide singleness into levels of attainment, degrees of truth and error, shades of honesty or dishonesty—or into an absoluteness that tries to ignore the world of tangibility. I recall the charges made in high human places that Goldsmith and his kind were mercenary and "in it for the money," when no such thing was true. No wonder the mystics swore their initiates to secrecy concerning "the hard teachings," upon the penalty of death. Initiates were forbidden to speak directly of "The Ratio" or "The Secrets." They needn't have been. The least mention of the Equation brings one's personal world to thunder and shake, and whoever tells of It makes himself a sacrifice, not always willing.

We are told that there is nothing hidden that will not be revealed, nothing covered that will not be uncovered. Now I speak directly about the Balance and its Equation. I have waited in this human experience until the human charges can make no difference to me. Now it makes no difference *how* I reap the world's trash or treasure. They are the same, no more real (or unreal) than anything else in my world. I have waited until everyone can see there are no human motives in this statement of the final covenant—and never have been.

We are told that every human imbalance (sin) is "forgiven" with the simple living of the grand Balance and its Equation, whether it is intellectually comprehended or not. With all my heart I know this is true. I watch the simple and childlike who live the Equation grow old with grace, dignity and peace. Their bodies may appear to anguish, but their hearts still romp with angels. I see those who do not live it—though they have attained to mighty places in the hierarchies of intellectualism—wither and die without a trace of Joy, without anything done for their world. God reveals the secrets of the Living Equation to children and hides them from the worldly.

53

ZEN BUDDHISM AND WESTERN ABSOLUTENESS

Zen Buddhism and Western "absoluteness" are equivalents. Zen brings us to negate everything but Isness Itself. So does the absolute view.

The second position, the "is not a mountain" aspect of development, as it is lived in the world, is represented in the illustration of Da Shan by the town of Metadelphia and its extreme neighbor, nearby Absoluty. In Absoluty, even the houses have walls that reach the clouds, negating everything pertaining to the senses and allowing no light to break through the non-thought of thought, or thought about non-thought—the "way of negation." Only Is is, quite beyond the evidence of the senses. No explanation is given in Metadelphia as to why "is-nots"—sin, sickness, and death—continue to *seem* despite the rigors of absoluteness. One may hear the philosopher say, "I don't have to explain an illusion."

Just beyond the walls of Metadelphia is the meadow of simplicity. With the help of the Child within, we climb Metadelphia's wall, or pass through it, when we surrender the weight of the egotistical intellectualism performed in the name of a non-existent ego. Beyond the wall one comes consciously to the Child of himself, skipping freely, joyfully, bounding from flower to flower, high place to high place, living the Equation's Balance all the way to the peak of realization—or non-realization, as the Taoist might say. There one learns why Is appears to include "is-not," and what to do about it. The Child allows us to move on to the third position—the mountain again. This time we see the new heaven and earth. The old views are understood and no longer have the power over us they had before.

54

OCCLUDING STATES OF MIND

How we feel about things influences what we see in the world, no question of that. Envy, jealousy, anger, hatred, greed, lust, fear, insecurity and "love" are some of the occluding states of mind. Who can see the garden's morning blossom when he is frightened for his life? Who can enjoy a birdsong when he's angry?

Well now. We aren't so quick to recognize what these states of mind do to us. There are countless other occluding mental states as well. The engineer's bent for orderliness; the religionist's and metaphysician's predilection for study; the psychic's concern with things psychic; the scientist's examination of cause and effect, all tend to overlook the uncaused and mysterious. They overlook the obvious. The metaphysician's search for meaning behind words overlooks the reasons for the words themselves. The religionist's concern for his organization holds him to that sense of things—which might be out on the edge of things. The organizational metaphysician's loyalty to his group prevents his discovery of balance—if the group isn't at the center of things.

Human science has discovered evidence of a fifth "force" in nature, but to this point makes little connection between the perception of those forces and the human condition itself. Religious subjectivists generally ignore the connection, trying mightily to deny dualism, still unaware of the good reason for its appearance in the scheme of things. He calls half of him-

self unreal, pretending to ignore tangibility rather than understand it. Human science very nearly touches the limits of
microcosm and macrocosm but fails to connect its findings to
life itself, unaware that scientific search is an examination of
living Consciousness.

This is the general rule I'm writing here, and there are certainly many individual exceptions to it. Whoever finds the
Child of himself becomes an immediate exception. The Child
is the Guide, unafraid to move on with his seeking and finding. The Child looks both ways, so to speak, and sees the principles of the objective studies as clearly as those of the
subjective. The Child takes us back to the beginnings of the
scheme of Life, through the reasons for theology, onward to
the reasons for (and examination of) subjective thinking, still
onward to a lived, experienced *balance* for ourselves in the
world—thence to confirmation. Confirmation is the provable
"link" between tangibility and Ineffability. Much of that link
lies beyond the limits of sense, but not beyond the Heart-Child
within us. The Child brings us to the victorious end of the human struggle for wealth, health, dominion and power.

The Child leads us straight to Itself. The Child is the Self
of us, the *soul*. The Child is Life *itself*. The Child is *identity*
made in the *image* of God. The Child is precisely what the avatars discovered, marveled at and identified AS—none more
beautifully than the historic Jesus.

Natural human arrogance has us believe we are coming to
understand God. Actually, we are coming to comprehend the
pure, perfect, unfallen Image of God. That much understood
is a quantum move in the right direction. *God* understands
God. Life is destined to understand Life—and is subservient to
God.

Religionists understand words like these, but old in-line scientists and metaphysicians struggle wih them. Life *is* God,
some of them say. Well of course, but God is *more* and that lies
beyond the limits of thinking. Thinker, thinking and thought
are one, but thinking and thought are subservient to Thinker.
By analogy, the television set and its functioning are one tele-

vision set, but the functioning is within the set—and so is the picture, subservient to the Whole.

55

BEING OPEN TO THE NEW

The eternal Now appears in linear time as newness. We anticipate newness and accept it willingly, adjusting to it as seems appropriate.

"Education adjusts to new wisdom," said Han. "See how scholars rewrite their papers and begin new subjects. Governments adjust to new wisdom, albeit often unwillingly. See how they increasingly protect the rights of the governed. Science adjusts to new wisdom. See how quantum mechanics is working miracles in its midst. Technology adjusts to new wisdom. See how the small nations have learned to compete with the large. In the world of people, only churchdom, especially churchdom, refuses to adjust to new wisdom. It holds to the old creeds and dogmas the way the shell of the cicada holds to the emerging spirit within itself. In time, the living spirit emerges and the shell is cracked asunder. The groups that will survive in the days ahead are the groups who allow the little voices of living spirit to be heard challenging the old ways. Love survives because it adjusts."

56

PILGRIMAGES

"We have endured many storms," Han said to the little group. "You have listened to my words and heard them well." Lee and Mary smiled in agreement. The minister nodded as well. The soldier sat motionless.

Poking the fire, the soldier said, "You have said many things that you haven't written about, friend Han."

"One can't write everything," Lee said softly, as much to himself as to the others.

"Aren't the written words what brought you here, soldier?" Han asked.

"I suppose so," the soldier answered slowly. "Your written words said something to the heart of me, so I came to hear more. I was a stranger and you took me in." He twisted the stick in his hand. "I listened and I heard."

"Have you heard beyond the words?" the old man asked.

"Yes," the soldier answered. "Yes, indeed. What I heard has brought the written words to life."

"Pilgrimages are always rewarded," Han said.

"Yes," the soldier smiled. "Ten times ten."

The metaphysician asked why the pilgrimage is rewarded.

"Because they require more than your thought," Han answered. "They require your time, your effort and your substance. They are like sending a root out into a fertile place; they are like turning a leaf toward the morning star. What good is a living fountain in your midst if you don't drink from it?"

57

THE DIMENSIONALITY OF GOOD

Evil has fewer dimensions than good.

I stand in front of a mirror and make some comparisons. The image there looks just like me. If the lighting were dim, one might be hard pressed to tell which was the real and which the reflection.

But the images aren't the same. For instance, we know the image in the mirror is reversed. My right eye is its left eye; my left ear is its right ear. The clothing is reversed, too. The candy stripes on my Hawaiian pants are leaning to the right on me and to the left in the mirror.

There is yet another difference as great as the difference between light and darkness: The image in the mirror has no authority. It can't see. It can't smell the aftershave lotion. It can't
hear the songs I sing as I shave. It doesn't feel the nick of the
dull blade nor the hot water in the tap. The image in the mirror doesn't hear me saying, "Thank God I'm not the body
alone. Thank goodness Life is so much more than the body!"

Exactly as the image in the mirror doesn't have the same
abilities as the one standing in front of it, so evil in the world
doesn't have the <u>dimensionality</u> of good in the world. Exactly
as the image in the mirror is limited to much less than the one
standing before it, so "evil in the world" has nothing remotely
resembling the POWER of "good in the world." The sight of
cancer may be terribly frightening, but I have learned something out of hard experience: The sight of the least little good
that we ENACT in the world is capable of DOING much more
in the world positively than the appearance of cancer
negatively.

The key is the word *enact.*

58

THE VISIT WITH THE MAGISTRATE OF
ABSOLUTY TOWN

There is a fine line between subjectivism's absoluteness and
the LIVING of subjectivism in the world. That line has grown
into the great wall that surrounds Metadelphia and its little
suburb, Absoluty. To reach the peak of Da Shan, we can't stop
forever in metaphysics.

Speaking to Lee, Mary and the soldier, Han said, "You must
visit the exalted How Boo How, magistrate of Absoluty. He is
the chief absolutist. He is in non-charge of no-one, because
there is no one to be in charge of, he says, even though he is

the magistrate of Absoluty. To be absolute is to be absolute."
Han continued, "To be absolute is to *begin* with God, *stay* with
God and never leave the consciousness of God. Yes, we must
be absolute, but there is more for us to do than that."

"That is what you do," Mary said. "That is also what you advocate we do. So, why do you want us to visit the magistrate
of Absoluty?"

Old Han answered, "The Absolutist often calls himself God.
'How can I be anything else,' he will say, 'since there is nothing
but God in all existence?' "

"He is right, isn't he?" Lee asked.

"Go and visit the magistrate, How Boo How. Ask him every
question you wish. He will answer. Then, when your visit is
over, come and tell me whether these teachings at the pond are
the same or different. If you conclude they are different, tell
me how they are different."

When the three arrived at the magistrate's office, the soldier
put a question to him quickly. "Are you God?" he asked.

"Since there is nothing but God, how could I be anything
else?" said the absolutist. "There is nothing but Being being,
ever. God is all."

"Then, what am I to call you?" the soldier asked.

"People call me Magistrate How Boo How."

"Our friend Han tells us that God is all in all, magistrate.
What. . . ."

"I say exactly the same," the man in the golden headdress
answered quickly and confidently. "I know this about the
Truth: *Being is being the being that Being is being.*" The words
tripped from his tongue like hammer blows.

"And am I that same Being also?" the soldier asked.

"Yes, you are," the magistrate answered, smiling broadly.

"What do you think Jesus meant when he said that God was
greater than he?" Mary asked.

"My dear Mary, Jesus said 'My Father and I are *one*,' " the
man with the golden headdress replied.

"But he added that his father was *greater*. Perhaps he meant
that in the way a mathematician might say that the plane and
the sphere are one, but the sphere is greater than the plane."

"I do not think about dual matters such as greater or lesser,"
said the magistrate. "I remain in my metaphysical bliss, where

I and God are the same one. What I see is God, and if it isn't
God, then it doesn't exist and has no reality. That is that. Your
friend Han talks about simplicity. I agree with that simplicity
and you can, too. I keep things as simple as being the Being
that God is being— and I *stay* there."

"Is this room, filled with the smells of medicine and old age,
part of your metaphysical bliss?" the soldier asked bluntly.

"I neither see age nor smell medicine," the magistrate said
with an air of self-righteousness, eyes closed, head lifted toward the ceiling. Then, as if he sensed the soldier's thought,
he added, "I see no ceiling. There are no ceilings in Mind.
There is no age in Mind; there is no one who needs medicine
in Mind. All is infinite Mind and its most infinite manifestation. I know this. I *am this* and I *remain* this eternally!" Ah
yes, the magistrate of Absoluty is straight and forthright with
words.

"Yes, yes!" said Mary, in agreement. "You used the word
manifestation. Is this room my manifestation or yours?"

"If you see anything that isn't perfect just as it is, that is
your problem, not God's," the magistrate said.

Mary smiled. "Oh, I agree with much of that. Nothing but
God is *happening* and that is precisely what lets us see Good
in everything—even in illusion."

"There isn't any illusion in Mind, my dear," How Boo How
intoned contradictorily from under his golden headband. "The
illusion isn't real because God has nothing to do with illusions." The magistrate was beaming even if the ceiling wasn't.

"If there is no illusion in Mind, what is the illusion I see?"
Mary asked.

"You don't see an illusion, my dear. You just think you do,"
said the magistrate.

"Is my thinking that I see an illusion also an illusion?"

"Yes."

"Haven't you contradicted yourself?" Lee, the soldier and
Mary asked simultaneously.

"I have done no such thing. Mind doesn't contradict itself,"
said the absolutist.

"Then what did you do?" asked the soldier.

"What do you mean, what did I do? If God didn't do it, it

wasn't done," the magistrate said from beneath his great headdress.

"Oh my," Mary whispered. "Words can be so intimidating, can't they? In the name of metaphysics, everything can be affirmed or denied at will. Fortunately that doesn't change the Truth."

"Speak up!" said How Boo How. "I didn't hear you."

"Mind hears," said the soldier. "It is the meatman whose ears are solid and unhearing."

"Yes," said the magistrate, "but I am not the meatman. I am infinitely more than that!"

"Yes, we are more than the physical appearing," said Mary, "but what is the physical appearing?"

"Nothing! Absolutely nothing at all—and you children must understand, it is that view of the meatman's nothingness that heals the meatman!"

"Ah so?" Lee asked. "Then it is our knowledge that the illusion is an illusion that allows us to see the illusion more nearly as it is?"

"Absolutely!" said the Magistrate.

"But if it is an illusion that doesn't exist, what difference does it make what it looks like or doesn't look like!" asked the soldier.

"That is the Zen of it, my young argumentative friends. That is the mystery."

"*What* is the 'mystery'?" the soldier asked.

"That is for me to know and for you to determine," the magistrate said. A servant entered the room bringing the magistrate's meal and the first meeting ended.

The three young people sat in the courtyard discussing their conversation with How Boo How. "It seems to me he is saying exactly what Han is saying at the pond," said the soldier.

"Oh no he isn't!" Mary said, "There are gigantic differences. Han is saying more."

"What?" asked the soldier.

THE SECOND VISIT

The talk with the magistrate of Absoluty resumed. "What of the hungry, unhappy people here in Absoluty?" asked the soldier.

"I do not see hungry, unhappy people," the magistrate smiled. "I see only love and beauty here, and that is all there is to see!"

"Do you see me, too?" asked Mary.

"Why, dear, you *know* I see you, as sweet as you are. I see you as the perfect child of Tao."

"Did you see the man who served your meal while we were away?"

"Well, of course, I saw him. He was complaining about his paltry wages, profaning his employer all the while. I told him that he should see the positive side of his employer, not the negative."

"Then you responded to the scene at hand?" Mary asked.

"Well, of course I did, dearie. I just told you what I said."

"Did you do more?" Mary asked.

"There was no greater gift I could have given that poor man than setting him on the positive, uplifting course."

"That was a wonderful gift," Mary said, "but Master Han at the pond tells us there is more than that to do."

"Good for Master Han," said the magistrate haughtily, turning to leave.

"Don't you wish to know what?" the lady asked.

"I never ask questions," the magistrate said curtly. "I am not interested in the illusory scene at hand."

"Do you visit your banker?" asked the soldier.

"He comes to me, my friend," the magistrate answered from under his golden wrappings. "The mountain comes to Me, you see. I have dominion. That is why I am the magistrate of Absoluty."

So ended the second visit with How Boo How. At the pond, Han asked if the three had perceived any differences yet. They had, but they were not sure precisely what. "Then visit again," Han said.

THE THIRD VISIT WITH THE MAGISTRATE OF
ABSOLUTY

As before, the students were admitted to the magistrate's room, but warned that no argument or dissension would be permitted. "Did we argue?" asked Lee.

"I thought we pursued questions," the soldier said. "Master Han said that many metaphysicians call it an argument when someone doesn't agree with them."

Magistrate How Boo How was wheeled into the small room. He smiled at the group.

"We hope everything has been fine with you," Lee said tremulously, feeling intimidated.

"Everything is perfect. There is nothing but God going on. There is nothing but good. Nothing but love," said How Boo How, beaming from under his headdress.

"What is love?" asked Mary.

"I am love. I am love itself! I am nothing but love," the magistrate answered quickly and confidently. "I begin with love and I stay with love—and so should all of you."

"How do you know we *don't?*" asked the soldier. "If your view of me. . ."

"Just a figure of speech, my friend. I don't see you as anything but love either," said the Magistrate of Absoluty.

"How does love act?" Mary asked.

"As love, of course. Love acts as God acts. I act as God acts—and so should you."

"If God is all in all, there is no other action going on but God's Self-action, is there?" the soldier asked.

"You are correct, my soldier."

"Tell me, what have you done about the war in Afghanistan?" the soldier asked abruptly.

The magistrate looked at the soldier incredulously. He hesitated, as he rarely did. "What do you mean, what am I doing about the war in Afghanistan? What kind of question is *that?*" The magistrate had asked his first question.

"I mean, what are you doing about warfare in the world?" the soldier explained. "There *appear* to be people at war all over the earth. I know the *appearing* is an unreal illusion—and that an illusion is an illusion—so I wonder what you are doing about the illusion of warfare. Or of poverty. Or of terrorism. Or of sin, sickness and death. But, specifically, I really want to know what you are doing about the starving people of the world."

"Oh my goodness, my man," the magistrate began, a sound of patronage in his voice. "I live in another world entirely. Don't you know you are asking questions about empty, meaningless things? Do you not yet understand that your friend Jesus said that he was not of *this world* of illusion? Don't you realize that he told us not to have anything to do with this world?"

The soldier smiled. "That same man asked us to go out into this illusory world and *do* whatever we can for it. I am asking you what you are *doing* for this world."

"My argumentative friend. I am being the Being that Being is being. What are you being?"

"I am being that too, friend How Boo How—what else can I be?—but I am *doing something for the illusion.* What are you doing for the illusion?"

"I am denying the reality of the illusion, my upstart friend! And you should be doing the same thing."

"I am," the soldier said quietly, "and more. What are you doing for the illusion besides denying it?"

"Absolutely nothing. I don't have to work for an illusion. There is nothing to be done for an illusion. There is nothing to heal. There has NEVER been anything to heal. God is all and God is good and God is perfect and God doesn't need to be healed."

"Ah so, Magistrate How Boo How, you have answered our questions. Now we know why Han wanted us to visit you."

"The world is a powerless illusion!" the man swathed in headbands roared on, unaware that his visitors were leaving. "I am LIVING the BEINGNESS of God! You should live the BEINGNESS of God too, my three argumentative friends. What am I doing about the starving Ethiopians, indeed! I am not making a *reality* of NOTHING for one thing, and neither should you."

"Yes, but we all live in Nothing's house and eat Nothing's food, don't we?" Mary said, softly. "How Boo How is TALK-

ING about the allness of God, but not living it." Mary's words were unheard by the Magistrate.

At the pond, Han asked, "Have you found a difference?"

"Yes, friend Han, we have found a great difference. The difference between talking about love in the world and living love in the world."

"Ah so," said the Master of Kwangse Province, "Next you will find the Child within. THAT is the Wonder of wonders. THAT is the One who works marvels in this world and the next. THAT is the One who lives eternally, giving more to his world than words."

THE ZEN TRAP, THE TAOIST TRAP, THE ABSOLUTIST TRAP
The Semantic Games of Subjectivism

Nothing is more ridiculous than a theological argument among theologians, especially if they use a common book to support their differences and can't even agree on exactly which verses to use nor on how to interpret the ones they do use.

Ah, but nothing is more *absurd* (or funny) than an argument among metaphysicians. The reason for the absolute absurdity lies in the fact that metaphysicians argue about things they say don't exist and can't happen.

The danger of metaphysics (and perhaps the reason the rabbis of old discouraged the study of subjectivism) is that one can so easily entrap himself in his own semantic game and begin believing himself and his words.

Metaphysicians who have discovered the inner nature of things are, sooner or later, brought to express that knowledge to others—if only because "others" see their light and come asking questions. One can spot the metaphysician who is entrapped at the absolute level because he has stopped asking questions. He has begun believing he must find every answer within his own objective/subjective head, so to speak. He denies the "outside," calling it an illusion. The metaphysician, old or new, finds that his subjective words have quantum power in his experience, compared to the former use of those same words "out there" in the world. Right there, the unwary metaphysician, establishing the "God is absolutely ALL" position, spends the rest of his life explaining (and trying to understand) that position—and, without realizing it, never moves beyond it. He may even hold to that lordly place telling of the *simplicity of Allness* and the inability of words to capture his thoughts, all the way to his "seeming" grave, but he stays right there at the semantic bend of the river, content to see himself able to joust verbally with "others" and hold his own. From that point, unless the subjectivist is willing to *move on*, he measures his progress, not by new insights and new Light of the Absolute, but by his ability to hold to the "God is ALL" (or whatever else) position. "I am God and not man!" he proclaims against the greatest odds—enjoying the battle.

This is the Zen Trap, the Taoist Master's Trap, the Absolutist Trap. While it is absolutely necessary that we come to this correct conclusion—God is, indeed, all in all—we are expected to go beyond it. "It is a mountain; it is not a mountain; *it is a mountain again.*" The subjectivist who has not recognized the third position can't get there by merely claiming to be there.

Ah, but there is Something Beyond.

The Child within us is beyond. The Child within us remains unacknowledged and undiscovered by the Zen advocate, the subjectivist and Taoist.

"Nothing is beyond INFINITY," says the Absolutist.

God is beyond Infinity to infinity. The Child I am is beyond infinity. For goodness sake, even experimental mathematics is beyond infinity. If science can get beyond infinity, why can't we? We can.

"Nothing is beyond ALL," says the absolutist.

God is beyond All—or any other *concept*. The Child I am is beyond all.

"See the trap that semantics can become," said Han, old master of Kwangse Province. "See that trap and go beyond that trap. But one doesn't go *beyond* it, without working his way *through* it. THAT is the hard part. THAT is the Zen of the matter. That is also why we get busy and get going and get beyond the glib flow of words that settles nothing out there in the world—and frequently misleads others. Leave the endless talking to entrenched metaphysicians and theologians. We begin the DOING. We complete the INTERFACE."

The paradox that so baffles us at the metaphysical and transcendental level is that the interface of DOING requires the concomitant use of words that don't matter. Try to get a metaphysician to DO anything for the world and he'll tell you everytime, "There is no world to illumine or instruct. There is no world to heal." Those words are only half the Truth. Ah, but at least they are half the Truth, half way up the mountain. Indeed, we get our subjectivism correct—that only God is happening—then we put our knowledge to work on the illusory scene.

THE WORLD IS A PERFECT VESSEL AND WHOEVER TRIES TO ALTER IT, SPOILS IT. LaoTse, 500 B.C.

The view that there is no world to heal and no persons to instruct is a perfect view—almost. But there is a View *beyond* that view, as the real masters have told, including LaoTse, Jesus and many others. The greater view simply hasn't been widely "seen" yet.

"Oh, yes? What?" the minister, metaphysician and philosopher ask in unison.

There is a world to be *understood* rather than denied. When it is understood, we understand the *reasons* for the illusion of a world in need of healing.

Nothing is done for this world of illusion by the view that there is no world to heal nor persons to illumine. (If the absolute view of metaphysics really "worked," the illusive world would not appear to be on the brink of a common disaster in every field of human experience.) To arrive at the near-final conclusion that the world is all right (despite the tenacious claims and holds of world-belief to the contrary) is a wonderful *and necessary* second step, but Truth is an *ongoing* revelation that ultimately tells us why the appearing appears. Subjectivism without the Child within is a dead thing, even as religion is. Without the Child, religion and metaphysics are like stillbirths in the world. The final light from the third step (the step beyond metaphysics) tells us what we are *to do for the il-*

lusion. When we know this, we set out to do it. And until we do that, we haven't done anything.

To paraphrase the enlightened Zen saying once more (Mountain; not a Mountain; Mountain again): First there is a world to heal and many ignorant people to be instructed; then we see there is no world to heal nor persons to be illumined; finally, the world is understood *for why it appears,* and our real action begins, with *much for us to do in each position.*

These are the apparent steps along the way up the mountain of Da Shan. The minister often bogs down in the first step, the absolutist most certainly in the second. The illumined are those who have continued to move on and have found the Child within themselves. The Child *is* the third step, and those who have found It are already gathering into a joyful new community preparing the way for mankind's recognition of the Child-within-Everyman. Messiah! This Community spans the universe in a sweet camaraderie of *simplicity and childlikeness.*

But, let the reader understand: The Child within us can be acknowledged and found anywhere along the objective or subjective way. Within religion or outside it. We do not leave or forsake either science, religion, metaphysics or "the world." Rather we *understand* them and include them *to infinity,* perceiving whatever is real of their activities and truth. The Child within does this for us! Wherever and whenever the Child enters our conscious recognition, That One takes us quicky through the objective, subjective, male, female, first, last, above and below "steps," without ignoring or ridiculing them—and brings us to a marvelous Balance and a unitive knowledge of Godhead. In that balance, where the marvelous Equation is learned and lived, we live our subjectivism in the objective experience, accomplishing wonders—and mankind doesn't even see us doing it!

The first step laughs at the second. The second step holds itself mighty and superior, doing nothing in the world that it calls an illusion. The second step deceives the elect and denies both the first and third steps with all the vigor it possesses. Religion and metaphysics without the Child neither eat the oats they profess nor allow the world to. But the Child IS the third step—and *includes* the lesser steps to infinity. The Child within us leads the way to Godhead here at hand.

Han and Mary were talking at the pond. "Friend Han, you have said that the subjective (metaphysical) view of the Perfect World is only half the truth. What is the other half?"

"The objective truth," answered Han.

"And these two are the whole Truth?" asked Mary.

"Oh no," Han said emphatically. "Godhead and Its Selfhood, the Child, are the whole Truth. They are much greater than the sum of their parts."

The soldier said, "The subjective view of the second step seems to be diametrically opposed to the objective view of the first step. How can these contraries exist side by side? They are like positive and negative. Shouldn't they neutralize one another, like matter and anti-matter?"

"In the world, people think they do," the old man smiled. "But, here we appear to be sitting in an objective world, talking to ourself at the pond. Yet, we sit here talking of subjective things. Therefore, I see that my subjective idea does not neutralize nor eliminate my objective world—even though there are times I would like mightily for it to turn the picture around completely. Ah, but *when* I found the Child within myself—so much closer to me than I had ever thought of God being; closer than any concept of an Ever-present Being—the Child showed me how to live my subjectivism *objectively* right here in this world of appearances. When I learned this, my world came alive."

"I speak of these unfoldments as happening sequentially—as three steps—but that is only a concession to time and words that a linear world demands. *The three steps are happening simultaneously in non-time, for all of us, within one omni-dimensional Godhead.* The non-day of non-time will arrive in this linear sense of things, as the masters and prophets have declared—and then I shall see as I am seen."

Han smiled. With a firm countenance and eyes ablaze, he added, "Meanwhile, as long as I appear to be here in this linear sense of things, I will continue to do everything I can do for my world and for the images of myself I see within it. I shall not stop short with religion alone. I will not withdraw into arrogance and blindness in the subjective world of my own viewing. I shall do for my world as long as I can. I will run as long as I can run, and walk as long as I can walk. Then I will crawl on my knees if I can. But as long as I am 'here' and 'now,' I am here for God's divine Purpose. That Purpose is not without *action* to help men find what I have found and do what I have done."

A thoughtful silence followed at the pond. "Does that answer your question?" Han asked the soldier.

"Yes. My God, yes," the soldier said.

59

___

THE BRIDGE

As one approaches the bridge, he is concerned with the difficulties that beset him on the side where he stands. While he is on the bridge, he is conscious of the troubles he is leaving behind. When he reaches the other side, he is intrigued with the New Land and quickly forgets the troubles behind. The wise man knows the value of the mental bridge, the progression, and how to lead the weary across it. Talk of the other side is cheap and fools many, but directions that point to the bridge and across it are invaluable—and rare. Our journal records the directions we take and have taken, allowing us to help others in precise words that reach beyond the sterile, antiseptic generalizations of religion and metaphysics. In this action, our science, religion and metaphysics come together and the three are one.

60

THE LOVE LETTER OVERTONES

There are those among us who think that unless we go around thinking about our job, our mission, our discipline all day, that we are not doing our duty. I remember a time when I put rubber bands around my arm to keep me God-mindful—as though I were a separate being with a mind of my own to bring into line. There are also those who think they can't possibly "pray without ceasing," as the Bible adjures. The following illustration is an eye-opener for such folks. It will also be a help to discouraged journal tenders who think they can't write or that they have nothing to say.

Imagine a young man busy at his desk, writing a letter to the young lady of his dreams, asking her to marry him. Imagine the intensity of this work—the most important letter of his life! He has decided, after much thought, the letter is the best way to do it. Why? Because the letter will say exactly what he wants it to say just as many times as she reads it, but he could say it out loud only once—and not half as thoughtfully. I think our man feels the lady may need a bit of persuading.

Now, as our friend sits there writing, his boss comes in and sees him busily engaged in writing an important letter. The boss understands and permits it. Question: Does our friend see the boss come into the room? Of course. He speaks to his employer with a crisp, "Good morning," and goes on with the letter. Because every word is important, he tries twenty beginnings before he selects just the one he wants: "My dearest Susan." When coffee-break time comes, he works right through it. When lunch time arrives, he hurriedly puts the letter in a drawer and heads for the elevator. As he walks up the busy street to the cafeteria, he passes store windows that are ordinarily an invitation to investigate. He sees them, but this time he walks on. On the street corner, he passes a heated argument that would ordinarily stop him, but he walks on. He is not unconscious of the shop windows or the argument, but he simply has more important things on his mind. He is, to use my expression, in the "writing mode of mentation."

At the cafeteria, he walks down the line, quickly selects his food and finds an empty table. In a few minutes a friend stops and sits with him. They converse as usual, but the thing most on our young man's mind is the half-written letter in his desk. That fateful letter can mean so much! Soon he is back at his desk and at work. The matter in his head is still "the letter" and what he hopes it will accomplish.

Our friend does whatever work is required of him on this particular afternoon, but the letter is physically before him whenever possible and, finally, as the work day ends, the letter is finished, tucked into an envelope and taken to the corner mailbox.

The matter isn't finished yet. That night in front of the television set, the young man thinks about the reception his words may have when the letter arrives and what the response might be. He calculates the day of the letter's arrival and how she will open and read it. He anticipates her response. He watches his favorite television show, but he is still mindful of the letter. His dreams are a pleasant turmoil.

I present this little story about the love letter in connection with journal tending. The connections and parallels are identical in many ways, but not in all ways. We don't have to worry about how well we write in the journal. It's just important that we get ourselves into the "journal mode" of writing because it is "the journal mode" *that allows us to be receptive to the Glimpses and Glimmers of the Light of Life. The mode of thought is important, not what we write in our journals and letters.* Ah, but the writing improves and flows as the mode opens us to more light—and we are introduced to paradox. More about paradox in other places.

Question: Was the young lover in the mode *before* he sat down to write? Yes, yes, yes. That's WHY he sat down to write the letter. He thought about it for weeks before he actually wrote it. The mode preceded the writing for umpteen days, off and on. I have discovered, with my journal, that the mode is with me constantly now.

Consider: Did the mode, the mood, stop when the young man went to lunch at the cafeteria and the letter was only half written? No. It went with him and allowed him to be "in the world but not of it." He walked right past the windows that usually interested him so much and past the argument that he might have taken sides in otherwise. Did it keep him from making selections along the cafeteria line? Obviously not. Nor did it keep him from visiting with the friend who sat down. So it is, the journal mode of mentation doesn't interfere with our worldly activity of making a living. Rather, it *helps* us to get through the human scene without so much hassle and without getting caught up in meaningless, sidetracking activity.

Consider: Did the mood end when he put his pen or typewriter aside, folded the letter and dropped it into the mailbox? Not at all. It continued. The mood of that letter continued until something happened in his experience to *confirm* its reason for having been written. That night our friend even dreamed of the letter and its recipient.

Dear friends, if such an innocent thing as writing a love letter can do so much for a man of the world, how much more do you think your journal word to Godhead, and seeing good in Its perfect Everyman, might do for you? The journal mood begins right here and now, before you even pick up a pen to write a single word. *You are in it the moment you begin looking for good in the images of Awareness.*

Now, listen again carefully. It's the mode of mentation that allows the glimpses and glimmers, not necessarily *what we write* at all. We do not get trapped into thinking we must create the Great American Novel or win a Pulitzer Prize for literature before we're successfully into the discipline of journal tending and its mode of mentation!

THE POWER OF THE JOURNAL

When one makes contact with the Muse of Ideas or the Muse of Truth—even the naked muse of sensual gratification and emptiness—it is possible to hear Something INSIDE and write it for the world OUTSIDE. In my first days at journal tending, I would put myself down at the notebook and turn to a new page, or I would put a clean sheet of white paper in the typewriter, take a deep breath with eyes closed and vow to write "something worthy of God."

IS IT IMPORTANT TO KEEP A JOURNAL?

Why keep a journal? It can become one of the most important activities in our life. There is a synergistic power in writing. For instance, twenty-five years ago I began talking about awareness, using that very word in my small experience. Now my external world hangs on "awareness" as if it were a flagword to all wisdom in the human sphere of things. That word and its significance arrived in my experience as I wrote in my journal. I began using it in conversation—and eventually wrote a book about it. Now, many years later, the ideas in that book are becoming common knowledge in the world, and it all started as I sat with pencil in hand.

One will notice that a Glimpse comes and, *if we COMPLETE the transaction,* that Glimpse enters our world to enlighten it. That is how it works—as it has been proven to me time and time again. Our world is SUBJECTIVE. It is in our hands. If anything is to happen to help our view of the world, it begins right here with us. How? As we complete the INTERFACE. We get the Glimpse. We live it, tell it, give it, share it as quickly as seems sensible, and in the doing, we put ourselves in the position to RECEIVE more Glimpses to give—and our world is steadily "improved"—awakened—seen as it really is— as Life *confirms* our Glimpses.

I don't think one even begins to realize *how much he can do for his world* until the subjective nature of things is comprehended at least in part. This knowledge arrives slowly, "line upon line. . ." but now it rushes in as if a floodgate has been lifted, acknowledging and confirming my willingness to give what I have been given. Throughout the day—and at every turn—there is an event, a "happening," that proves once again that *"my" world is here in my hands, and if the Light of Life is to be seen in it, I am to BE the Light of Life for my world.* It isn't false Light we try to be, as a satanic influence in the world trying to emulate the works of God, the action that brought the Angel of Light to be cast down. Rather, we await the Glimpses and tell of THEM. I let the human experience of years count as nothing, and tell only of the Glimpses, the REAL and the GOOD and the TRUE. That is, I'm GIVING my light, my Glimpses and Glimmers, to "my" world and watching the world take that Light and start LISTENING TO GOD! THIS is what journal tending is all about.

"Listening to God" is the MODE that writing in the journal

puts one into! Therein lies the value of writing and journal tending. WHAT we write isn't half as important as the MODE which writing puts us into. In those moments we are not caught up in the world, but are quiet and receptive. In those moments we aren't frantically reacting to the scene, but sitting still, expectantly anticipating Good even as we write a simple statement of tenderness or beauty we have already seen. THAT is the mood of the writing mode.

ABOUT THE JOURNAL MODE

What I call "the journal mode" is nearly, but not quite, the same mental mode we get ourselves into when we are reading metaphysical papers and studying our books, searching for Light. The very mood that has us sitting back and pondering a statement, contemplating the meanings of things, is what does the good work of Light's arrival in our subjective metaphysical work—and that work, as often as not, has little if anything to do with what's written on the page there. It's the MODE, not the information. So, understand it is the journal mode that matters, not what we write—albeit, what we write often comes out of the mood. So, again: we tend the journal, not to inform anyone, not to inform ourselves, but to live in the Light from out of which our Glimpses come.

I can tell you, it is possible to get into this state of mind and stay there perpetually! THIS is to pray without ceasing! If one should wonder where "tranquillity" is—the peace that is beyond understanding—he will find it in the contemplative mode of mentation.

JOURNAL TENDING AND SUBJECTIVISM

When one sees the world objectively and wishes to do something for that world, the best he can ordinarily do is to write a letter to the editor or write a book, and hope an individual here or there will read it and heed. The odds are a million to one against the world hearing and responding. *Ah, when subjectivism dawns and one comes to perceive that all tangibility is within himself, the world is changed even as the words are written onto the paper of his journal.* There, the mere knowledge that one is writing to his Selfhood propels his thoughts and ideas into the external world where their validity will be confirmed.

61

WRITING AND THE COMMUNITY

Dear William,
   My life has become new since I started keeping a journal. I have filled half a dozen notebooks, but better, I have opened a hundred new doors inside myself. My family and friends have taken on a new respect for my ideas because I can present them so much more courageously. . . .

My dear friend Bill,
   . . . my journal time has become the most precious time of my day and my life. It is my talking-to-the-Child time when the answers to the mysteries are given. . . .

Dear Bill,
   . . . thoughts clarify and expand . . . answers to the most agonizing problems come. . . .

. . . writing does all the things that meditating did for me, and so much more. Meditation was renewing. Writing is equally renewing but with something to show for it in the pages of my notebook.
   . . . my wife tells me she hears what I am saying now.

Bill, you started me keeping a journal twenty years ago. Since then, I have taught classes and have introduced your ideas to many people.

Dear William, can you possibly know how the Muse has come to me through writing? Yes, she does . . . directly.

. . . writing from the memories of childhood has opened the doors to new light I didn't know existed. The meanings of memory and time have brought those golden times back again. . . . growing awareness comes with sitting down and being still for a time with my notebook.

. . . I wrote and asked what I was to do with all the things I have written. You gave me Hilde's name and asked that I write.
She and I have become the closest friends. I live for her letters and this Christmas we are planning to visit. It will be the first time in years I have had anyone to enjoy Christmas with.

. . . William, you told me about the man who lived alone in the mountains of Tennessee. We exchanged letters, telling of our appreciation for Truth. I have introduced him to my friends here in Seattle and I know he gets half a dozen letters every month. He writes that he isn't lonely anymore. . . .

. . . Rachel suggested that I write John D. . . I was surprised to know a doctor was interested in metaphysics. We have become good friends and I look forward to his notes. . .

. . . I am continuing to keep in touch with Trudy, whom I met at Woodsong. We became immediate friends. How silly the years I wasted keeping my Glimpses to myself for fear my own world wasn't ready to hear my own thoughts. Now I recognise Glimpses to be immaculate perceptions!

. . .Bill, tell me what I am to do with these thoughts. I have no one to share them with.
Dear friend Brian, would you mind dropping a note to Mrs. Ann K. in Spain? She says she is alone and frightened. Tell her some of the things you've told me. No fancy words are necessary for her because she reads between the lines as you and I do. Tell her of the courage you found after your experience and how your loss turned out to be great gain. . .

. . . I am writing both Ann and Michael. I find Michael's poems beautiful and freeing. I have introduced Michael's words to Ann and she feels as I do. . .

Dear Reverend B. I know you are busy, but they say busy people are the ones to call on when you want something done. . . . she (Ann) lives in a nursing home near you and is quite alone in the world. When you next feel the depression you tell me is so recurring and devastating in your life, will you make it a point to go by and take a gift to that lady? Any little thing you might have around that you don't need but feel she might appreciate. . . . There is a reason for asking you to do this, and the reason is very special.
. . .I did not wait for another round with depression but did as you suggested immediately and took Ann Frances a small gift. I learned that she is from England...so well educated and without a friend here in the United States.

Following letters: I have taken a radio to Ann Frances . . .
I have discovered two members of Ann's family who have
moved to Canada. I have informed them of her plight and encouraged them to write. . . They tell me they will get in touch.
. . . Ann received the tape recorder your Rachel sent and especially enjoyed the tape of the thunderstorm . . . I must tell
you that my son has come out of his shell completely. He has
gotten over his discomfort of going with me to the nursing
home and has fallen quite in love with Ann. It is the first time
I have seen him show any respect for older people. . .
. . . We are taking Ann for long rides and are planning to
house her visitors from Canada for a time during the holidays.
She has met the lady that you suggested visit her and is busy
herself writing of her childhood and memories. I have never
seen her more happy. . . . Ann is a gifted writer, so full of wit
and wisdom. . . . Jack (son) is beginning to keep a journal of
our time with Ann.
. . . Ann passed on quietly this morning. There is a notebook
of beautiful things here which she has written for you and
Rachel. She has copied an entire book that was out of print
because she thought you should enjoy it, too. She was very
much alone in this world when you first suggested I visit her
. . . under her bed was a box of letters from new friends who
brought excitement to her life and she equally to theirs . . .
Bill, my life has become so much richer because of Ann, you
and Rachel and all the others of like mind. . . .

Dear William and Rachel,
I am writing a poem each morning as my gift to the world.
I may be just a rag picker in the eyes of the world, but I am
tending the most beautiful heaven on earth as far as I am concerned . . . as I do my chores in the park, I keep an eye open
for someone to share my thoughts with. It is amazing how a
"Good morning" brings a smile to the face of a stranger. Of
all men, I am most blessed.

Dear Bill and Rachel,
I have received several letters from rare and beautiful peo-

ple and I am sending them each a poem and a gift.

Dear Bill,

. . . I will be meeting some of my new friends this summer and my heart sings in gratitude. My poems are to be published.

. . . now that I'm outputting a little, I find new Glimpses coming with regularity. I went for years without new inner light and now Light walks with me everywhere I go. Why was I so slow learning of this marvelous way?

Rachel and William . . . you have introduced me to a new community of wonderful people. It is a community without leaders and without followers. We are all children, everyone equal as Children of Light . . . child-people who try to walk with Love and share true love with one another.

. . . I thought we were just sharing our love with one another but when George fell ill, Mary sent me a gift of money! Susan and her husband came down from Washington to take care of my affairs . . . enough to meet the immediate needs . . . such unselfish love!

. . . years ago you wrote to tell me that the Truth would be just as valuable in my affairs as I valued the Truth in the world. I had no idea what you meant. I thought I had given my whole life to the pursuit of Truth, but learned that all I had given to my world was little more than a selfish pursuit of Truth to please myself. . . . I read constantly, every book that came along, but that is as far as it went. I did not put the Truth to work in the world until you suggested I "get off my dead ass" and start doing something "for the world" that was refusing to give me anything . . . shocked me . . . I needed that slap . . . and now I have discovered part of the true principle of supply. . . . I am giving a tangible value to the Truth with my efforts for others and with my substance, as much as I can . . . there have been rewards a hundred times beyond anything dreamed, in ways I never expected and still can hardly believe.

. . . I am giving smiles and good cheer to the people around me here in the retirement home. My life has turned into a blessing too big to believe. I give my glimpses too. . .

Mr. Samuel, how do I get into this "community of correspondents"?

Begin a journal of your own insights and memories of the marvelous events of your life. Record your Glimpses with whatever words you can. Then expect *someone to appear for you to tell them to. God will take care of the rest.*

Dear Bill, when I withdrew from my church, my church withdrew from me. . . . I am getting along in years and have begun to wonder about things.

Dear George, go back to church.
. . . Never!
. . . *George, I know a most lovely lady who says she has no one to talk the Truth with. Write her. Here is her address:*

Dear Bill, I have gone back to church in a way I never thought I would . . . but it is a congregation that lives all over the country . . . an unseen congregation of old and young with whom I try to share my experiences and views of Truth.

. . . Bill, this little group of people has come together in correspondence most amazingly. We have never met, and likely
never will, but we are more intimate and more helpful to one
another than any group I have ever known . . . some of these
people have just begun a study of subjectivism . . . but they
have everyone found the Child of themselves and our joy is
marvelous. Yes . . . this is my own inner world happening.

*Dear Michele, the churches do a better job of taking care of the
children, the elderly and the needy of the world than the metaphysical groups do. Churches generally tend non-members and do
some work for the world. Most metaphysical groups don't even tend
their own members in need, much less the stranger in another
land. Look for yourself and see how many homes for the elderly or
orphanages are provided by the metaphysical groups who insist that
every edifice have a sign saying, "God is Love" or "Divine Love
always has met and always will meet every human need." Can you
imagine a Christian Science practitioner working in a soup
kitchen to serve starving street people? There is much profession of
love from some groups with very little living of Love out in the
world. Someone should tell them this? No, not really. "They" are
my own subjective viewing, so the problem, subjectively, lies right
here with me. So, what am I doing for my street people and my
subjectivists who do not appear to be living their love? This book
is my way of DOING something for my world which so often appears in human, tangible need. This effort is my effort to put a
tangible VALUE on Truth by living it with all my might. I give
words when that seems important, but Rachel and I give our substance and our shelter when someone is hungry and tired. You do
these things too, Michele, and your rewards will be quantum! You
will see, as I have, that if we want to see marvels happen in our
own subjective experience, the action starts right here as our Self.
Our viewing is loosed or unbound when we TEND it as we have
been admonished to.*

Dear Mr. Samuel, I am helping my world by refusing to see
the reality of sin, sickness and death. Your book, *A Guide to
Awareness and Tranquillity,* has taken me to a state of meta-

physical bliss in which I have lost all consciousness of the world
. . . however, I am faced with a personal difficulty pertaining
to what the world calls health. . . . I miss my husband so!

Dear Marie,
There is a big step beyond metaphysical bliss. That is the dis-
covery of the Child within who knows what to do with that bliss.
The first step to find the Child within is to be conscious that the
Child EXISTS.

William, I have never, ever heard of "the child" in all my
study. You lose me when you write about "the child."

You are right, Marie: There is nothing in subjectivism's litera-
ture about the Child or the Child's way to live in the world. It is
supposed to be that way, I think. There is nothing in the Symphony
about how to read the music on the printed page. The Symphony
merely makes the notes readable. The Child and the Equation re-
quire our DOING, ACTING, BEING, LIVING, beyond mere
reading, talking and professing. . . . yes, there is a step BEYOND
reading holy books. LIVING them comes next.

62

ABOUT LOVE AND THE FLOW

If we intend to reach the top of the mountain, it is essential
that we let go our inhibitions concerning love for our fellow
man. This isn't to say that we let go our restraints concerning
sexual activities and become libidinous, trying to "love" everyone sexually, without restraint. This is the charge historically
leveled against those of us who advocate that we love our
neighbors without inhibition—the accusers suspecting or believing they will see their own desires fulfilled in our actions.

We love without *spiritual* restraint. Why? Because "others"
are our own image carried to all possibilities. As Alphabet, I
can love all the letters. As a specific letter, I can look "outside"
my letter-self and love the other letters, knowing we have Alphabet in common, knowing we all live and move and have
our being within the Alphabet-I-am.

But the metaphysician and mystic are prone to equate Alphabet with God. The Ineffable is beyond Alphabet, more than Alphabet, the basis for this Awareness which "Alphabet" is. As Alphabet, Awareness looks one way, down the spiral, and perceives the countless letters of itself; it sees them making groups of words, bound together into sentences and paragraphs and books of ideas. There is no power *there,* but there is authority in the Alphabet/Awareness that observes the letters. This observation is the "downward spiral," as I put it. Not downward in the sense of wrong or incorrect or not preferred—but only the "outward" look as it spirals into more of itself, of itself, more of itself to infinity. This love of the image reproduces the image of the lover, the object of its love. Neither good nor bad.

As Alphabet looks the other way, upward to the Ineffable and Unknown-but-to-ItSelf, Alphabet sees nothing tangible and uninhibitedly loves that Ineffable Beyond-seeing as the Source of Awareness. The upward spiral allows Alphabet to FEEL the immeasurable love of the Infinite *which loves Awareness* as its own Self-perceiving, disclosing Self to Self. This "upward spiral" culminates not in the birth of images, but in the rebirth of the adored Child within. This birthing comes as an enwrapment most poignant and sweet. We feel as the Original Child Self of us. Oh, it is powerful and real, this feeling! This Love of God for Me *allows Me to love the images of myself to infinity.* I do not, must not, interrupt this flow. I let love given to Me flow into all others. All others flow into me and I give that adoration to Source. I do not, must not, interrupt that flow. I keep nothing for Myself, but give it to Godhead from whence it came. The Joy given to me is passed along to my Others; their joy is passed to Godhead—and I am the FLOWING between. That "between" lies in the bosom of an adoring, loving God.

Do you see?

The feeling I feel is God adoring Me.

The feeling I give to myself (others) is God adoring me.

The feeling others give to me is God's adoring love for me.

The feelings I give to God are God's love reflected by my actions of adoration for God and mankind.

"So, where does sex fit into this, Sam? My glands are overpowering me. My son's glands are about to overpower all the women in the neighborhood. What do I tell my son about love? What do I do with this powerful urge to make physical love to all the people on earth now that I have found the virile Child of myself?"

My friend, you listen to and *hear* what was just said about feeling. Really HEAR it. And, listen, listen: chief among the things that one does NOT do, is use God's love as an excuse to justify sex with any and everyone who walks into view.

"But my subjective Selfhood is beyond the moral laws of society, Samuel. I am a Law to mySelf. I can find those very words in many places, including the Bible. Anyway, if love doesn't justify sex, what does?"

You make a good point, old friend. Just so it is love for God that determines our sexual pursuits and not the human desire to enjoy the body's orgasm. That desire is what the glandular pursuit is about and it culminates in an itch scratched for a few minutes and another image on the scene.

The upward spiral of adoration culminates in the inner Child's return. The Child's unrequited love for all mankind pushes us to new levels of accomplishment for the world. When the Child reawakens within us, It holds rein on the sexual pursuits intended to make a conquest of another. The enlivening love which the Child feels is from God and from man, to God and to man. It transcends sexual feelings as Alphabet transcends a line of verse. The verse may be beautiful, but the Alphabet contains all verses to infinity.

As the Child atop the mountain, I am the point of the Flow. It moves through Me to everyone. It returns through Me to Godhead. I be that point steadfastly and feel the Love which God is. God is Love.

63

THE MYSTICISM OF JOURNAL TENDING
A special word to writers about Understanding

Words can be deceivers.

Words are man-made symbols of symbols.

One may turn from the word to the symbol (or from the symbol to the word) and find himself one step closer to Reality. Then he looks behind the symbol (or the word) and *there* *IT* is, arriving as a Glimpse of light.

From the Glimpse, we see the world from Zen's final position and see the symbol in the new Light, to find it changed or somehow different—which means, whatever words (symbols of symbols) we write NOW will be different from those written before we first turned from the symbol of the symbol. *The words we write become clearer and simpler because they are a distillate from our earlier intellectual confusion and indecision.*

This is why, with glimpses, I am able to say more every day and write more now than I ever dreamed possible. This "more" may be less in numbers of words because, being the distillate, *it is to the point* and easy to comprehend by the heart of mankind. It goes to the heart of the matter directly, whether the intellect comprehends or not. The Child is enlivened.

Oh, there is certain to be the usual intellectual argument within myself, especially if the words are poorly written. If one doesn't want argument in the world, his words should "make sense" to the intellectual view. And one should not *want* argument! Argument may shake the intellect, but it doesn't explain it or lessen it. Contrariwise, argument brings the intellect to use all excuses to maintain its old position and justify its cherished existence as the human authority. The intellect rises no higher than the intellect. Its domain is the tangible world. Like Herod, it slaughters whatever threatens it or doesn't compute intellectually. So, we get our words to make sense as much as possible and then let intellectualism rail as it likes—while we remain true to the Glimpse and heed the Heart's vista of Truth. The Heart KNOWS and, in the end, *prevails.*

We read correct words, expecting Heart *confirmation.* Confirmation comes with healing on its wings.

Then we turn from the symbol of symbols to reinterpret the world. The world is a step closer. We hear ourselves saying, "As I be lifted into new Glimpses of Light, the world I see is lifted likewise."

To say this another way: I have learned to address the heart of those with whom I talk, *using the intellect's own rules to do it, thereby avoiding an unnecessary argument with ego and arrogance!* I speak to the Child that's there before me, using the Child's own words. The Child is all that's *real*. The Child, the heart, is the Same Me.

Before the mist lifted, my words were directed to the intellect where they could be understood by the intellect, but the intellect is capable of going no higher than the arena where words were created as symbols for things.

After the mist lifted, my words were directed to the Heart, with full knowledge they must pass through the intellect which permits only what it will.

There is a good reason why we think we have insight so long before we really do. The intellectual knowledge of things isn't the full knowledge of them. But, listen listen: neither the intellectual understanding nor the Heart's understanding is the Truth Itself. Truth is *more* yet.

At some point (a point of travail for most of us), the Truth-beyond-the-limit-of-the-intellect comes quietly onto the scene. Line upon line, precept upon precept... Lo! The scene becomes a Scene, new each moment, wonderful beyond the ordinary.

"Let him who has ears to hear" . . . understand what is written here before he publishes words that sound as if he knows when he doesn't.

NOW I know why an arrogant belief of understanding puffs us up with human satisfaction and personal pride long before Understanding consciously arrives. That time of understanding-before-Understanding is an impertinent and vainglorious time which has been addressed in so many ways in the literature of the world. This unrecognized vaingloriousness is especially deluding to those of us who fancy ourselves mirrors of

the Light, teachers of Truth, ministers, priests and practitioners, writers, seekers along the pathway, instruments of God or
any of the nearly infinite human absurdities we get snagged
into believing *we are,* in our bewitching vanity of vanities.

The hooks of pride are so subtle, so evanescent and beguil-
ing that *none I know have escaped them.* But these hooks are
not *bad* either. They are ultimately understood and seen as a
necessary part of the Plan. They are our twisting in the wind
and writhing time; our wriggling out of the cocoon time; our
me-dying time. It is a terribly difficult time but a Good-be-
yond-good Time! It was the time I stuck my head farthest into
my own darkness, looking for light there but finding anguish
instead.

Ah, but fortunately, these were the times I intuitively knew
to disappear from the human scene *and write to no one but
God.* Thank God for that! Of all times, the mirage-in-the-wil-
derness time is not the time to spew words into the ears of
one's "others" or into print. Pity the minister who feels obli-
gated to speak to his congregation twice a week! Look at the
travesties pouring from the printers and presses, subjectively
all my own echoes of me-sense talking when I could have been
listening, the real Vision just beyond my arrogance, seen
through the me-sense darkly.

The question comes: Are *these* words any different? Yes,
yes—but I can't make anyone "out there" believe this. We let
the Heart tell us whether or not there is Authority behind the
words on these pages or any others.

Certainly Samuel is not the Authority of honesty. Authority
lies with the Life who looks and listens to catch Truth's
glimpses, here a little, there a little. The trees in the field minister with straightforward, unpretentious honesty. So must we.

Father, keep the me-sense and its self-righteous search for
Truth silent and subdued. Sound the Melody *beyond* the echoing canyons. In the contriteness of Me—the me-sense still—let
Me hear the Morning Stars singing. Then, Father of Light,
help me sing as I should, giving the melody to the wind.

These words mark a measure of the Song I hear today and

of the Joy I'm blessed to feel: Only God knows what words will be written tomorrow.

64

THE FROG, THE TOAD AND OLD DAN JONES

Just because someone has written a book doesn't mean the book's message is on target or the author an authority. Because one talks about the Child doesn't mean he has found the Child.

How does one tell the Mystic from the mystic? The genuine from the fraud? The one who knows from the one who says he knows? The one who knows from the one who THINKS he knows? There is a difference between these creatures, and it behooves us to know about the wheat and tares. The Child within helps us see the difference.

In Wetumpka, Alabama—or Toombsuba, Mississippi, I forget which—lived an old man, Dan Jones, who claimed to know the difference between a frog and a toad. "Toads hop. Frogs leap," he said, and wrote that into a book. Well now, generally speaking, that's true—provided one knows the difference between a hop and a leap. When does a hop turn into a leap? What's the difference between a large hop and a small leap? I suspect the difference is about the same as that between a Mystic and a mystic, a philosopher and a bullshooter, a person who talks Truth and one who lives it.

Dan was also considered to be an authority on mushrooms and toadstools—and he wrote about them in his book, too. He told me all about frogs, toads, toadstools and mushrooms in my early days on the river and I believed everything he said. One afternoon after a hard arrowhead hunt, I stopped by his home to show him my latest finds. His wife told me that Dan had passed on unexpectedly. Dan, she said, had gone into the woods, gathered the evening meal, prepared it with his own calloused hands, eaten it and died of poisoning. She and her son—who were still sickly when she told me this sad story—had barely survived. The last supper which Dan gathered, pre-

pared and with which he destroyed himself and his reputa-
tion, was frog legs and mushrooms.

I've thought about Dan a lot over the years; there is a lesson
leaping and hopping somewhere in his story. I feel about the
Truth the way the Jews once felt about their prophets. Let
what one says about the Truth be what he KNOWS from his
own heart-felt revelation. And let what one says about his revelation be said with all the honesty and accuracy possible.
Never mind that "talking out of the Spirit" stuff ministers and
teachers say is so wonderful when they are standing before
their captive audiences. Better that we put our revelations to
the test *first*, and when they have been confirmed—"heard in
the other ear"—we are at liberty to talk about them to *everyone*. If we believe the Spiritual Muse can tap into us while we
are at work on our journal or delivering the Sunday sermon,
then we'd better accept the corollary that the "debbil" can tap
in as well. I don't think God would consider it distrustful if we
put His Light (our Glimpses) to the test before we tell the
world. We'd better.

Another of the Jones boys, probably not related, led several
hundred of his followers to their suicidal death in the jungles
of South America. It is well that we understand there is no *external* authority in the end. Rather, the Christ Child *within*
each of us is the Authority we can trust. If an external authority—church, philosophy, government or whatever—*tells us
that* and gives us words in such a way that we can put them to
the test, then we can learn much from that source and trust
it. The Child within us will confirm those words and show us
how to live them honestly to everyone's benefit.

65

ABOUT CONFIRMATION or PROVING
THINGS TO BE TRUE

We have Glimpses that are wonderful and enlightening; then
we are to look into the world to CONFIRM those Glimpses.

The Glimpse may arrive today, but it may take a lifetime to see it confirmed in one's tangible experience.

How to say this so it won't be misunderstood? Out of the linear way things are comprehended, we've grown accustomed to believing that when the Glimpse of Truth comes to us, everything will be hunky-dory with never another problem along that line in our affairs. That isn't how it works. It is more like this: One catches a glimmer of something pertaining to "supply," say, but instead of our supply needs being filled immediately, we're more likely to have a bout with the very opposite—*which is often exactly what is necessary to bring us to put our Glimpse to the test.* It is intended that we live our Glimpses and prove them. The proof is its *confirmation,* the second coming of the Glimpse, so to speak, confirmed "in the other ear." Then, and not until then, can we speak *with authority* about it.

However, and please understand, we don't hold back giving our Glimpses. We tell them as best we can—as GLIMPSES—because they are ours alone to tell and give. But when we publish for the world, we hold our publications within the arena where we have lived the confirmation and heard in both ears. That is, we publish the things we have confirmed internally and externally!

I heard about the nothingness of the subtle and arrogant ego more than thirty years ago. I also learned the "secrets" of the Child and the Child's Equation years ago—but I've been looking for their CONFIRMATION ever since—and am just NOW given the AUTHORITY to publish them.

Let those to whom these words bring insight, know that *they must still confirm every insight for themselves, in their own experiential world, even as I have had to do!*

There is no presto in the Truth, as we all so want to believe. The REAL of us is on the PEAK of the Mountain; and we live this body in all ways that will confirm that Fact of Being. Then. . . .

66

ABOUT WORDS, THOUGHTS, STATES AND STAGES

Dear Terry,

The book you are studying *(A Guide To Awareness and Tranquillity)* is much like a primer of subjective thinking. *This* book cannot sound like that one because I have progressed since those days.

Yes, I have suffered enormously in my human affairs and have gained much because of that—BUT I MUST BE CAREFUL NOT TO LEAVE THE IMPRESSION THAT SUFFERING IS NECESSARY to perceive the Truth, even though it may well be. There are entire religious orders that speak to the necessity for personal suffering before one can catch the Glimpse.

I must not leave an impression in the other direction either, that the Truth is gained without suffering. I simply do not know if that is true or not. I have never met a person who has not suffered significantly in one area or another somewhere along the long pathway to awakeness—but that does not mean it is an invariable rule.

Another factor, Terry: Those who have come here to study were given all the graphics, formulas, "how to's" and "what I did's" that seemed appropriate when they were here. You already know this. But the Light I have awakened to declares forthrightly that the "how to's" and "the what I did's" *are not half as important as they seem to be to the intellectual nature of ourself.* Listen carefully: *There is another STATE OF MIND entirely which "does the good work" of bringing people to wakefulness.* I address that state of mind.

You tell me: (1) Should I write what I write out of that state of mind? Or, (2) should I write what I did to acquire that state of mind? (3) Shall I write what that state of mind did for me in my affairs? Or, (4) should I write what that state *allows me to see presently?* Where is the book that can do all those things simultaneously? Yet, this new book does most of that if you search for it with more than a single reading.

Here is another thought for you: There is a point in one's

ongoing development at which subjectivism hits like a ton of bricks. At that time, there are things one vigorously and vehemently chooses NOT to listen to—usually about suffering and other difficulties. You tell me, Terry, how am I to write and avoid offending those people and their new sensitivities?

There is a point along the way when methods take a backseat to perceptions. When one is concerned with methods, the perceptions sound like pie in the sky. When one is viewing perceptions, methods sound like foolishness because some of the new perceptions seem to do away with the importance of methods. It is terribly difficult to write words that cut through this particular dilemma of religion and metaphysics.

Dear Terry, there are enormous problems in writing a book that purports to tell of the Truth:

(1) Finding the words that are honest AT ALL LEVELS OF PERCEPTION, even though there REALLY are no levels of perception. To do this sometimes requires that strange sounding absolute language—but not always.

(2) Finding the words that do not create false hopes, even though grand hopes are justified.

(3) Finding the words, examples, illustrations, "how to's" and "what I did's" that cut through intellectualism without causing it to REAR UP in the process—thereby defeating the purpose of the book.

(4) How to do all this and, as if that weren't enough, KEEP THE BOOK PHILOSOPHICALLY, THEOLOGICALLY, METAPHYSICALLY AND SCIENTIFICALLY CONSISTENT THROUGHOUT!

And, as if all that were not enough, there is this consideration: How am I to establish meaningful and concrete modes of thought to replace those I would cast down, alter or destroy? It is easy to attack the things we know can't be right, but not as easy to see what should be there instead. It is one thing to talk about the "real Self" and another to find it!

Ah so, Terry, it is an enormous responsibility, this book we write—like walking a tightrope between two buildings—a single misstatement would plunge us straight to the pavement below. I have been led down too many primrose pathways to want to do that to others. "How to's" can become TOO specific, causing people to try to do things exactly the same way—which can often be self-defeating. Once I was determined to levitate because St. Catherine levitated when she prayed.

You are correct in saying that "the enlightened" ain't necessarily so enlightened they don't belch like everyone else. I belch with the best of them.

Love from Alabama,

67

JOURNAL TENDING

Thoughts about journal tending:

1. Journal tending began for me as a respite from the world, and at the same time, a way to examine my thinking. It eventually becomes a means of talking to God about everything—and getting the answers we need.

2. We keep our journal private. It's not for others to read. If we keep it to ourselves, we will be more honest in it. That isn't to say we don't share the thoughts that come forth there, because we do. The very purpose of the journal is to open the door to greater communication with the rest of ourself—above and below.

3. We don't worry about how well it is written! Journal tending is a means to Self-discovery, not an attempt to win the Nobel Prize for literature.

4. Never mind the punctuation, spelling, grammar and all that. Get the thoughts down first.

5. Phrases and single words can do just as well as whole paragraphs—if they remind us of some insight we might one day think about in greater depth and write in more detail.

6. Never mind neatness unless you are inclined that way. I'm not.

7. Especially, don't write in elevated, pedantic or Godly language if you don't want to write that way. Try not to write in the jargon of science, metaphysics or religion but in the fresh words you'd use with a friend.

8. We write as it is comfortable to write.

9. Use plain English.

10. Write simply.

11. Make illustrations!

12. Make analogies! Yes! Yes! Yes!

13. Get in the habit of *thinking* in parables, analogies, similes, parallels and illustrations.

14. Use non-verbal symbols if that helps picture the thought.

15. Diagrams are wonderful if glimpses can be put like that!

16. Remember, it isn't WHAT we write that ultimately becomes important, but it is the MODE of mentation that writing puts us into.

17. When you are writing about people, use their names. This doesn't sound like "impersonal metaphysics," but you'll see why this is important later. Our insights become our friends; they become ourselves—and we see the people we have insights *about* bloom in the light of those insights.

18. Put dates on all the entries. The reason for this becomes evident later—and is very helpful in the years ahead when you are looking back on the birth of an idea. Sometimes when I go back to an old page of the journal, I write in my current insights about the idea there, noting the date of the new addition. The dates allow us to see our growth right there on the printed page—and be astounded.

19. Never mind trying to write "absolutely"; write normally, as though you were talking to yourself or a friend. This is, in fact, what you are doing—talking with the Self. We don't have to use the language of any group. We don't write like Samuel or Eddy, Bohm or Goldsmith, but as OURSELF.

20. Write on scraps of paper, backs of envelopes, paper bags and whatever is available when the journal is not handy. Those scraps will amaze you one day. They can be written (or pasted) into the journal later.

21. You don't have to be meticulously regular in writing in the journal. We write when it seems good to do it, but it is a marvelous way to BEGIN a day. It can set the mood and establish the framework for the day if we choose to let it.

22. It is a good way to END a day too, like a goodnight prayer, if we make it that.

23. Journal tending BEGINS one way *and grows into quite SOMETHING ELSE!* MANY things else! Books can be written about this alone. History shows us that writers have been the ones who shaped the directions for entire civilizations.

Many, if not most of the founding fathers of this country were journal tenders—and look at what their words have spawned!

24. Those of us who are disposed to, begin with Ineffability, God, as we write; and if we are faced with problems, we bring that Pure Principle, God, "into" those problems.

25. Dialogue writing! Most wonderful part of it all. Conversations between God and oneself, or between oneself and the Original Child within—and, eventually, between the Child and Godhead. The "Han Discourses" are just such writing as I talk to the Self within and without.

26. Whether we write a little or a lot, makes no difference. It is good to write as much as comes to be written if you have the time. But we understand there are days to write and days to read, days to watch the river flow and the flowers bloom, days to work our tail off and days to rest, days to talk and days to listen. You will find that the "writing mode of mind" *becomes constant* whether you are actually holding a pen in your hand or not.

27. We mark certain pages (for instance, on those days when much is coming but we haven't time to write it all). The marked pages are for going back to (under certain circumstances) and finishing later.

28. We mark the FLOW DAYS. I put a mark in the top corner of such papers because I know there is something special there to be further understood.

29. We mark the days when Light occurs! Oh yes, I put a special mark at the top of such papers, because whatever was being written is a part of "the bridge."

30. We even mark the very places on the page when Light "comes." And, remember, sometimes the light that comes doesn't seem related to the words on the page at all—and may not be. It was the mode of mentation that allowed the light through.

31. We note the sundry *intuitions* that come as we write—over in the margins, or wherever we can spot them again. As with the previous entry, those intuitions may or may not be related to the material we were writing about.

32. The journal is especially helpful on down days when we're feeling lousy. A little writing on such days and the juices begin flowing again. Those are sometimes good days to write to a

friend because the very thought of that one can be uplifting. That one is *us*.

33. There are days to write in the journal, days to read it, and days to do both.

34. As I said earlier, but repeat, we keep our journal from the eyes of others who don't know what we're doing. There are exceptions sometimes if it seems good to let someone read our special thoughts, but the journal should be kept from prying eyes. It is better to *say* what is in our journals than to have others read it. The day will come soon enough when our inmost thoughts will be published and we stand naked before the world.

35. *Ask questions* in the journal! Try to answer them from the "God Perspective." This is not to play at being God, but is to "let that mind be in us which was also in Christ."

36. Write as much as possible, especially at first, from the old, questioning position. Then dare to answer as the Wisdom of God! Why? Because Awareness IS the Wisdom of God.

37. Very important: We make two GLIMPSE and GLIMMER sections! One for the ones we can remember from our past experiences. This requires patient recollections but is a joy to do. Memories of wonderful things come back to us—little things we haven't thought about in years. And don't worry about the bad things coming back. We all have a way of being grateful that those things are over. Or, if they are not over, they tell us what we are to "unbind" in our experience. The other section is for the NEW Glimpses that begin to happen more and more often as we get into the writing mode of mentation.

38. Journal tending is MEDITATION in the act of happening.

39. Journal tending is CONTEMPLATION, happening on the spot.

40. Journal tending, if we are writing about the good we see, is PRAYER—and it can become "unceasing."

41. Journal tending is "entering into the Shekinah."

42. Journal tending is "entering the Secret Place of the Most High" because it is the doorway to and from our inmost thoughts.

43. Journal tending leads one (allows one) to be "in the world but not of it." Who can worry about what to do tomorrow when he is writing about the beauty in front of his nose at the moment?

44. Learning to type might be helpful, but the entries must be spontaneous and loose. If you make the switch from a pen to a typewriter, it doesn't take too long until the typewriter no longer stands between you and your thoughts.

45. I can see that a personal computer with a word processing capability would be a marvelous adjunct, especially one with a printer to keep a written record of your thoughts and ideas. It is important to be able to see the whole journal, so to speak— and to be able to "just open it" on those "certain days." The computer is especially good for those who are to become published writers. When an electronic typewriter came into my experience, it was a wonderful day—and I bless the people who helped me buy the rabbi. (The rabbi is my word processor— Rabbi Moses Goldberg is his name, processing words is his game. The printer is Mrs. Goldberg. The electronic typewriter that preceded the personal computer is Nelly Magnolia Calhoun, from Mississippi.)

46. In the journal, have an IDEAS OUT OF THE BLUE section. These are ideas for things to do immediately in the world.

47. Perhaps have an INTUIT section. I remember the way "continental drift," the effects of weather, cosmology, etc., came to me while I was in the process of writing in my journal. All of these intuitions later proved to be right.

48. Have a PEOPLE TO HELP SECTION! Put four stars on this!

49. Have a PEOPLE TO WRITE section, too. Four-star this!

50. Journal tending is an interface with the Child within and God. It is a holy time because we are right down to the nitty gritty of LIVING.

51. The journal is the PLACE where the outside begins to become like the inside. (Much about this is explained elsewhere in the book.)

52. The work in the journal is always supply work for oneself and the world. It is right in the middle of the flow—give/receive, receive/give, to God, to mankind, to Self.

53. Journal tending is subjectivity in action!

54. Journal tending is balanced activity, between inside/outside.

55. Write about things BEAUTIFUL or TENDER or CHILD-LIKE in preference to things scientific, religious or metaphysical. Why? Because they are easier and much more fun to write—and do a better job opening us up and getting us into the RECEPTIVE MODE.

56. Notice the difference between receptive mode as opposed to the worried mode, fearful mode, struggling mode, etc. The journal helps in all these situations.

57. Journal tending is the place where intangibility becomes tangible. This is explained in detail elsewhere.

58. Journal writing teaches us to go to GOD *WITHIN and allows the Child to express Itself outside.*

59. I have found it most helpful to write like this: I write whatever thoughts seem appropriate and honest; then I read the sentence and listen to it as though I were a listener listening. This is a wonderful way to write, of course, because it immediately permits anyone who can talk to another person to write as beautifully and tenderly as he would carry on a conversation with someone he loves.

Remember, the best way to begin a journal is to start a list of Glimpses and Glimmers. This fits perfectly into the Equation, the whole picture of GIVING AND RECEIVING.

Dear Reader, how many more journal thoughts can you add to this list? There must be a hundred I've missed here.

68

IDENTITY AND THE GENUINE COMMUNITY

The physical body itself is the first hierarchy of completeness to which Light/light flows in time and space. This is to say, our own physical body is the *first part of the wake immediately behind the Ship, the first grain of sand atop Da Shan.* In retrospection—in the people, places and things arena—the last thing we really know is ourself. The first and last body one has under control is his own.

We get ourself straight and then comes dominion. Birthright! Authority.

From here grows the genuine community—the harvest the avatars have spoken of.

We love our mankind unrestrictedly and give to those who come to us and receive from those who are given to us. We give our Glimpses and Glimmers to our entire WORLD of people. We receive from Everyone (God's images) and from the world.

Balance is perceived as existing in and from Source. Balance takes care of this physical body as this body takes care of its world of people.

While I have been very slow learning these things and have unwittingly lived virtually every imbalance to find balance again, I know God tends this body-in-time until this Message becomes clearly written in the world. I am at it, Father!

JOURNAL ENTRIES

When one becomes nothing of himself, he finds himself and knows himself, even as he is known of God.

One doesn't need to try working miracles with the Truth. Rather, let him try to understand himself and, in the process, miracles will happen, miracles not bound to the framework of the wanter and needer, the wisher and seeker. It is pointless to do aught but get to know the Selfhood made in the image of God; then we know, as nearly as can be known, what God is via that Self's self-examination. God will disclose what is necessary as we work to expound the glimpses and glimmers. The Community grows THEN. The companion comes THEN. The help comes THEN.

69

"SILLY SOLIPSISM!" SHOUTS THE PREACHER

"Everything comes to me by way of my own perception," said Han. "For instance, my own eyes have seen all I have seen. My own ears have heard everything I have heard. Only my fingers have touched whatever my fingers have touched. Every thought I have ever heard has been considered, or not considered, right here within this head as I experience my own sensations. This is self-evidently true for all of us, isn't it?" asked Han.

No one spoke. "Now, I hold a leaf in my left hand and the minister's sacred book in my right. How do I know the book is a sacred book? Is it sacred because the book has words that say it is sacred? How can I believe that? How do I know the Bible is infallible? Because the preacher and his church say so? Because the book says that it is infallible? I look at the leaf. How do I know it is a leaf? Because I have looked and heard and seen and have become able to discern that it is a leaf and not a stone. Am I able to tell this is a sacred book because I have heard it is not like the other books that exist? Do I believe it is a sacred book because of the beauty and truth I have found there, or do I believe it is sacred because the teachers and ministers tell me it is, just as their teachers and ministers told them before?"

Everyone was listening intently, especially the preacher.

"Where have I determined these things about the leaf and the book?" Han continued. "Within my own head. And how did I learn what I know of the leaf and the book? Within my own head. Can I believe the written word is sacred because the written word says it is? I can believe the leaf is good because I know about leaves. I can believe the leaf is green because it is green, but can I believe the sacred book is sacred because the minister and his church say so, or because the book says so?"

The preacher was plainly annoyed but said nothing.

"If mankind has designed the alphabet to express the principle of words, and if mankind has created the words to speak of ideas and things, can I believe that the words which have been put together and called sacred are sacred because mankind says they are or because the words say the words are sacred? And if the words say that God is the source of the words, how does that make the words any more sacred than the leaf? Is not God the source of everything?"

The preacher clenched his fists.

Han said, "Ah, but even if the words are sacred, there is

something more sacred than they are. Do you know what that is?"

The soldier, sitting beside the preacher, threw up his hands in disgust. "I don't even know what you are talking about or trying to say," he said.

"Where do I see the leaf?" asked Han.

"In your head," the soldier answered.

"Where do I see the preacher's text?"

"Same place," the soldier said.

"Where do I decide what shape the leaf has and what color it is?" asked Han.

"In your thick head," the preacher said.

"And where do I read the words that say the words are sacred?" Han asked.

"Where you see everything," the soldier answered. "Inside yourself."

"And where do I know the leaf is not connected to the tree any longer?"

"Within your question-asking, cantankerous nature."

"And is that the place where the holy text is read?"

"Yes, the same place," the soldier replied.

"Have I ever seen or heard of the sacred text or the leaf or anything else, outside myself?"

"Perhaps there is a way that information comes directly into the heart," said the minister, "without having to go through the senses."

"Yes," said Han. "And where but here within myself would I become conscious of the heart's knowledge? Would that knowledge be within me or within the self of another?"

"Within yourself," the soldier said wearily.

"If I hold the leaf and ignore it, would I discover its qualities?"

"No, damnit!" the soldier muttered.

"And if I hold the sacred text and ignore it, will I know of the arrangement of words within it?"

"No."

"So, how can the arrangement of words become sacred to me without my own intent and without my willingness to believe?"

"I suppose they can't."

"So, are the words sacred by themselves or with my consent?"

"For God's sake, Han, I don't know! I am lost. What are you trying to tell us, old man?"

"I am not trying to tell you anything," the teacher answered. "I am telling myself something. I see only my own sensations when I see you."

"And I see only mine when I see you," the soldier said, tired of the matter.

"I don't *know* that you see *anything*," said Han. "I know only that I see. Everything meaningful to me begins and ends here as my own sensation."

"Bullshit!" the preacher exploded, unable to contain his anger. "That is oversimplified solipsism; pure, silly solipsism, just as the theologians labeled it years ago!"

"Ah, there we have it," laughed Han, clapping his hands. "The theologian calls it silly because this fact of Being insists that nothing is more whole than the Awareness within which images appear. Silly solipsism says that an image is an image is an image. What is this Bible but an image—an engraved image—I hold in my hand? And which is more holy, the book in my hand or the Life that perceives and encompasses and lives that book?"

The preacher's anger grew. "Are you trying to tell me the Bible is not the Word of God?" he asked incredulously.

"It isn't the only word of God," smiled Han.

"Oh my God!" the pudgy preacher shouted. "I can't believe my ears. Are you trying to tell us that the Word of God is not holy?"

"No," answered Han patiently. "Everything that is, is equally divine because everything exists within Divinity. But the book in my right hand is no more whole than the leaf in my left—and all things together are not as holy as the Whole Awareness that sees them."

"This is contrary to everything I have been taught," the minister said, shaking with rage.

"But contrary to nothing you have *learned*," Han smiled.

"It is contrary to *everything* I have learned, you Oriental heathen!" raged the preacher.

"No," Han smiled broadly. "It may be contrary to everything

you have heard, but just because something has been heard doesn't mean it has been learned. What is heard is learned when it has been put to the test and proven."

The preacher slapped his knee in frustration. "That is how I know the Bible is holy, you fool! I have proven it and proven it and proven it!" He shook as he spoke.

"And that is how I know the leaf is just as holy," said Han.

The people sat wide-eyed, awaiting the next blast from the minister. With a visible effort to control himself, he asked, "Why are you telling us these ridiculous things? What is your motive?"

"I remind you that I am telling myself these things," the old teacher said. "But I say them aloud so my listening selfhood may see that our link to God is direct and doesn't have to be funneled through the words of a book one holds in his hands."

"My God, man!" the preacher began, "Do you realize what would happen if men stopped believing in the Holy Bible?"

"I am not suggesting that men stop believing in the Bible or any other book, my friend; only that they come to see that their interface with God is direct and not irrevocably tied to the words of any book—nor to a church or anything else. Like you, I have books that are meaningful to me, but my link with the subject of those books is direct, as is my interface with Truth. The Bible may point to the stars, but I see them with my own eyes."

"But the Bible says . . ." the preacher began and stopped. He stood up. Pounding his fist into his hand, he glowered at the group. "This is the worst kind of heathenism!" he said finally. "I think all of you are tools of the devil. All of you are deluded! I am leaving before I do something I will regret."

Everyone watched as the minister stormed down the path toward the village. It was not the first time this had happened. Many had come to visit Han over the years, begging his views, only to leave in anger the moment their beliefs were threatened. Han shook his head in sadness. "I didn't speak to myself very well today, did I?" he asked.

"You spoke very well," Mary replied softly. "You just didn't listen. That is our deafness thundering down the path. The minister's fists are clenched around his most cherished illusions. He will be letting them go one day."

"Perhaps," said Han. "Then, those who follow him blindly may let them go as well."

HUMAN GOVERNMENT

Totalitarian governments, right or left, disparage God. Why? Because their control over church people is not complete. Exactly so, churchdom in the world unwittingly disparages the subjective idea because the people who truly find subjectivism cannot be controlled very well either. The subjectivist is as weird to the common man as the quantum physicist is to the ordinary scientist. Yet, subjectivism discovered and lived will eventually be as catalytic in the human experience and all of its institutions, and do as much for them, as the subjectivism of quantum has done (and will do) for the sciences.

Unchallenged religion, like unchallenged government, has led to racism, concentration camps and sycophantic, half-sleeping followers pushed into one holy war after another. Now, another Holy War looms, perhaps the last. Only the Child within us escapes the final oppression of exclusive externalism. "I alone am escaped to tell thee" are the words the suffering Job heard. (We might note that the marvel of the American system is the citizen's right to challenge external authority when it seems wrong to him—and this right *is guaranteed* to him in writing by his government!)

Church government, which generally considers itself superior to human government, would do well to let its lowly members challenge a few of their leaders and some of the church's ancient creeds and dogmas that have been clearly outgrown. The humanly ungovernable Child within us will be up and out one day very soon as linear time goes, and, when it is, every organization will be reorganized.

I doubt if words that tell of the Child within us could be published in the Soviet Union where external authority is supreme. I know *these* words I write could not be published by the individual in the Roman Catholic Church or the Christian Science Church without that individual being taken to task. But the Child within us is already free of human government, living and moving and having Its being in our heart of hearts! Now, the knowledge of the Child doesn't mean that we—as the rediscovered Child—don't vote or support our church and country. We don't withdraw from anything. It means more nearly that we are viewed as a peculiar people, not quite so governable by external authorities and their institutions. We will be taken to task by everyone who hears and fears our Self-discovery. The prophets saw this coming—as did Jesus. "Blessed are you when men shall revile you and persecute you and say all manner of evil against you falsely" (for the Child's sake).

The point being made here? That church governments anywhere in the world, including the United States, are just as dictatorial and demeaning, *when they feel threatened,* as any secular government has ever been. The recognition of the Child within us is coming soon to challenge all exclusively objective modes of mind. The egocentric turf protectors, the priests, rabbis and ministers clutching their numbers, will bellow and shout and bring their houses down on their heads *because the people they lead like sheep will perceive that the Child is indeed alive within themselves as it is in us.* And exactly as the prophets said, ". . . great will be (the Child's) reward in heaven, for so persecuted they the prophets before you."

Bottom line: It is natural for the objective world to try to hold to the status quo and to subdue the subjective idea if it can. Subjectivism has been put down successfully by churchdom many times before. It was a subjective uprising within Judaism that gave birth to Christianity. But what do the rabbis teach about the subjective idea today? That it is dangerous! Judaism warns the rabbis who would like to explore the deep things of God that subjectivism can safely be studied only with a proven prophet. And what do the organized Christian sects teach of subjectivism? See for yourself. Virtually nothing.

Now that the physical sciences are in the process of rediscovering metaphysics once more, in quantum mechanics, it remains to be seen what they will do with it; but if the past forty years are an indication, there seems little reason to doubt the prophets' predictions. Perhaps it is poetic justice that it may very well be the concretized egotism of mankind, led by its organizational leaders—ministers, rabbis, mullahs and priests who know nothing of subjectivism whatever—who, with their frightened, uneducated flocks, will appear to do the "devil's" final work of tearing down the houses whose foundations lie on objective sand.

Quantum information is arriving now. The world is being flooded with information that is certain to induce new modes of thought, if mankind is to survive the upheaval. The old things will certainly pass away. There will be a new heaven and earth to be seen with the eyes because it is here already, unseen.

The Child within us survives. Those of us who have found that Child will be non-judgmental onlookers, doing what we have been given to do to help our new world. And we will do it against great odds—successfully.

70

TEXTBOOK THINKING

When the great theologians came along to speak of Godhead, it seemed to the ordinary churchman that God was in danger of being abandoned. When subjectivism arose among the Jews and crystallized in the community of the Essenes, the threat to the establishment was plain. After the schism of Christianity, the subjective idea was stamped out of Judaism as thoroughly as it could be done. It is interesting that we find no mention of the Essenes in either the Old or New Testament today.

As Christianity grew in worldliness, the threat of subjectivism became apparent there as well—and the expulsion of all gnosticism from Christianity followed. Then came the subjective metaphysical groups who have, in turn, removed all meaningful subjectivism from their own subjective ideas—one of the mental miracles of modern times.

But, as it has been shown, all of this is exactly how it was supposed to happen. Throughout history, the Child within has been present, here a little, there a little. Today, the time approaches when quantum mankind, the tree of life, will be forced to turn within itself and re-discover the Child once more. But, lo, the very churches charged with leading the way

are themselves aimed at a single historic point in time, blind
to the Child within Everyman.

71

───────

THE GALILEO ILLUSTRATION PERTAINING
TO TEXTBOOK THINKING

As the reader knows, Galileo built a telescope and discovered that the planets were part of a great solar system. Then
he defied the teachings of the church by stating that the earth
was not the center of the universe. The church objected and
Galileo was accused of heresy. Doesn't entrenchment always
object to ideas that threaten it?

Fortunately, men of vision saw the wonder of Galileo's discovery, and (the story now turns to semi-fiction) a small and
dedicated group soon evolved to study Galileo's work. They
virtually worshiped the astronomer and his wonderful new
vista of the night sky.

Now, for the sake of an illustration, suppose Galileo had
written a statement called <u>Science and the Ten-Power Telescope
with a Map to the Stars</u> or something like that. The new organization, dedicated to protecting and promulgating Galileo's
view of things, used this book as its sacred text—a veritable
Holy Book. Then, as Galileo's band of faithfuls wrote stories
about their time with the astronomer, their body of books
slowly became a new canon for the astronomers of the world.

Galileo passed on—some say he is still here in another
guise—but his followers continued their veneration of the man
and the truth he wrote about. As the years went by, their organization grew in influence and the Galileans believe to this
day they have been shown the final view of the stars.

But some time ago pomp and ceremony began to take over
their organization, which, though the Galileans couldn't perceive it or even admit to its presence, began to have a significance all its own, as important to them as the ten-power view
of the stars.

Wherever Galileans met, their ceremonies were identical. The textbook was reverently removed from its golden container. The Prophet in charge stood on the right side of the podium and made certain that all words read from the new canon gave proper credit for its divine authority. The Interpreter, who read from selected books of the time, stood to the left of the Prophet. An order of ceremony—"refined and dignified, befitting our high view of the stars"—was established and enforced. Indeed, let the Prophet or Interpreter make a mistake in any part of the ceremony and there was much clucking. Members could tell immediately if a Byzantine, Roman, Lutheran or Anglican stranger was in their midst.

In the early days, the followers of Galileo had been an adventurous people, but strangely, few went out to build their own telescopes and look at the stars for themselves. Instead, in a strange set of mind, peculiar to this day, *the study* of the textbook, day in and day out, became equivalent, in their view, to looking at the real stars in the night sky. Goodness, they memorized their testament.

The story goes that in the umpteenth year of the group's existence, a young woman was inspired to build her own telescope, an act prohibited by the manual of organizational procedures. Using the bottom of a broken bottle, a coat rack and a broom handle, the young person contrived a telescope of nearly twenty power and was able to see twice as much of the heavens as the old master. The lady made careful note of all she observed, and eventually wrote a book detailing her new discoveries in the night sky. Her book was entitled, *Beyond Galileo's View of Things*.

The daring astronomer expected acclaim from the members of the society. After all, Galileo himself had written that one day others would look into the great panoply of stars and see beyond his "feint and feeble glimpses," as he put it—and certainly the lady astronomer had done that. But the recognition she expected never came. Instead, she was vilified, taken to task and called disloyal for writing views of the sky not in accord with the honored ten-power textbook.

"Of *course*, the *words* of my book are not in accord with Galileo's words," she objected, "but my *astronomy* is in accord. How can a ten-power view of things be in accord with a twenty-power view?" she asked. "Or how can I use the old ten-power words to describe the twenty-power scene? *I have seen more of the heavens, just as Galileo said we would."*

Her protestations availed nothing. She was cast from the society as a disloyal, disobedient apostate bent on destroying the organization dedicated to keeping the science of astronomy "uncontaminated and unfettered by human hypotheses," exactly as Galileo had been cast from and destroyed by the entrenched church in his day.

So it goes with organizations. Virtually all of them. See how the methods have crystallized into formal ceremonies in the nineteen hundred years of Christianity. Notice also how the ideas behind those forms have ceased to be understood altogether. Let someone go back to the original idea that stands behind the form, and he is looked at with awe. But let someone see beyond the limits of the symbolism—as with a more direct view of one's own Selfhood—and he is excommunicated from all churchdom because his words are not in accord with tradition or the established books.

Now, suppose another astronomer comes along who happens also to be a radio engineer. He hears the radio sounds emanating from space and builds the first radio telescope that allows him to *hear* things Galileo and his group had no idea existed. His hearing, along with his twenty-power looking, allows him to discern things that the Galileo Text *makes no mention of whatever.*

Furthermore, suppose the Galileo canon disdains all the astrological stories of the heavens and calls them "heresy" or "heathen ideology not based on science." It can be understood that the students of this text, after many years of conditioning, still echoing some ancient Brother George's sentiments about "heathen ideology" *are naturally prone* to condemn the new radio astronomy as "more of the same old heathenism." This is precisely what "loyal Christians" do automatically when they turn a deaf ear to anything scientific or mystical just because there is no clear mention of it in the Holy Bible or other authorized textbooks.

Just as the old astronomy had no concept of radio astronomy, for which no descriptions then existed to put in the holy books, so the subjective experience of "Illumination," to which every sage has alluded, had not dawned sufficiently for the rabbis to make clear and significant mention of it in the pre-Christian Talmud, nor for the Apostles to explain it sufficiently in their letters which became the new canon. To this day, consequently, church groups traditionally turn their backs at the mention of things "mystical."

Now consider: if the radio astronomy of "Illumination" goes without notice by those groups of earnest (but textbook bound) people, can there be any EXPECTATION of Illumination in their experience? The expectation of It seems one of the primary means of *recognizing* the Experience! ". . .say to yourselves: 'On which day will (the angels and the prophets) come'. . .?" Jesus said.

Consider further: Inasmuch as we now clearly perceive the subjective experience of Illumination to be a FACT of Divinity, and inasmuch as that Experience acknowledged seems requisite for the "Something Beyond Words" (about which my life and the lives of many others are dedicated to telling), then how can TEXTBOOK THINKING permit the door of human consciousness to be pulled from its hinges allowing Light of the Infinite to enter the dark places of human intransigence?

Jesus came bringing the subjective message to the Jews and was cast out by the established order. Then, the new Church which grew from the words of Jesus turned right around and divested itself of the subjective message as thoroughly as the Jews before them. A new subjectivism was born nineteen hundred years later in Christianity which, in turn, lost the subjective idea once again, and within a hundred years that new subjectivism, too, is virtually inactive in the world. So it is, the very religious "Science" that opened so many doors early in this century now refuses to open its own doors to the ongoing New Light which it first recognized. Indeed, just as Jesus proclaimed, "The first shall be last." Let those stalwart groups, once so earnest and honest with their beautiful "First Glimmers of the Morning Light" re-examine themselves.

This is no plea that anyone's organization be abandoned or that books be burned. It is a plea that church members of all groups everywhere reconsider what "loyalty" means. Loyalty to a leader's original words is not loyalty to the Divine Principle those words heralded. The writers of the Bible called for loyalty to God. And God, the dynamism of the Universe, is an ongoing Essence, constantly revealing Itself as new marvels and new glories.

Those who wonder what has happened to churchdom and why the churches are failing to meet the moral obligations they have been given, might see that in all nature the fields that are plowed and fenced are fertile only for a brief time—without NEW enrichment.

Not one word of the favored Bibles and textbooks of the world needs to be changed. They are the wonders they are. But churchdom must eventually allow its members to input from the depth of their own intrinsic freedom of Soul—and listen to the Heart of themselves which receives and tells of other enriching Glimpses of Light. The real communication is between God-Mind and Its Self-awareness. Direct. Pure, pristine and virgin. The glimpses of others, as told about in the holy books, are wonderful, but the glimpses that count most for each of us are the ones we have ourselves. They are between God and us and those whom we love.

72

THE NARROWNESS OF TEXTBOOK THINKING

The way of non-contention with the world was given to me. It doesn't struggle to reform things. Enlightened non-judgmentalism permits one to see the good in the world, perfect as it already is.

But there is something inside that shouts for me to shout. The rebellious boy-cadet—the soldier—would have me beat the drum. But at WHAT?

The Heart knows, yet it isn't likely that a drum roll thundered by Jeremiah himself would be heard by my deaf selfhood—that part of me that worships people and their books. So, to what shall I shout?

To the narrowness of textbook thinking. Yes, yes. I rail about the narrowness of textbook thinking. Mind you, this is *not* to have the textbooks rewritten nor to have their organizations reformed. It is a plea that my "others" (not outside myself) stop limiting themselves to the boundaries of books—even the holy books, even to this group's or that group's interpretation of the Bible. Oh, books are wonderful and the world is blessed to have them. I ask those who study with me to *begin* a journal at once—and many of those jounals have become more books and papers that circumnavigate the world. Oh no, it isn't books I rail at, but our disposition to give them values they do not have *of themselves.*

I would roll my drum only to call attention to certain tendencies of the unenlightened nature of us. Our revered scriptures and textbooks already do that, but to little avail! Chief among those tendencies is that deadening inclination to establish the words of our treasured books as immutable, eternal law—especially a law to those areas of the heart that we haven't fully understood yet and wherein we still need an honest guide. Mind you, *there is nothing wrong with this tendency to put faith in books!* We had *better* believe the automobile manual until we are familiar with the machine. But that manual isn't immutable law for all eternity. There comes a day when we drive *another automobile.* There comes a day when we fly a spaceship. To hold tenaciously to original *words* as though they were eternally sacrosanct, is to be doomed. How so? That action *forces* us to return to the same ignorance from which those very words assisted our escape. *This* is what I'm inclined to shout about.

Are the words of the Bible holy? Or, is it the Lord God and His Principle which are more holy than the human words that tell of them? We know the answer to that without thinking. Then, why the great veneration of sacred *texts?* Again, we know the answer. "But now they are drunk," said Jesus. "When they have shaken off their wine, then. . . ."

ONGOINGNESS

There is a definite and essential *ongoingness* within the bedrock stability of spiritual Essence. Movement within non-movement; wheels within wheels, so to speak. There is no way for the human community to view the dynamism of Spirit, of Essence, of Godhead as immobile and stagnant. But the nature of the old ego man is to hang onto comfortable beliefs and familiar traditions. Spirit reveals Itself as eternal newness. The textbooks sometimes speak to that newness, but "textbook thinking" precludes the living of newness because there are no *specifics* of that newness written about in the textbook. Textbook thinking leads to stagnation, as one can plainly see from the many closed societies of churchdom, all in argumentative disagreement with others over their interpretations of the Bible or Whatever.

Religious metaphysics is a clear case in point. It entered the scene asking mankind to look to a new Idea "whose time had come." People did. That old/new Idea of subjectivism was off and running. Since those days, the world pace has quickened. In its one hundred years, that new Idea—a restatement of subjectivism in an objective world—has seen more confirming movement on earth than in all the eons preceding. The transcendentalist's push at the door of understanding was surely responsible for much of that movement. Now, that Idea's organizations *themselves* stand with blinders on and ears closed to the very ongoing spiritual revolution they helped spawn. Present era metaphysicians are afraid to examine the fruits of their own once fertile field—their own progeny. Why? No one wants to be cast as "disloyal." "They left the field." "They have not given due credit to So and So" who gave no credit to her sources other than the Bible. And it all happened exactly the same way before when Christian churchdom broke away from the objectivism of Judaism.

In a human way this is sad to see. But, in retrospect I see how absolutely right it all is. From the present calcification of religion worldwide, is soon to come the final blossom for which the Tree of Life was intended. That flower will be the rediscovery of the Child within. A new Community is being readied.

73

ILLUSTRATION OF THE INCUBATOR

What do we know about Light? Virtually nothing. About God? Still less.

Let me make a parallel illustration that suggests why Everyman knows so little and may one day learn so much. Instead of people, imagine chickens. Instead of the world, imagine a great incubator with the light turned on perpetually and with us chicks scratching around looking for (or not looking for) comfort, first, and the meaning of life, a distant second.

Let's pretend that an incubator hour is more like a decade, and that for nearly eleven thousand years we chickens have been speculating about the nature of Reality, wondering which version is right. During our long search, the thinking chickens among us have concluded that our well-being has something to do with light. (It might be interesting to note here that the scientist chicken and the religious chicken have apparently opposing ideas. The scientist speaks about the light he can measure; the religionist about the Light of God that can't be measured.)

Well now, how do we stand in the great incubator today? What do we chickens really know about Light/light? There is a precise parallel here. What did we know of childhood when we were children? What does a fish know of water or a bird of air? What do those who have been in the light without realizing it know about the light?

Over the chicken-millennia, thousands of religions have come and gone. Four primary philosophies remain today, one for each corner of the incubator. In the corners are great organizations with grand gurus representing different points of view such as Eastern, Western, Jewish, Catholic and, now that science has found metaphysics in its quantum mechanics, we need to add another corner to the pyramid. Each view insists its way is the best way; some say, the only way. The chicks in the south are diametrically opposed to those across the way. The Eastern view is opposite the Western view. One can imagine how these differences arose by recalling the Illustration of the Pyramid. (See THE GLASS PYRAMID) We remember how those along the north wall see Polaris in a different overhead quadrant than do those near the south wall, and must necessarily describe its relationship to the pyramid differently. The four corners have a common root, but that is about all. Ah, but science has the world's attention. Religious metaphysics hasn't kept up in that respect.

Organizations, using this authority or that, have encouraged us to judge the other views as less enlightened than our own. It is difficult to believe that one claiming enlightenment would call another view heathen because that view sees the North Star at a different angle, but of course, many do. The struggle between science and religion seems unending, science presently dominating.

In search of the true message, some chickens like me have gone to every corner of the incubator and to half the religions—only to become more confused. The subjective East doesn't jibe with the objective West, and neither really knows what the other is talking about, but each seems certain of what the other is *not* talking about. For that matter, the traveling chick learns that virtually no one who calls himself "metaphysical" knows what metaphysics is.

Most of us chickens have no concept about the light that warms us, much less about the Light standing behind that light. We know what we've been told in our own little corner of the incubator—by our parents, our leaders and their holy books, our schools and organizations. Like the chickens, most of us think primarily of our comfort, self-satisfaction and ongoing titillation—which carefully includes the way we make a living. It is said that less than ten percent of the Western world is religious, though one doesn't have to be religious to have a concern for and interest in Truth. Still fewer concern themselves with subjective thoughts such as these, so we wonder what marvel brought the holy books into being or impels anyone to write these things to so small an audience. Yet through the years there have been correct words to guide us to the Light within.

As for the disputes about what the light of the incubator is (or what the Light beyond the light is), the grand gurus learned long ago that it is infinitely better, for their own sakes, to let the chickens debate the meanings of the words in the holy books rather than delve into the nature of Light/light. Leave theology to the theologians, they say. Debate invites schism and schism is hurtful to the organization and its power.

Reader, what DO metaphysics, theology and philosophy reveal about Light? Light is, after all, one of the things so close to us we don't notice it or really know what it is. The Light of Life can't be seen with mortal eyes. It can't be touched. What do people really know about the Light of Life? Like the chickens in the incubator, almost nothing. Only that It IS—and because It is, we are. One can get a powerful argument from philosophers and metaphysicians that even this much isn't certain.

Yet, there is an event that will surely bring every chicken to know about light immediately! When a great storm one day pulls the incubator's plug for a moment and everything goes dark, THEN every chicken in the place will know what light IS from experiencing what it is NOT. In the twinkling of an eye, the apparent ABSENCE of light—and the panic of that absence—will bring everyone to a full consciousness of light. Even those drinking beer, flapping the levers on pinball machines and watching their latest videos will know, from the least of them to the greatest, that light is an integral part of their well-being. And those who are meditating or pinching their noses in prayer, imploring Light to be more Light, will become acquainted with It also.

The Light of Life is just as close to us as the light in the incubator is close to the chickens. We were born into the appearance of time and space with/as It, and we have grown up with It whether we are aware of the fact or not. Light is here, unheralded and unnoticed, living us, supporting and warming us—the very spark of Being Itself. The Child of us IS that Light, here and now.

Strangely, for each of us individually and all of us collectively, life must be threatened and common disaster loom before we are willing to be earnest. The religions of the world have so cut and dried the believer's approach to theology, cosmology, cosmogony, debate and discussion (from fear of schism and disloyalty), that one doesn't learn until the end of his personal affairs that the grand gurus in the corners are no longer spokesmen for anything resembling the Original Message; that these servants of the "living Word" have, in the name of the printed word, dismissed the Living Child within themselves. The Biblical Apocalypse says these churches will have served their purposes in the final days of time. Perhaps so. When we see the bickering and warfare that passes for religion, metaphysics and "love"—Christians torching other Christians in the name of Christ—one only wonders when the destruction will be over.

There are unnoticed Lights in the world—religious and otherwise—individuals working diligently, able in marvelous ways to walk the precarious pathways *beyond* religion and metaphysics—no longer beguiled by the organized bewilderers. There are those who have climbed the barbed walls of orthodoxy and found the Child of themselves again. Those who have found the Child are able to tell us how to find the same Child within ourselves. They tell of the Self within, how to find Its Equation for living, how to receive It and how to give It. We seek these people out and listen to them.

The light in the world incubator has begun to flicker and flutter. I am reminded of the Carpenter who said the day would come when there are two are in the field, one taken up and one left behind. Two on a bed, one lives and one dies. Five in a household—three against two and two against three. Perhaps I have been shown some of these things because I know such days will come in the world's "time" if only when the individual faces his own transition. There will be those who are frightened and those who are not; those who will know what to do and those who won't. The unafraid will have found the BALANCE between inside and outside, above and below, first and last, male and female, objective and subjective.

These people may or may not be familiar with the words of the historic Christ Child, but they will know those words are true and faithful, having found the Child themselves.

The Child takes us to the Balance quickly. The Child tells of the Equation wherein life prospers with security, grace and decency. The Child takes us to the non-spatial place of Identity where we EXCHANGE the things Above and give them below, not theorize and talk about them endlessly; where we pass the reports from outside and give them inside. Those who stand on *that* High Ground will be (are) the final harvest and final seed of the Tree of Life.

"What about the rest of us, William?"

A good question. Who are "the rest of us"? What happens to our friends in a dream when we awaken? They were never more than the dream itself, the powerless straw dogs about whom LaoTse speaks. They are, until they find the subjective idea, the dead burying the dead, that Jesus spoke of. It is up to us to get THIS one I AM and *its subjective world* straight within ourselves. *This* one that reads these words gets his world straight. Then, "all mankind will be drawn unto me."

It is said that "Whatever is bound on earth is bound in heaven. What is freed on earth is freed in heaven." Could it be we take our subjective world with us, forgiven or unforgiven, freed or still bound? "You can't take it with you" has been the world's belief for so long. I often take my day's adventures into the dream at night. I often awaken to more clearly understand the things I've been dreaming about. Who is to say we can't leave the image of the Image to return to the Image? The essence of the Nag Hammadi Library says exactly that; subjectively understood, the Holy Books of the world say that—and now, agnostic science is looking at infinite possibilities and infinite dimensions, finding universes within universes, not unlike the New Jerusalem John foresaw.

My unseen reader friend, we have things to get straight, to understand and to DO in the days ahead. Let's get on with it while we can.

74

THE SHATTERED MIRROR

The end days and the tribulations always generate interest. Everyone has felt he must surely be living near that time. Could it be that the shattering of the mirror is what happens in the "end days"?

In time and space, matter is an image, including the body image with which we identify. The subjective state perceives the universe as the qualities and attributes of Whatever the universe actually is. Subjectivism is much like an unembodied, infinite awareness looking into a mirror of itself and seeing its possible qualities and attributes imaged. Or, as Douglas Harding describes in his book *On Having No Head*, it is as if the world of time and space were our head. But, as we recall, Godhead Itself is more than Its qualities and attributes—just as the nugget of gold is more than appears to the eye. There is no "gold" in "yellow," "malleable," "valuable" or anything else we perceive to be the qualities and attributes of gold, yet gold is what it is. Images, real or unreal, are what they are. Behind them stands Something Marvelous.

It becomes clear to the subjective mode of mentation that everything physical, however it appears—sounds, sights, feelings—"comes" from within the Self. Awareness may seem lodged in a form, but the fact is that all we perceive to be the form exists within Awareness.

Images are "after the fact," following in time. Awareness (Self) precedes the image. Intuitions and ideas, thoughts and feelings "come from" the Self-I-Am holding God's hand, so to speak, and they precede images. These thoughts, when awakened to, have a profound influence over the images following in time, especially over this immediate body. It is this "precedence"—just the heart-felt knowledge that the precedence exists—that "heals" the tangible body. My ability to see "health" in the place of "illness" increased when this simple light of *precedence* dawned.

THE SHATTERED MIRROR ILLUSTRATION

Imagine a lady who falls so in love with her image in the mirror that she forgets the one standing in front of the mirror. We would call her foolish, wouldn't we? Essentially, this is what the world has done, worshiping, gathering and controlling matter, unaware of the Self that precedes matter in time and space.

Suppose the man with no head fell so in love with the universe he could see and hear *(and BE, as metaphysicians so love to add)* that he forgot the *Ineffable Awareness* doing the perceiving. Is this man any different from the woman in love with her image? Perceiving Awareness to be one's personal possession is the humanistic solipsism of much of Metadelphia. It rightly perceives everything to be within awareness, but deems "my" awareness in the time and space equation to be the end of the matter.

The time has come for Everyman to turn from the mirror of matter's enchantment and find the Child within. The Child will tell one all he needs to know about images, the world of matter. Subjectively, *one's own discovery of the Child can preclude the world's confirming upheaval!* Armageddon doesn't have to rattle everything. The choice is ours individually. It is following that objective/subjective battle, individually, wherein the objective world is re-examined carefully through subjective eyes and one begins living his subjectivism objectively in the world, that we and our world find Peace. Dominion! The New Covenant. No more teachers or temples. Messiah at hand!

My reader friend, we do this individually first; then the world, following in time sequentially, is seen *confirming our discovery!* This is a Mystery, most marvelous. This is the Mystery of Messiah, who comes to deliver our subjective world from the grip of illusion.

Let whoever reads these words, please understand their meaning if he can. If "you" are to see "your" world improve, the improvement begins with "you." I have found that, despite my many human weaknesses and follies, it is possible with God's grace to envision and see "the new heaven and earth" already spread over the face of Everything—and to perceive it right here in the world, no matter the human circumstance or one's personal condition.

The Tree of Life (quantum man) is soon to bloom, shatter and seed. The Child preceded all this and will survive. Life survives. The mirror will be broken, whether we are ready for Awareness without an object or not.

In the end of our discovery, as we scale Da Shan the mighty mountain of understanding and finally realize that we truly *do* stand atop God's mountain of dominion, it becomes extremely troubling to perceive that we *alone* are responsible for bringing our subjective world from the wheel of rebirth in time and space. "My God! How can I do that?" is the question I asked in disbelief. But we are to do it, and eventually we do. This dawns on us, line upon line, precept upon precept, here a little, there a little, until finally, and after much denial and reluctance, we are convinced. Then, we get busy.

This book is part of my effort to do for the world as I can. You can begin where this effort ends. *You* are the final stage of the rocket to the Star beyond stars.

Our confirmation of the job *finished,* is the appearing of Everyman searching for and finding the Child within himself—and *becoming* the Child in conscious fact. That one works to bring his world to what is called "salvation" and "life more abundant."

BOOK CONCLUSION

SUBJECTIVE / OBJECTIVE; OMNIJECTIVE

Objective/subjective isn't the whole of the appearance of things. The life of us with all of its perceptions is more nearly omnijective. Or dimensions of perspective *within* dimensions— much as point, line, and plane are dimensions within one another, and all included subjectively within (or from) the sphere's universal point of view.

To use that analogy: Imagine all points of view to infinity happening simultaneously. The point of view of the point perceives itself (point) subjectively and all other points (that make up "lines" of thought) as objective—as "out there." But to the line, all points of itself are subjectively "within 'my' consciousness" and all other lines (and their points) are "out there." Lines that intersect have a common and subjective "something" akin, like people who have common interests.

The plane (even a plane of thought) perceives its own inner nature (of lines) as "within" and all other planes as objectively external. In addition, it sees itself joined with each of them at whatever their lines of intersection. The plane finds itself "related" to all planes at the subjective juncture—like a common "life" existing between them, making them "one" at that line.

The sphere perceives all these points of view, lines of thought and planes of thinking *subjectively* as its own functioning going on.

I do not know why the feeling of a cosmic *body* comes to mind every time I pursue this line of thought, but it does. I get a consistent intuitional "picture"—a Deific Body of Consciousness with which I interface at the level of awareness, conscious and unconscious. It is as if my little point of OBJECTIVE view (body) is like a life-cell circulating within the Body—human peregrinations being but an examination of, and function of, the Deific Body. (I am not the only one to whom this parallel has occurred. There is a discussion of these ideas in the mysticism of Judaism.) My developing SUBJECTIVISM somehow touches—I almost said encompasses—the WHOLE of Deity's nature, albeit that Whole Being seems "past finding out" such that it doesn't (can't) *quite* "make sense" to the point, line or plane's perspective.

What I formerly perceived as "my out there" world is a reflection of my own withinness—that inner world and its reflection interfacing at the "point of awareness" I am. *The point makes its own world,* so to speak—its "out there" reflecting all possibilities from the ridiculous to the sublime and only a portion of those possibilities actually "real."

I have an intuitive feeling that "death" is not only unreal but merely a progression along this linear way in time, from point to line to plane, and so on. The cell (to use that analogy) "perishes" within the stream of life, but the stream is enriched by the cell's temporal and finite existence—but what is really happening is not so "mortal" as that. Whatever consciousness of the stream which the cell becomes aware of before its move from temporal cell to its greater nature, continues and expands *enormously* as the *stream's* awareness. Now, "the stream of life" (Everyman) has intimations of its greater dimension, even as now I have intimations (maybe more than intimations) of things for which there are no words—only overtones.

In this way, I perceive "my" omnijective awareness to be in the hands of omni-dimensional (and no-dimensional) Godhead, forevermore. This Awareness-I-am (and the reader is) is the perception of the Divine Mind. As that perception, I am charged to be an honest observer, a faithful witness—*not a perpetual judge of good and evil.*

This, I understand, is why the universe forever appears as *qualities and attributes* of Something greater—that "Something," I choose to call Godhead or Deity.

Additionally, this explains how and why one is brought to understand that these qualities and attributes are not Godhead Itself, but what Godhead *knows* Itself (its qualities, characteristics and attributes) to be.

Overmind knowing Itself.

Overmind Knowing what *knowing* is.

Thence to account for the (point's, line's and plane's) viewing of "evil": Overmind knowing what It is NOT, and could never be—the correlation that "explains" the appearances of an unreal, powerless "evil" or "error" "in the world."

This Awareness (or call it "life") is "knowing" going on.

When I identify as the one who owns awareness (i.e., as the possessor of knowing, the owner of this life) I cannot distinguish between IS and IS-NOT.

When I end my enthrallment with the pseudo-possessor's beliefs, I know as nearly as possible "as I am known" and find myself intuitively aware of which is wheat and which are tares—even why the need for such an apparent dualism.

There has never been a *real* possessor of Awareness other than Ineffability, Godhead, Isness, Truth. Yet, in order that Awareness be aware that awareness is not the whole of God but *less*—or, in order for Awareness to know beyond the limit of intellectualism—it does for a necessary time (the duration of its own making) struggle diligently to believe it IS God. That struggle marks the upper limit of the human experience—transpiring only in its own time and measure of eternity for the purpose of rediscovering the Child within.

Bottom line here: The human experience is theology's necessary descent into hell (is-nots) that allows us to rediscover, thence *know* beyond human frailty and its intellectualism, the Divine Nature of being. The ultimate simplicity of it is boggling. How would any of us have known what the light of the sun is without suffering the long emptiness of the dark night? Who would know what security, peace, health, joy, beauty or anything else *really is*, had he not tangled with the chimerical, contradistinctory opposites? We left the Child in adulthood in order to rediscover It and KNOW Its reality and dominion. We live the appearances of death in order to know the eternal nature of Life.

ABOUT IDENTITY, IN LIGHT OF SPHERE

In the Mind's Eye I see the Infinite Sphere and Its Self-Awareness, two that are One.

At its very center, I see the Point of Light, the Infinite Sphere's spiritual Image and Likeness—pure, perfect and immaterial.

Inasmuch as this Point's essence has been "given" Life (which is to say, IS the Image of Life), the living Image sees the images of the qualities and attributes of (1) Infinite Sphere and (2) Infinite Sphere's Image or Self-awareness. That is, the

Divine Man is empowered (1) to see, to look "within" Himself and perceive the Perfect Image in toto—His knowledge of IDENTITY, and (2) to look "outside" Himself at the divine Qualities and Attributes in their sequential form, separate and apart, intertwined and interrelated. But "outside and inside are a single one" to Sphere. INSIDE is the Image, outside are images of Image and images of images to infinity. "The KINGDOM OF HEAVEN is within."

Now understand, "outside" includes the first image of oneself, the "tangible" body. That body is finite image of Image! IMAGE is the REAL Identity; body is the first image of that Image. "Outside" includes images of images to forever. But "outside" is BEHOLDEN to Inside. DOMINION was given to Image, not image.

Once, in blind arrogance, I wrote that I had stopped identifying as image or Image. I acknowledged GOD to be all in all, without need of image or Image. But I was wrong. Absolutely wrong. I should have known the Lights of the world couldn't have been wrong, every one. Even the word "identity" means identical, but the identical Image is what GOD knows GOD to be—this is the Twin—and there is no power in the IMAGE unless it is given to it by God, exactly as the Christ Light said for Himself and His view of "others." I do not know where my arrogance came from that would deny God the privilege of Self-perception, but I lived that attempt. NOW I know that deep "within" IDENTICAL IMAGE is the Light of Godhead, because THAT is what motivates and directs me.

Who is this "me" that is motivated and directed? It looks like an image of an image called William, but it is the Soul of the Divine Identity, IMAGE of God. It is the GOD-view, not the man-view. The man-view, the image of image-view, is compounded of arrogance and ignorance until it is understood and surrendered.

Now I see why the Christ Light of history and His first followers said time and again that one must not love the world but love God. The world is image of the body's images moving toward the macrocosm—and contains all the compounds that comprise materiality. And THAT "matter" is only half substantial, half true—that "half" rooted in the image of the Image. The image of the Image is not a lie; it just isn't the Image itself, just as the Image is not God itself. Just as the Image is beholden to God, so the body and its actions are beholden to Image, the Child, the soul of God!

Listen gently, Reader. Let one not worship Image because it is holy or because it has dominion over everything that creepeth on the earth, but let one worship the INEFFABLE GODHEAD. (The me-sense point of view may very well be the CREATOR of tangible matter and its forms, not God! The mirror "creates" the lifeless images within it.) "Don't call me good," said the Light of Life. "Call no man good." "Don't worship me," he said. "Worship God." John echoed those words. So did the prophets.

Jesus said also that when you see Him who was not born of woman, to fall on your knees and worship that one. IMAGE comes to image one day in time because Image is being image in timeless Alreadyness. When *that* one comes, that one brings testimony of GODHEAD. Jesus heralded THAT Light within one. Mankind has turned this process around to venerate the linear herald of Light.

Yet the historic Jesus identified correctly AS that Light and said that all mankind who recognized that Light Within could do the same as he, and more.

In my personal experience at this "time," the Image is breaking through the ignorance and humanity of me more and more frequently, telling me what to do about "the world" and its images; this seems to be to live the Equation in the world, but most especially to be prepared to do something for my images who are given to Me in the time ahead, even as I have been faithful to them in the time past. "As I get the beam out of THIS Eye," the Divine Alchemy renews this view of the world. Not just for me, but for Everyman.

The world view ending will not be the end of anything, but the CONSCIOUS Presence of Everything which is ALREADY "spread over the face of the land"—and the events of a linear history in time will be like the wink of an eye and a dream we dreampt of our images upon images having power when they didn't really.

THE INNER SELF

It is one thing to read about the inner Self, but it is quite another thing to find it. It is one thing to hail the inner Self as Image of the Supreme, the only Truth and Identity, but it is another matter entirely to *find it*. It is one thing to proclaim that "naught but Reality is going on," but quite another matter to live that Reality in the face of "unreality," be tested by it, and then *find* oneself the Son of the Living God, recipient of the Heritage.

There are at least five pathways to that Reality, and metaphysics is only one of them—perhaps the most difficult of them all. Many enter into the door of "modern metaphysics," but few get beyond the inclination for study, to flow with the way of wisdom to its end and Beginning. Many succumb to the verbal power they find they exercise in the world, the me-sense swollen and large because others think them intelligent.

Many enter the door of churchdom and its organization, but few get beyond the social and intellectual entrapments. Few lift themselves from the words of the Bible to the Spirit which the Bible confirms, thence to follow the way of devotion to the peak and the Beginning. Many succumb to the authority they entertain or to the social world they enjoy. The church is a comfortable bend in the river where men grow confident in their objective humanness rather than their subjective divinity.

Many enter the doors of science, but few find the Spirit for which matter exists, the Spirit which matter demonstrates and confirms.

Many walk the roads of psychology, education, government, business and their enterprises in the world, but few are willing to renounce the world and its riches or to let go their pride of accomplishment.

THE RIGHT AND THE LEFT

Han was leaving. It was time to go home, he said. He spoke to his little group for the last time. "In the world, the right and left are extremes that come together without our realizing it. My right is my arrogance. My left is my ignorance. My arrogance pretends humility and my ignorance pretends wisdom. They come together and are the mirrored images of one another, like holding my hands behind my back. But, listen, listen. Beyond these two, and by far the most important, is the HEART *between* them and superior to them. The inward flow from either hand leads directly to the Heart and Its perfect balance. The outward flow from the Heart leads to the hands and the hands give to the world.

"In the world one hopes for a peace between right and left, East and West, rich and poor, young and old, male and female, but permanent peace isn't found at the political or social level of things. Peace is with the Child of God, three steps beyond government, two steps beyond religion and one beyond wisdom and metaphysics. We find the Child. We live the Child's sweet Equation and are swiftly carried to the top of the mountain. There, the world under our feet, we find 'the peace that passeth understanding.' When we find THAT peace, our world rushes to confirm it. When our world confirms peace, we have been victorious.

"Our work isn't done when we reach the peak of Da Shan!" said Han, almost shouting. "Our work is done when we look roundabout and the world, seeing what we see, has confirmed our understanding and our Peace!"

"Will I ever see that day with mortal eyes?" the soldier asked.

"I don't know," the old teacher answered. "I don't know. That is up to you."

The Child enters the world and is found to be Wisdom itself. The old man leaves the world whispering, "I don't know. I don't know. It is up to you." The Balance is untouched by either event. We find the Balance and be it. One day we look out and *everything* confirms Godhead, no matter how it appears to others. Then we understand how it is that ". . .these stones shall minister unto thee . . . Cleave a piece of wood and, behold, I am there."

We think Truth and the Child's Equation flows outward. We

think Truth and the Child's Equation flows inward. We tap our foot and drum our fingers to the rhythm of the Flow. For the most part, the church mice leave us alone, but we know what to do about them if they don't. Truth speaks to the Child of us directly!

The angels and the prophets bring Light and Life.

THE ROLE OF THE CHILD WITHIN US

We are watching television, and an unexpected scene brings a tear to the eye. The emotion we feel is the Child stirring within. Subtly, *unnoticed thoughts inward toward the Child* and *outward to the scene at hand* combine in stillness to elicit a movement of the Child within—and we *feel* it. What hasn't been common knowledge is that the Child lies at the seat of simple, honest emotions that have to do with the tender things, the true things, the good things of the human condition.

We see the enthusiasm of a puppy whose whole body wiggles in tail-wagging excitement, its head nuzzling the hands and feet of a friend. The response we feel from the center of us is the Child within confirming that the joy outside IS the joy within, one joy. What hasn't been common knowledge is that our empathy comes from the Original Child of us, the Good of us, eager to prove It is ever here as the Real.

We see something as we round a turn of the pathway and are tinged with some distant nostalgia, a statement within reminding us of a pleasant time in our affairs or a happy place we know. What hasn't been common knowledge is that the seat of feeling within us is the Child's domain and that our response to the unfolding view, in fact or in memory, is the Child's reminder that we *are* that Child, *not merely the body that walks the pathway or thunders hell-bent and unthinking through a human experience.*

We see the sight of dolphins and porpoises playing alongside the ship of life. Suddenly we *feel* their joy and freedom, their uninhibited playfulness, and we are relieved. What hasn't been common knowledge is that their joy and zest is our joy and zest. If we had not learned what joy is, we would not recognize it in the world—and it is the Child of us that responds, *feeling* the same joy and zest. Our body is renewed. What hasn't been common knowledge until now is that it is the living Identity of us, the immortal Child who is stirring within, telling us It is willing to be up and out and into our affairs, bringing us up and out of the old nature to take us home to the Real again.

We see two old folks walking slowly, hand in hand, for their evening stroll. Suddenly something within us responds—goodness knows what we feel, but it is very good. It is warm. It is refreshing and delightful. It is in response to the *Child's lessons learned* somewhere along our old man's line of life. *But the Child is the responder to the scene at hand,* telling us that we are not the unfeeling, dispassionate aging person we thought we were. Rather, we are the Child within that doesn't grow old. We live and we know we live. We are coming *back* to our senses again. What hasn't been common knowledge before is that we are not the old person looking on the scene at hand, but we are the Child, the Awareness of God, looking at the subjectivity of Godhead.

Sometimes it is the Child that dreams our dreams for us— dreams to be thought about a little. It seems to me that some of my dreams do not come from the inmost Child of Me but out of my old worldly imbalances, hinting at something for me to *unbind* in the world I am. Something to forgive and forget. But on the mornings when I awaken to freshness and eagerness, I can be sure the Child has been at Its work during sleep, being instructed by the Father of Life.

Now, ever so slowly, line upon line, in these days at hand we are becoming aware that the Child within is the REAL of us, the IDENTITY that walks hand in hand with God, and we are beginning to let that trustworthy Child lead us. The Child I am speaks to me and writes these words. Nothing I can write of myself will be worthy of that Inner One made in the Image of God, but with the Child's help I try. The response one feels to these thoughts and ideas comes certainly from the Heart, the Child, not at all from the dying nature of the unreal man who ridicules and laughs at the idea of an eternal ongoingness of Life. The Child laughs, too—oh, how he laughs and claps his hands!—but not in derision or hurtfulness. The Child laughs in honest *confirmation* that the Heart of us *lives* and is eternally about the Father's business.

And I shall write my law in their inward parts and write it in their heart; and will be their God, and they shall be my people. They shall teach no more every man his neighbor and every man his brother, saying "Know the Lord" for they shall all know me from the least of them unto the greatest of them, saith the Lord, and I will remember their sin no more. (Jeremiah)

The wolf also shall dwell with the lamb, and the leopard shall lie down with the kid; and the young lion and the fatling together; and a little child shall lead them. (Isaiah)

Verily I say unto you, Except ye be converted and become as little children, ye shall not enter into the kingdom of heaven. (Jesus)

While ye have light, believe in the light, that ye may be the children of light. (Jesus)

Ye are all the children of light and the children of day. (Paul)

Suffer little children to come unto me . . . for such is the kingdom of God. (Jesus)

It is the Child that sees the primordial secret in Nature and it is the child of ourself we return to. The child within us is simple and daring enough to live the Secret. (Chungtse)

For where the beginning is, there shall be the end. (Jesus)

The children of the promise are counted for the seed. (Paul)

We are the children of the promise. (Paul)

I have no greater joy than to hear that my children walk in truth. (John)

Who is that Child, my friend, if it isn't the one buried beneath the adulthood of yourself? We look for the Child and the Child stirs to tell us It lives. We reach for the Child and the Child comes running into our gut to respond and say, "I am come!" We begin to see small wonders again, the way we saw them as children. We *acknowledge* these wonders as *gifts from God* and, lo, they come more frequently. We gird up our loins and *dare tell others* of the gentle Child within them, and our wonders increase and grow apace. We thank God for the Child of Life by telling our subjective selfhood of the Child they are. Imperceptibly, bit by bit, we let the inner Child lead us to the right hand and to the left. Imperceptibly, our reliance on external authority gives way to the Light of Life within ourselves, and we quarrel no longer with any man. Then we see the Child in all men, even the arrogant and scornful, even the feeble and sick. As we look for the Child in ourselves, we see It in all men and see them coming alive as well. *THIS is to give God what is God's.*

UNDERSTANDING TIME AND THE END DAYS OF TIME'S DOMINION

Now it is, in these late days in the ongoingness of mortal life, that the attention of the one who survives will be turned to the Child within himself. He will be comforted and profited in his worldly affairs, and in his heart he will grow wealthy. As this Child-consciousness grows in the world and as these renewing people communicate with one another around the earth, writing and telling *their own glimpses and glimmers of the Child's joy*—no longer reciting the words of others as proof of their own wisdom—there will be a remarkable synergistic assembly of feeling within humanity beyond the grandest hope of anyone. Out of this unexpected synergism of Light, like a plant sending up a tall stem with a great flower on it, so the world will send up a newness of Child-people, blooming as a flower of Renewed Life—just like a fall flower finally coming to bloom in the late days before the frost. After nearly eleven thousand years of human time, God's Tree of Life is coming into bloom. There will be a special Joy beyond joy felt by those who are part of this Flower of Life, the offspring of Godhead, seed from the Original Seed.

But listen, listen. It is the Tree that blooms, not we ourselves. Those who are led by the Child become the Living Blossom of Life here on earth—a new brotherhood, a new Community without leaders or temples, subservient to naught but the Child and its Source. This flower may be shaken by the laughter, envy and scorn of the incredulous, and assaulted by pseudo-authorities whose power appears to be threatened. But the Child is a threat to no one. Before us lies a brief and severe time when the flower is shaken by the wind and the petals seem to be scattered again and when those who are not holding fast to the inner Child's hand will wonder who the real prophets are. But from the Flower will come the Seed that will be taken up for the reseeding and ongoingness of tangible life. The tree will perish, but the seed will live.

How do I know this is so? Because it has been shown to me

by the Child I am—and I see confirmation of the Divine Process and Its Equation in all nature. All one must do to know these things are happening already, is to look and see that they are happening. Line upon line now, but soon precept upon precept, more than a little here and a little there, the New Community already begins to flower and be seen by Everyman, first fruits of the Tree of Life—from out of which comes the Seed eternal.

All tangibility, all Da Shan and the life teeming on its slopes, is the subjectivity of God, not man. The Life that reads these words is the Awareness of God, not man. The synergism we feel in the community of our families and most meaningful groups is only a fraction of the Divine Energy and Light of Godhead's Life soon to be felt by those who summon forth the Child within *and dare to become that Child.* The downward human spiral of energy that culminates in selfness and the reproduction of human life will turn around to spiral upward and out, bringing with it the incomparable Energy of Life in its wholeness, joined with the Groom—and this joy is yet to be experienced by men and women. It is reserved for the final flowering of Life. It begins with the Child within. We get busy and find It. We live the Equation, giving and receiving, receiving and giving to all mankind. We write and tell of the Child's Glimpses because we are ourselves the only ones who can tell our own Glimpses of Light—they come to us immaculately and individually and to no one else. We are charged to give them to our others. The Glimpse contains the pollen of Life and we give it freely. We accept it and pass it along. We live God's Equation with joy.

As it might be said in the East, the night of Brahman falls as soon as the harvest of the Seed is accomplished. The Morning of the New Day comes quickly.

EPILOGUE

THE APPLE TREE BLOOMED LAST WEEK

Woodsong's little orchard is an endless delight, especially in the spring. The apple tree bloomed last week. Each bloom opened onto an unobstructed scene and looked roundabout to see the world. Today, most of those blooms have shattered and fallen to the ground. The few that remain no longer have the unobstructed view but peer out through the new green leaves. The first blossoms saw the world, the last see mostly the leaves of their own branch.

The first flush of Truth is like the unobstructed opening bloom of spring, able to see so much. The apple tree's last blooms don't see as far but—listen softly—*they produce fruit just as certainly!*

Could it be that the present days are like the tree full of complicating, obstructing leaves—like business activity, family responsibilities, government, world argument, self-doubts, fears and the like? Yes, we look through leaves of the world. And could it be that we are trying to converse with blossoms surrounded by the complex, complicating world? Yes. But we are still addressing the Heart of Selfhood, the Child within— the innocent and pure in heart. When I tell my "others" (myself) of the expansive view, I'm fully aware how the leaves stand before us as distracting, contradictory and *tangible* obfuscations.

Listen, Child Heart of Myself. Hear of the simplifying Open Spaces! Hear of the Unobstructed Spirit! The grand View is just beyond the leaves.

AFTER THE STORM

When the apple tree bloomed last week, it was so proud of itself! Now, after the wind and the rain, its petals lie scattered on the ground. The tree may be tempted to think it has fallen from grace again and is back where it started, but it isn't. It isn't! Why not? Because the fruit follows the bloom and the fruit contains the seed!

Gentle reader, if, anywhere along the way, you have felt a stirring in yourself while reading this volume, be of good cheer. That was the Child blooming again! What follows inevitably in your experience is the fruit and the seed.

POSTSCRIPT

Now the reader is asked to begin rereading Book One immediately. Those twelve chapters will become clearer this time and you may feel that you are reading an entirely new book. With the second reading, the Related Papers can be read concurrently—as the reader chooses. You are then perceiving your own insightful overtones, determined by your experience, your needs and your choice of readings. The book will be ever new—and your experience likewise. There are Mysteries and Secrets contained in these pages, all of them related to the Divine Imprint *already present in the reader's heart.*

PUBLISHER'S WORD

The author invites the earnest reader's correspondence. He will respond as promptly as his schedule of writing, travel, speaking, artifact hunting and fencepost leaning permits. Many unpublished pages of his work remain to be shared; many delicate points that could not be included in this volume await those who write.

There is a growing Community of men and women of all ages around the world—without human leaders, without followers—who are finding and living the subjective idea, eager to correspond with the like-minded, exchanging Glimpses and glimmers. We come from all disciplines, all religious denominations, East and West—theologians, psychologists, mathematicians, teachers, business people, homemakers, artists, musicians, poets, naturalists, gardeners, ministers, priests, rabbis and at least one fine young poet who is a paper picker and loves his world mightily.

The exchange of letters becomes synergistic, as you will see—and must surely be the beginning of the final "generation of prophets" spoken of in the literature of the world.

Address correspondence to William Samuel, Mountain Brook Publications, Box 7474, Mountain Brook, Alabama 35253.

The publication of subjective literature, the "top-down" way to think, is rare. There is only a miniscule market for it at the moment. **Your help in placing this volume into the hands of those who will benefit from it and into the bookstores and libraries in your community will be greatly appreciated.**

THE PUBLISHER

OTHER TITLES BY WILLIAM SAMUEL

A Guide to Awareness and Tranquillity

The Awareness of Self-Discovery

The Melody of the Woodcutter and the King

Two Plus Two Equals Reality

Notes From Woodsong, Essays